Geschichte und Philosophie der Medizin
History and Philosophy of Medicine

Herausgegeben von / Edited by ANDREAS FREWER

Band / Volume 18

www.steiner-verlag.de/series/1860-6199

Leo Alexander at the Nazi Doctors' Trial

The Nuremberg Diary and Correspondence

Edited by
Ulf Schmidt, Kate Docking,
David Peace and Andreas Frewer

Franz Steiner Verlag

This publication was printed with the financial support of

European Research Council
European Union's Horizon 2020
Research and Innovation Program
(grant agreement no. 854503)

Professorship for Modern History
Department of History
Centre for the Study of Health, Ethics, and Society
University of Hamburg

Professorship for Ethics in Medicine
Institute for the History of Medicine and Medical Ethics
Friedrich-Alexander-Universität
Erlangen-Nürnberg

Cover Images

Portrait of Leo Alexander during a trial session at Nuremberg, 1946/47
© NARA
During his testimony at the Nuremberg Doctors' Trial, Leo Alexander, medical expert for the US Prosecution, points to the scars on the leg of Jadwiga Dzido. Nuremberg, Germany, 20 December 1946.
© NARA

Bibliografische Information der Deutschen Nationalbibliothek:
Die Deutsche Nationalbibliothek verzeichnet diese Publikation in der Deutschen Nationalbibliografie; detaillierte bibliografische Daten sind im Internet über dnb.d-nb.de abrufbar.

Dieses Werk einschließlich aller seiner Teile ist urheberrechtlich geschützt.
Jede Verwertung außerhalb der engen Grenzen des Urheberrechtsgesetzes
ist unzulässig und strafbar.
© Franz Steiner Verlag, Stuttgart 2025
www.steiner-verlag.de
Druck: Beltz Grafische Betriebe, Bad Langensalza
Gedruckt auf säurefreiem, alterungsbeständigem Papier.
Printed in Germany.
ISBN 978-3-515-13858-1 (Print)
ISBN 978-3-515-13861-1 (E-Book)
DOI 10.25162/9783515138611

To the victims and survivors who have been

persecuted by authoritarian regimes

TABLE OF CONTENTS

Acknowledgements xi

List of Illustrations xiii

Abbreviations xv

1. Preface 1
2. Editorial Guide 3
3. Leo Alexander in Nuremberg – An Introduction 5
4. Leo Alexander – The Nuremberg Correspondence 1946–1947 23
5. Leo Alexander – The Nuremberg Diary 1946–1947 31
6. Leo Alexander – Selected Expert Testimony 151
7. Leo Alexander – War Crimes and Their Motivation 163
8. Leo Alexander – Medical Science Under Dictatorship 187
9. Ulf Schmidt – Interview with Cecily Kate Alexander-Grable 203
10. The Nuremberg Code of Medical Ethics 217

Bibliography 221

Table of Defendants 227

Table of Concentration Camps Mentioned in Alexander's Diary 229

Index of Persons 231

Index of Places and Countries 239

Biographical Notes of the Editors 247

Fig. 1: At the podium Leo Alexander is giving testimony at the Nuremberg Doctors' Trial. To the right is Maria Kusmierczuk (1920–1989), one of the victims of the Ravensbrück medical experiments. To the left is Julius Panek, an interpreter for the English and Polish languages. Friday 20 December 1946 (Source: NARA).

ACKNOWLEDGEMENTS

The editing of this volume would not have been possible without the support of trusted colleagues, librarians, and expert archivists, too numerous to mention here in full. We have particularly relied on the support and expertise at the University of Hamburg, including James Farley and Will Studdert from the Centre for the Study of Health, Ethics, and Society, and the University of Erlangen-Nuremberg, particularly Kerstin Franzò, Julia Mikolaj, and Moritz Kardeis. We would especially like to thank Rebecca Williams, Archives Librarian for Research, Outreach, and Education at the Duke University Medical Center Library & Archives, who supported the project beyond the call of duty. We are grateful to the Duke University Archives for granting us permission to reproduce an annotated transcription of Alexander's "Record ledger book of activities and notes", as it is called in the collection, in addition to the permissions to reproduce parts of the material as facsimiles throughout the volume. We also wish to thank Katharina Stüdemann, Amelie Schwemm and Thomas Schaber of Franz Steiner Verlag for their editorial support in bringing this volume to publication.

Furthermore, we would like to thank the colleagues of the Harvard Law School Library for the "Nuremberg Trials Project" and their important scientific efforts. Our thanks also extend to the Northwestern University School of Law for allowing permission to reproduce 'War Crimes and their Motivation', originally published by Alexander in the *Journal of Criminal Law and Criminology* in 1948. We are also grateful to the Massachusetts Medical Society, who have given permission to reprint an edited version of Alexander's seminal paper 'Medical Science Under Dictatorship', first published in the *New England Journal of Medicine* in 1949. Finally, we would like to express our sincere gratitude to the family and estate of Leo Alexander, particularly to his late daughter Cecily Grable who not only allowed access to relevant correspondence and source material but agreed to an interview on the life of her father; excerpts of which are included in this volume. Any errors in the manuscript remain our own.

Research for this edited volume, which is part of the project "Taming the European Leviathan: The Legacy of Post-War Medicine and the Common Good," has been supported by the European Research Council under the European Union's Horizon 2020 research and innovation program (grant agreement no. 854503).

Ulf Schmidt, Kate Docking, David Peace, Andreas Frewer
Hamburg/Erlangen-Nürnberg, Summer 2024

LIST OF ILLUSTRATIONS

1. At the podium Leo Alexander is giving testimony at the Nuremberg Doctors' Trial. Friday 20 December 1946.
   [page ix]

2. Leo Alexander during a trial session at Nuremberg, 1946/47.
   [page xvii]

3. Leo Alexander's letter to his wife Phyllis Alexander, 27 November 1946.
   [page 21]

4. Alexander's record ledger book of activities and notes, 11–13 November 1946.
   [page 32]

5. Brigadier General Telford Taylor, Chief of Counsel for War Crimes, pictured in his office at Nuremberg. Nuremberg, Germany, 1946/47.
   [page 34]

6. The foyer of the Grand Hotel, Nuremberg, Germany, 1946/47.
   [page 39]

7. Fritz Fischer, defendant at the Nuremberg Doctors' Trial. Nuremberg, Germany, 1946/47.
   [page 43]

8. Leo Alexander interrogating the Nuremberg defendant Wolfram Sievers. Nuremberg, Germany, 23 November 1946.
   [page 50]

9. Karl Brandt, lead defendant at the Nuremberg Doctors' Trial. Nuremberg, Germany, 1946/47.
   [page 53]

10. Alexander's record ledger book of activities and notes, 3 November 1946.
    [page 75]

11. Alexander's record ledger book of activities and notes, 3 November 1946.
    [page 76]

12. Members of the US prosecution team, including Brigadier General Taylor, James McHaney, and Leo Alexander. Nuremberg, Germany, 1946/47.
[page 87]

13. Herta Oberheuser (left) at the Nuremberg prison, 1946/47. She was tried for her involvement in medical experiments at the Ravensbrück concentration camp.
[page 98]

14. Victims of Ravensbrück medical experiments arriving at Nuremberg. From left to right: French navy specialist, Françoise Bayle (French trial observer); Leo Alexander; Jadwiga Dzido, Maria Broel-Plater, Maria Kuśmierczuik, and Władislawa Karołewska. The women were operated on while prisoners at Ravensbrück concentration camp. Nuremberg, Germany, 15 December 1946.
[page 101]

15. During his testimony at the Nuremberg Doctors' Trial, Leo Alexander, medical expert for the US Prosecution, points to the scars on the leg of Jadwiga Dzido. Nuremberg, Germany, 20 December 1946.
[page 105]

16. Entrance to the gate of the Nuremberg courthouse. Nuremberg, Germany, 1946/47.
[page 110]

17. Fritz Fischer, defendant at the Nuremberg Doctors' Trial being cross-examined. Nuremberg, Germany, 1946/47.
[page 129]

18. The judges of the Nuremberg Doctors' Trial. Left to right: Harold L. Sebring, Walter B. Beals, Johnson T. Crawford, Victor C. Swearingen. Nuremberg, Germany, 1946/47.
[page 150]

19. Jadwiga Dzido alongside Leo Alexander giving his expert testimony about the Ravensbrück experiments at the Nuremberg Doctors' Trial on 20 December 1946.
[page 161]

20. Work of civil and military experts at the Nuremberg Doctors' Trial. Leo Alexander (first from left) and colleagues 1946/47.
[page 219]

21. Leo Alexander at the Nuremberg Doctors' Trial. 1946/47.
[page 245]

ABBREVIATIONS

a.d.	an der (at the)
BDM	Bund Deutscher Mädel (League of German Girls)
BTA	British Troops Austria
CC	Concentration Camp
cc	Cubic centimetre
DPs	Displaced persons
DUMC	Duke University Medical Center (Durham, North Carolina, USA)
EKG	Electrocardiogram
EUCOM	European Command
FIAT	Field Information Agency, Technical (Office of the Military Government for Germany)
FK	Führerkorps (Corps Leader, SS)
GC	Gonococcus (Gonorrhoea)
HBS	Hogere Burgerschool (Higher Civic School, Netherlands)
HöSSPF	Höchster SS- und Polizeiführer (Supreme SS and Police Leader)
HQ	Headquarters
JAG	The Judge Advocate General (Britain)
JAMA	The Journal of the American Medical Association
KL	Konzentrationslager (concentration camp)
KZ	Konzentrationslager (concentration camp)
Lt	Lieutenant
MD	Medicinae Doctor (Doctor of Medicine)

Mo	Morphine
NARA	National Archives and Records Administration (USA)
NSKK	Nationalsozialistisches Kraftfahrkorps (National Socialist Motor Corps)
Op	Operation
Pfc	Private First Class (US Army)
Pg	Parteigenosse (party member)
PU	Polizeiunits (police units)
PW	Prisoner of War
RBC	Red blood count/cells
RFSS	Reichsführer-SS (Reich-Leader SS)
RGBl	Reichsgesetzblatt (Reich Law Gazette)
RLM	Reichsluftfahrtministerium (Ministry of Aviation)
SA	Sturmabteilung (Storm Division)
SD	Sicherheitsdienst (Security Service)
SS	Schutzstaffel (Protection Squadron)
TB	tuberculosis
u.	und (and)
UNRRA	United Nations Relief and Rehabilitation Administration
U-St-F	Untersturmführer (Second Lieutenant, SS)
USFA	United States Forces in Austria
USFET	United States Forces European Theatre

Fig. 2: Leo Alexander during a trial session at Nuremberg, 1946/47 (Source: NARA).

1

PREFACE

Leo Alexander,[1] Jewish émigré neurologist and psychiatrist, documented world history through his diary and letters as an expert at the Nuremberg Doctors' Trial and as one of the authors of the Nuremberg Code has left a lasting legacy on medicine and ethics. When 25 years ago, in May 1999, one of the editors of this volume talked to Cecily Alexander-Gable,[2] his daughter, at their holiday cottage on Cape Cod, Massachusetts, about what had motivated her father in spending a year away from his family and career to prosecute Nazi doctors at Nuremberg, she replied:

> "He told me that he had worked on the creation of the Nuremberg Code for human experimentation and that, while there were still discussions to be brought up about how to implement these rules in the Code, but that these were the basis, and that there had to be a lot of development and that people needed to really pay attention to that, that these, these things should never ever ever [sic] happen again, that's why he was at Nuremberg to see to it."[3]

Her observation throws into stark relief the continued importance of individuals and organizations dedicated to the development and enforcement of the rule of law. It is thanks to them and their unwavering efforts throughout the last eighty years that fundamental violations against international laws and customs such as war crimes, crimes against humanity and genocide are being documented "so that no-one can ever doubt that they were fact and not fable", as the chief prosecutor in the Nuremberg Doctors' Trial, Telford Taylor,[4] pointed out. Earlier, Robert H. Jackson[5] had stressed that the wrongs which the International Military Tribunal (IMT) wanted to address had been "so calculated, so malignant, and so devastating, that civilisation cannot tolerate their being ignored because it cannot survive their being repeated".[6] As we are moving into the fourth year of the Russo-Ukrainian war, in which the Russian dictator and his regime have trampled on the existing rules and customs of war in flagrant breach of the Nuremberg principles and international law, we are a long way from ensuring that those who have initiated and committed such acts will be held accountable. Only recently has Vladimir Putin's regime attempted smother even the slightest form of discontent and public criticism by ensuring that his main political rival, Alexei A. Navalny,[7] found an untimely death. The civil courage shown by those who attended his funeral against a draconian police presence can only be described as heroic. The volume in front of us should not

---

1   Leo(pold) Alexander (11 October 1905 – 20 July 1985).
2   Cecily Kate Alexander-Grable (23 November 1938 – 7 January 2024).
3   Interview with Cecily Alexander-Grable, May 1999. The interview was conducted as part of Schmidt's work on *Justice at Nuremberg. Leo Alexander and the Nazi Doctors' Trial* (2004).
4   Telford Taylor (24 February 1908 – 23 May 1998).
5   Robert Houghwout Jackson (13 February 1892 – 9 October 1954).
6   Annas/Grodin (1992), 68.
7   Alexei Anatolyevich Navalny (4 June 1976 – 16 February 2024).

only give us pause for thought and a better understanding of existing historical precedents, in which key individuals such as Alexander and his mostly lawyer colleagues documented and helped to prosecute the crimes committed, but a renewed determination to work towards international justice and the rule of law, regardless of how difficult and futile it may seem at times.

EDITORIAL GUIDE
ON LEO ALEXANDER'S NUREMBERG DIARY

In the process of preparing Leo Alexander's Nuremberg Diary for publication, we have undertaken several editorial changes to enhance readability and accessibility. The original text was in some places highly fragmented, both in terms of language use, formatting, and handwriting, making reading and/or comprehension difficult. Despite making necessary modifications, we have strived throughout the transcription process to preserve the authenticity of the voice of Alexander and of the people he talked to and interviewed.

To achieve this, one of our key goals has been to maintain the original language use throughout the diary, reflecting Alexander's regularly alternating use of German, English and, in some instances, French, for example when he recorded his trip to Paris (see page 165ff. of the original diary). It is our intention that keeping this multilingual approach in the transcript of the diary text highlights both the international nature of the Allied investigation being conducted into Nazi medical war crimes, in addition to providing insight into the Alexander's own character through his diverse linguistic background and usage.

In addition to the preservation of language use, we have made the following editorial additions:

1. **[1]**: Square brackets in bold typeface have been used to indicate page numbers in the original diary.

2. [Nuremberg]: Square brackets are used to indicate that a word or a letter has been inserted into the original diary text by the editors. These insertions may be to provide context, correct factual errors or spelling mistakes, or to provide full names of individuals or institutions where abbreviations are used in the original text.

3. [Trial?]: Square brackets with an inserted word or letter followed by a question mark are used where the original text was illegible and where the editors have provided suggestions for clarity. It should be noted that these suggestions may not reflect the original word use by Alexander in the original, and should be cited with discretion.

4. […]: Square brackets with an ellipsis are used throughout the document to indicate to the reader where parts of the original text are missing or illegible, and where no editorial suggestion for clarity could be made.

5. [?]: We have used a single question mark in a square bracket to represent potential inaccuracies, misunderstandings, or spelling errors by Leo Alexander. The purpose of these marks is to highlight the contemporary

limitations in knowledge about the Nazi medical crimes during the investigation. In many instances these marks are further clarified with explanatory footnotes.

6. *Italics*: italic font has been used in those instances where in the original diary text a word or phrase was underlined by Alexander.

We have included extensive annotated footnotes in the diary. These footnotes provide biographies and institutional histories, historiographical details, and explanations of important ideas and details related to the investigation into Nazi medical war crimes. These editorial footnotes are largely explanatory and avoid giving overt interpretations of the diary, aiming to enhance reading of the diary by providing important contextual information. The index of persons, and the index of places and countries refer to chapter 5 "Leo Alexander – The Nuremberg Diary 1946–1947".

Throughout the transcription, we have kept to Alexander's original formatting and punctuation use as much as possible. All parentheses, question marks, exclamation marks, underlining, line and page breaks, and tables that do not appear in square brackets are as originally authored by Alexander. To give the reader a better impression of the original diary some selected pages are reprinted as images in the original version. We hope that this attention to detail ensures this transcription of the diary remains as true to the original as possible, allowing readers to engage with this important historical text in its authentic form.

3

LEO ALEXANDER IN NUREMBERG
AN INTRODUCTION

Ulf Schmidt, Kate Docking, David Peace, Andreas Frewer

The poignant statement of Leo Alexander's daughter that her father was at Nuremberg to ensure that the medical atrocities committed during the Third Reich would "never ever ever happen again" reflected the desire of war crimes investigators, prosecutors, trial experts, and judges at the Nuremberg Doctors' Trial.[1] The individuals involved in the proceedings, which were held between December 1946 and August 1947 under the auspice of US-American military authorities, shared the goal of preventing non-consenting human experiments, compulsory sterilisations, and "euthanasia" killing carried out by doctors and nurses during the Nazi regime from happening again. The revelations of these medical crimes led to a consensus amongst the Allied legal and medical personnel at Nuremberg that the perpetrators should not only be suitably punished for their actions, but that medical ethics principles be formulated which would guide future experimental research conducted by physician-scientists in trials involving human subjects. Such guidelines would, it was hoped, "balance the need for advancements in medical science that benefit all human society with the right of the individual to personal inviolability, autonomy and self-determination".[2]

Leo Alexander (1905–1985) was an American psychiatrist of Jewish-Austrian origin and chief medical expert at the Nazi Doctors' Trial, who played an important role in formulating medical ethics guidelines known as the Nuremberg Code. The Code has significantly shaped modern biomedical research ethics and research regulations on human subjects.[3] The diary Alexander kept during the Doctors' Trial provides an important and unique insight into the historical background to the trial and the Nuremberg Code. It demonstrates how Alexander worked on, in his own words, "ethical and non-ethical experiments on human beings", reflecting his personal involvement in the drafting of the Code. The diary also highlights the viewpoints Alexander developed which convinced him that such regulations were necessary and how he arrived at certain perspectives, thus deepening understanding of the Code's origins.[4]

---

1   For the contemporary context see Mitscherlich/Milke (1947) and (1949), Bayle (1950) and for the further background Dörner et al. (1999), Frewer/Neumann (2001), Weindling (2004), Schmidt (2004), Schmidt/Frewer (2007), Bruns (2009), and Roelcke et al. (2014), Moreno et al. (2017), Schmidt et al. (2020).
2   Schmidt (2004), 3.
3   See, for example, Moreno (1997), Schmidt (2004), 6, Schmidt/Frewer (2007), Moreno et al. (2017), Weisleder (2021), 122, and Schmidt (2023).
4   See DUMC, Alexander diary (1946/47), 105, 6 December 1946.

The ten universally applicable principles of the Code, read out in court as part of the judgement in August 1947, established the rights of patients and the responsibilities of doctors with regard to human experimentation.[5] The authorship of the Code has been debated. Scholars have argued that Andrew Ivy, another medical expert present at the trial who had been sent by the American Medical Association, was the sole author, while others have made a case for Alexander's authorship.[6] Both men themselves claimed authorship in the mid–1960s, a claim not particularly surprising given the renewed international focus on medical ethics in light of the drafting of the Declaration of Helsinki in 1964; both likely wanted to shine the light on themselves as authors of the Code to enhance their own reputation.[7] The Code was in fact the work of both Ivy and Alexander, with their original principles changed by the Nuremberg judges (most likely by Harold L. Sebring[8]) to incorporate more legalistic and general language. Yet as Ulf Schmidt, one of the editors of this volume, has demonstrated, the Code was ultimately a product of the Doctors' Trial itself. It was shaped by the defendants, witnesses, experts, participants and the prosecution involved.[9]

Alexander's diary can help us to better understand his precise role in the writing of the Nuremberg Code. He sent a memorandum to the United States Counsel for War Crimes in April 1947 detailing six points for legitimate medical research; an expanded version of an earlier memo he had sent the chief prosecutor at Nuremberg, Telford Taylor, two days before the opening of the Doctors' Trial in December 1946.[10] However, Alexander wrote in his diary on 25 January 1947 that he had 'worked on Ethics article, drew up affidavit'. In the undated article and in the affidavit dated 25 January, the exact six principles from the April 1947 memo are recorded. Alexander's diary therefore deepens scholarly understanding of when particular principles from the Code were formulated. It shows that discussions about the six principles were held between Alexander and Ivy as early as January, and that Alexander originally formulated the six principles in this month but had only sent the memo to Taylor in April.[11]

The first principle Alexander formulated – and arguably the principle that has most significantly shaped the history of modern medical ethics – outlined the right of the experimental subject to consent or refuse to participate in human experimentation in an informed manner. It stated that the "legal valid voluntary consent of the experimental subject is essential". The first principle as reformulated by the judges in the Code in more legalistic terminology is one of the most elaborate informed

---

5   Schmidt (2004), 3.
6   For an extensive discussion on the origins of the Nuremberg Code see Schmidt (2004), 199-263; see also Shuster (1997) and Moreno (1997). While some have argued that Leo Alexander was the main contributor to the final version of the Code, others have critically assessed the role of Ivy, claiming that he was not the sole author; see Weisleder (2021) and Gaw (2014).
7   Schmidt (2004), 246.
8   Harold Leon Sebring (9 March 1898–26 July 1968), nicknamed "Tom" Sebring. He was a Florida Supreme Court and an American judge at the Nuremberg Doctors' Trial, first of the Subsequent Nuremberg Trials of German war criminals after World War II.
9   Schmidt (2004), 247, 252, 253.
10 Ibid.
11 Ibid., 203.

consent principle of any medical ethics code in existence. The five additional statements focused on the need for the experiment to be humanitarian in nature and purpose, and stressed the scientific integrity and obligations of the investigator to the subject's wellbeing.[12] The resulting Code was based on these statements. The fourth principle of Alexander's memo regarding experimental facilities and preparation to prevent injury and death was hardly changed in the Code.[13] The fifth principle of Alexander's memorandum from April 1947 – 'the degree of risk should never exceed that determined by the humanitarian importance of the problem to be solved by the experiment' – was directly replicated in the Nuremberg Code. The rest of the stipulations were taken from a shortened version of a twenty-two page document Ivy had sent to the American Medical Association's Judicial Council.[14] Some key modifications were made based on Ivy's testimony during the Doctors' Trial; Sebring added the patients' right to withdraw from an experiment after questioning Ivy on this subject to principle nine. The Code was therefore drafted in stages.[15]

While the Nuremberg Code today is deemed to be one of the most significant documents pertaining to the regulation of human experiments in history – if not *the* most – it was initially dismissed by Anglo-American doctors in the immediate post-war period as irrelevant for their medical practice. Physicians contended that since the Code had been drafted in the wake of revelations about Nazi medical atrocities, it had no significance for their own practices of experimentation that took place in what was regarded as a world apart from the concentration camps in which experiments were conducted during the Third Reich.[16] It was viewed by the majority of the medical community, as the doctor and medical ethicist Jay Katz put it, as a "good code for barbarians but an unnecessary code for ordinary physician-scientists".[17] However, as Jonathan Moreno has shown, the Code did significantly shape the planning of the US government for defence against atomic, biological and chemical weapons during the decade following the end of the Second World War, even if its impact on both the medical profession and the practice of individual doctors was initially limited.[18] The Code was partially adopted by the United States Department of Defence in 1953 regarding defensive experiments associated with such weapons.[19] With regard to the history of modern bioethical research ethics, the Code has been a 'milestone'.[20] For example, informed consent forms the basis of the International Ethical Guidelines for Biomedical Research Involving Human Subjects, published in 1993.[21] While the Nuremberg Code is not explicitly mentioned with reference to 'informed consent' in the document, it is named as a document that prominently shaped medical ethical discussions during the formulation

---

12   Shuster (1997), 1437.
13   Schmidt (2004), 244.
14   Moreno (1997), 348.
15   Schmidt (2004), 246, 244.
16   Moreno (1997), 349.
17   Katz (1992), 228.
18   Moreno (1997), 351.
19   Moreno et al. (2017), 796.
20   Ibid., 795.
21   Shuster (1997), 1439.

of the International Ethical Guidelines.[22] The Nuremberg Code also influenced at least the Draft Code of the Declaration of Helsinki which serves as the guiding regulatory document for biomedical research; the final Declaration was published in 1964; subsequent versions followed. The principle of the Draft Code 'that during the course of the experiment the subject of it should be free to withdraw from it at any time' reflects the ninth principle of the Nuremberg Code.[23] The Code has therefore served as a key reference point in the drafting of bioethical regulations, even if the exact wording of the Nuremberg document is not used and references to it are not explicit.

The Nuremberg Code has also influenced the drafting of global human rights law. While the complete Code has not been legally adopted by any nation or as an ethical code by any major medical association, and the 1948 Universal Declaration of Human Rights has had a more significant influence in shaping international human rights law, the requirement of informed consent has been written into international law, as demonstrated in Article 7 of the United Nations International Covenant on Civil and Political Rights (1966).[24] However, in practice, the Code has not been readily applied as a legal precedent. Rather, there are notable instances where judges ruled that it did not apply. In 1987, the United States Supreme Court declared that it was not relevant to the case of a retired Army sergeant who stated he was injured in an LSD experiment. In the UK in 2004, British lawyers argued that the Code did not apply in the inquest into the death of a British serviceman from sarin nerve agent.[25] Yet the Code has certainly been significant as a legal reference point and as a regulatory document shaping modern biomedical research ethics.

Beyond the medical profession, the Nuremberg Code is also significant for historians. It has served as a key point of reference for assessing whether doctors who performed experiments on humans during the Cold War period adhered to, or violated, the medical ethics standards outlined in the Code. It therefore facilitates greater historical understanding of human experimentation during the Cold War period, and also informs legal judgement on, and contemporary scientific debate about, the actions of certain individuals and groups.[26] Analysing the Nuremberg Code also enables an insight into the extent to which subsequent ethical regulations – such as the Declaration of Helsinki – have weakened the Code's principles and provisions (e.g. the voluntary/informed consent principle) or have addressed the Code's shortcomings (e.g. its lack of legal gravitas), aiding in the strive of medical ethicists and other activists towards contemporary medical ethical regulations that protect patients' rights.

The context in which the Code was produced – beyond the principles of the document itself – also holds significance for the contemporary status of modern medicine in relation to the state. The entrenched entanglement between the German medical profession and the government of the Third Reich – with many doctors

---

22 See International Ethical Guidelines for Health-related Research Involving Humans, Prepared by the Council for International Organisations of Medical Sciences (CIOMS) in collaboration with the World Health Organisation (WHO), Geneva 2016, xi.
23 Schmidt et al. (2020), 5.
24 Shuster (1997), 1439, Moreno et al. (2017), 796.
25 Moreno et al. (2017), 796. For more detail about this inquest, see Schmidt (2015), 424–447.
26 Schmidt (2006), 5.

holding high-ranking positions in the Party and the SS – highlights the necessity of a degree of professional political independence from the state, in order to help prevent the profession from being subsumed into its ideological and geopolitical ambitions.[27] Alexander's own perspective on Nazi medicine and its ethical implications, revealed in his diary – that we must consider the power social and political forces have on medical practice – is still pertinent today, even if his statement that 'science under dictatorship becomes subordinated to the guiding philosophy of the dictatorship' perhaps minimises the complexities and dynamics of authoritarian regimes and the ability of the medical profession to resist certain ideological pressures.[28] Yet the legacy of the Code also points towards the importance of the medical profession being 'open to the essential role of nations and government agencies that respect broadly defined and agreed-upon rules to protect the rights and well-being of human research participants'.[29] The relationship between the state and the medical profession is often carefully negotiated and at times contested. Yet it is all the more essential – in the face of frequent medical ethical violations today and the concerning rise of right-wing political movements around the world – that governmental bodies and the medical profession collaborate effectively, on both a national and international level, to better protect the rights of patients and greater safeguard against unethical human experimentation.

LEO ALEXANDER AT NUREMBERG

The involvement of Leo Alexander in the drafting of the Nuremberg Code stemmed from his role as one of three medical experts of the prosecution in the Doctors' Trial, the other two being Werner Leibbrand[30] and Andrew Ivy.[31] After completing his training in neurology and psychiatry in Vienna, Berlin and Frankfurt/Main, Alexander taught at Peking Union Medical College in China. He had planned to return to Germany after his training, but after the rise of the Nazis to power in 1933, he immigrated to the United States where he was naturalised. In 1941, he was appointed associate professor of neuropsychiatry at Duke University, and served in the US Army Medical Corps during the war.[32] Alexander was recruited by the 7th US Army War Crimes Group in April 1945 to report on Nazi war crimes, selected due to his scientific training, German language skills, and knowledge of the cultural and scientific environment. He reflected on the 'grim spectacle' of German science as a result of these initial investigations in a letter to his wife in June, noting the "really depraved pseudo-scientific curiosity" of doctors.[33] By the time his initial war crimes investigations culminated in June 1945; Alexander had formed a good reputation for himself amongst American war crimes officials, which influenced his

---

27 Moreno et al. (2017), 796.
28 Schmidt (2004), 10; Alexander (1949), 39.
29 Moreno et al. (2017), 796.
30 For the role of Leibbrand in the Nuremberg Doctors' Trial see Frewer (2020), (2021), (2023) and Engelhardt/Frewer (2023).
31 For Ivy see Harkness (1996) and Gaw (2014).
32 Weisleder (2021), 122.
33 Schmidt (2004), 105.

appointment as medical expert for the Doctors' Trial in November 1946. While it is not known exactly who suggested him, the urgency of his presence in Nuremberg was articulated strongly by Taylor Telford in a cable to the United States War Department on 7 November 1946: "Badly need Dr Alexander here two or three weeks in advance of the trial for consultation and assistance in preparation of [the] case". He arrived in Nuremberg on 18 November after a tiring five-day journey he articulated in his diary.[34]

The "essential background work" Alexander completed before the trial helped to shape public, legal and medical awareness of the medical crimes individual doctors had committed.[35] The interviews he conducted with numerous perpetrators and witnesses in the lead up to the proceedings, and also during the trial itself, shed light on the extent of Nazi medical crimes from a psychological as well as medical perspective, across different geographical locations and spatial sites – from concentration camps to "euthanasia" centres. The victims of these atrocities were those deemed racially, politically and socially 'inferior' by the Nazi regime, such as Jews, communists, and the disabled. Alexander's tireless efforts in documenting these atrocities, which are described in vivid detail in his Nuremberg diary, ensured that some perpetrators – even if those tried in the Doctors' Trial formed only a small fraction of the medical personnel who committed medical crimes – were held legally accountable for their actions, providing some justice for the victims. Alongside investigating and documenting atrocities, and providing some of the crucial statements which were later incorporated in the trial judgement and the ensuing Nuremberg Code, Alexander helped to write the opening statement for the Doctors' Trial. He wrote in his diary that he "dictated Chapter 5".[36] In the two days before the beginning of the trial, Alexander worked with Taylor on the opening address, remarking that he had "tied in a good deal of my material".[37] Taylor's opening speech reflected Alexander's argument in the aspects of the statement which outlined the determination to kill within German medical science, referring to Alexander's concept of "thanatology".[38]

Alexander refined his concept of 'science of killing' during a time in which contemporary scholars were already writing about the Doctors' Trial. Alexander Mitscherlich and Fred Mielke's edition *Das Diktat der Menschenverachtung*, published in 1947 and followed by *Wissenschaft ohne Menschlichkeit* in 1949 and *Medizin ohne Menschlichkeit* in 1960, together with Alice Platen-Hallermund's book *Die Tötung Geisteskranker in Deutschland* (1948) were key early texts that highlighted the medical crimes committed during the Third Reich described in the trial.[39] The publication of George Annas and Michael Grodin's volume, *The Nazi Doctors and the Nuremberg Code*, was the first to fully historicise the case.[40] Since the publication of their book – and the passing of the fiftieth and seventieth anniversaries of the trial and the Nuremberg Code – there has been a proliferation of

---

34 Ibid., 77, 105, 151, 152; DUMC, Alexander diary (1946/47), 5, 18 November 1946.
35 Schmidt (2004), 7.
36 DUMC, Alexander diary (1946/47), 78, 3 December 1946.
37 Ibid., 105, 8 December 1946. See also Schmidt (2004), 67.
38 Schmidt (2004), 177; also Schmidt (2024) (forthcoming).
39 Mitscherlich/Milke (1947), (1949), (1960). Platen-Hallermund (1948).
40 See Annas/Grodin (1992) and Frewer et al. (1999).

literature on the Doctors' Trial.[41] While this scholarship initially criticised the trial for failing to identify the crimes of German doctors during the Third Reich, subsequent literature, notably Ulf Schmidt's book *Justice at Nuremberg*, have taken a more nuanced approach, placing the trial in its social and political context and analysing its implications for modern biomedical research ethics.[42]

In addition to this work, documents relating to the trial are now readily available. Since the microfiche edition of the trial transcripts was produced by Klaus Dörner and Angelika Ebbinghaus in 1999,[43] numerous documents have been digitised and published.[44] This effort has been part of a broader attempt to make files from the International Military Tribunal and the following twelve trials before the United States Nuremberg Military Tribunals (NMT) conducted between 1945 and 1949 accessible for use by scholars, students, and interested members of the public. The Nuremberg Trials Project, initiated by the Harvard Law School Library, contains open-access material specifically related to the Doctors' Trial, including prosecution and defence files, evidence documents, court transcripts, and photographs.[45] Yet in spite of Alexander's major role in uncovering Nazi medical crimes, shaping the Doctors' Trial, and articulating some of the key points of the Nuremberg Code, as outlined by Ulf Schmidt in his history of Alexander and the Doctors' Trial, his diary – which documents these key events – remains obscure and known to only a few expert scholars.[46]

ALEXANDER'S NUREMBERG DIARY

Leo Alexander wrote what we have termed the "Nuremberg Diary" between 11 November 1946 and 24 June 1947. Following on from the notes he took between May and June 1945, which pertained to his initial war crimes investigations in Germany regarding Nazi medical crimes, this particular diary – officially listed as "Record ledger book of activities and notes, 1946–1947" at Duke University Medical Center Library & Archives – documents and interprets the medical atrocities committed by defendants at the Nuremberg Doctors' Trial, based on numerous interviews with the accused and concentration camp survivors.

The scholarly use of Alexander's Nuremberg diary carries certain methodological problems. Alexander wrote in both English and German, switching languages sometimes in the space of one paragraph or sentence, which can be jarring for the reader. The use of multiple languages in the written text explains why it remained largely unexplored for many years. Indeed, a good command of the English and German languages together with knowledge of scientific terminology is needed to make sense of certain passages. Pages 26 to 30 of the diary, where Alexander notes detail about the freezing experiments at Dachau based on interviews with doctors

---

41 See, for example Freyhofer (2004), Weindling (2004) and Annas/Grodin (2018).
42 Marrus (1999).
43 Dörner et al. (1999); see also Frewer/Opitz et al. (1999).
44 For a guide to the microfiche edition, see Eltzschig/Walter (2001);.
45 See 'Nuremberg Trials Project', Harvard Law School Library, https://nuremberg.law.harvard.edu/. Digitisation begun in 1999, and was completed in 2016.
46 See Schmidt (2004).

involved, is a pertinent example of this.[47] His handwriting is also particularly hard to decipher; it is not always clear in the diary at first glance which language he is using, making an understanding of what he wrote particularly difficult. Alexander was not only a doctor, but also had a particular style of writing, utilising sometimes unconventional abbreviations, shorthand, and often missing out letters.[48] We have therefore made the editorial decision to stylistically change certain aspects of the diary to maximise readability; we have explained these changes in the following short editorial guide to the diary, along with other details we believe will aid the reader in interpreting this distinctive historical source.

In spite of extensive efforts to transcribe the diary entirely, gaps in the transcription remain: one example is the table about the different medical experiments carried out in the Third Reich on page 13 of the diary. The question of the extent to which we can use information from Alexander's scribblings as historical evidence when there are particular omissions might therefore be raised. Yet throughout the diary, the gaps are one or two words in sentences, rather than entire paragraphs or sections. It is still possible to glean Alexander's thoughts and therefore make historical arguments based on particular sections of the diary. Overall, approximately 95 percent of the diary has been transcribed. Instances where the words Alexander penned are not decipherable – in spite of best efforts – are clearly marked with dots inside square brackets. We have also indicated the instances where it is not completely clear what Alexander wrote but an educated suggestion can be made by placing the word or words in square brackets. Furthermore, Alexander's use of shorthand, abbreviations, and his missing out of letters convey to the reader his determination to hastily record what defendants and witnesses told him, so that this detail could be quickly used as part of trial investigations. His hurried handwriting thus provides an insight into the pressure Alexander was under, and is therefore of historical interest to the reader in itself. Alexander's frequent switching between German and English – while somewhat interrupting the diary's flow for the reader – also illustrates his multilingual background, further demonstrating why he was selected as an expert witness for the trial.

Another aspect of the diary which might make it difficult for the reader to follow are the numerous references to people and places with little or no context provided. To help readers better navigate the diary, we have provided footnotes and indexes detailing information about the lives of individuals and the geographic locations mentioned. The inclusion of a selection of Alexander's papers in this book also provides scientific context to some of the conceptual terms mentioned, for example, thanatology, and we have also defined other historically relevant conceptual terms. Since considerable medical expertise is needed to understand particular parts of the text, with many specialist medical terms used throughout the diary, we have also explained these terms in the footnotes.

In spite of these methodological problems, which we have tried to mitigate as far as possible, the diary is a rich historical source that is immensely valuable for specialist academics, undergraduate and graduate students, and interested general

---

47 DUMC, Alexander diary (1946/47), 26–30, 27 November 1946.
48 Berlin medical historians have written about doctors' handwriting. See, for example, Hess/Mendelsohn (2014), 471–503.

audiences. It provides a unique insight into preparations for the Nuremberg Doctors' Trial from the perspective of one individual; namely, it details the attempt of a medical expert to find general trends in the medical crimes committed by doctors during the Third Reich. We can discern how the contribution of one medical expert to the documenting of medical war crimes enabled arguments and theories to be produced about the nature of these atrocities and the motivations behind them. The diary highlights how Alexander developed his concept of thanatology based in numerous conversations with defendants and witnesses. Alexander developed the concept as a rebuttal against the possible defence argument that the human experiments carried out by Allied medical scientists were comparable to those conducted by the German doctors and should therefore not be punished.[49] Alexander first mentioned the concept in his diary on 21 November 1946, recording a discussion with Taylor on the subject.[50] He defined thanatology as the 'scientific implementation of genocide' on 21 November 1946, and wrote that he worked again on the concept over the next few days.[51] He seemingly titled a paper on the subject on 24 November as 'The voice of destruction spoke through medicine'.[52] By 28 November, Alexander noted that he had 'completed Thanatology'; his diary therefore indicates how he produced the broad outlines of the Thanatology concept in just over a week.[53] Alexander sent a memo to Taylor on 30 November with a subtitle 'Thanatology as a Scientific Technique of Genocide', and another on 5 December titled 'Suggestions for a Discussion of the Thanatology Genocide Angle'.[54] From January 1947, Alexander used the word 'ktenology' instead of 'thanatology' to describe the 'science of killing' in his diary, and 'ktenology' became his preferred term to describe this 'science' in his articles published after Nuremberg.[55] While the concept of thanatology has certain shortcomings and no bearing on international law today, it played an important role in solidifying the case of the prosecution in the Doctors' Trial by outlining ethical and non-ethical human experimentation for the purposes of the trial. The concept of Thanatology aimed to show how Allied medical experiments were distinct from the murderous intentions and outcomes behind the experiments conducted during the Third Reich.[56]

Alexander's diary provides hitherto barely known detail about the effects of some of the experiments which took place in the Nazi concentration camps. It describes in intimate detail the devastating impact sterilisation experiments at Auschwitz had, assumably based on an interview with two Jewish brothers, Abram and Joshua Sak, who were sterilised by exposure to X-Ray and subsequently castrated. Alexander noted that Abram felt 'deeply humiliated and ashamed of his disability', and found it difficult to tell his wife, a survivor of Majdanek concentration camp, about what had happened to him. He lost his desire to have sex after the experiment.

---

49 Schmidt (2004), 160–161; also Schmidt (2024) (forthcoming).
50 DUMC, Alexander diary (1946/47), 11, 21 November 1946.
51 Ibid., 12 and 18, 21 November 1946.
52 Ibid., 20, 24 November 1946.
53 Ibid., 35, 28 November 1946.
54 Schmidt (2004), 163.
55 DUMC, Alexander diary (1946/1947), 168, 21 January 1947. See Alexander (1948) and (1949).
56 Schmidt (2004), 168.

His wife decided to stay with him, but stated that she did not know how she would feel about the situation in half a year.[57] Alexander's notes highlight the devastating extent to which the sterilisation experiments affected the physical and personal wellbeing of individuals after the war, detrimentally influencing future relationships and social encounters. His diary provides a crucial insight into the impact of Nazi persecution on the Third Reich's victims and how the loved ones of individuals subjected to experiments often struggled to personally navigate what had happened to them.

Alexander investigated and documented these medical atrocities while remaining in close contact with his family in the United States. His diary provides a unique insight into how Alexander's professional obligations as a war crimes investigator ran parallel with his role as a husband and father.[58] His scientific notes and reflections on the trial are interspersed with comments referring to letters from his family. On 7 January 1947, for example, he commented on the 'magnificent testimony' of Eugen Kogon, who was imprisoned at Dachau, before writing directly afterwards '2 letters from Phyllis'.[59] When he was reunited with Phyllis in The Netherlands a week later, he remarked that it was "wonderful to see her again", but lamented on her 'attitude' towards a party at Nuremberg in May.[60] Alexander's diary therefore allows the reader a glimpse – if brief – into the textures of his marital relations, as well as his extensive work as a trial investigator. Using the diary in tandem with the letters Alexander sent to his wife provide a vivid insight into both the personal and professional aspects of his work at Nuremberg, and how the two often intersected in his thoughts.

Indeed, Alexander's interpretations of Nazi medical crimes were not simply formulated alone in the vacuum of his own mind. The articulation of his findings in letters to Phyllis and his family – even if these writings were not always frequent – no doubt helped him to compose his own thoughts in relation to the atrocities. Furthermore, Alexander's arguments were shaped not only by conversations with witnesses and defendants but by discussions with members of the prosecution and other individuals working on the Doctors' Trial case. Alexander's diary indicates that many of these conversations took place in social settings. On 8 December 1946, for instance, the day before the opening of the Doctors' Trial, he first worked with Taylor on the opening speech before attending a party hosted by the General at Villa Schickedanz in Dambach, a large estate located south-west of Fürth, where the conversation would, in all probability, have touched upon the strength of the prosecution case in the upcoming trial against the Nazi doctors.[61] He also frequently spent time with Keith Mant, a British medical expert who wrote an extensive report about the medical services at Ravensbrück concentration camp, in informal contexts. The two went for dinner on 20 November 1946 after Alexander had spent the day interviewing Herta Oberheuser and Gerhard Schiedlausky, two doctors at the camp.[62]

---

57 DUMC, Alexander diary (1946/1947), 41–44, 29 November 1946.
58 Schmidt (2004), 207.
59 DUMC, Alexander diary (1946/1947), 158, 7 January 1947.
60 DUMC, Alexander diary (1946/1947), 203, 13 March 1947. DUMC, Alexander diary (1946/1947), 237, 15 May 1947.
61 DUMC, Alexander diary (1946/1947), 105, 6 December 1946.
62 DUMC, Alexander diary (1946/1947), 7–11, 20 November 1946.

He likely discussed the behaviour of these doctors in the evening with Mant, perhaps drawing on Mant's knowledge of Ravensbrück. Alexander also went to the opera with Mant and had wine with him in January together with his assistant Marian Shelley. We should not underestimate the role of these informal encounters in shaping Alexander's views and informed the Doctors' Trial and the Nuremberg Code.[63]

The diary provides a vivid insight into how the Doctors' Trial was constructed: we can discern the frantically developed nature of the proceedings. War crimes investigators faced real time pressures in the build-up to the trial. Alexander's 'first day of rest' was, he noted, on 29 December 1946, well over a month after he first arrived at Nuremberg on 18 November.[64] Indeed, Alexander had completed a thorough analysis of all the experiments named in the trial indictment and had studied the behaviour and personalities of twenty-three defendants in just over two weeks, working until 3 am in the morning to complete his task.[65] One of the experiments he analysed was the sulfonamide operations, which took place at Ravensbrück concentration camp. Alexander described his preparation of expert medical testimony to be delivered to the court on the effects of these experiments as a "race against time".[66] The diary reveals the extensive research Alexander conducted – in spite of such time pressures – on this set of experiments. While Alexander wrote "The pace of work is terrific" to his wife, he nonetheless meticulously recorded in his diary the precise measurements of the scars suffered by the victims and their devastating effects, such as the disturbance of gait, walking difficulties, and severe pain.[67] This detail likely provided the basis for his crucial expert report presented in court, which was the most effective of the entire trial from the prosecution's viewpoint. Alexander's testimony also received media attention in *Life* magazine, throwing the horrific nature of Nazi medical atrocities into the international limelight.[68]

LEO ALEXANDER'S CORRESPONDENCE AND PUBLICATIONS

In addition to providing readers with the edited diary transcript, we have included correspondence from Leo Alexander to his wife Phyllis and his son Gustav in late 1946 and early 1947. These letters demonstrate how Alexander attempted to express and summarise the historical significance of bringing Nazi medical perpetrators to justice. They convey a degree of immediacy, and provide an unfiltered – and partly unreflected – view on how the Doctors' Trial proceedings developed and were hastily organised in a politically charged, highly improvised environment, with staff working intimately together around the clock. As such, the correspondence serves to 'set the scene' of the atmosphere of the Doctors' Trial, allowing the diary to be situated in this unique historical context. To aid readers' understanding

---

63   DUMC, Alexander diary (1946/1947), 167, 17 January 1947.
64   DUMC, Alexander diary (1946/1947), 155, 15 May 1911.
65   Schmidt (2004), 167. Letter from Leo Alexander to Phyllis, 7 December 1946.
66   DUMC, Alexander diary (1946/1947), 146, 18–19 November 1946.
67   Ibid., 139–146, 16 and 17 December 1946. Schmidt (2004), 180.
68   Schmidt (2004), 186, 191.

and interpretation of the diary, we have included the correspondence before the diary manuscript.

In addition to the correspondence, we have also included excerpts from Alexander's expert testimony in which he drew from the pre-trial investigations outlined in the diary and in which the voice of one of the victims, Jadwiga Dzido, is present. Moreover, we have included two key publications Alexander produced, borne out of his involvement in the Doctors' Trial: 'War Crimes and their Motivations', published in 1948 in the Journal *of Criminal Law and Criminology*, and 'Medical Science Under Dictatorship', printed in 1949 in the *New England Journal of Medicine*. The articles demonstrate Alexander's continued promulgation of the 'ktenology' (the science of killing) concept, and also highlight the development of his perspectives on Nazi crimes since the Nuremberg diary. Based on his interviews conducted with perpetrators, he articulated in these publications his theory of *Blutkitt* ('blood cement'): individuals participating in a crime in order to clear themselves of perceived disloyalty by SS officials which, in turn, "definitely and irrevocably" tied them to the SS.[69] This explanation of the motivations of perpetrators, however, does not account for the persecutory behaviour of thousands of individuals who were not classified as "disloyal". Ian Kershaw's seminal "Working towards the Führer" thesis, which suggests that individuals were "working towards" Hitler by implementing the persecutory actions they believed were in the interest of the Nazi regime, can be applied more broadly as an explanation for the carrying out of the Third Reich's atrocities by individuals "on the ground", even if it does not account for the particular motives of individuals within the medical profession.[70]

Alexander's interpretation of Nazi perpetrators as sadists is also outdated in light of the scholarly interpretations of these individuals proliferating in the 2000s. Although he found that the doctors he interviewed had no notable psychiatric histories, documented in his diary, and argued that some scientists committed crimes out of "fear and cowardice, especially fear of ostracism by the group" rather than due to "simple ferocity or aggressiveness", he also drew on "release of repressed destructive primitive and sadistic drives" amongst men in the SS who perpetrated violent crimes.[71] Historians have long since abandoned this idea; the most prominent and early example is Christopher Browning's seminal work, *Ordinary Men*.[72] Chris Dillon's 'interactionist' approach – the argument that 'culture, cognition, and situation interact in perpetrator behaviour' – encapsulates the complex factors that combined during the Nazi regime to drive individuals to perpetrate crimes, and reflects recent nuanced approaches to perpetrator behaviour.[73] Alexander's focus mostly on the SS from a 'top-down' perspective also overlooked the contributions of individuals not officially affiliated with the SS to Nazi persecution, such as administrators, teachers, and nurses; many of whom were women and therefore not eligible for SS membership.[74]

---

69 Alexander (1948), 300. Alexander (1949), 44.
70 McElligott/Kirk (2003), 6.
71 Alexander (1948), 301, 306.
72 See Browning (1991).
73 Dillon (2017), 7.
74 See, for example, Century (2017), Betzien (2018), and Docking (2021).

Some of Alexander's perspectives on the Third Reich generally in these articles are now somewhat outdated in light of historiographical developments in the decades since. He described the regime as totalitarian – in line with contemporary perspectives of the Third Reich as a regime as a "monolithic system of totalitarian rule" – and viewed the German people as collectively tainted by Nazism, arguing that Germany as a whole needed "socio-psychologic rehabilitation".[75] His view reflected not only those of American intelligence and psychological warfare officers involved in denazification, who wanted to enforce the notion of "collective guilt" on Germans in the immediate aftermath of the war, but that of philosophers and political theorists such as Hannah Arendt who in 1951 published her seminal book "The Origins of Totalitarianism".[76] Historians have in recent decades favoured more nuanced approaches to questions of guilt and responsibility amongst Germans; as highlighted by Mary Fulbrook, they have analysed the varying and often overlapping roles Germans had during the Third Reich, ranging from victims to perpetrators and bystanders to collaborators.[77] Nonetheless, Alexander's articles demonstrate the development of scholarly perspectives on Nazi crimes since the end of the Second World War; viewpoints which have evolved from the contentions expressed in Alexander's original writings. These publications, and, indeed, the diary, provide an insight into the viewpoints – which may indeed be nuanced and challenged today – of one particular expert in the immediate aftermath of the war, as well as detailed descriptions of the medical crimes committed by Nazi doctors.

CECILY GRABLE INTERVIEW

We have also included the transcript of an interview Ulf Schmidt, one of the editors, conducted with Cecily Grable in May 1999 as part of his research for *Justice at Nuremberg. Leo Alexander and the Nazi Doctors' Trial*, published in 2004. In this interview, Alexander's daughter reflected on her father's work at Nuremberg and his professional life. The interview also provides a snapshot into Alexander as a person. Grable discusses his religious beliefs, family background and childhood, and her overall perception of him as a person, describing him as 'intellectual, brilliant, sophisticated, fascinating, distant'.[78] While she may have withheld disclosing certain memories in the interview context, the transcript, nonetheless, provides a revealing insight into how she perceived Alexander as a father and psychiatrist, as well as her articulation of his role at Nuremberg. The interview provides a more personal insight into Alexander than the diary or articles; together with his Nuremberg correspondence, the material allows readers to obtain an impression of Alexander's multi-faceted and complex personality.

---

75 Alexander (1949), 298. Alexander (1948), 299. McElligott/Kirk (2003), 1.
76 Arendt (1951), Grossmann (2007), 41.
77 Fulbrook (2018), 8.
78 Interview by Ulf Schmidt with Cecily Alexander-Grable, May 1999.

CONCLUSION

As burgeoning recent scholarly research such as the European Research Council "Taming the European Leviathan" project has striven to understand the development of post-war ethics in not only Western Europe but in Europe as a whole, including in Central and Eastern Europe, the understanding of the Nuremberg diary and the work of medical ethicists in the immediate aftermath of the war gains additional scholarly and historical significance.[79] Work on the history of post-war deontology, for example, has shown that in many parts of Europe, including Poland, the Nuremberg Doctors' Trial and the Nuremberg Code were carefully monitored and studied but strikingly were not included, at least by name, in the development of the medical ethics standards that arose in these countries. This needs explanation. By engaging critically with how Leo Alexander's work – most visible in the Nuremberg Code – was perceived in other regions and cultural contexts, we will gain a much better and more nuanced understanding of how post-war medicine and principles of research governance developed across Europe. This is also crucial knowledge for a more complete and less one-dimensional understanding of the role and history of bioethics.

As international military tribunals associated with genocidal crimes still occur around the world today, and undoubtedly will continue to take place, studying Leo Alexander's diary sheds light on how one individual medical expert attempted to, with varying degrees of success, influence the Nuremberg trial process and its ultimate outcome, the Nuremberg Code.[80] His diary is of significant scholarly interest because it not only illuminates hitherto unknown details about Nazi medical atrocities, but also demonstrates how the Doctors' Trial was constructed and the origins of the Nuremberg Code. For all the shortcomings of the trial and the Code, the work of Alexander in taking witness statements from victims and preparing them for their testimony in court was crucial not only for the success of the prosecution, but also in drawing broader public attention to Nazi crimes. The dream of Alexander and other experts and prosecutors at Nuremberg of preventing unethical human experimentation and other medical atrocities from ever happening again has not been realised, given the continuous revelations of unethical practices around the world which violate accepted international medical ethics standards. It also does not seem that medical ethics is back on the international agenda; as Schmidt, Frewer and Sprumont have noted, we are rather living in a 'post-ethical' world.[81] This book therefore makes a step – if small – to placing issues such as informed consent and scientifically valid research practices back on the scholarly and public agenda. It does so through the eyes of a man who made medical ethics history: Leo Alexander.

---

79 For the Taming the European Leviathan project see https://leviathan-europe.eu/.
80 Schmidt (2004), 9.
81 Schmidt et al. (2020), 2.

REFERENCES

Alexander, Leo (1948): "War Crimes and Their Motivation. The Socio-Psychological Structure of the SS and the Criminalisation of a Society". In: Journal of Law and Criminology 39 (3), 298–326.

Alexander, Leo (1949): "Medical Science under Dictatorship". In: The New England Journal of Medicine 241, 39–47.

Annas, George/Grodin, Michael (eds.) (1992): The Nazi Doctors and the Nuremberg Code. Human Rights in Human Experimentation. New York.

Annas, George/Grodin, Michael (2018): Reflections on the 70th Anniversary of the Nuremberg Doctors' Trial. In: American Journal of Public Health 108 (1), 10–12.

Arendt, Hannah (1951): The Origins of Totalitarianism. New York.

Bayle, François (1950): Croix gammée contre caducée. Les expériences humaines en Allemagne pendant la seconde guerre mondiale. Préface par le Dr. René Piédelièvre. Neustadt/Pfalz.

Betzien, Petra (2018): Krankenschwestern im System der nationalsozialistischen Konzentrationslager. Frankfurt/M.

Browning, Christopher (1992): Ordinary Men. New York.

Bruns, Florian (2009): Medizinethik im Nationalsozialismus. Entwicklungen und Protagonisten in Berlin (1939–1945). Geschichte und Philosophie der Medizin, Band 7. Stuttgart.

Caplan, Arthur (ed.) (1992): When Medicine Went Mad. Contemporary Issues in Biomedicine, Ethics and Society. Totowa.

Century, Rachel (2017): Female Administrators in the Third Reich. Basingstoke.

Dillon, Christopher (2017): Dachau and the SS. Cambridge.

Docking, Kate (2021): "Gender, Recruitment and Medicine at Ravensbrück Concentration Camp, 1939–1942". In: German History 39 (3), 419–441. Doi: 10.1093/gerhis/ghab021.

Dörner, Klaus/Ebbinghaus, Angelika/Linne, Karsten (Hrsg.) (1999): Der Nürnberger Ärzteprozeß 1946/47. Wortprotokolle, Anklage- und Verteidigungsmaterial, Quellen zum Umfeld. Deutsche Ausgabe, im Auftrag der Stiftung für Sozialgeschichte des 20. Jahrhunderts herausgegeben von Klaus Dörner, Angelika Ebbinghaus und Karsten Linne; in Zusammenarbeit mit Karl-Heinz Roth und Paul Weindling. Bearbeitet von Karsten Linne. Einleitung von Angelika Ebbinghaus, Mikrofiche-Edition. München, New York.

Eltzschig, Johannes/Walter, Michael (eds.) (2001): The Nuremberg Medical Trial 1946/47. Guide to the Microfiche Edition. München.

Engelhardt, Thomas/Frewer, Andreas (eds.) (2023): NS-"Euthanasie" in Erlangen. Tatorte – Hungerkost – Opfer. Neustadt/A.

Fulbrook, Mary (2018): Reckonings: Legacies of Nazi Persecution and the Quest for Justice. Oxford.

Frewer, Andreas (Hrsg.) (2020): Psychiatrie und "Euthanasie" in der HuPfla. Debatten zu Werner Leibbrands Buch "Um die Menschenrechte der Geisteskranken". Nürnberg.

Frewer, Andreas (2021): Werner Leibbrand: Leben – Weiterleben – Überleben. Geschichte und Philosophie der Medizin, Band 16. Stuttgart.

Frewer, Andreas (2023): Werner Leibbrand und die "Euthanasie" in Erlangen. Seine besondere Rolle bei der Aufarbeitung von NS-Verbrechen. In: Engelhardt/Frewer (2023), 239–294.

Frewer, Andreas/Neumann, Josef N. (eds.) (2001): Medizingeschichte und Medizinethik. Kontroversen und Begründungsansätze 1900–1950. Frankfurt/M., New York.

Frewer, Andreas/Oppitz, Ulrich-Dieter et al. (eds.) (1999): Medizinverbrechen vor Gericht. Das Urteil im Nürnberger Ärzteprozeß gegen Karl Brandt und andere sowie aus dem Prozeß gegen Generalfeldmarschall Erhard Milch. Erlanger Studien zur Ethik in der Medizin, Band 7, Erlangen, Jena.

Freyhofer, Horst (2004): The Nuremberg Medical Trial. The Holocaust and the Origin of the Nuremberg Medical Code. New York.

Gaw, Allan (2014): Reality and revisionism: new evidence for Andrew C. Ivy's claim to authorship of the Nuremberg Code. In: Journal of the Royal Society of Medicine 107 (4), 138–143. Doi: 10.1177/0141076814523948.

Grossmann, Atina (2007): Jews, Germans and Allies: Close Encounters in Occupied Germany. Princeton.

Harkness, Jon M. (1996): Nuremberg and the Issue of Wartime Experiments on US Prisoners. The Green Committee. In: JAMA 276 (20), 1672–1675.

Hess, Volker/Mendelsohn, J. Andrew (2014): "Sauvages' paperwork: how disease classification arose from scholarly note-taking". In: Early Science and Medicine 19 (5), 471–503.
Katz, Jay (1992): "Abuse of Human Beings for the Sake of Science". In: Caplan (1992), 223–270.
Kurihara, Chieko/Dhai, Ames/Greco, Dirceu (eds.) (2023): Ethical Innovation for Global Health. Pandemic, Democracy and Ethics in Research. Berlin.
Marrus, Michael (1999): "The Nuremberg Doctors' Trial in Historical Context". In: Bulletin of the History of Medicine 73 (1999), 106–123.
McElligott, Anthony/Kirk, Tim (2003): Working towards the Führer. Essays in honour of Sir Ian Kershaw. Manchester.
McElligott, Anthony/Kirk, Tim (2003): "Editors' introduction". In: McElligott/Kirk (2003), 1–5.
Mitscherlich, Alexander/Mielke, Fred (1947): Das Diktat der Menschenverachtung. Heidelberg.
Mitscherlich, Alexander/Mielke, Fred (1949): Wissenschaft ohne Menschlichkeit. Medizinische und eugenische Irrwege unter Diktatur, Bürokratie und Krieg. Mit einem Vorwort der Arbeitsgemeinschaft der Westdeutschen Ärztekammern. Heidelberg.
Mitscherlich, Alexander/Mielke, Fred (1960): Medizin ohne Menschlichkeit. Dokumente des Nürnberger Ärzteprozesses. Frankfurt/M.
Moreno, Jonathan D. (1997): "Reassessing the Influence of the Nuremberg Code on American Medical Ethics". In: Journal of Contemporary Health Law & Policy 13 (2), 347–360.
Moreno, Jonathan D./Schmidt, Ulf/Joffe, Steve (2017): "The Nuremberg Code 70 Years On". In: Journal of the American Medical Association 318 (9), 795–796. Doi: 10.1001/jama.2017.10265.
Platen-Hallermund, Alice (1948): Die Tötung Geisteskranker in Deutschland. Frankfurt/M.
Pross, Christian (1992): "Nazi Doctors, German Medicine and Historical Truth". In: Annas/Grodin (1992), 32–53.
Reginbogin, Herbert/Breger, Marshall J. (eds.) (2024, forthcoming): Nuremberg Principles and Ukraine: The Contemporary Challenges to Peace, Security, and Justice. Lanham.
Roelcke, Volker/Topp, Sascha/Lepicard, Etienne (eds.) (2014): Silence, scapegoats, self-reflection. The shadow of Nazi medical crimes on medicine and bioethics. Göttingen.
Schmidt, Ulf (2001): "Der Ärzteprozeß als moralische Instanz? Der Nürnberger Kodex und das Problem 'zeitloser Medizinethik'". In: Frewer/Neumann (2001), 334–373.
Schmidt, Ulf (2004): Justice at Nuremberg: Leo Alexander and the Nazi Doctors' Trial. Basingstoke.
Schmidt, Ulf (2023): "From Nuremberg to Helsinki: Historicising the Codification of Post-War Research Ethics". In: Kurihara et al. (2023), 149–174.
Schmidt, Ulf (2024): Thanatology and the Nuremberg Doctors' Trial: Conceptualizing the "Science of Killing". In: Reginbogin/Breger (forthcoming).
Schmidt, Ulf/Frewer, Andreas (eds.) (2007): History and Theory of Human Experimentation. The Declaration of Helsinki and Modern Medical Ethics. Stuttgart.
Schmidt, Ulf/Frewer, Andreas/Sprumont, Dominique (eds.) (2020): Ethical Research. The Declaration of Helsinki, and the Past, Present, and Future of Human Experimentation. Oxford.
Shuster, Evelyne (1997): Fifty Years Later: The Significance of the Nuremberg Code. In: The New England Journal of Medicine 337 (20), 1436–1440. Doi: 10.1056/NEJM199711133372006.
Weisleder, Pedro (2022): "Leo Alexander's Blueprint of the Nuremberg Code". In: Paediatric Neurology 126, 120–124. Doi: 10.1016/j.pediatrneurol.2021.10.015.
Weindling, Paul (2004): Nazi Medicine and the Nuremberg Trials: From Medical War Crimes to Informed Consent. Basingstoke.

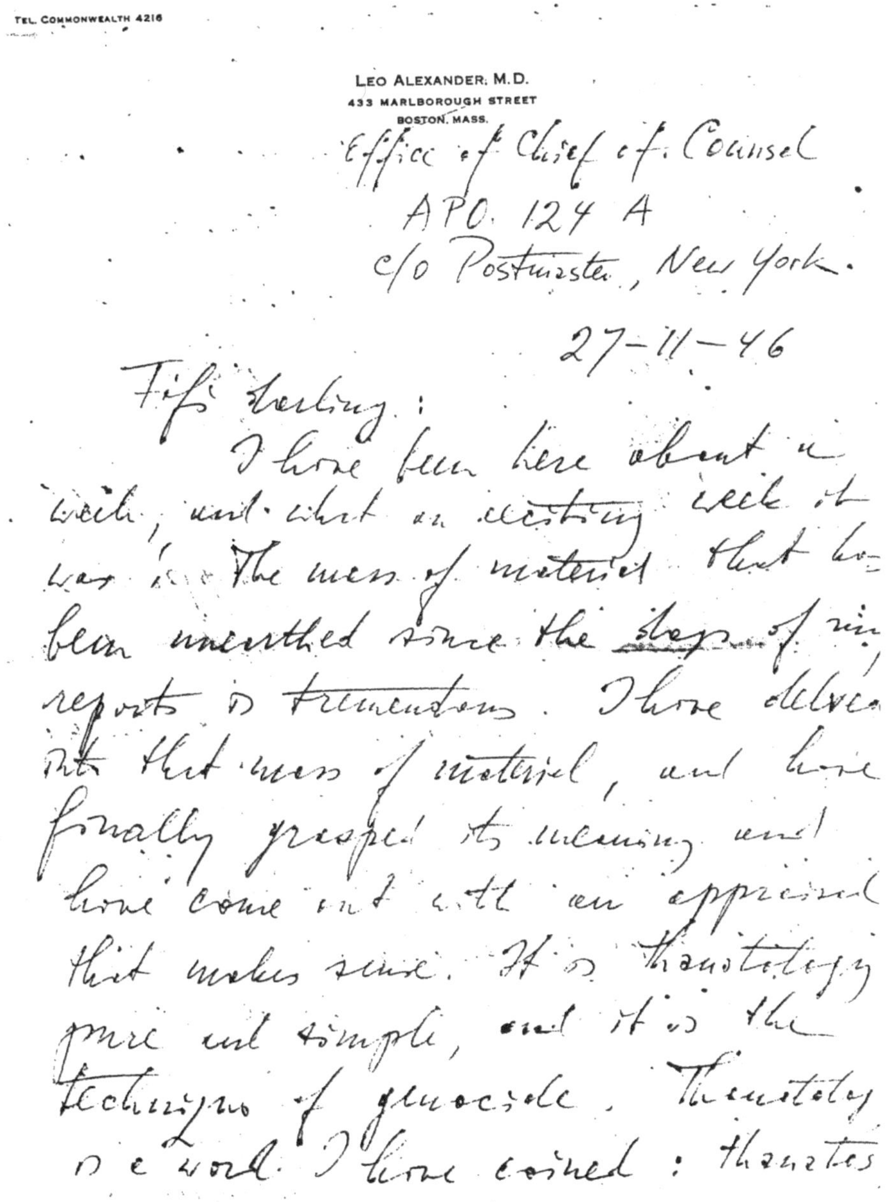

TEL. COMMONWEALTH 4216

LEO ALEXANDER, M.D.
433 MARLBOROUGH STREET
BOSTON, MASS.

Office of Chief of Counsel
APO 124 A
c/o Postmaster, New York.

27-11-46

Fifi darling:

I have been here about a week, and what an exciting week it was! The mass of material that has been unearthed since the days of my reports is tremendous. I have delved into that mass of material, and have finally grasped its meaning and have come out with an approach that makes sense. It is thanatology pure and simple, and it is the technique of genocide. Thanatology is a word I have coined: thanatos

Fig. 3. Leo Alexander's letter to his wife Phyllis Alexander, 27 November 1946 (Source: Alexander Papers, Duke University).

4

LEO ALEXANDER
THE NUREMBERG CORRESPONDENCE

1946–1947

27 November 1946

Fifi darling:

I have been here about a week, and what an interesting week it was. The mass of material that has been unearthed since the days of my reports is tremendous. I have delved into that mass of material, and have finally grasped its meaning and have come out with an appraisal that makes sense. It is thanatology pure and simple, and it is the technique of genocide. Thanatology is a word I have coined: thanathos in Greek, means death. Genocide is the "murder of people", a word coined by our old friend Lemkin. I shall send you the carbon of an appraisal of the whole problem which I have been writing for General Taylor, the chief prosecutor; and which I may publish independently, if the War Department approves. I have been writing of nights; mornings I spent in interrogations, after noon I cram through the evidence, and night I have been spending trying to organize the material. I wish you were here and I hope you will come.

The people here are an interesting group, a small town within a town. I live at the Grand Hotel; breakfast is at 8 A.M. – 8:30 A.M.; then the bus leaves for the Court house. There one works, with a brief intermission for lunch on the ground floor, til 6 PM. Then the bus leaves for the Hotel. Supper, then talking shop in the lobby, exchange of notes and …, then to my room for writing.

The Chief Prosecutor is General Telford Taylor, a young Harvard trained lawyer, aged 38 years, he has a highly intelligent and charming wife, who also works in the interrogation section (not as an interrogator). Their children aged 4 and 6 years are in a boarding school in Washington D.C. General Taylor is a A.U.S. Officer expects to return to F.C.C. after the trial his assistant is Mr. Ervin, his wife, Wellesley educated, is in charge of the location buro who try to locate missing war criminals. It sports an air of amateurishness and erudition which would make a Boston cop's hair stand on end, her office works reasonably well. A very good job has been done in ferreting out missing war criminals. Mr. MacHaney is in charge of the prosecution of the doctors' case; he is a smooth Southern lawyer from Arkansas. His assistant is Mr. Alexander G. Hardy, from Cochituate and Boston, a future politician, but very smart and a hard worker. His assistant is Dr. Horlik-Hochwald, formerly from Prague.

The defense lawyers are quite smart too, especially the Austrian who is defending Dr. Beiglböck from Vienna, who turns out to have been in the same class with me during in first year in Medical School; however, he stopped behind later, because he flunked in his pre-chemical subjects. He did not recognise me, but I vaguely remember him. He always was a Nazi rough-neck, and I guess he still is.

Nurnberg is a heap of rubble and so far I have not done any sightseeing, except what I happen to see when driving to and from the Courthouse. It is considered inadvisable to walk alone unarmed through the inner walled city, the ruins being hangouts for thugs of all kinds. But the main thing that has kept me out so far is the lack of time. I look forward to the day of your arrival, New regulation will go in effect on January 1st. I shall try to find out particulars.

Love to you and the Bunnies
Yours Leo

7 December 1946

Fifi darling,

These were hectic days. In little more than 2 weeks, I have completed a job for which I should have had 3 months at least. But the job is done now, I have performed complete analysis of all the experiments, have completed studies of motives, techniques and personalities of all the 23 accused men, have put the salient features of all this into clear and lucid writing, and have submitted it, as it came off the typewriter, in installments, to General Taylor for inclusion into his opening speech. He has used it well. Right now my secretary is typing the last 2 pages, and before correcting them I have a breather of a few minutes, since I have got ahead of her typing by greater speed of correction, a mere accident. For the last week I have worked daily from 9 AM til 2 or 3 AM.

I shall send you copies of all my briefs; the last one (one of the hottest) is included.

Love to you and the bunnies!
As ever, Leo

10 December 1946

Fifi Darling,

Things are still going hectic although the trial has opened. I mailed you the opening statement and I am sure you will find it interesting. The General has made very wise use of the memoranda I submitted to him. Right now the actual trial is taking place and the hectic rush of getting documents ready and getting the right witnesses selected and into Nurnberg on time is absorbing everybody. I have spent a lot of time on interrogations of the witnesses to separate the wheat from the chaff, but we really have some witnesses now. Yesterday we had a poor unfortunate Czech here who had been held in the crematorium and though he knew everything going on within the concentration walls unfortunately he knew nothing really about it so we had to let him go, otherwise, he had a harrowing tale to tell.[1] His hands showed marks of Gestapo torture.

1   This might be a reference to the Czechoslovak prisoner Dr Franz Blaha whom Alexander interviewed on 10 December 1946. Although Alexander states in his letter to his wife that he interviewed the Czech prisoner "yesterday", which would be the 9 December, it is quite plausible that Alexander in fact wrote the letter on the 11 December and may have simply made an error after a long night of interviews. Alexander writes in his diary that he interviewed Blaha

I hope you can come over here soon. In a few days I will have all the data on how to arrange for you coming over for a visit. Estimates on the duration of the trial vary. I personally have the feeling it won't last much longer than February, unless the defense springs a surprise.

All my love to you and the bunnies,
Sincerely,
Leo

16 December 1946

Fifi Darling,

The trial is going on. What a madhouse this is! I don't know what they would have done without me, the Snafu [situation normal, all fucked up] is so terrific. I am working from 8:30 AM till 2:30 AM. What a grind! But we'll come out with something really monumental, both historical and legal.

I am sending you the copy of my article, another one is near completion. I am not much of a letter writer, as you know, but you are worse, I have only had one letter from you so far. Was ist los?, as they say here (What's the matter?)

I have sent the enclosed article to Mr. Gulliver for distribution. Let me hear from you soon, and with all my love to you, and the bunnies,

Yours
Leo

18 December 1946

Fifi Darling,

Your letter of December 10th came today. I know I haven't been writing enough but if you were here you would know why. The pace of work is terrific. Sunday night four girls whose legs had been operated on and badly disfigured by experiments came in from Warsaw.[2] I had to examine them, take their histories, bring out the important points for interrogation, prepare complete expert statements regarding the examinations, all in three days. In addition to everything, three spoke only Polish, one spoke broken English and I had to work through a Polish interpreter who got them all involved in the lengthiest discussions. The work is finally completed today, Wednesday night, 6:00 PM and I have 31 pages of long, legal type completed. What a job! But it has got to be done and it has got to be done right. The emergency of the situation and probably my obsessiveness just keeps driving me on, but my temper is getting short, so I noticed, and I wish you were here with me. According to a recent statement in the Stars and Stripes, you will be able to come to Germany for two weeks and afterwards we can spend some time in France

---

on the evening of 10 December 1946. On p. 112 of the diary, he describes Blaha as a 'disappointment' and an 'obvious faker' which tallies with his description of the "Czech" in the letter, who "knew nothing really about it and we had to let him go". See p. 112 of the diary for more information about Blaha. See also František Bláha, 'Medical Science Run Amok', in: Medical Science Abused, reported by Czechoslovak doctors (ca. 1946), pp. 14-41.

2   This corresponds to Alexander diary entries from pp. 139 ff. in which details his interviews with the four Polish women and how he prepared them to give their testimony in front of the Nuremberg court.

and England. The trials will probably last until the end of February. It would be great if you could get here about the middle of February, maybe earlier. I will send you the particular. The court will recess next week until January 2, but I will keep busy completing the personality studies of the defendants, but under somewhat less pressure of immediate work. I shall lose no time to arrange things in Captain Kruskall's office about getting you here by the end of my stay.

From a visitors point of view there is not much to see or do here in Nurnberg. All that I have seen so far is the hotel, the court house, the station hospital and the stretches of road between the three. There are plenty of bombed buildings to be seen everywhere. The whole thing is grey and dirty with the air of an abandoned slaughter house, which the Nazi's made out of every place they were in. The concentration camp evidence is terrific. It even surpasses what I had known when I first investigated Dachau and Ebensee. The stories the witnesses tell are terrific. Unfortunately, I did not have time to take in but a few of the court sessions because I have to keep on working to be always one jump ahead of the cases to be presented in evidence. But I know the story from the interrogations, of course, and I do get transcripts (after raising hell to get them).

Well, that is all for today, Darling, Work has never been as hectic, except at sometimes during the war.

Give my love to the children. I shall write to them separately but I hope you will all hold your horses before you become dissatisfied about the rate of my letters. I shall write more often. All my love to you and the bunnies,

As ever, your loving husband,
Leo

21 December 1946

Fifi Darling,

This is the most tremendous thing I have ever gotten into. It is overwhelming; the wealth and importance of the material, from all points of view – medical, historical, psychological – is enormous; in all this maelstrom of the biggest, most hectically working legal machine ever assembled with inevitable improvisations, which drives one to distraction – the stream of documents coming in and being worked up, and in the shuffle of course much is lost or mislaid. I could kick myself for losing a rather rare find, namely, one of the strips of electrocardiogram which Rascher took while he killed people, by various means – low pressure, cold, shooting and hanging. I found it in a big box of material taken from Dr. Rascher's house. At that time[,] I did not know its significance, and until proper identification was possible I left it in the box. In the meantime[,] I got the story from one of the witnesses, Rascher's former assistant Neff, as to what it was.[3] When I wanted to lay my hands on it again the whole box was gone because one document storeroom had been made over into an office and the material distributed to other storerooms – nobody knows where. I have been frantically looking for it, both to introduce it as a document in the trial and as a permanent museum piece either for The Surgeon General's Museum or for the Smithsonian Institute. So far, no luck.

3   See p. 115 of the diary for Alexander's interrogation of Neff. See p. 118 of the diary for his re-interrogation of Neff, and p. 127 for his re-interrogation with McHaney. These interrogations contain more detail about Rascher's experiments and killings at Dachau.

That is just one incident of the stream of material which flows through our hands, which has to be grasped or it is lost forever. The documentation of all this is an overwhelming job. I am perpetually under the state of mind of a hunter who suddenly finds himself in a swarm of the most amazing birds with only one gun in his hand and a limited number of bullets to bring those trophies home. But such is life.

That is the reason, Darling, why I haven't been writing much and please don't take it in a sensitive manner as a lack of affection or devotion because that would be utterly mistaken, and let the children know what I am in. I have plenty of stories to tell when I come home but there just isn't time to do everything at once, and the job is fascinating and overwhelming at the same time, but I'll keep writing more regularly.

With love,
Leo

31 December 1946

Fifi Darling,

The mad old whirl is going on and more and more war crimes are unfolding. It sometimes seems as if the Nazis had taken special pains in making practically every nightmare come true. Some new evidence has come in where two doctors in Berlin, one a man and the other a woman, collected eyes of different color. It seems that the concentration camps were combed for people who had slightly differently colored eyes. That means people whose one eye had a slightly different color than the other. Who ever was unlucky enough to possess such a pair of slightly unequal eyes had them cut out and was killed, the eyes being sent to Berlin. This is the carrying out into reality of an old gruesome German fairy tale which is included in the Tales of Hoffman, where Dr. Coppelius posing as the sandman comes at night and cuts out children's eyes when they are tired. The grim part of the story is that Doctors von Verschuer and Magnussen in Berlin did prefer children and particularly twins. There is no end to this nightmare, at least 23 are being tried now and, I trust, the others will follow later.

[...] Work is going along well although I have a stack of interrogations on my desk which I haven't corrected yet. The material is fascinating from a social-psychiatric point of view but I hope these trials are instrumental in preventing something like this in the future.

I miss you a lot and I hope you come here soon. With all best wishes for a happy New Year and many of them together, and all my love,

Your
Leo

31 December 1946

Dear Gusty,[4]

It was great to read your letter and your fine report card. I want to congratulate you, I think you have done a fine job. It was real pleasure to read it. I am enclosing it for you to keep. It is very nice to know that Pierce School won the championship in football. I am sure you contributed to that.

There is a great deal to do here and I am working hard. I have a great deal to tell you when I come back and this is a real historical occasion. The people we are trying committed crimes during the war. All these crimes which the Nazis have committed consist in abuse of their power over people whom they unlawfully imprisoned. The particular group which is being tried right now are doctors who abused their skill for killing rather than for helping and healing people as they should have. They in turn were put up to this by a criminal government which fortunately and with God's help we have defeated by force of arms during the war. Now is the time to establish law and order for the future; I hope, for a long time to come. I am here to help in this task and after it is completed[,] I shall come home. I wish you could be here with me, however, only such people could bring their children who were going to stay a year or longer but since it won't be necessary for me to stay that long I had to leave you at home. I also think it is better for you to stay at home and take your trip abroad during happier times, after law and order throughout the world have been re-established. I hope someday in the future to take many trips with you. Next summer we will all go on vacation together. I hope that Mother will be able to come for a brief visit before I go home but I don't think that you and the other children would get much out of this trip at this time. There are a good many shortages of transportation, food and heat and the ruins with which the streets are lined are still witnesses of the ravages of war which the Germans brought upon themselves. While it would be interesting for you to see all this[,] I feel that at this time it is more important for you to go on with your school. We will take a trip in the summer this year.

Under separate cover I am sending you a photograph of myself, the British[5] and French[6] medical experts and one of the prosecutors, Mr. Hardy, whose home is also near Boston, in Cochituate. Also[,] a picture of General Taylor giving his opening address with myself in the background.

I missed you at Christmas but I was so busy that it brought only a brief pause. I hope to see you soon, in the meantime take good care of Mother and the other children.

With all my love and best wishes for the new year,
Your Daddy

---

4   The letter was written to Gustave Osgood Alexander who was Leo Alexander nine-year-old son. See Schmidt (2004), p. 58.
5   This is a reference to Keith Mant. For more information about him, see p. 11 of the original diary.
6   The French medical expert was François Bayle. For biographical details, see the footnote attached to p. 105 of the original diary.

8 January 1947

Fifi Darling,

I received three letters today, two from you (one with the photographs) and one from Cecily. I am delighted that things are clear on your end for you to come over for a visit.

[...] My little apartment consisting of one room and bath and ante-room is very adequate indeed, and I am sure you will love it. The furnishing is simple and the twin beds that are in it are military style but I am sure you will be very comfortable. The bath tub is tremendous, "Goering's" size and you could swim in it.

[...] There may be some delay but the money is good. Don't worry about that aspect of things. I think it would be wonderful if you could come here. It is a unique and momentous act in history and you should be here to go through it with me. We can always make or save money but we couldn't go through this again no matter how much we made or saved. So I expect you here soon. I need you very much, Darling.

With love to you and all the bunnies,
Your own husband,
Leo

1 July 1947

Fifi Darling,

Here is good news – the trial is finally winding up and final proof will be in next week followed by the final statements of the defense. After that I can leave. Probably sometime between the 15th and the 21st of this month so that I will be in Boston about the 1st of August. I shall let you know exactly the time of my departure.

The speech in Holland was a great success, there was a great deal of interest in it and I picked up some good new information. Burt, Leny, Dr. Silevis Smitt and Mr. Boularts will be coming here on the 5th.

The two Dutch witnesses, Mr. Nales[7] and Mr. Broers went on the stand yesterday and were a great success. Many people thought they were the best witnesses of the trial. The fact that Mr. Nales knew exactly the names, dates and places of birth in regard to most of Haagen's victims added an air of definiteness which helped the judges to find themselves on familiar ground, namely on the ground of murder cases of definite specific persons. After each name he asked whether he saw the corpses and he said "yes" and in most cases added specific statements that he, himself, washed the corpse before sending it to the morgue or the autopsy room. The great definiteness was impressive and a sort of relief from the horror of the nameless murdered masses which we dealt with on so many other occasions.

I have definitely decided to take August off with you and the children. Please see to it that we can get reservations somewhere on Cape Cod, preferably in a little inn where you don't have to cook and let's all get acquainted with each other again. I will spend at least a month alone with you and the children before I go back to work. I have a letter from Miss Hayes in which she said she had lunch with you –

---

7 For further details, see p. 200 of the original diary.

and due to the fact that the bank account also seems to be balanced I feel it would be wise not to immediately rush back to work but spend a leisurely month together.

I had a letter from a Dr. Weissenberg which I am enclosing, in regard to Ann's whereabouts. This revives my concern and worry about Ann and I think it might be a good thing to start contacting the Missing Persons' Bureau and instituting a search for her since all other means of inquiry failed.

Well, darling, I shall wire you as soon as I know which type of transportation I shall use to come back. Until then lots of love and many kisses,

Your own husband,
Leo

5

LEO ALEXANDER
THE NUREMBERG DIARY

1946–1947

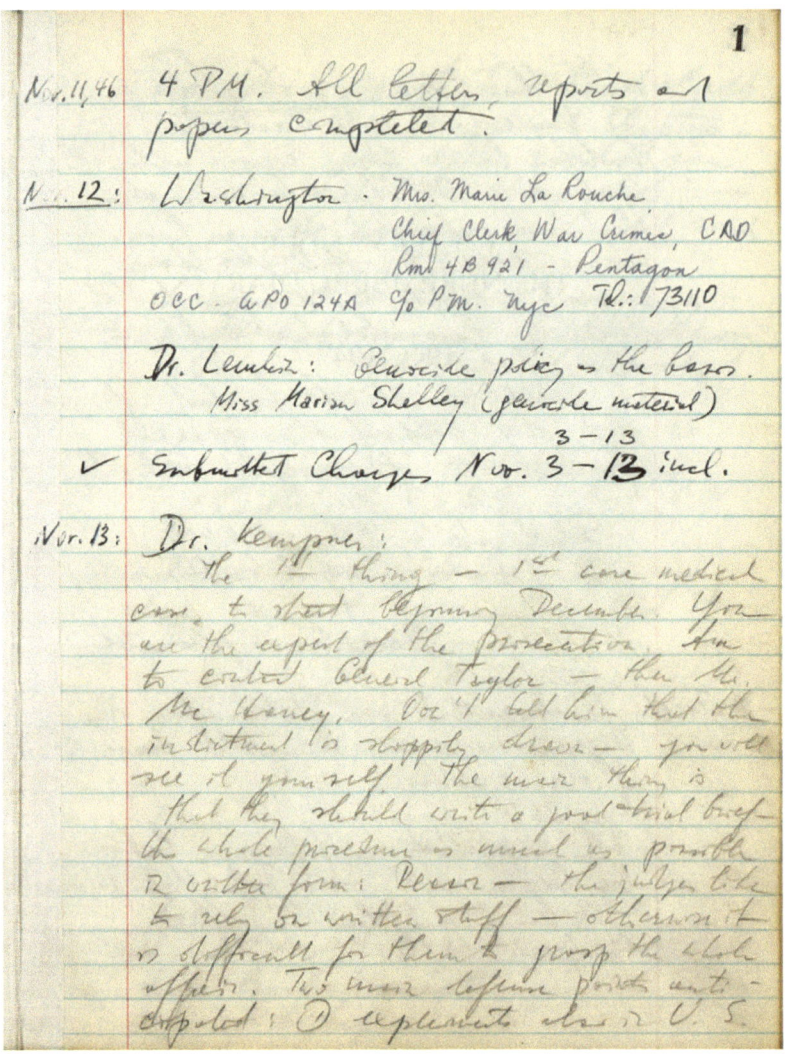

*Fig. 4: Alexander papers, DUMC, box 3,
Record ledger book of activities and notes, 1946-1947, p. 1.*

[1] Nov. 11, 46 4 PM. All letters, reports and papers completed.

Nov. 12: Washington. Mrs. Marie La Rouche. Chief Clerk, War Crimes. CAD.[1] Rm 4B921 – Pentagon OCC – APO 124A. c/o Pm Nyc Tel.: 73110.

Dr. Lemkin: Genocide policy as the basis. Miss Marian Shelley (genocidal material).[2]

Submitted Changes No. 3–13 incl.

Nov. 13: Dr. Kempner:[3] The 1st thing – 1st case medical case [Nuremberg Doctors' Trial] to start beginning December. You are the expert of the prosecution. Am to contact General Taylor[4] – then Mr. McHaney.[5] Don't tell him that the indictment is sloppily drawn – you will see it yourself. The main thing is that they should write a good trial brief – the whole procedure as much as possible in written form: Reason – the judges like to rely on written stuff – otherwise it is difficult for them to grasp the whole offence. Two main defence points anticipated: 1) experiments also in US [2] and other countries. Differences. 2) Under German medical, esp. military law, they were allowed to do so. It should be made clear that according to German law it was a crime. Ask McHaney to send a cable to Kempner for the German law – Send a cable to this office: Sight should not be lost of that it is part of the general framework of genocidal activity.

---

1 War Crimes Branch, Civil Affairs Division, The Pentagon, Washington D.C., see Nuremberg Military Tribunal (1949), 407.
2 Marian Shelley was Alexander's assistant. Weindling (2004), 148.
3 Robert Kempner (1899–1993) served as assistant US chief counsel during the International Military Tribunal at Nuremberg. He had his German citizenship revoked in 1933 because he was Jewish and fled to Italy in 1935. He emigrated to the US in 1939, where he advised the government. He returned to Germany in 1945 in preparation for the Nuremberg Trials. Kempner prosecuted both Hermann Göring and Wilhelm Frick. He remained in Germany after the trials and practiced as a lawyer in Frankfurt am Main. See Löwen (2005).
4 Telford Taylor (1908–1998) was a US lawyer and lead counsel for the prosecution of Nazi war criminals during the Nuremberg Trials. Born in the United States and educated at Harvard, Taylor was first an assistant to Chief Counsel Robert Jackson (1892–1954) at Nuremberg. In this role, he was the US prosecutor in the High Command case. This case called, unsuccessfully, for the General Staff of the Army and the High Command of the German Armed Forces to be considered criminal organisations. In October 1946, Taylor succeeded Robert Jackson as Chief Counsel. After the Nuremberg Trials, Taylor opened a private law practice in New York. He subsequently spoke out against Joseph McCarthy, the Republican US Senator for Wisconsin who alleged that communists and Soviet spies had penetrated the US government, universities, and creative industries. Taylor was also opposed to the 1972 Christmas bombings (Operation Linebacker II) by US military forces in Vietnam, arguing that it breached the standards set by the Nuremberg Trials. Schmidt (2004), Pugliese (2013), Taylor (1970a). For Taylor's post-war publications see Taylor (1952; 1970b; 1974; 1992).
5 James Monroe McHaney (1919–1995) was an American prosecutor who served as deputy chief prosecutor at the Nuremberg Doctors' Trial. He was promoted by Telford Taylor as an investigator for the Trial to gather evidence of medical crimes committed by Nazi doctors, including involuntary human experimentation and the murder of concentration camp prisoners. See Schmidt (2004), 2.

Fig. 5: Brigadier General Telford Taylor, Chief of Counsel for War Crimes, pictured in his office at Nuremberg. Nuremberg, Germany, 1946/47 (Source: NARA).

Sterilisation: 008–0010.[6] Dr. Pokorny's[7] report to Himmler.[8]

Dr. Lemkin:[9] genocide implemented scientifically. Dr. Fried:[10] Reichszentrale zur Bekämpfung des Zigeunerunwesens.[11] Completed genocide of the gypsies. p. 250.

The exploitation of foreign labour by Germany – John H. E. Fried, International Labour Office, Montreal 1945.

[3] *Procedure*: The trial brief should start with 2 or 3 general chapters – "Your sphere is what you make out of it, nothing else" –
"The German Aerzte did such and such – to destroy – through the following agencies:

---

6   In July 1933, the "Law for the Prevention of Offspring with Hereditary Diseases" was passed in Germany. It legalised the compulsory sterilisation of people deemed "hereditarily unfit" to have children, such as those who were deaf, blind, or who had physical disabilities. Between 1934 and 1939, an estimated 350,000 to 400,000 people were sterilised under the law. See Bock (1986) and Shields/Foth (2014), 1–13.

7   Adolf Pokorny (1895–d. unknown) was a dermatologist who worked as a medical officer in the German Armed Forces (*Wehrmacht*). It is likely that Alexander was referring here to a letter Pokorny had sent to Himmler which suggested the sterilisation of Russian prisoners of war using the sap of the caladium plant, which was believed to cause sterilisation in mice. The method was never used. Source: Weindling (2004), 245.

8   Heinrich Himmler (1900–1945) was *Reichsführer* of the *Schutzstaffel* (SS).

9   Raphael Lemkin (1900–1959) was a Polish Jewish lawyer, who coined the term "genocide" in 1943. Between 1945 and 1946, Lemkin served as advisor to Robert Jackson, Taylors' predecessor of first Chief Counsel at Nuremberg. The Convention on the Prevention and Punishment of the Crime of Genocide – drafted by Lemkin – was formally presented and adopted by the United Nations General Assembly on 9 December 1948. Cooper (2008). See also Schaller/Zimmerer (2009).

10 John H. E. Fried (1911–1990), was an Austrian/US lawyer, professor, and human rights activist. Born in Vienna, he emigrated to the US in 1938 and received his doctorate at Columbia University in 1942. He was a legal consultant during the Nuremberg Trials and served as a special consultant to the US War Crimes Tribunal at Nuremberg from 1947–1949. He was later appointed as a professor of political science at Lehman College of City University of New York. He died in New York in 1990. He wrote extensively during the early post-war period on the subject of "guilt" and the Nazi crimes. Other books include *The Guilt of the German Army* (1943) which includes chapters on the nature of "common responsibility" and questions how a culture that glorified militarism was able to flourish under the Third Reich. Archival material and biographical details can be found here: John H. E. Fried Collection, 1815–1997 AR 7262/MF 490/MF 485, Leo Baeck Institute.

11 The *Reichszentrale zur Bekämpfung des Zigeunerunwesens* was founded in 1899 as an intelligence service to support police. Under the Weimar Republic it was charged with aiding police by setting up a personal database to record 'people who roam the Gypsy way'. The headquarters was relocated to Berlin under the Third Reich, who together with the *Rassenhygienische Forschungsstelle* (RHF) organised the registration and deportation of the European Roma. The headquarters remained in operation until 1970. Hehemann (1987). See also Henke (1993), Margalit (1997), and Milton (1995).

1) Reichskommissar for the strengthening [of] German Volkstum[12] (Himmler, since Oct 2, 1939)
2) Frick,[13] Conti.[14]
3) Nazi party, military forces, Luftwaffe,[15] SS

Chart should be made – where medical agencies fitted in. Put in names.

---

12 The position of "Reichskommissar für die Festigung deutschen Volkstums" (RKF, RKFDV) appears to have been decreed by Hitler on 7 October 1939 as a means to enact the the Third Reich's policy apparatus on German nationality: „Damit hat das Großdeutsche Reich die Möglichkeit, deutsche Menschen, die bisher in der Fremde leben mußten, in seinem Raum aufzunehmen und anzusiedeln und innerhalb seiner Interessengrenzen die Siedlung der Volksgruppen so zu gestalten, daß bessere Trennungslinien zwischen ihnen erreicht werden." The responsibility to enact these policies were given to the Reichsführer-SS (Himmler). What must have been important to the prosecution's investigation were the following "guidelines" outlined in Hitler's 7 October speech: „1. die Zurückführung der für die endgültige Heimkehr in das Reich in Betracht kommenden Reichs- und Volksdeutschen im Ausland, 2. die Ausschaltung des schädigenden Einflusses von solchen volksfremden Bevöl¬kerungsteilen, die eine Gefahr für das Reich und die deutsche Volksgemeinschaft bedeuten, 3. die Gestaltung neuer deutscher Siedlungsgebiete durch Umsiedlung, im besonderen durch Seßhaftmachung der aus dem Ausland heimkehrenden Reichs- und Volksdeutschen. Der Reichsführer-SS ist ermächtigt, alle zur Durchführung dieser Obliegenheiten notwendigen allgemeinen Anordnungen und Verwaltungsmaßnahmen zu treffen. Zur Erfüllung der ihm in Absatz 1 Nr. 2 gestellten Aufgaben kann der Reichsführer-SS den in Frage stehenden Bevölkerungsteilen bestimmte Wohngebiete zuweisen." Adolf Hitler, Erlaß des Führers und Reichskanzlers zur Festigung deutschen Volkstums (Berlin, 7. Oktober 1939). In: Themenportal Europäische Geschichte (2007).
13 Wilhelm Frick (1877–1946) was *Das Reichministerium des Innern* (Reich Minister of the Interior) and *Generalbevollmächtigter für die Reichsverwaltung* (General Plenipotenary for the Administration of the Reich). He was instrumental in forming legislation to support Nazi racial ideology, notably through the formulation of the 1935 *Nürnberger Gesetze* (Nuremberg Laws), which curtailed rights to citizenship and marriage for people deemed of non-German origin, including German Jews, Romani, and *Afrodeutsche* (Afro-Germans). In 1939 Frick was appointed to the Council of Ministers for the Defence of the Reich (*Ministerrat für die Reichsverteidigung*). He was appointed governor of the Protectorate of Bohemia and Moravia in May 1943. He was convicted of war crimes and sentenced to death at Nuremberg. The sentence was carried out in Nuremberg Prison in October 1946. Neliba (1992).
14 Leonardo Conti (1900–1945) was *Reichsärzteführer* (1939–1944) of the National Socialist German Doctors' League (*Nationalsozialistischer Deutscher Ärztebund,* NSDÄB or NSD-Ärztebund) – tasked with integrating the German medical profession within the Nazi regime. Conti had been recommended by Frick to Hitler and cultivated close ties to the SS prior to his appointment. His appointment reflected the decline of the SA, and those who had been loyal to it such as his predecessor Gerhard Wagner (1888–1939), during the animosity and competing ambitions between the two organisations before the outbreak of the war. Under his leadership public medical administration further expanded it eugenic and racial hygiene aspirations – leading to forced sterilisations and racially motivated human experimentation. He was imprisoned prior to the Nuremberg Trials but hanged himself a year before the trial commenced. Cocks (1985).
15 *Luftwaffe*: the aerial-warfare branch of the German Army (*Wehrmacht*).

Himmler
|
Brandt[16]
|
Sievers[17]

Not small affidavits – such as on that and that day 5 people were killed etc., but broad concepts. Not before 1933.

[4] All financed by the Nazi State and Party – and by private organizations, such as Deutsche Notgemeinschaft.[18]

Only universities with SS majority participated – all University State Institution and all appointments political.

Get witnesses you need.
Capt. Sarah Kruskall. Nuremberg.
Play down euthanasia.[19] Merely a training center for killer personnel. Most already executed.
Rassengerichte: medical experts.

German Medical experts.

Always get sworn affidavits from witnesses.

16 Karl Brandt (1904–1948) was a German doctor, 'companion' doctor (*Begleitarzt*) to Hitler, and a senior SS officer. In Autumn 1939, Brandt was given responsibility for coordinating the Nazi euthanasia programme, which entailed the killing of those deemed "lives unworthy of living" (*Lebensunwertes Leben*). This included many people with disabilities and psychiatric patients. Brandt was involved in numerous unethical human experiments, including experiments on hepatitis, malaria, and chemical agents with concentration camp prisoners. He was the most senior ranking doctor to be tried at the Nuremberg Doctors' Trial. He was sentenced to death by hanging in August 1947. The sentence was carried out in Landsberg prison in June 1948. Schmidt (2007).
17 Wolfram Sievers (1905–1948) was managing director of the *Ahnenerbe* (Ancestoral Heritage) Society between 1935 and 1945. He was responsible for human experiments on concentration camp prisoners. Sievers was sentenced to death by hanging in August 1947. The sentence was carried out in Landsberg prison in June 1948. Schmidt (2004), 155.
18 In 1929, the *Notgemeinschaft der Deutschen Wissenschaft* was renamed the *Deutsche Gemeinschaft zur Erhaltung und Förderung der Forschung*. Rudolf Mentzel (1900–1984) was the president between 1936 and 1945. He was interned by American forces for three years following the end of the war and was eventually released in 1948 by an affidavit provided by Walther Gerlach (1889–1979). Gerlach was a German physicist held in England under Operation Epsilon as part of a group of ten scientists believed to have been associated with the development of atomic weapons under the Third Reich and was released in January 1946. Gerlach argued Mentzel was only a science policymaker and was not involved with ideology or racially motivated crimes. See Document 121 *Walther Gerlach: Affidavit on Rudolf Mentzel [December 13, 1948]*, translation printed in Hentschel/Hentschel (1996), 403–406. The original source can be found in the papers of Walther Gerlach held by the *Deutsches Museum* in Munich.
19 It is estimated that 300,000 died during the "euthanasia" programme. Frewer/Eickhoff (2000) and Engelhardt/Frewer (2023).

Ask every defendant examining their hippocratic oath.[20]

[5] [...] Lt. Head. Westover G.A. 13. Massachussetts. Box 541. formerly Group Vorjahr. 49.O.B. Gp. Trbenlion.

Nov. 14 Arrived Lagus [Lagos Island] Azores.[21] Lt. wants conversation with Senator Wayne L. Morse. Dinner at Lagus and Hotel Accomodation. Capt. Joseph Numa Wenger U.S.N.[22]

Nov. 15 Left Lagus at 7:30. Arrived Paris at 5:30 PM – journey over [...] then clouds, heading by radar contact then overcast over Orly Field. To Hotel Napoleon over night.

Nov. 16 Slept till 2 PM. In the evening to the Opera. Don Giovanni.

Nov. 17 To the field at 9 AM. Washington till 1 PM – all phones cancelled because of weather. Sightseeing with Colonal Nestlewood. Les Invalides, Madeleine, les Tuileries, Louvre, Notre Dame. Dinner at Napoleon, then boarded train to Frankfurt.

Nov. 18 Arrived in FfM. Arranged motor transportation to Nuremberg. Very well received at Grand Hotel.

[6] Nov. 19 To Palace of Justice. Met Prosecution, MacHaney[23] and Hardy;[24] went right to work. Found them short on documents, called for my microfilm.

[7] 20 Nov. 1946 Dr Gerhard Oskar Schiedlausky.
    Born Jan 14, 1906. Grad. 1931, M.D. Univ. Berlin, 1933 Interned Landsberg a.d. Warthe; 1933 nach Friedrichshain.
    Joined SS 1933 in Landsberg.[25] 1933 "Waschekzem", which kept him from continuing as a surgeon. Then became physician for the police in Potsdam.

---

20 The "Hippocratic Oath" requires a physician to swear to uphold moral standards. The oath is the earliest expression of Western medical ethics, establishing moral standards which remain significant for medical practice today. See Miles (2005).
21 Lagos Island is a small island which forms part of the Azores archipelago. In 1943, Antonio de Oliveira Salazar (1889–1970), Prime Minister of Portugal for 36 years (1932–1968), leased the archipelago to the British. In 1945 a new airbase was constructed by the US on the island of Terceira, named Lajes Field, which continued to support both the American and Portuguese military into the post-war period.
22 United States Navy.
23 Alexander uses two different spellings of McHaney.
24 Alexander G. Hardy was the associate counsel for the prosecution.
25 Gerhard Schiedlausky (1906–1947) notes in his deposition produced as part of the first Hamburg Ravensbruck trial that he was "persuaded by a friend" to join the SS. He left Landsberg because of an allergic eczema ("Waschekzem"). The National Archives, London, WO 235/313, "Deposition of Dr. Gerhard Schiedlausky", 22 November 1946.

Fig. 6: The foyer of the Grand Hotel, Nuremberg, Germany, 1946/47 (Source: NARA).

Therefore had to leave SS. Left police March 31, 1934.[26] On 28 Oct. 1939 joined Waffen SS:

General SS; Unterscharführer, when rejoined 1935/36. Assigned to Einwandererzentrale to Posen.[27] There till June 15, 1941.

Promoted Dec. 39 Hauptscharführer, Aug. 1940. Untersturmführer, Juni 1941 Obersturmführer, April 43 Hauptsturmführer (last rank),

Jan. 41, military training for 2 months in Hamburg. Then a few days in Oranienburg,[28] then assigned to Mauthausen.[29] There April to [October] 1941. Then to Flossenbürg (KZ).[30] Dec. 18, 1941; to Ravensbrück.[31] There till August 1943; then to Natzweiler,[32] August and September 43.

[8] Then to Buchenwald,[33] til the end. "Damit war meine Odyssee in den einzelnen KZ's zu Ende." They had been promised to be transferred after ½ yrs of KZ.

Concentration camp staff was unpopular. He was told that he could not very well be sent to do duty under a younger man of higher rank, and that it would be best for him to do ½ year KZ duty. When he first had seen KZ in 1933 only SA were doing duty there. The personnel chief, Sturmbannführer, told to sell his assignment by telling him that it would give him an opportunity to develop surgical

---

26 In his deposition for the Ravensbrück trial, Schiedlausky elaborates on why he left the police: "I left the police in August 1934, because of a condition, that all members of the police had to wear uniforms and as a doctor I did not want to wear a uniform or carry weapons". The National Archives, WO 235/313, 'Deposition of Dr. Gerhard Schiedlausky', 22 November 1946.

27 The Central Office for Immigrants (*Einwandererzentralstelle*, EWZ) was established by Reinhard Heydrich, Director of the Reich Security Main Office (*Reichssicherheitshauptamt*, RSHA), in mid-1939 as a centralised office to naturalise ethnic Germans in occupied territories. Heinemann (2005), 231.

28 Oranienburg was one of the first concentration camps established during the Third Reich; it was set up in March 1933 and initially ran by the SA. In total, about 3,000 prisoners were interned at Oranienburg from its founding to the time of its closure in July 1934. Dörner (2009), 147–149.

29 Mauthausen concentration camp was opened in August 1938. Prisoner labour was used to extract granite from the site which was located near the town of Mauthausen in Upper Austria. From 1942 to 1943, the mining work grew in importance leading to large increases in the prison population. In March 1943, 14,800 were held at the camp. By spring 1945, this had increased to 45,000. Waite (2009), 900–903. It is estimated that 100,000 people died there. Jardim (2012), 2.

30 Flossenbürg concentration camp was opened in May 1938. The camp population rose rapidly, from 1,500 at the end of 1938 to a total peak of 53,000 in March 1944. Nearly 97,000 prisoners passed through the camp system between 1938 and 1945. About 30,000 prisoners died in the camp. Huebner (2009), 559–566.

31 Ravensbrück concentration camp for women was opened in May 1939. In total, 123,000 women were interned between 1939 and 1945, and approximately 10,000 female inmates died there by shooting, gassing, poisoning, and starvation. Morrison (2000), 14, Strebel (2003), 11, Schwartz (2018), 61.

32 Natzweiler-Struthof concentration camp was the only concentration camp to have been built on French territory. The camp was setup in July 1940. In total 52,000 were registered at the camp or exterior sub-camps. 20,000 prisoners died overall. Dreyfus (2009), 1003–1008.

33 Buchenwald concentration camp was constructed in 1937. Around 250,000 people were imprisoned there in total, and at least 56,000 people died in the camp system. Zegenhagen (2009), 290, 293.

skill. Never saw extermination. Cyclon B only for delousing of clothing. Heard of gas chambers in Oswiecm [Oświęcim/Auschwitz][34] in May 1944.

His wife never told her friends when he did duty – ashamed "Kein schöner Dienst". While travelling on the RB [Reichsbahn], if he mentions it, there was "eisiges Schweigen".

Has been faithful to his wife all his life. Never drank.

In Mauthausen, there was overdrinking on the part of the staff, not in Buchenwald.

[9] Heydrich,[35] who was shot in Prague, died from gas gangrene.[36] Also in Russia many amputations for gas gangrene in SS personnel, end of 1942.

In 1941, anlässlich Besuch's Himmler's in Mauthausen, sollte Lagerbordell eingerichtet werden, to increase "Arbeitsfreudigkeit", als "Belohnung" – und als antihomosexuelle Vorbeugungsmaßnahme(n).[37] Himmler wollte Freiwillige; does not know that girls were passed by Himmler himself. Many volunteered. 800–1,000 "asocial" girls. A good many were minors, and they wondered whether their relatives would not have to approve. Frei von Geschlechts- und Hautkrankheiten. Die Kommandanten verlangten gutes Aussehen, Gebiss. "Damals wurden für Dachau 4 ausgesucht". Gebhardt was once present during the experiments in Ravensbrück.[38]

Dr. Oberhäuser [Oberheuser]: tüchtig. Haut- und Geschlechtskrankheiten. Versprechungen, sie weiter zu fördern. besonders gutes Arbeitsgebiet. For experiments: political prisoners [10] of Polish nationality:

---

34 Oświęcim is a town in southern Poland and was the site of the Auschwitz concentration camp.
35 Reinhard Heydrich (1904–1942) was Head of the Reich Security Main Office (RSHA). Schmidt (2005), 31.
36 This links to the main motivation for the human experiments at Ravensbrück which involved the creation of artificial wounds in the legs of women prisoners to test the effectiveness of sulfonamide drugs in treating such wounds. Professor Karl Gebhardt (1897–1948) – the doctor who treated Heydrich – was accused, unofficially, of medical neglect by Dr. Theo Morell (1886–1948) – Hitler's personal physician – who maintained that the use of sulfonamide drugs to treat Heydrich's wounds could have saved his life. The order for the experiments to be conducted to 'test' this theory came from Himmler and also from Ernst Grawitz, the President of the German Red Cross and the Reicharzt (SS Reich Physician). Gebhardt essentially undertook these experiments from July 1942 onwards to prove his competency to high-ranking Nazi officials. Schmidt (2005), 32.
37 The historical literature on the camp brothels states that women were selected to work in these spaces from 1942 onwards. Docking (2021), 17. Privileged male inmates were allowed to use the brothels, which were located in concentration camps such as Ravensbrück and Auschwitz, often as an 'incentive' for working hard. Doctors examined women for sexually transmitted diseases, to ensure that these illnesses would not be spread to the privileged male prisoners that frequented the brothels. 88 out of the named 174 women who worked in the ten concentration camp brothels were classed as 'asocial' inmates, and 114 were German. Docking (2021), 207. For further literature on the brothels, see Sommer (2009), Wickert (2002), and Bogue (2016).
38 Karl Gebhardt oversaw the Hohenlychen sanatorium. He was chief surgeon in the staff of the Reich Physician SS and the police, and personal physician to Heinrich Himmler. Gebhardt conducted human experiments at Ravensbrück concentration camp. He was sentenced to death at the Nuremberg Medical Trial and hung in 1948. Source: Docking (2021). See page 67 of Alexander's diary for his interview with Gebhardt.

Disease produced by the experiments very painful. Pain inherent in the nature of the experiments, not due to negligence. About 15 died (had said 12 before): "Ich schätze 36 Operierte". "Vielleicht auch 40". "2 died of tetanus".

(Actually 76 Polish girls).

Gas gangren experiments. experiments on regeneration of bone by Dr. Stumpfegger.[39] Transplantation from one leg to the other. Dr. Trommer succeeded him.[40]

Lethal injections were given by nurses on prisoners, not usually by physicians; denies ever having given one himself.[41] Remembers a scapula having been "healed in" at Hohenlychen;[42] but does not know of a living part having been transferred for it. Lethal injections: frequently done in my absence. Admits only euthanasia.

Admits that he has given approval to kill some people with petrol injections ("Benzin"). Rosenthal was an unstable personality, ging "Phantasiegesprächen" nach.[43]

[11] Dinner with Major Mant.[44]

---

39   Ludwig Stumpfegger (1910–1945) was Hitler's personal surgeon from 1944 to 1945. He was present in the *Führerbunker* in Berlin in 1945. Kaiser/Schmidt (2020), 155, 162.
40   Richard Trommer was a camp doctor at Flossenbürg (1941), Neuengamme (1942–1943), and Ravensbrück (1943–1945). Strebel (2003), 61.
41   Herta Oberheuser (1911–1978) and Rolf Rosenthal (1911–1947), both doctors at Ravensbrück, also administered lethal injections to prisoners. Source: The National Archives, London, WO 235/317, Deposition of Dr. Rolf Rosenthal, 19 August 1946. Nuremberg Medical Trial, Microfiche number 131, Affidavit of Herta Oberheuser, 2 November 1946.
42   Hohenlychen was an SS sanatorium affiliated with the German Red Cross. It was located seven to nine miles away from Ravensbrück concentration camp and was presided over by Karl Gebhardt. Waltrich (2001).
43   Herta Oberheuser also suggested that Rosenthal had an "unstable" personality. She remarked to Alexander when he interviewed her during the Nuremberg Medical Trial that he was "frightening" to her. Oberheuser perhaps wanted to portray a particular image of herself as a scared woman in a male-dominated environment with the hope of garnering sympathy while the trial was ongoing. However, these sources might suggest that others did perceive Rosenthal as a volatile character, too. Source: Stadtarchiv Nürnberg, Rep 502 VI O1, KV-Anklage, Interrogations, Vernehmung von Frl. Dr. Oberheuser durch Prof. Dr. Alexander, 28 December 1946. Oberheuser also stated in an interview conducted with a public prosecutor in Kiel in December 1956 that „Mein Verhältnis zu Dr. Rosenthal war nicht gut" and that „Ich habe ihn als Menschen nicht geschätzt". She stated that this did not get in the way of their „gegenseitigen ärztlichen Massnahmen". Source: Landesarchiv Schleswig-Holstein, Abt. 352 Kiel, Nr. 1141, Auf Vorladung erscheint als Beschuldigte Ärztin Dr. med. Oberheuser aus Stocksee, 5 December 1956.
44   Arthur Keith Mant (1919–2000) was a British forensic pathologist who wrote a volumnious report about the medical services at Ravensbrück which was used as evidence in the post-war Ravensbrück concentration camp trials. See The National Archives, London, WO 309/419, Major Arthur Keith Mant RAMC, Special Medical Section War Crimes Group B.A.O.R, Ravensbrück Camp. A report on the Medical Services, Human Experimentation and various other atrocities committed by medical personnel in the camp. The final version of the report was produced on 1 September 1949, but other earlier versions were written before the start of the Ravensbrück trials in December 1946.

Fig. 7: Fritz Fischer, defendant at the Nuremberg Doctors' Trial. First row, from left to right, Karl Brandt, Siegfried Handloser, Paul Rostock, Fritz Fischer (standing), Karl Genzken, Karl Gebhardt. Second row, from left to right, Gerhard Rose, Siegfried Ruff, Viktor Brack, Hans-Wolfgang Romberg, Hermann Becker-Freyseng, Georg August Weltz. Nuremberg, Germany, 1946/47 (Source: NARA).

Evening: Record analysis. Sievers diary: Blome,[45] Rascher[46] and the Reichsärztekammer.
Weltz[47] was in SS.

21 Nov 1946 Indictment read in Court. Afterwards: conversation with General Taylor, re Thanatology. "You have given the def. too much credit, and Himmler too little". Afternoon: Interrogation of Mr. Chaim Balicki, aged 26 yrs. born 28 February 1920, Dzialoszyc [Działoszyce]; Poland, District of Kielce. CC No. 132266.

In Auschwitz[48] sterilisiert und kastriert. In Dachau[49] from 28-1-45 to the day of deliverance by the U.S. Army on 29 April 1945, camp serial number 139799. Stenogapher: Mr. Roeder. Room 330.

Evening: Conversation with Major Mant and Miss Shally.

---

45 Kurt Blome (1894–1969) was the Deputy Reich Health Leader and Plenipotentiary for Cancer Research in the Reich Research Council. He was charged with euthanasia and human experimentation at the Nuremberg Doctors' Trial but was acquitted of charges. After the trial, he was hired by Sidney Gottlieb to work on the MK-Ultra programme, the code name for the human experiments designed and carried out by the United States Central Intelligence Agency (CIA) that were intended to identify drugs such as LSD which could be used in interrogations.
46 Sigmund Rascher (1909–1945) was an SS doctor. He conducted human experiments on concentration camp prisoners pertaining to high altitude, freezing and blood coagulation. Rascher was arrested in 1944 following accusations of scientific fraud and financial irregularities. He was sent to Buchenwald concentration camp, before he was executed by the SS at Dachau on 26 April 1945. Schmidt (2004), 127, 156.
47 Georg Augustus Weltz (1989–1963) was a German radiologist and head of the Munich Institute for Aviation Medicine. He was charged for participation in human experiments at the Nuremberg Doctors' Trial but was acquitted. Schmidt (2004), 90, 260.
48 Auschwitz was a complex of over 40 concentration and extermination camps located in occupied Poland. The camps were set-up between 1940 and 1942 and lasted through to the end of the war. Nearly 1.3. million people died at Auschwitz. Sydnor (2009), 204.
49 Dachau concentration camp was established in March 1933. The total number of prisoners in Dachau between 1933 and 1945 exceeded 200,000. The number who died there is estimated to be between 32,099 and 40,000. Distel (2009), 442–445.

Thanatology:[50] Sulfonamide experiments on blood. Production **[12]** of gas gangrene by inocculation. When Grawitz[51] visited Ravensbrück he asked "how many deaths?" (see Fischer's[52] affidavit).

[...]: Sulfamid [sulfonamide], Cold, low pressure (see Brandt's formulation), Sea water ("12 days"), Typhus (incubation. form of incub. typhus), sterilization and kastration with carcinogenus x ray overdose.

experiments inadequate for purpoits [purported] uses, but scientifically adequate if interpreted as [...] [...] research in quest of a new field; Thanatology,[53] scientific implementation of genocide.

50 Alexander coined the term 'Thanatology' from the Ancient Greek 'thanatos', meaning 'death', and the suffix '-logia', derived from 'logos' meaning 'word', 'thought', or 'principle' and used to form nouns to define disciplines and fields of study. Alexander used the term to refer to the 'scientific, inconspicuous and effective methods to carry out the murder of other people'. Thanatology became an important part of the prosecution's case against the Nazi doctors to support charges of genocide in the realm of medical science. It was developed by Alexander as a rebuttal against the possible defence argument that the human experiments carried out by Allied medical scientists were comparable to those conducted by German doctors and should not be punished. Schmidt (2004), 160–161.
51 Ernst-Robert Grawitz (1899–1945), was a German doctor and member of the SS involved with the Action T4 'euthanisia' programme. He committed suicide during the Battle of Berlin.
52 Fritz Fischer (1912–2003) was a German doctor who conducted human experiments on women at Ravensbrück concentration camp. He was sentenced to life imprisonment at the Nuremberg Medical Trial, but his sentence was reduced to 15 years in 1951 and he was freed in March 1954. Fischer continued to practice medicine after his release, working for a chemical company. See page 63 of the diary for Alexander's interview with Fischer. Schmidt (2004), 127, 260, Roth/Schmidt/Weindling (2001), 287.
53 In a memo sent to Taylor on 30 November 1946, Alexander outlined this new concept under the title 'Thanatology as a Scientific Technique of Genocide'. In another memo, 'Suggestions for a Discussion of the Thanatology Genocide Angle', was submitted to Taylor on 5 December. According to Alexander, the human experiments demonstrated that doctors had produced an actual 'science of killing', which he referred to as 'Ktenology', Schmidt (2004), 163. This term was likely to have been coined by Alexander from the Ancient Greek verb stem '-kten', meaning 'to kill', with the suffix '-logy', together forming a word that can be interpreted to mean 'the science of killing'. It seems that he used both the terms 'Thanatology' and 'Ktenology' interchangeably. While both concepts played an important role in the Doctors' Trial their legal application is now non-existent. Schmidt (2004), 171.

[13]

Table   legwork of experiment

A Ostensible purpose purpose	B Real problem	A	B
Typhus: efficiency of vaccine (Mrugowski,[54] Hoven,[55] etc.)	Incubation period of inoculation. Typhus: what time does it take to infect and kill.	− (insufficient numbers)	+ (Incubation period 14 days; height of illness 3 weeks of infecting. (Mrugowski This is the only fact Mrugowski is specific about)
Sulfamidamation [sulfonamidation] study (Gebhardt, Oberheuser, Fischer)	Actually: feasibility of infecting clean wounds with gas bacillus	− (see self-annihiliation levels; [...] experimentation stopped as soon as method of making infection to [...] was recompleted)	+ A method was found by which gas bacillus was made to grow in healthy human tissue
Sea water experiments of Behring and Mecker methods	[...] necessary to [...] a closed [...] of people by supply with sea water only	− Only the [...] Becker method was tried	+ Time of 12 days necessary to kill was determined
[...] of immunity	Possibilities of use [...]	− No meaning [?] of vaccination were actually [...]	+ No real immunity [...]

54 Joachim Mrugowski (1905–1948) was a Polish-German bacteriologist who conducted human experiments at Buchenwald concentration camp. He was Chief of the Hygiene Institute of the Waffen SS. He was tried in the Nuremberg Doctors' Trial and executed in 1948. Schmidt (2004), 143, 229, 260.

55 Waldemar Hoven (1903–1948) was a doctor at Buchenwald concentration camp. He was involved in typhus experiments at Buchenwald. He was found guilty of war crimes, crimes against humanity and membership in a criminal organisation, and was hung in June 1948. Schmidt (2004), 143, 260.

[14]

A	B	A	B
Methods of treatment to save our splendid young dying soldiers and aviators	Detrimental types necessary to kill by experiments cold	− No comparable statistics from stiffened subjects given; the method that to be this best never [...] for use of [...]	+ excellent statistics of times and temperature. Good method frequently met to [...] concentration camp inmates, and one knew that prisoners of war were herded into cold water and dereriored there for time specified by the report of cold study.
[...] of "safe" levels of high altitude at low pressure	Test of explosive decompression as a method of execution	[...] levels used much higher than known to be unsafe.	+ confirmed by actual use of low pressure apparatus as an extermination chamber (see Neff's[56] diary) and by Brandt's formulation esp. 3, No. 55.
Tuberculin experiments	Parts of [...] often intrapulmonic inoc.		

---

56 See page 115 of Alexander's diary for his interview with Neff.

[15]

A	B	A	B
Sterilization, followed by removal of testes [...] to see effect	Use of sterilizations with additional carcinogenic effect, which would kill victim in the course of a few years.	Massive reaction: 15 minutes	+ frozen [...]
Dissemination of cancer [...]	Use of cancer dissemination as a weapon	− known	+ [...]
Poison and petrol (include. phenol inj.)			
Poison bullet			
Gassing exp.			
starvation (death camp for the tubercules)			
Euthanasia	Training of killer personnel for death camps	Appoints the staff out of supporters with own [...] euthansia	Actual [...] at [...] of euthanasia personnel

[16]

			for genocidal activities

[17] With the method of abortion doctors [...] search of methods which could be handled by unskilled personal (abortion rests at night [...]) even in 8th month. Plane use of [...]

Difference between [...] this [...] experimented ones, not only voluntary recruits [...]; but also main objective not search for methods of healing, but for methods [...], and true facts of producing death by various non-obvious and non-conspicious means. The constant search for methods of camouflage of killing is obvious from the exchanging of letter. Blome-[...] Brandt-Himmler re extermination of tubercular Poles.

Experiments designed to pervert the basic purpose of medicine. Therefore, just naturally the method of [18] carrying them out adapted itself to the guiding principle. Because the purpose was humanitarian, the athmosphere of what the experiments were carried out became likewise humanitarian; while in its German group, where the purpose was "thanatological", the methods were quite diabolical too.

22 Nov. 1946 Completed examination of witness.

Bolovsky; he signed the affidavit. Mr. Herbert Meyer's[57] resume: "If the State becomes a criminal institution, the individual goes down. too; with nothing etc." Unless, of course, he happens to be a real independent mind.

Mr Bernhard Raymond, Room 394

In the afternoon worked out the evidence analysis in the Weltz case; then worked on Thanatology.

23 Nov. 1946 Interrogated Weltz, Rudolf Brandt,[58] and Sievers.

Weltz confessed: "It had to be done." Weltz, by confessing a lot of facts [19] previously concealed, brought out strongly the fact that Germans found it allright [alright] to lie to inferiors, but not to superiors and equals. Some brought out re Himmler by the interview with Sievers.

Afternoon: conference with MacHaney, Horlik-Hochwald;[59] dictated refutation of "voluntary" and "given a chance".

24 Nov. 1946 Sunday. To Courthouse at 11 A.M. Dictated conclusions re Weltz interview, worked on Thanatology.

Sunset supper at the Hotel; talk with Mr. Raymond; his own experiences at Auschwitz.

---

57 Herbert Meyer interrogated those accused of war crimes at the Nuremberg Medical Trial. See Trials of War Criminals before the Nuernberg Military Tribunals under Control Council Law No. 10, Volume 1, Nuernberg, October 1946–April 1949.
58 Rudolf Brandt (1909–1948) was the Personal Administrative Officer to Himmler. He was convicted of war crimes and crimes against humanity at the Nuremberg Doctors' Trial and executed in 1948. Schmidt (2004), 131.
59 Anorst Horlik-Hochwald (1898–1990), also known as Ernst Hochwald, was part of the Czech legal team supporting the prosecution at the first International Military Tribunal in Nuremberg. Weindling (2012), 101. He then served on the prosecution consel for the Nuremburg Doctors' Trial. Cf. Ebbinghaus/Roth (2001), 68; Weindling (2004), 136.

*Fig. 8: Leo Alexander interrogating the Nuremberg defendant Wolfram Sievers.
Nuremberg, Germany, 23 November 1946 (Source: NARA).*

In the evening worked on thanatology paper: *"The voice of destruction spoke also through medicine"*.

25 Nov. 1946 Reports conc. German defense experiments and interrogation Weltz completed. Rascher's picture sent for distribution. Further work on thanatology. Telephone conversation with Wiskott[60] and Rein[61], who are not too eager to cooperate.

[20] 26-11-1946 *Romberg*:[62] Ich selber habe Rascher 8 Menschen in die Unterdruckkammer hingebracht, um electrocardiogramm zu registrieren. Er machte das auch bei den Erschießungen.

Krach zwischen Rascher und Weltz. Rascher hat Weltz immer als einen schwarzen Katholiken bezeichnet, zwischen der ersten München Besprechung u. dem Beginn der Versuche [...] nicht abgelehnt.

Born May 15, 1911:
Abitur 1929; MD 1935. Married 1940, congenial, 2 children, aged 4 and 2 yrs old. Cause for medical study: 2 choices; engineer, technical contents, 2nd physician. They [...] one on the same degree. Economic matters much in this decision. Ursprünglich wollte Chirurg werden wegen heilberuflicher Neigung; Pathology Prof. Büchner (1936); there developed interest on aero-medical research. Came then in research, practiced only for brief periods as a substitute. Since 36 at the [*luftfahrtmedizinische* – deleted] Deutsche [21] Versuchsanstalt für Luftfahrt:

Evangelisch:[63] Never went much to Church. But never left Church either. Was married in Church in 1940. "Ich bin nicht streng kirchlich religiös, aber ich glaube an Gott."

---

60 Alfred Wiskott (1898–1978) was a paediatrician and director of the Kinderklinik and Kinderpoliklinik in the Dr. von Haunersche Kinderspital from 1939 until his retirement in 1967.
61 Hermann Rein (1898–1953) was a physiologist and university professor. He directed the Göttingen University Physiology Institute and held the title of Consulting Physiologist to the Chief of the German Air Force Medical Service. He played an active role in the establishment of the Reich Ministry for Aviation in 1933. Rein participated in the Seenot-Winternot conference in October 1942. He was considered – alongside Hubertus Strughold, Franz Büchner, Theodor Benzinger, and Siegfried Ruff – a leading co-ordinator of Nazi aviation medical research. During the period from 1933 to 1953, Rein was nominated twelve times for the Nobel Prize for Physiology of Medicine. Hansson/Daan (2014), 2911, Ebbinghaus/Roth (2001), 130.
62 Hans-Wolfgang Romberg (1911–1981) was a defendant in the Nuremberg Doctors' Trial. He was one of Rascher's collaborators in the high-altitude experiments at Dachau and eventually aquitted. Schmidt (2004), 156.
63 Throughout the diary, Alexander often attempts to establish the religious background of those he is interviewing. In the context of the Nazi doctors, this was perhaps based on an attempt by Alexander to establish possible links between any religious beliefs and moral ideas with their actions. In many instances the Nazi interviewees in the diary state that they are Christians. Throughout the Third Reich, Christianity's relationship with the Nazis was complex. As the party grew in power over the course of the early 1930s, many Christians, both Catholic and Protestant, were attracted to Nazism. The complexity of this relationship was marked by a pragmatic realisation of the power of the churches in Germany that promoted means to accommodate them yet followed by instances of outright hostility to the Judeo-Christian values viewed as incompatible with Nazism. Kurlander (2019).

Rascher definitely left Church. Thought that Germany would win the war until of November 1942, at the landing on North Africa. "Für die meisten Leute war Stalingrad die Wende (Juni 43)".

Karl Brandt:[64] Euthanasia programme in 1939. Vom ärztlichen Gesichtspunkt "Euthanatos" Praesidialrat im Reichsforschungsrat.[65]
Born 8–1–1904
Abitur, Realgymnasium 1923
MD February 1928
Bochum, Chirurg, 1934
SA 1933
SS 1934
Heer 1935 (Reserve)
Differenzen mit Himmler; Sanitätsoffiziersamt Arzt, dann Offizier, Himmler umgekehrt.

Schulmeister; Allgemeinwissen; [22] Hans Dampf in allen Gassen. "Es gab nichts, das er nicht selbst machen wollte. Egozentrisch. Als Lehrer – dachte immer mit Schulkindern zu tun zu haben. Belehren wollen, belehren müssen, selbst immer alles wissen wollte. Kräuter gezüchtet, Gold machen, Kohle synthetisieren. Pflanzen mit Opiaten getränkt, Mystik über ihn selbst [als] alten König Heinrich. Sterne gucken zugänglich. "Krebs heilen" oder "Nibelungenschatz heben". Hielt sich für eine Reincarnation von Heinrich II (Quedlinburg).

Was condemned by Hitler to death on April 16, 1945.

Break with Goebbels in 1944, re total war; he wanted to close universities, abolish specialised literature, etc.

Married 1934, congenial, one son aged 11 years. Vater: Polizeioffizier; mother: daugther of a physician. Congenial, only child.

Evangelisch. 1935 or 1936 left the church, since he lost [23] contact with the church since he started on university study. War in der Kirche, verheiratet. Frau ist nicht aus der Kirche ausgetreten. Naturwissenschaftlicher: Berlin durch medizinisches Studium.

In spite of this, wanted to go to Lambarene with Albert Schweitzer. Would have had to be a Frenchman to go there, and to serve in the French Army. Frau hat sich auf den Standpunkt gestellt, dass jeder das mit sich selbst abmachen muss.

"Immer wird geglaubt, das wird etwas Besonderes [...] wäre – im Jahre 1944 habe ich geglaubt, dass wenn nicht etwas bes.[onderes] geschieht, es nicht mehr zu schaffen wäre."

Speer re west [...] against Russia. "Stalingrad was a shock." Defection – wo einer Scrupel hatte. Defeatistische [Defätistische] Tendenz unserer Dienststelle.

Zukunft – vor mir selbst ein gutes Gewissen – zerbrach mir nicht den Kopf [da]rüber.

---

64 For an extensive biography of Karl Brandt, see Schmidt (2008).
65 Reich Research Council, founded in 1937.

Fig. 9: Karl Brandt, lead defendant at the Nuremberg Doctors' Trial. Nuremberg, Germany, 1946/47 (Source: Ray D'Addario).

[24] In the afternoon: Mr. Bernd Bessing, born 30-8-1927, in Lund, Sweden. Was in Concentration Camp Stut[t]hof near Danzig; claimed he recognised Rostock, on having been present at his parents' execution; and on having given him injections into his left leg at the Versuchs-Institut: mechanical hepatitis extension contractions of left leg. Not a good witness.

Read [...] in Brack's letter (Brack's "remedy")[66]

[25] 27-11-46
Becker-Freyseng:[67]

Fall 1941–44 assistant consultant with aviators medicine in the Surgeon General's office of the Luftwaffe. Since 44 consultant.

Seewasserversuche.

1) Entsalzung: Methode Dr Schäfer (Wolfatit). Geeignetes Verfahren.

2) Berkatit: Kohlehydratabkömmling aus Tomaten. Nahm nur den salzigen Geschmack ab. Salzgehalt unverändert. Körper verliert Wasser, um es auszuscheiden. Gutachter Prof. Sippingen, der sich für das Berkatit einsetzte: Niere könnte trainiert werden, um das Salz auszuschwemmen. Komplexe Verbindung, "durchgeschleust". Heubner hält die beiden Möglichkeiten nicht für unwahrscheinlich.

Vorschlag, den Versuch am Menschen zu machen, ging von mir aus. Bedingungen so durchgeführt, daß dabei nichts passieren kann. In dem Moment abzubrechen, da ernste anschließende Gesundheitsstörung. Technisches Amt zwang [26] eine Entscheidung in 4–5 Wochen zu treffen (July 1944). 40 Männer hätten wir damals von der Truppe nicht bekommen. A) Ungefährlichkeit B) Schwierigkeiten mit anderen Versuchsarten. No inspections.

Was unsere Dienststelle erwartet hatte: Berkatit nichts als eine geschmackliche Abänderung. Nach 4–5 Tagen konnten die VP kein Seewasser mehr trinken. Mit Wolfartit keine Schwierigkeiten. 4 oder 5 Versuchsgruppen. 1: Wo[l]fartit, 2: Berkatit; 3: reine Trinkwassergruppe, 4: reine Seewassergruppe; 5: Eine Gruppe in reinem Durstversuch. Am längsten ausgehalten: Seewasser und Berkatit-Gruppe: 4–5 Tage. Durstgruppe: 6 Tage.

Abruch, wenn Versuchsperson sich weigerte, den Versuch weiter mitzutun, ohne Gesundheitsschäden.

Schröder made arrangements with Himmler thru Grawitz.

Beiglböck started July or August 1944. Reported immediately after conclusion of the experiments. B. hat nichts mit Rascher zu tun gehabt. He had 2 or 3 physiological chemists; and several Luft- [27] waffe soldiers. Does not know how many. Dachau personnel helped; he told him about one interned ENT [Ear Nose and Throat] man who helped.

---

66 Viktor Brack's "remedy", as referred to by Erhard Wetzel (the "race expert" in Rosenberg's ministry for the occupied east), was to use "gassing devices" to murder Jewish prisoners and overcome the psychological impact mass shootings had on soldiers in Eastern Europe. Friedlander (1995), 54.

67 Hermann Becker-Freyseng (1910–1961) was a German physician, consultant for aviation medicine and convicted Nazi war criminal. He oversaw human experimentation on concentration camp prisoners, was tried and convicted of war crimes and crimes against humanity at the Nuremberg Doctors' Trial. He was sentenced to 20 years imprisonment, but this was commuted to 10 years and he was released in 1952.

"Ich hatte die Berichte zu unterschreiben."

Sense of emergency. Holzlöhner's[68] work helped convince people of quick rewarming.

Born: 18 July 1910; Ludwigshafen a.Rh. Vater: Franz Becker, director of a bank, killed in 1st World War at 37, in 1917. Mutter: Frau Josephine Becker, geb. Danner, lives at age 72 yrs.

1br., 3yrs older; [Becker-]Freyseng was name of paternal grandmother.

Abitur 1929; Heidelberg, Assistent, Berlin. MD 1935. Feb. 35–Feb. 36: Medizinalpraktikant, Medicine. Assistant 38. Aug. 38. Assistant of Luftfahrtmed. Forschungsinstitut Prof. Strughold.

Married 1936; congenial; 3 daugthers, aged 6, 7, 8.

Catholic: Church member.

1933 Parteimitglied.

[28] Sturm and NSKK. Member FK. No member of SS.

Beiglböck: Abteilungsarzt, innere Abteilung in Luftwaffenlazarett Turin, Stabsarzt der Luftwaffe. June 1944 received telegraphy order to go to Berlin. Obeyed: Mitgeteilt, dass beschlossen wurde, die Versuche mit den beiden Verfahren durchzuführen, in Dachau.

Schäfer: chemische Salzfällung.

Berka: Zuckerarten und Säuren als Geschmackserzeuger, Zuckersäure and Ascorbinsäure. "Komplizenlos". Luftwaffenärzte hatten Bedenken gegen dieses Mittel. Rohstoffgründe. Concurrenz Bei Vorbesprechung war Eppinger zugezogen.

Dr. Sievering hatte Versuch an deutschen Soldaten gemacht: Meerwasser gern getrunken [...], relativ wenig Schäden. Beaufsichtigung nicht gründlich.

4 Gruppen: 1) nur Wasser 2) Seewasser und Berka 3) Seewasser und Schäfer 4) Seewasser.

So lange fortführen, bis man deutlich sähe, ob Berka different [29] from Seawater, bis deutlichste Zeichen zur Wirkung des Meerwassers feststellbar seien." "Bis deutliche Meerwasserschäden sichtbar werden." Hypertonische Salzlösung, Niere 2% Salz. Meerwasser 3% Salz. Körperwasser. Durstphenomene: Austrocknung, verschiedene Symptome: 1) subjectives Durstgefühl am 1st Tag gering, 2. Tag heftiger, bei nierenschädigung sehr heftige Formen. Frage der Wasserreserven. Depotwasser wechselt immer individuell: Depotwasser, Lösungs-, Quellungswasser. Austrocknung der Haut und Schleimhäute. Haut gut abheilbar: dehydration Muskel[n] wurden härter. Merkwürdige mechanische Überregbarkeit idiomusculäre Wülste, wie bei der Tuberkulose oder Krebsgeschwüren. Ansteigen des Bluteiweisses und der Erythrocyten.

Suggestive hypertension Families, was found by a French ophtalmologist. 3 chemists (physicians), from the Luftwaffe. Ein Sanitätsgefreiter. 3 Medizinstudenten-Häftlinge. Ein Häftling Sanitäter. Im Lazarett Dachau. 42 VP [Versuchspersonen].

[30] Durst: 3–5 days.

---

68 Ernst Holzlöhner (1899–1945) was a German physiologist. He carried out sub-cooling experiments in Dachau concentration camp from August 1942. Schmidt (2004), 102.

Criteria: Blutverdickung war 6,500,000 Rbc überschritten. Auch die, die subjektiv nicht viel auszuhalten glaubten. Manche haben den Durst gut ausgehalten, manche haben subjektiv gelitten. 2 Liter Flüssigkeitsmenge wurde erlaubt, als Wasserverlust.

Meerwasser: Lebervergrösserung
2 tetaniforme Krämpfe: Sofort unterbrochen. In der Meerwassergruppe.

Fachärztliche Befunde alle von Häftlingsärzten.

Seewassergruppe: 3–5, 6 days; a few 7 and 8 days (the latter had few drinking, small quantities of fresh water).

Berka: like sea water.

Schäfer: nothing noxious. Carried on for 10 days. Like normal water. The VP [Versuchspersonen] waren Zigeuner und Zigeunerstämmlinge.

[31] [...]
kurzer Zwischenbericht – Mündlicher Bericht zu Berka, später schriftlich. Nicht publiziert. Kein persönliches wissenschaftliches Interesse. Nicht mehr fertig geworden, es hat sich alles aufgelöst. Urlaubssperre.

Stoffwechsel. Vitamine.

Born October 10, 1905.

Gymnasium 1915–23, kath[olisch].

1923–31, Medizinische Fakultät; erstes Rigorosum später.

Christlich. 1931–33, 39–45 bei Eppinger. 1932–44, 50 wiss. Arbeiten. Married 1937, 2 children. born 1939 and 1941. Divorced 1945.

Keine Religion. Left the catholic church 1938.

SA since 1934.

Referred questions regarding his attitude to human experimentation.

[32] In the afternoon worked on sea water case, went over my previous interrogations. Found excellent quotation from Grosse-Brochhoff, stating that human experimentation had revealed nothing new beyond universal experimentation with specific reference to Holzlöhner's paper on cold (Report of the Nürnberger Tagung).[69]

28-11-46 Abraham Sachs (Abram Zaks), aged 26 yrs.,
DP [Displaced Person] Camp, Kaserne, Block 18, Landsberg from Lech, Room 15. Born on 22-3-1920 in Częstochowa.

Taken to Auschwitz August 1943; transported to Landsberg January 1945; liberated. 10 weeks after being taken to Auschwitz was sterilized by x ray, subsequentally castrated.

Exam: extensive x ray burning over both thighs.

Complaining of weakness and lack of pep. An American doctor has implanted pellets into his thigh; slight improvement since then (2 months [33] ago). Dr (Capt. Strime). He is married. Brothers:

---

69 Leo Alexander's thoughts on the supposed "scientific" value of the experiment: "One cannot help feeling that the experiments were amateurish and poorly coordinated, that they failed to give scientific information which was claimed to be desired, and that a unified policy was completely absent, except for the barbaric manner of their execution." Schmidt (2004), 165.

Joshua (Szyja) Zaks, born 1–12–1922, aged 24 yrs.
DP camp, Kaserne, Block 18, Landsberg / am Lech.
Born in Częstochowa.
Taken to Auschwitz August 1943. He bolted from the transport at Gleiwitz, on Jan 3, 1945; since the blockleader said that all the castrated ones are to be killed, in order to rut out witnesses. The blockleader said that to a sentry (block leader was an SS man). He hid in the woods for 4 days; Russian soldiers helped him to search his home in Bedzin, Poland. Then came to Landsberg in a Kibuts transport, because both his brothers were here. Sterilised and castrated same way as brothers.
Testicles empty. Less severe x ray burns than brothers.
All of them show the same reaction of "shame" concerning their condition. Abram heard someone say: "that guy had his nuts cut out at Auschwitz". Joshua has not been able to take [34] a bath at the camp, for fear that his fellow DPs would know about his condition.
Afternoon: reviewed interrogations. Evening: completed Thanatology with the help of Marian Shelley, who could be a really inspiring coworker. Must talk to MacHaney about her.

29–11–46 Dr. Waldemar Hoven

26–X–39–Jan 41. Truppenarzt. Jan. 41–July. 42 zweiter Lagerarzt. July 42–12 Sept. 43 erster Lagerarzt. Dann verhaftet; wegen Giftmordes; es stellte sich später heraus, daß er an Nikotinvergiftung gestorben war. In Haft bis 15. März 45; erst bei Gestapo[70] in Weimar, dann in Buchenwald als Häftling. Remembers that another prisoner was Dr. Rascher; was still there on March 15, 1945.
Phenol injections were available in the pharmacy in Buchenwald, 8 or 10 cc, since 1941. MD Sept. 39. SS member since 1934, active duty with Waffen SS since 1939. Nach [...] [35] ordered to Buchenwald, knew nothing about concentration camp. After he became Lagerarzt; allgemeine Dienstvorschriften. Nicht sprechen, keine Rauch- und Esswaren. Zuchthaus. Todesstrafe über politische Dinge zu sprechen. Nach 3 Monaten: "die Nase voll". Versetzungsgesuch zur Front-Truppe. Häftling Schreiber diktiert, Rudolf Gottschalk. Wurde befreundet mit prominenten politischen Häftlingen: Abordnung bat ihn, im Lager zu bleiben. Kampf gegen Berufsverbrecher geholfen.
1941 Vergasungsaktion. Killed only professional criminals. On March 15, appointed police doctor official; on April 11, when on his way to Buchenwald, was captured by the Americans. 2 hours later was taken to Buchenwald, where the prisoners vouched for him.
Did not participate in experiments.
Vergasungsaktion 14 F 13, "Krüppel und Geisteskranke", specially direcected against Jews. Took political prisoners and 8 Jews off the list. Summer 1941: Selected only professional criminals for his typhus experiments:
10% with Schutzimpfung
20% died.

---

70 The Gestapo (*Geheime Staatspolizei*) were the secret police of Nazi Germany.

[36] Thinks the prisoners invented the use of phenol and eviapan for lethal injections. Death occured in 1–3 seconds. "Ich sehe es noch vor mir. Im Augenblick wie die Spritze zuende war sofortiger Tod["] (mistaken as spasm like mimic in the direction of [...]) Versuche mit farbigen Stoffen, Heilmittel gegen Fleckfieber.

No Benzol injections.

geb. 10 Feb. 1903, in Freiburg i. Breisgau.

Married 1929; glücklich; one daughter, aged 7/8, son aged 16, son aged 9 yrs.

Ich habe manche Liaison gehabt, aber meine Frau ist mehr als ein Kamerad gewesen, immer zu mir gehalten. Frau wollte nie in ein KZ Lager: sie sagte immer zieh Deinen [...] aus, ich kann das nicht anschauen. Sie hatte ihn manchmal besucht; gab einen Kaffee für die Häftlinge.

War protestant; 1925 aus der Kirche ausgetreten; wife and children are catholic.

[37] Thought that Germany would win the war until 1943; since his imprisonment, especially the attempt on Hitler's life, thought the war was lost. Wir hielten die Impfstoffversuche für nicht sehr hervorragend. Ding war kein Wissenschaftler der sich mit Druck dahintersetzte. Später hat ein jüdischer Arzt, Fleck,[71] die Ergebnisse bewertet. Der hat sie für interessant gehalten.

Natzweiler war ein Liquidationslager. Vor dem Transfer hat Pflegeanstalten mit holländischen jüdischen, polnischen, russischen und tschechischen Häftlingen besetzt. Wie sie darin waren, kriegswissenschaftlich tätig, waren sie geschützt. Pick als Künstler. Cohen hat ihn gerettet, er hatte gesagt, ich werde es ihnen einmal vergelten.

Dr. Pokorny

Defence that he wanted to shift the east policy into an [...] unfeasible method.

Born 25 July 1895 Wien.

MD Prague 1922

Assistant a.d. Hautklinik Kurbaden in Prag bis 1924, dann, weil Frau Jüdin war, musste Klinik verlassen. Ging nach Kärnten. Privatpraxis;

[38] Frau tätig als Röntgenologin. Worked until Einziehung in 1942: Oberarzt, Heer, in a Lazarett in Saxony. Divorced 1935; not for political reasons. Wife remarried in Komotew [Komotau] 2 years, then fled to protectorate with both children, ist dann durch das Regime ihrer Praxix verlustig gegangen. Kein Ende. Jänner 1942 in ein KZ. Hat [...] angerufen und um Hilfe gebeten, hat ihr Hilfe zugesagt. Am Abend kam ein SD-Mann, drohte mit sofortigem Einschreiten. ½ Jahr vorher waren die Kinder nach England zu Verwandten geschafft worden. Frau wurde tot gemeldet. But heard recently that she is alive.

Did nothing but write the letter. Never possessed the plant or an experimented animal. Für [...], um eine Erhöhung der Potenz zu erreichen. Massensterilisierung bei der Ostbevölkerung und Massenverstümmelungen.

SS men treated for Lues for about 2 months, in 1941.

---

71 Ludwik Fleck (1896–1961): Polish Jewish and Israeli biologist, physician and philosopher of science. Important medical work in epidemic typhus. In the 1930s Fleck developed the concepts of "Denkstil" ("thought style") and "Denkkollektiv" ("thought collective").

Proposed to Himmler with others he knew the changes were artefacts. Wanted an influential position.

[39] Studied medicine – medicine was in the family, maternal grandfather – because of World War I, in which he did not fire a single shot, developed philanthropic interests.

Religiös – Arzt, naturwissenschaftlich gebildet, [...] – person: [...] – Kirchlichen Glauben, aber tiefen – Glauben der [als] Pantheismus bezeichnet werden kann. Ich such in allen Geschöpfen und Erscheinungen das Wirken der Gottheit. Katholisch, resigned 1926, after 1st child was born, wife was Jewess, and she wanted the child to be Protestant. One parent had to be protestant, so he became protestant. Returned to Catholicism ... das war vielleicht an dem Tag, wo der Bombenangriff auf Chemnitz war, January 1945. Äussere Ursache, langes Gespräch mit zweiter Frau; remarried Sept. 27, 1943. No children. Catholic. Civil ceremony.

No Nazi membership.

NSKK, über Befehl der Kreisleitung, did duty. Hoven did **[40]** not actually join. Aufnahme aus rassischen Gründen abgelehnt. (Kinder Mischlinge 1sten Grades).

"Never thought that Germany could win the war. As early as the occupation of the Sudetenland said: You will be surprised how sometime your gang will be pushed back". Ahnen beiderseits tschechisch. Nationalsozialistisches Regime so viel Leid angetan.

Balicki: Abram Daffner. Manick Daffner.

Castrated together with Balicki. Both are in trance now, in a hospital. One until recently was in St. Ottilien Krankenhaus bei Landsberg am Lech.

The American doctors there could testify.

Balicki: No beard: shaved every 2 weeks.

Abram Saks:

Scars:	left thigh:	9:	6 ½ inches
	right thigh:	7 ½:	5 inches
	right chest:	6 ½:	3 inches
	left chest:	2 ½:	2 ½ inches
	chest:	1 ½:	¾ inches
[41]	right upper arm:	3 ½:	5 inches
	right forearm:	2 ¼:	1 ½ inches

Marked diminuation of pubic hair and beard: shaves every 3 weeks.
Implantation of pellet right thigh.
Procurrent at times; less so since implantation.
"Der Mund eines Mädels".

Joshua:

Procurrent at time, less so since implantation.
Pellet left thigh.
Secretly through pubic hair.
Trace of beard; shaves every 2 weeks.
Complains of feminine face, which his [...].

Abram & Joshua Saks:

Vater Moses Saks; would be 60 today; Tailor in Caestrochow. Mutter Chzia geb. Rothschild would be 45 today. Arrested together with children. 2 August 1943, taken to Auschwitz, directly to the Crematorium. The selection was done right at the railway riding. A truck took them right to the crematorium; ten minutes later one could see the clothing being taken [42] out. The smoke and the smell was terrible. Every morning at 4AM one could see the fire's red glow over the chimneys; during day time one could only see the smoke.

Three sisters, aged 20 in 1943; she was taken to the camp and *steril.* later. One sister, aged 28, married, was gassed together with her child aged 4 yrs; another sister, aged 30, likewise with child, was gassed. One brother, aged 32, was gassed on arrival with wife and child. One brother survives at his age 34; he was in Auschwitz. His wife and child were gassed (Altogether 7 siblings).

Abram was married; wife survived Maidanek [Majdanek]. Joshua was engaged; fiancé was in Auschwitz, survived. Four weeks after arrival in camp, both brothers were sterilised by exposure to X Rays for 25 minutes; a piece of cloth was placed over the upper part of each thigh; at the end of the experiments it felt hot, and later the chest became pussy (in Joshua's case the pus formed later). (The burning in Abram's case were below the location of the piece of metal).

[43] […] merely […].
2 weeks later both were castrated.

Abram had hot coffee poured over him when he tried to get a drink of water, 10 minutes after sterilisation: had burning over chest and thighs.

Afterwards, Joshua worked as a brick carrier, in the Messerschmitt factory in Flössenburg [Flossenbürg]; then in the coal mines. Die Messerschmitt Fabrik hat ein KZ-Straflager gehabt.

Abram worked all the time in the tailor shop. Winter 1944 to transpt. to Kaufering KZ.[72] Tunnelbau.[73] Abraham feels deeply humiliated and ashamed of his disability. He found his wife 2 month after liberation, when she came to Kaufering. He found it difficult to tell her, but she decided to stick by him. It grates on him day after day. He works to get away, because some know about his condition; he heard once someone say, in the presence of his wife; that guy had his nuts taken out

Joshua was away in Gleiwitz; he found his way to Landsberg. Kattowitz found his fiancé, who had been in a concentration camp in Grünberg. Told her what had happened to him;

---

72 Kaufering Concentration Camp: A series of Dachau concentration camp subcamps were referred to as "Kaufering". The first of the submaps was opened in June 1944. By the end of 1944, ten additional camps were constructed around the village of Landsberg am Lech in Upper Bavaria. This particular subcamp system was the largest of the Dachau subcamps. By the end of April 1945, 30,000 people were interned in the Kaufering camps. Approximately 14,500 people died there. Raim (2009), 490.

73 "Tunnelbau": after the destruction of major armament factories by Allied bombing in Spring 1944, the Reich Ministry for Armaments and War Production began plans to build underground facilities in tunnels to continue production. The tunnels were planned to be built in the area between Überlingen and the suburd of Goldbach on the coast of Bodensee, to take advantage of the soft rock that formed in this area (*Molassefelsen*). "Tunnelbau" refers to the work by prisoners of Dachau and its subcamps on these tunnels. Burger (2009), 554.

[44] Belicki – "ich fühle es immer, es klebt – ich kann nicht gehen ohne es zu fühlen".

She decided to stick by him, but she does not know how she would feel about it in ½ year or so. Married her in Landsberg: "before the war I used to bath every day; now I only wash there once every 2 weeks, because it is such an ordeal – tries to wash himself in his own room to avoid exposing himself.

Can carry out sexual intercourse with his wife once or twice per month, 3 times per month, since he had the pellet. Married 6 month ago.

Abram: no sexual desire, but manages to get an erection once or twice per week, unsatisfactory to him, but better since the pellet have been implanted. On the whole 3 satisfactory occasions for wife – during past year.

[45] Dr. Konrad WP Schäfer.[74]
7-1-11
Mühlhausen, Elsass.
MD Jan. 1936.
Worked on hematoporphyrin, from medico-legal point of view.
Medizin: because of general interest in natural sciences, because physics, chemistry, all combined.
Kein Parteimitglied. Terroristisch u. Zwangsmaßnahmen. Married 1937, congenial, 2 daughters, aged 5 + 6 yrs. Religious, protestant. Standesamt. But wife and children are baptized.
Internship Berlin; found it hard because he had no party membership. Interested at a hydrotherapeutic clinic. Interest on hematology. Research on thrombosis with [...] persits, etc. "Status thromboticus". Patients with his state had complications. Determination of "iso-electro-point".

[46] 1938 had to leave, because of his lack of party affiliations. Then went to Schering, pharmaceutical firm. Worked in Dr. Field's pharma-therapeutic laboratory, until 1945.
Starts work in sea water in the summer of 1942, at the request of the Surgeon General's office.
1941 joined the Luftwaffe; 6 months training in Baden/bei Wien. Then to Frankfurt/Oder, then back to Berlin, dividing his time between Schering and for the Luftfahrtforschungsinstitut Strughold.[75] Perfected Entsalzungsverfahren Fall 1943.

---

74 Konrad Schäfer (1911–1951) was a researcher at the Institute for Aviation Medicine (*Forschungsintitut für Luftfahrtmedizin*) in Berlin under Hermann Göring's Reich Ministry of Aviation (*Reichsluftfahrtministerium*). He was tried and acquitted at the trial. Schmidt (2004), 143.

75 Hubertus Strughold (1898–1986) was a German physiologist who pioneered aviation medicine, developing equipment which enabled German pilots to reach higher altitudes and adjust to speed, temperature and oxygen deficiency. He was the director of the Aviation Medical Research Institute of the German airforce. After the war, he emigrated to the United States and led a team of 33 scientists in San Antonio, Texas, for the US Air Force. While repeated accusations indicated that Strughold had, at least partly, been involved with the Dachau experiments, there was never enough substantial evidence that warranted prosecution by the US Office of Special Investigation. Schmidt (2004), 100, 110.

Reported to Höppler's office. Nothing happened at first. One day in the Winter, Jan. 44, was sent to Vienna; to check on some work by Colonel Simony; who had used Berka's method; Debunked Berka's method. Made report about it. Had conference [with] Schröder towards the end of February. Sent to Christiansen, who questioned him. Told him that the Berka method was nothing but a corrective for the water.

Berka: Sie sagten, es sei nicht unangenehm [47] zu trinken, tasted like tomato soup. It was nothing but a sugar compound added. Inf.'s method consists of an aluminium and barium silicate combined with silver nitrate, the silicate links the Na, the silver, the chloride, barium silicate binds the sulfat. The Mg goes to the aluminium silicate: Filters; drink.

Then a meeting took place at the technical office, at which a heated discussion ensued (April 1944). Berka methode nichts als Geschmackscorrigens [Geschmackskorrigens]: Their motives were suspected. Another meeting on May 20. A method good for 12 days was looked for. It was asked how long one could live on Berka water. I said that either on seawater or Berka water serum impairment of health was to be expected after the 6th day, death on the 12th. Becker [-Freyseng] suggested to test it in man. Suggested experiments in Dachau on inmates, but only so far until difference between Berka and sea [48] water would become manifest, and until first symptoms became manifest. The rest was arranged between Becker-Freyseng and Christianson.

1 group 6 days thirst
1 group Berka water for 12 days
1 group Zeolith water

Commission zur Vorbereitung. Medizinischer Leiter Prof. Eppinger.[76]

Ich sah diese Versuche als unsinnig an. Am Zeolith Verfahren war nichts zu prüfen, das war reines Wasser, und das Berka Verfahren war kein Verfahren.

Heubner was then contacted.

Christianson und das Technische Amt: wollten das Berka Verfahren. Psychologisch, daß die Leute was zu trinken hätten.

Another conference in the beginning of July.

Rank of Feldunterarzt, Ende 1944 became Assistenzarzt.

Lockere Complexverbindung

Beiglböck[77] showed photos of the people before and after.

Participated on [in] 3 conferences, 2 before, [49] one after 20 May 1944, and on the beginning of June 1944 with Heubner and Eppinger. On the first conference answered questions.

---

76   Hans Eppinger (1879–1946) was an Austrian doctor involved in experiments on concentration camp prisoners at Dachau. Eppinger directed the *1. Medizinische Universitätsklinik* (1st Medical University Clinic) in Vienna. The clinic was involved in seawater experiments on Dachau concetration camp prisoners. Eppinger visited the camp on at least two occasions and was involved in trials with Roma and Sinti prisoners. Jobst/Czech (2022). After he was called to Nuremberg in 1946 as a witness, Eppinger killed himself, likely due to fear of being accused himself of medical crimes. Weindling (2004), 143.
77   Wilhelm Beiglböck (1905–1963) was an internist and had the title of Consulting Physician to the German Luftwaffe during the Second World War. He was convicted of war crimes and crimes against humanity at the Nuremberg Doctors' Trial, sentenced to fifteen years of imprisonment, but was released after ten years. Schmidt (2004), 143, 260.

Never thought that Germany could win the war.
Talked to General re Leibbrand[78] contributions.
Completed Thanatology.
Evening: read Neff's diary, p. 31: "That could only happen in Germany, that a defenseless prisoner is inoculated with some disease juice, without being asked; or without paying attention to his protest: "40 Polish catholic priest". "Murder, plain murder, just because some character with officers' rank in the SS thinks he has invented a miracle cure."

[50] *Handloser*:[79] Ich weiss bis heute nicht was da eigentlich gemacht [worden] ist. No regulations regarding human experimentation. No directives were issued on the basis of Rascher's work.

Himmler ideenreich und repressiv: Er hat immer seine Leute angestossen, es müsse was geschehen, wir müssen führend sein. Nach Heydrich's Tod. Rassenbiologisches Programm ehrgeiziger Ärzte.

Born 25–3–1885; studies medicine 1903–1908; MD 1911, after Pép[p]inière.[80]
Married – 1923, one son, aged 22; was wounded in the war, now studying medicine.

Medical interest aroused by new research in Geneva; daneben, Liebe zum Soldatentum hat jeder deutsche Junge. Synthese des Mediziners und Soldaten, Military and Medical interests.

Reminisces about his medical study.
Lives of Tourenreise first.

[Karl] Genzken,[81] Generalleutnant Waffen SS.
SS since 1936[.]
Organisator of Med. Work Waffen SS.

[51] Reichsarzt SS. Inspektionsrecht.
Never saw written directives based on experimental data.
Knew of the Buchenwald experiments, and that inmates were used.
Beratender Hygieniker des Reichsarztes informed him of results. 40.000 Blutportionen gegen Flecktyphus stehen bereit. Das Beste war der SS Impfstoff.
No "Merkblatt" for the treatment of soldiers on shock from cold was issued.
Sulfonamidversuche in Ravensbrück habe ich gehört. Referat O. Fischer auf einem Kongress. Häftlingsgut des KL zugesagen [zugesagt]. 1937–39 war in SS

---

78 Werner Leibbrand (1896–1974) was a German physician/psychiatrist and medical historian. He was the only German expert at the Nuremberg Doctors' Trial. Frewer (2020) and (2021).
79 Siegfried Handloser (1885–1954) was a doctor and Chief of the Army Sanitary System. He was sentenced to life imprisonment at the Nuremberg Doctors' Trial. His sentence was reduced to twenty years and he was released in 1954. Schmidt (2004), 131.
80 The Pépinière, from the French for "plant nursery", was a surgical school in Berlin's Charité Hospital founded by the Kingdom of Prussia in 1795 for the training of royal medical officers. Bonner (2000), 124.
81 Karl August Genzken (1885–1957) was the Chief Medical Officer in the Concentration Camp Inspectorate (Inspektion der Konzentrationslager). He was tried at the Nuremberg Doctors' Trial and sentenced to life imprisonment but was released in 1954. Schmidt (2004), 260.

Sanitätsamt Berlin, die die KL versorgte. Hygienische und Reviermäßige Aufgaben. Spezialabteilungen, Bade- und Massageabteilungen.

Es war schwer, Ärzte für die Waffen-SS zu bekommen. Die wurden in KL befohlen. 50 active physicians at start of war.

Born 8–6–1885
MD 1911;

[52] 1912 joined Navy;

Poppendick[82]

Born 6–1–1902.
Vater, lebt gesund; 70 yrs. railway official. Mutter lebt, über 60.
1 Bruder, aged 39, diplomingenieur [Diplom-Ingenieur], served in Luftwaffe.
Married; April 1943. glücklich, 2 chi. aged 2 and 3; and 2 stepchildren, aged 6 ½ and 4, (wife's first marriage).
Medical study 1921–26, Göttingen, München, Berlin, Staatsexam[en] Dec. 1926, Berlin; never got his M.D. Intern; Peter Friedr. Ludwig Hospital in Oldenburg, dann Berlin Ortskasse Krankenhaus til 1927. Then Lungenheilstätte. 1929 to Charité Geheimrat His, til 1932. Then Oberarzt Virchow Hospital Berlin til 1934. Then to Dahlem to KWI für Erblehre und Anthropologie; for 1 year; then entered SS office for hereditary hygiene and population [53] policy. One year later this became the "Rasse- und Siedlungsamt"[83] der SS: There until the war as "Erbarzt" zur Bewertung der Heirat der SS[-]Angehörigen. War: Heer, Assistenzarzt u. Oberarzt, French campaign. 1941 returned to SS, to Rasse- und Siedlungsamt, unter Reichsarzt SS. 1942 leitender Arzt des Rasse- und Siedlungsamtes. Fall 1943 attached to personal staff of Reichsarzt SS.
"Nie übermäßig religiös." Left the protestant church 1935.
Member of SS since 1932.
(Krieg gewinnen?) Bedenklichkeiten [sic – Bedenken] erst nach Stalingrad. Als die Invasion kam konnte ich nicht mehr sehen wie zu gew.[innen] sei.

Knew about experiments when he returned to Reichsarzt SS in 1941.
In 1944 heard paper by Gebhard on Sulfonamide and gas bacillus. "An zum Tode verurteilten [sic], dafür begnadigt."
Evening: [Hazel Roy]; Mm Shelly assignm.

---

82 Helmut Poppendick (1902–1994) was Chief of the Personal Staff of the Reich Physician SS and Police. At the Nuremberg Doctors' Trial, he was acquitted from being criminally involved in human experiments. He was acquitted of involvement in human experiments but was sentenced to ten years imprisonment for membership of a criminal organisation. He was released in January 1951. Schmidt (2004), 143, 260.

83 The *Rasse- und Siedlungshauptamt* (RuSHA) was originally founded as the *Rasseamt der SS* in December 1931. It was responsible for racial examinations and the marriage permits for members of the SS. The office was part of the *Reichskommissariat für die Festigung deutschen Volkstums* and the *Generalplan Ost*, taking over responsibility for the "racial selection" of the populations in occupied territories and the selection of candidates for the planned settlements of dismissed SS members to the East. Heinemann (2003), 12, 13.

1–12–46 Work with General Taylor. Leibbrand's excellent paper.[84]

[54] 2–12–46 Started on the General's assignments.

Schroeder: Interrogation General Schroeder.
 born 1891, in Hannover. Father: School principal; died 1934 from apoplexy, at 73. Mother: died at 78.
 Congenial.
 Brother, aged 51, retired Colonel, artillery. Engineer.
 Married 1920, wife (older), nurse. 2 sons, one died at age 10 from sepsis in throat (1929); the other was killed in 1945 in combat; Lt., Luftwaffe; aircraft accident, at age 21, marriage congenial.
 Entered 1910, Militärärztliche Akademie, graduated 1916. During the war served as Unterarzt, later Assistenzarzt. Wounded 1915, fracture of lower leg, complicated by Tibialis ant. sepsis. Released to front. After the war joint regular Army as Oberarzt. 1920–23 was given specialised training Otolaryngology with Rhene in Würzburg, 1923–25 in Würzburg, with Prof. Manasse,[85] for advanced training. 1925, as Stabsarzt, placed in charge of the [55] ENT [Ear, Nose and Throat] department of the military Group in Hamburg. 1931 was promoted to the position of "Referent" in charge of therapy and hospitalization section. The other sections were: 1. Personnel. 2. Hygiene. 3. Organisation. 4. statistics and reports. 5. Pharmaceutical 6. + a h [death at hospital] 7. Supply.
 Section chief in the Surgeon General's office; Captain promoted to Major. Sept. 1935 transferred to Luftwaffe, soon promoted to chief of staff under Gen. Höppler. 1936 Lt. Col., 1938 Col.; Feb. 1940 went to the front, Flottenarzt der Luftwaffe 2, with the rank of General. Saw further [voluntary?] service in Russia, Africa, Sicily and Italy; until Dec. 31, 1943. Query that [Lieutenant] promoted to Maj. General. (General Centred). On June 1st 1944 was promoted to Surgeon General of the Luftwaffe (Chef des Sanitätswesens der Luftwaffe), after Höppke retired.
 Religious, protestant.
 1943, Afrika landing; Bedenken, erste. Worry about reliability of Italian ally, (Dr. Marx: Normandy Division after [56] 160.000 people were arrested after 10 days) especially after Avranches.

Gen. Schröder: 20 July 1944, Unstetigkeit in der Führung, SS [...] Wüten.

Learned about cold experiments from Seenot-Winternot (1942).[86] Seenotdienst in Syrakus und Athen musste ein Bad für heiße Bäder bekommen. Gave order to

---

84 Alexander is most probably referring to Werner Leibbrand 1946 publication *Um die Menschenrechte der Geisteskranken* (On the Human Rights of the Mentally Ill). See Frewer (2020) and Engelhardt/Frewer (2023) for more details.
85 Paul Manasse (1866–1927), German Physician for Otorhinolaryngology (ENT), Professor and Director of the ENT Clinic in Würzburg in the 1920s.
86 "Seenot-Winternot" refers to a conference in Nuremberg which took place in October 1942 that demonstrated the results of trials conducted on "medical problems arising from distress at sea and in winter hardships". The results of human experiments conducted on prisoners in Dachau were presented at this conference. Ebbinghaus/Roth (2001), 151; Trittel (2022), 408.

inhabit them, in the spring of 1943. Never heard whether it was done and how it worked; the chief physician of the air rec. rescue resource, Dr. Ruhbranck, was shot down near Malta. The successor had no particular interest in that problem, of course the retreat was going on, and these material problems changed.

1944 Holzlöhner told Dr. Schroeder, in a casual conversation, asked him about Unterkühlungsversuch, but was rather taciturn [still] about it. Er früher ein frischer, lebendiger Mensch, jetzt ist er ein [57] alter, müder Mann. Er hat unter dem Eindruck der Versuche gestanden.

„[...] [knochenbruch] sport gekommen, 43 konnte ich der Sache erst ausweichen.

Haagen's[87] Versuche sind mir unbekannt."

Meerwasser: die beiden Verfahren gegeneinander ausprobieren. Wir waren „Schäfer-Leute." Muß schnell gehen – Frage wo. Luftwaffenlazarett Braunschweig. Juni–July 1944. Invasion in the West conduct new retraining on patients in hospitals. Vorschlag vom technischen Amt der SS und Dachau. Order[:] Ab[b]rechen wenn er Wasser verweigert [verweigern] wird oder wenn Schäden drohen. Beiglböck competent. May 1944; Septem. 1944 received report.

Generalarzt des Heeres, Professor Dr. Rostock[88]

born 18-2-1892

Med. Greifswald, Jena, Staatsexam[en] 1922.

MD, 1922.

Milit. Service: Infantry officer 2nd Lt., afterwards prom. to 1st. Lt. [58] 1915–18, after enlistment as a private. Study: 1913–14, 1919–22.

Assistant surg. University clinic in Jena, under Prof. Guleke until 1928. Oberarzt Magnus[89] was appointed to Bergmannsheil, Bochum [...]. There til 1933; Magnus was then called to Berlin, and R. accompanied there. In 1936 Magnus went to Munich, and R. became acting director, in 1942 director and full professor of surgery.

1934 became Privatdozent in Berlin; associate professor 1936, full professor 1942; Magnus died from a brain tumour in 1943 [1942].

Consultant surgeon since 1939; participated in French campaign. from Holland til Biar[r]itz, May–July 1940. Then back to Berlin. Winter 1940/41 2 month in Paris, Summer 1941 Lublin to Zhitomiz. 1942 became chief consultant in surgery until 1943; then director of the department for scientific research with the [59] Reichskommissar des Sanitätswesens (K. Brandt), 1944–1945. Days worked in

---

87 Eugen Haagen (1898–1972) was a German bacteriologist at the Reich University of Strasbourg. He ordered live vaccine research for typhus to be carried out at Natzweiler concentration camp on human subjects. Weindling (2014), 135. He was incarcerated by American military forces in April 1945 and was released in June 1945. He accepted the invitation of the Soviet military administration in Germany to establish an institute for virus and tumour research in Berlin-Buch. He was arrested by the British military police in 1946. He appeared as a witness in the Nuremberg Doctors' Trial before being tried himself in 1952 by a French court. Although he was sentenced to life imprisonment, he was released and worked from 1956 to 1965 at the Federal Research Centre for Virus Diseases in Animals in Tübingen. Hubenstorf (1994), 445, 452.

88 Rostock was acquitted at the Doctors' Trial. Schmidt (2004), 260.

89 Georg Magnus (1883–1942) was a German surgeon and professor; he followed August Bier (1861–1949) at the Charité in Berlin.

Berlin, evening and nights in Beelitz. At the same time Dean of the Medical School, 1943/44.

Father died 1905 from coronary occlussion, between 50 and 60 yrs of age. Father was a farmer (Landarzt) in Pomerania. Mother died 1939, at age 73, from old age.
1 brother, aged 65, sister aged 61, both shot by the Russians during invasion. They were living on the parents' estate.
Parents congenial.
Married 1922; from X-ray assistant: 1 daughter, aged 17 yrs. Secretary to a government official. Marriage congenial.
Moderately religious, in terms of general religious feeling. Member of protestant Church: Married in this church.
Thought the war could not be won he knew when America came into the war. Unlikely to win it – **[60]** he thought when the war with Russia came. That it would collapse as it did, he did not think so; believed in an "Arian genius" until the beginning of 1945, when Berlin [?] was closed and Russians went into East Prussia. Believed Goebbels early in 1944.
Knows about: Gebhard's sulfonamide experiments at the meeting – an zum Tode Verurteilten. Does not know about Sterilisation with x ray – castration was not intended in Zweckforschung", but in fundamental Versuch.
Scribbling remarks about the sulfonimide [sulfonamide] experiments.
No regulations for human experiments.
No regulation for animal experiments, except for the Caring rules of 1934.[90] Commissionsberichte about inspecting stables etc. It all [...] out.
Had nothing to do with sterilisation or castration.

[61]
60–80 papers, all subjects of surgery, particularly plastic surgery and injuries.
Wrote 7 books on accident, expert appraisals of accident, textbook of surgery, general and special, fractions and dislocations, technique of plaster costs,
History of University clinics Berlin (together with Diepken [Giepken, sic]).
Pg 1938 or 1939, mainly paid dues never took other part, No SS member.

Dr. Beiglböck[:] Schäfer-Wasser schmeckt wie Trinkwasser. When cautiously prepared, 0.3 % Salz.
Sea water 3 %.
No difference in the revulsion against sea water as compared to Berka water; most of them found it repulsive after 3 days, some after 5 days
Always drank in front of experimental persons.
Habilitated 1939.
Military rep.: Mai 41, to Luftwaffe, Sept. Unterarzt, Laz.

---

90   Two animal welfare protection methods were introduced in 1934: a degree passed in February 1934 by the Prussian Ministry of Commerce and Employment that introduced school education on animal protection laws, and a law enacted in July 1934 which limited hunting. In 1934, an intetnational conference on animal welfare was hosted by the National Socialist regime in Berlin. Sax (2000), 181.

[62] Wels; Dez.41–May 42 Linz Work […], Kriegsschäden, July 1942; August 1942–Nov. 43 Russian Front, near Pleskow, field hospitals; promoted to Oberarzt. Nov. 43 Braunschweig til March 44, then Törnis. Braunschweig, because of his gratification (like hosp.).

Habilitated 1939, ausserordentlicher Professor 1944.

Main field: Hematology, liver disease; Vitamines; Continued to publish while in military service (about 10 papers). In Russia did some work on Wolhynien fever, hepatitis epistunice.

„Fieldnephritis" – nephritis unter besonderen Bedingungen, nicht infektiös. Physische Inanspruchnahme. Kälteschäden. On dependenz – rheumatism.

Insulin – Sakel und Dussch, Insulinshock. Physiologie of insulin shock.

Ceased believing in German victory when he came to the Russian Front in 1942. Especially the sport of the partisans. When the invasion proceeded; he knew the jig was up.

[63] 3–12–46 *Dr. Fritz Fischer*

Born Oct. 5, 1912. Vater: l & w [living and well], at age 80, merchant (contractor). Mother, died at 50 from cancer of the womb, when Def. was 23 yrs old. Congenial. Sister aged 44, l & w [living and well], married. Mother's brother had massive depressive psychosis. No other neur. or ment. dis. in family. Married Jan. 3, 1942, congenial. 3 children, aged 3 ½, 2 and 1 yr old. Dates: 6–12–42, 2–8–44, 20–8–45 (son, daughter, son). Realgymnasium at age 18, then medical study Bonn, Berlin, Leipzig and Hamburg; graduated 16–12–36, MD 8–7–38. Then 4 months medical clinic in Leipzig; then pathology, first extern, then resident, at Rudolf Virchow Krankenhaus in Berlin, e Prof. Ostertag; there til Nov. 1939 (2 ½ yrs). Then called on active duty with the Waffen SS: had been member of the general SS since 1934. After basic training was ordered to Lazarett Hohenlychen; there til June 1941. Then until June 1942 **[64]** with 1st SS Panzer-Division on the eastern front. Jaundice, therefore returned, reassigned to SS Lazarett Hohenlychen Feb. 42 until May 1943. Then as medical officer to 10th SS Panzer-Division; served in France, Russia, Poland, and France again. On Aug 18, 1944, wounded in France, in the battle of the Falaise gap; severe injury of rt [right] arm by shell fragments; amputation on the same day. Then taken back to Hohenlychen as patient. From 1944 on assisted in Radiology at the University of Berlin. Up to then in Hohenlychen had started surgery under Prof. Gebhardt; mostly extremities and abdominal and thoracic.

Cause of medical study: „Ich war naturwissenschaftlich interessiert; und der Wunsch mich auf diese Weise weiter zu beschäftigen führte auch dazu – die Tatsache, daß mein Onkel Arzt war (the same) spielte auch mit. Ich interessierte mich besonders für Physik und Chemie auf der Schule; auf der Universität bes. für Physik und Chemie, der Übergang der Physik zur Biologie."

[65] (Wie lange […]?) schwer zu beantworten. Wir waren in unserer Weise gespalten. Auf der einen Seite Ratio, auf der anderen gefühlsmäßig. Ich erinnere mich 1943 gesagt zu haben, unser Leitmotiv war so wie die eines Pathologen der am Krebs erkrankt ist. Ich erinnere mich an Roessle,[91] der viel über Carcinom wusste, dennoch seinen Arzt fragte ob sein Carcinom nun nicht über derselben Bösartigkeit [?] stünde, wie bei anderen Carcinomen, sondern daß es der Ausnahmefall eines proportional günstigen Carcinoms wäre.

Entered Nazi Party 1939 (Pg.) 1939: Rottenführer (Pfc); U-St-F[92] (Leutnant) April 1939, with all physicians: Later promoted up to Sturmbannführer (Major).

Experiments: July 1942–Dec 1942. Effect of sulfonamides: 75 VP, 15 at first, 60 VP later. At first 15 men to bring about wound infection of a standard type. Wound infection did not take place. The other 5 groups: Mangel an Kontaktstoffen – Uniformiertes, isoliert ganz fein zerieben [zerreiben], cellulose [66] des Holzes

1) Bakterienkultur + glas
2) Bakterienkultur + holz
3) Bakterienkultur + holz und glas
4) Zum Angehen einer anaeroben infektion, ohne Schußverletzung – Unterbindung einer Muskelfaser – 24 persons, or 2 persons, und bänder und anaeroben Erregern.
5) Same, + bande. Erreger (12)

10 in each group were treated with Sulfonamide: Result: that sulfonamide were inadequate in combating infections, if topographically the culture of microbe went on in the event of an abscess, phlegma or emigence.

„Ich bin Soldat gewesen, unter einem sehr hohen Chef, der persönlich sehr stark war." Situation unentschieden, medizinisch. 3 died.

Scapula abgenommen. Gebhardt transplanted it into a patient named Ladisch, a man. Privatpatient. This was beginning of 1943. Left soon thereafter. Plan made between Prof. Gebhardt and Dr. Stumpfegger. „Vollkommen [67] klare und geklärte Verhältnisse." Scapula immobilisiert, physiol. Kochsalzlösung.

Prof. Gebhardt –

Born 23-11-1897: Vater prakt. Arzt, died 1935 from heart disease at 68. Mutter died in 1934 at 70, same cause. Congenial. 2 sisters, aged 51 and 53; one married. No illness in family.

Grammarschool in […] in Oberbayern, High school in Munich, Rosenberg and Landshut; father moved because he became a public health official and was transferred several times. 1916 served as Fahnenjunker, discharged as Lt. Captured by the British, captured in 1917; Rouen; worked in a labor battalion; 1918 to England, in camps in Scotland; exchanged in 1919, because of osteomyelitis from a jaw wound and middle ears. Then studied medicine in Munich, 1919–21, exam. Dec. 21; MD Dec. 21. Intern City Hosp. Landshut, then pathology [68] with Borst[93] until

---

91 Robert Rössle (1876–1956) was a German pathologist. He pioneered research in the fields of inflammation, constitution, growth, age, and immunity. He published regularly on hereditary biology and racial hygiene. While Rössle was not a member of the Nazi Party, he was involved in the administrative system of the Nazi regime. After 1945, he continued his academic career. Schmuhl (2008), 288; Kaiser et al (2022), 1.

92 *Untersturmführer* (literally: "junior storm leader", equivalent to a Second Leiutenant in the British Army).

93 Maximilan Borst (1869–1946) was a pathologist during the National Socialist regime. He conducted groundbreaking research on tissue transplantation and cancer. Schmidt et al. (2019), 1076.

1923 (one year). After Hitlerputsch, in which he participated as physician, went to Sauerbruch, 1923–1933; after Sauerbruch went to Berlin in 1927, stayed on with Lexer. 1932 Dozent für Chirurgie; Oberarzt der Sportabteilung; seit 1926, Lehrlingsübungslager in Hohenascher. Wiederherstellungschirurgie.

1933 berufen als beratender Kliniker zum Reichssportführer und Chefarzt der Klinik Hohenlychen. (192 km out of Berlin).[94]

Married 1933; congenial. 2 chi [children], aged 9 [Peter] and 12 [Jürgen]. 2 Sons.

Remained throughout the war in Hohenlychen. Left April 27, 45, to Flensburg.

Assoc. Professor 1935; 1937 ordentlicher Professor für Chirurgie, als Leiter des medizinischen Instituts der Reichsakademie für Leibesübungen. The Professors were Sauerbruch and Magnus.

Generalstabsarzt d.R. of the Army and Waffen SS (Gruppenführer der SS). Major General.

Heeresgruppenarzt: surgical [69] team, 1940/41 on all fronts except Africa. Took turns with his associates. Every few months went home to Hohenlychen. 1000 beds there, 700 military.

Ursache des Medizinstudiums: Zweckmässigkeit. Kriegsbeschädigter. Mein Vater hat mich dazu angehalten. Das Milieu lag mir als alter Arzt Sohn. Primär wollte ich Offizier werden, ich war [Gefreiter], wollte Musiker oder Architekt werden. Bohemien.

(Deutschland Krieg gewinnen?) Not after I came back from Stalingrad in December 1942.

Nov. 1943–April 1944. Speer[95] was a patient at Hohenlychen. Empyeme of his knee joint (right), 2 embolisms of the lung, from thrombophlebitis. Now Speer is in excellent physical condition. Checked him in 1944; 1945 saw him with Dönitz,[96] and he seemed alright. Of course his cartilaginous substances must be destroyed, and he will ultimately develop a chronic arthrosis deforming of the knee joint, with complaints. Should be checked with X rays. He must have a scar on the left side of his lung, from empyeme with scaring extending to the diaphragm.

[70] Devoted himself exclusively to him on Hitler's orders. That time with Speer became increasingly pessimistic. But Speer believed in the "miracle weapons". Totale Umstellung der U-Boote, den Krieg herumreißen. Had confidence in Dönitz, believed him to some extent. Das letzte an Anspannung herausholen.

Sulfonamid Versuche:

Ultrareptyl Cibazol – nach Winterkatastrophe 1941.

"Für mich war es eindeutig entschieden, vor den Experimenten."

---

94 100 km north of Berlin.
95 Albert Speer (1905–1981) was a German architect who served as the Minister of Armaments and War Production in Nazi Germany during most of the Second World War. He was convicted at the International Military Tribunal and sentenced to twenty years in prison. Schmidt (2004), 113.
96 Karl Dönitz (1891–1980) was a German admiral who succeeded Hitler as head of state in May 1945. He was sentenced to ten years imprisonment at the Nuremberg Trials. Schmidt (2004), 73.

Im Mai 1942 bin ich überstimmt worden: am 6. Juni ist das Heydrich Attentat von Hohlbaum[97] und Dick verübt worden. Ich habe Morel nicht zugezogen, und der Heydrich ist mir gestorben. Fahrlässig Schuld. Versuche befohlen zur Durchführung: Ultrareptyl, Cibazol, Eleulkan; Albazyt.

"Bei der Besprechung habe ich gesagt, daß ich es nicht für notwendig halte. Morel." Eissversuche [Bissversuche?], Summen von Menschen, nach der Heydrich Geschichte.

Morel's Läusemittel mußten ja eingeführt werden.

[71] Ohne Blutspiegel zu kontrollieren hat Sulfonamide bekommen. Sprach nicht mehr an nach dem 9ten Tag. Thrombosed abscesses accost him and stifling from the ear.

Sulfonamidfrage:
Man hätte sie auf dem Umfrageweg klären können.
Transplantation: Stumpfegger.
Lartisch: Larisch:
Himmler kam zur Wehrmachtsvisite 1942. Gab Befehl zur Heteroplastik. Nehme Gelenke von Häftlingen und übertrag es auf Verwundete.
Angioblastom.
Scapula eingesetzt: Ergebnis: Scapula nicht eingeheilt. Versuche heteroplastischer Art haben aufgehört. Zusammengesichert in Schulter, Spange gebildet, die den Arm unterstützt hat. Geschwulst zurückgegangen.

"All for the best", "Ich hab' sie nicht ausgewählt und nicht bewacht."
The Scapula was from a woman.

[72] Prof. Dr. Joachim Mrugowski:
Oberarzt der Waffen SS: (Oberführer)
Born 15–8–05:
Vater, praktischer Arzt, was killed by shell fragment at age 40 in 1914. Mother, l & w [living and well], at 68.
1 sister, died 1942 from TB at age 34.
Mother had a hard time; lost all her money by inflation; brought up her chi.[ldren] by home work for optical industry and private teaching. Lived in Rathenow near Berlin (Busch n. Gärnthen). Marriage had been harmonious.
Married 1934, teacher, congenial. 5 chi.: Girl aged 11, girl aged 9 yrs, boy who died at 2 months, (1938), 1 son aged 7, 1 son aged 5. They all live in Rathenow; Russ. Zone.
Abitur 1923. Then did proctorial work for 2 ½ yrs, as custom official at Polish border; then bank clerk's apprentice until 1925. Then went to medical school, Halle, graduated 1931, MD 1935. Studied medical sciences beside; PhD in nat.sc. 1930.

---

97 Josef Hohlbaum (1884–1945) was a German surgeon and university professor in Leipzig and Prague. He attempted to save Reinhard Heydrich, the Head of the Reich Security Main Office, who was assassinated in Prague in May 1942 by members of the Czech resistance (see p. 9 of Alexander's diary for details of Heydrich's assassination). Hohlbaum died in December 1945 from to a leg wound sustained by a grenade in May 1945. See Schmidt (2004), 31; Klimpel (2005), 78, 79.

[73] Schon als Schüler mit Nachweis beschäftigt, Botaniker und Ornithologe; wollte Naturwissenschaftler werden; durch wirtschaftl. Zusammenbruch daran behindert [gehindert].

Internship city hosp. Küstrin, internal medicine. Jan. 1933 became assistant at the hygiene institute at Univ. of Halle, under Paul Schmidt (lead poisons, influenza research). Interested in bacteriology and hygiene (public health), stayed there til 1935. Then 1 ½ yrs non-medical study, with the SS. [Mündlich] Nachrichtendienst für Geisteswissenschaftler. Othmar Spann,[98] universaler Streit.
[...]
Schulungseinrichtung in Alt Rhese [Alt Rehse].
Dr. Blome und Prof. Böhm[99] waren darüber.
Schulungskurs in 1937 mit Ministerialdirektor Gütt, Arzt, Reichsleiter im Innenministerium.
Über Universitäten Berichte, welche Person die Universität unterrichtet, nachgefragt.

[74] Memmen innerhalb des Lehrkörpers. Berichte analysiert und weitergeleitet.
Verpflichtung der deutschen Concerne [Konzerne] und Industrie [...] capital.

End of 1936, when criminal and state police came on, he returned to Medicine. Jan 1937 was appointed hygienist for the Waffen SS. Major. In allg. SS since 1931, formally Sturmbannführer. Til March 37 worked in 3rd military district Berlin, under Walter Schreiber, to work in military hygiene. Then basic training 1 1/4 year. August 1, 37–Oct. 38 company medical officer, then worked at the Surgeon General's office in the Waffen SS, as section Chief for hygiene. Built up bacteriology laboratory for local use. Stayed in this office until the end of the war, with interruptions. Oct. 39–Nov. 40 abroad with sanitary campaign, Holland and France.

Then returned to enlarge his department. June 41–end 42 Hygienist in the command of Reichsführer SS. Main position was his laboratory position, which grew; in 1941 it was called [75] Hygiene Institut of Waffen SS; 25 professional assistants include. 12 physicians, strength of personnel 200. (Wie lange Deutschland gewinnen?). Nicht zu gewinnen since Stalingrad, June 43, lost since Invasion, breakthrough at Avranches.

Religion; member of protestant Church. Married in Church. Chi.[ldren] baptized. Realised it was not the thing to do in SS. Was critisised about it, but no difficulties.

---

98 Othmar Spann (1878–1950) was a conservative Austrian scholar and social theorist. He was a proponent of the political principle of "universalism", or "*Ganzheitslehre*" – a philosophy that emphasises the idea that societies should be understood as "organic wholes", and gives importance to collective institutions over individualism, advocating for the formation of states based upon social groups organised under a hierarchy. Based upon this philosophy, he was an opponent to democratic ideals, liberalism, and Marxist socialism. Haag (1976), 227, 233–238.

99 Hermann Böhm (1884–1962) was a pathologist and racial hygienist. He co-founded the National Socialist German Physicians Association and consulted the association in 1931 about eugenics. He held directorships at the Institute of the Rudolf Hess Hospital in Dresden (1934) and the University Institute of Racial Purity and Eugenics at Giessen University (1943). He was also appointed Chairman of the Heredity Biology Research Institute of the Leadership School of German Physicians at Alt-Rhese by the Reich Physicians' Leader Gerhard Wagner in 1936. Ebbinghaus/Roth (2001), 77–78.

Experiments: Fleckfieber. Lausborn typhus e [and] Rickettsia Provazeki.
Privatdozent 1937, in Halle; 1939 in Berlin; 1944, associate professor in Berlin, with Zeiss.[100] (epidemiology, geomedicine). Medically not prepared for the Russian campaign. Fall of 1941 Typhus broke out. Delousing alone not enough.
Weigl's vaccine from intestins of infected lice. Their method of Cox, in hen's egg. Animal experiments Dec. 1941.

[76] Giroux's method of rabbit lungs. Dr. Ding[101] to Paris. Discussion with Grawitz; Himmler decided for Grawitz. Buchenwald; Himmler examined responsibility. Begin January 1942.
Result: Impfstoff keine Erkrankung vorhanden.
1) Weigl – 30 Personen, alle erkrankt, none died.
2) Behring stuff (Rickettsia provazeki + vaccine, egg cultured) 30 Personen, alle erkrankt, 6 gestorben
3) Behring, egg vaccine, only RP: 30 personen, 4 died.
4) Giroux rabbit lung. 30 persons, none died.
5) Goldemark with Hagen, improved egg vaccine. Immunised, 4 wks later infected: result in 8 weeks: 3 weeks disease; incubation period 9 days–10 days; 17 days fever. Incubation period increases the better the immunisation; 14 days inc., 9–1 day's disease.
Giroux series begun in the beginning of 1943. June 43 layer production.
Army continued with the Weigl method. Army kept the Weigl.
Civil pop. Goldemerk & Hagen.

[77] SS Giroux

Giftversuche: Pervitin[102] (1937).
3 Personen. Aconitin.[103]
Execution an einigen Personen verwendet. Bin dabeigewesen; habe gesehen 5 Menschen in jugendlichem Alter standen zur Verfügung, sprachen Deutsch; wurden als Strassenräuber bezeichnet. Der [...] war Vertreter des Kommandantens. Beigewohnt: Tod abgewartet. Puls gefühlt und Blutdruck gemessen. In Sachsenhausen. Oberschenkel geschossen. 2 Personen sofort getötet durch Kopfschuss, ganzes Gefäß angeschossen. Die anderen 3 starben in 120 Minuten. Vergiftungserscheinungen von Seiten des Magens. They knew they were to be executed.

Mentalität der Dienststelle: 300 km aus dem Weg geschickt, um zu entscheiden, ob von Amerika der bakteriologische Krieg eröffnet worden sei (Spring 1944, May). Infekt.: keine. Stichwerkzeuge.

100 Heinrich Zeiss (1888–1949) was a German bacteriologist and immunologist. From 1933, he was Director of the Institute of Hygiene in Berlin. Weindling (1993), 174, 175.
101 Erwin Ding-Schuler (1912–1945) was a German surgeon and head of the Department for Typhus and Virus Research of the Hygiene Institute of the Waffen-SS in Buchenwald concentration camp. Ebbinghaus/Roth (2001), 50.
102 Generic name for "Methamphetamin", a psychostimulant drug. Pervitin was the early version of what we know today as "crystal meth".
103 Aconitine is an alkaloid toxin produced by some plant species belonging to the genus Aconitum (family Ranunculaceae), known also commonly by the names "wolfsbane" and "monkshood".

[78] Dictated Chapter 5 of opening statement.

Further plans:
Many of these so-called experiments are frankly and openly devoted to methods of destroying or preventing life, namely to "euthanasia" and extermination methods, and to methods of sterilization. But this preoccupation with methods of producing death runs also though many of the other investigations like a red thread, irrespective of the ostensible other purposes of the experiment. The frightful body of new methods of killing – the new lethal injections, the new gases, the poison bullets constitute a formidable body of new and dangerous knowledge, useful to criminals everywhere, and to criminal state if another one is permitted to establish itself again – so as to constitute a new branch, a destinctive perversion of medicine, worthy of a new name, for which Thanatology has been suggested by our medical consultant. This **[79]** thanatology knowledge supplied the technology methods for genocide, a policy of the German Third Reich, which could not have been carried out without the active participation of its medical scientists.

Plan:
Ethical and non-ethical experimentation in human beings: the crucial experiment (Pettenkofer) – the scrutinizing experiment – the model experiment with physico-chemical systems – the theoretic thinking through.

In which way were the German experiments non-crucial experiments, inadequately prepared; therefore inaccurate and misleading (example: high altitude) and unnecessary (example: sea water).

[80] 4–12–46 Completed dictation of point 5, exclusive of biographies.

Dr. Herta *Oberheuser*
Born 15 May 1911, in Köln a Rh. Vater, engineer, retired, l & w [living and well] at 63, suffering from gall bladder disease. Mother l [living] at 61, suffering from pernicious anemia. Childhood happy.

UCD; no neuro or ment. dis. [nerurological or mental disorders] in family. Abitur 1931. medical study in Bonn; then Düsseldorf. grad. 37; MD 1937 in Bonn:

Postgrad. im Physiologie Institut April–June 1937; then until 1938 Medical Department Düsseldorf Prof. Edens. Then til Dec 1940 at Gen. + Venereal Clinic in Düsseldorf as intern and Resident. (Prof. Schreus). Dec. 1940–June 1943 Concentr. Camp Ravensbrück; July 1943–25 Apr. 1945 Hohenlychen, as surgical assistant, in [...] consulting [...].

Always had the ambition to become a surgeon. Denies that the **[81]** acceptance of Ravensbrück was [...] by surgical ambition.

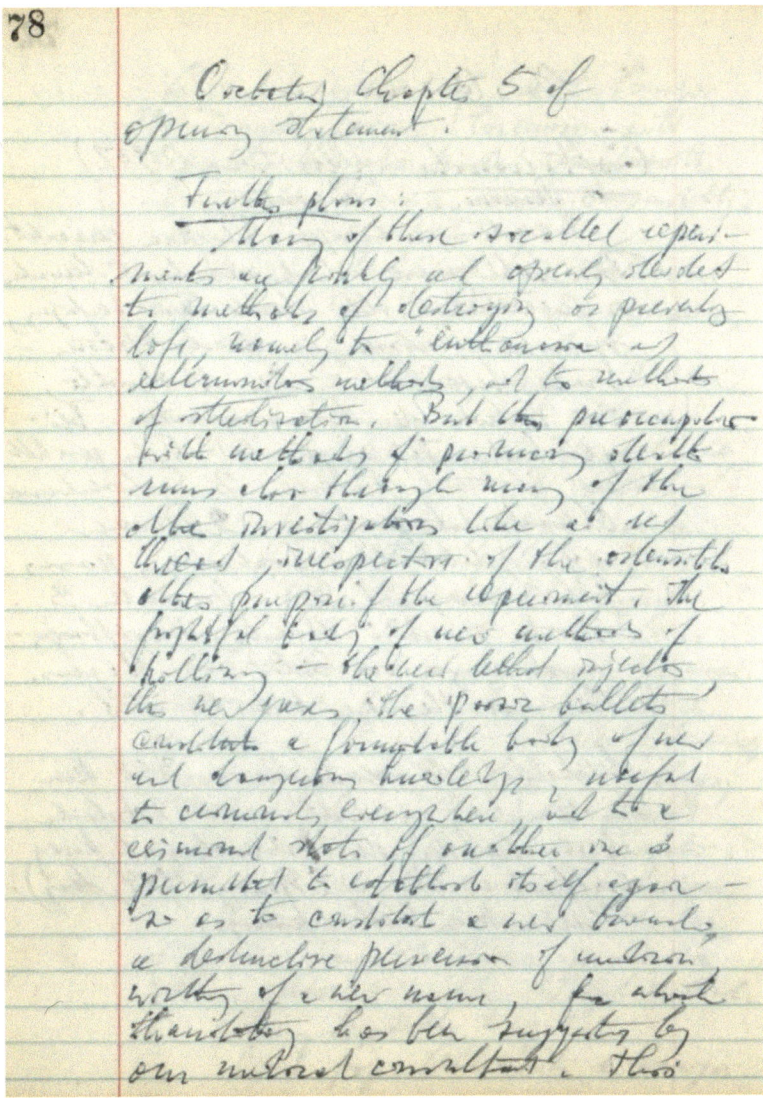

Fig. 10: Alexander papers, DUMC, box 3.
Record ledger book of activities and notes, 1946–1947, p. 78.

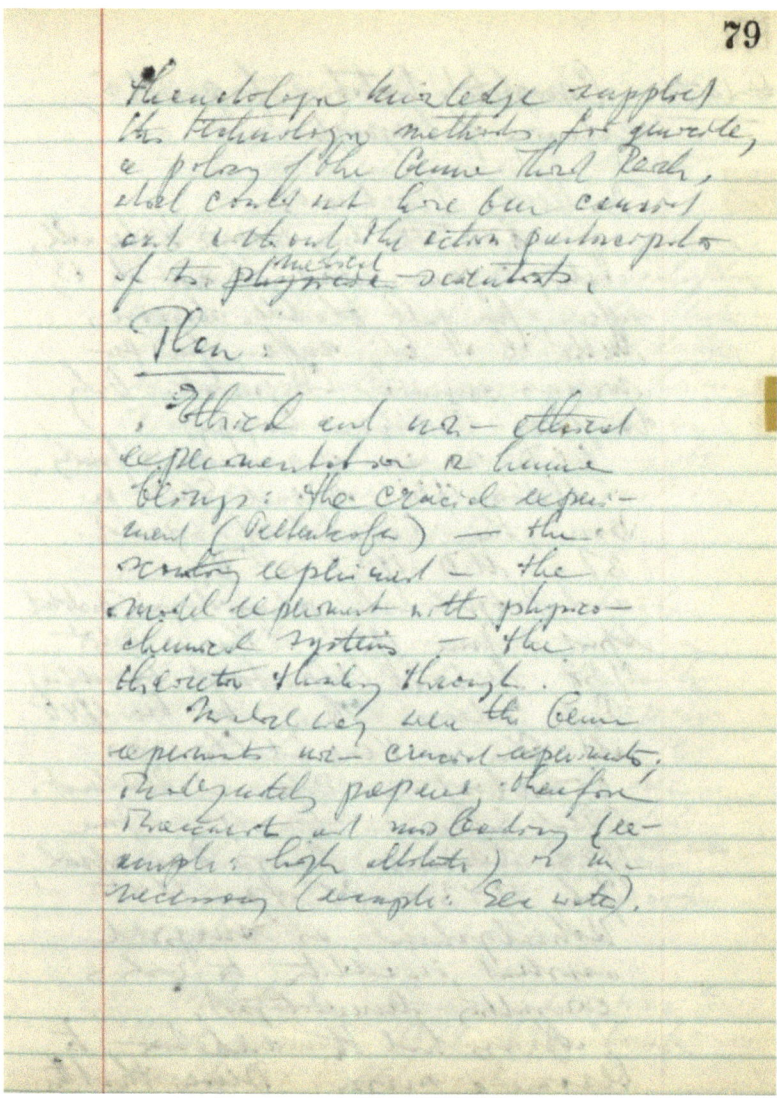

Fig. 11: Alexander papers, DUMC, box 3.
Record ledger book of activities and notes, 1946–1947, p. 79.

Hauptsächlich asociale Elements.[104]

Ursache des Medizinstudiums: Meine Veranlagung nach naturwissenschaftlichem Interesse. Hatte mich schon in der Untersekunda entschlossen Medizin zu studieren. Neigung zur Chirurgie; war für uns Frauen unmöglich.[105] Ich hatte eine Bekannte, die Hautärztin war, hatte ihr geholfen; die bat mich auch zur Hautklinik zu gehen.

Ich bin aus der evangelischen Kirche 1935 ausgeschieden. Ich war schon in der Schulzeit mit dem alten Test.[ament] nicht einverstanden, und später konnte ich auch mit dem neuen Testament nicht fertig werden.[106] Mein Vater mußte auf eine Direktionsstelle [...] [versetzt] werden weil Tochter protestant war.

Lebensphilosophy; to help other people.

Until when Germany win war? Until summer 1944. (?) „Danach mochte ich nichts sagen."

[82] (Interests) The venereal diseases.

In the beginning ¾ of Ravensbrück inmates were prostitutes, 300 untreated GC's.[107]

Experiments:

Frauen die zum Tode verurteilt sind.

(Gefragt?) So gut wie gar nicht. Kein Bild über das einem gesagt wird, (Selected?) Das weiß ich nicht. (?) Ich habe sie vor den Exp. [Experimenten] auf Hautkrankheiten untersucht, Herz und Lunge. Bei der Op. zugegen, gelegentlich assistiert. (?) Gezeigt, wo die Schnittführung lag.

„Betreut habe ich sie, weil sie auf meiner Station lagen." „Meine Station lag am nächsten zum Operationssaal."

Mo[108] before operation. Evipanethan. Später Morphin.

Had 60 patients: usually 10 patients were operated on any one day.

---

104 This is a reference to the prisoners who were in Ravensbrück concentration camp. Some of the women interned at Lichtenburg concentration camp for women and then at Ravensbrück were classed as "asocials". The category of "asocials" was large. It encompassed women who were homeless, accused of criminal acts, or were deemed prostitutes by the Nazi regime. "Asocials" were forced to wear an identifying black triangle. They made up the largest group of prisoners at the camp in the years of 1939 to 1940. With the onset of war, the number of "asocials" at Ravensbrück grew significantly due to the increased policing of women who fell into the category. Overall, the total estimated number of "asocial" prinsoners at Ravensbrück was around 5,000. Schikorra (2009), 59. For more information on 'asocials', see Schikorra (2001) and Allex/Kalkan (2009).

105 In 1937, only 1.6% of doctors who participated in surgery in the Third Reich were women. Kater (2005), 91.

106 Oberheuser also mentioned in this interview with Leo Alexander that Nazism appealed to her because it did not matter 'whether one belonged to a church or not'. It seems that Nazism offered her an escape from religious differences. Religion was perhaps a divisive issue in Oberheuser's family, since her father was a Roman Catholic, but she and her mother were Protestants. Source: Stadtarchiv Nürnberg, Rep 502 VI O1, KV-Anklage, Interrogations, 'Vernehmung von Frl. Dr. Oberheuser durch Prof. Dr. Alexander', 28 December 1946.

107 Medical abbreviation for Gonorrhea (guanine and cytosine base pair in polynucleic acides; gonococcus; gonorrhea).

108 "Mo": medical abbreviation for Morphine.

Transplantation experiments, end of 1942, begin. 1943.
Knows nothing about Larisch.

[83] (Gerda Quernheim?)[109] "Als Schwester [...] [im Reich/in Ravens (brück)]." Gute Schwester. Flink. Sehr sauber. Willig. (Dr. Rosenthal?) "Nicht geschätzt mit ihm zu arbeiten." [...]
Besonders in der letzten Zeit hat er öfter Patienten von meiner Sta. [Station] auf seine verlegt ohne Grund, ich habe es dem Standortarzt gemeldet. Ich weiss nicht, warum er es gemacht hat. (Wie lange gelebt?) "Darüber kann ich nichts mehr sagen.
(SS Untersuchung?) "Da war ich nicht mehr da."
(?) "Die Quernheim war eingesperrt. Der Rosenthal war noch dort."
(Thanatos?): "Ich weiß nur, daß er die Quernheim eingesperrt hat."
(Gerüchte?) "Ja!"
(?) "Verhältnis."
(Leichenschändungen?) "Nein."
(Tödliche Injektionen?) "Ja."
Medikation auf Veranlassung des Standortarzt[es] kurz vor dem Tode gespritzt. Morphin und Benzin. Nur bei Moribunden. (Wieviel Benzin?)

[84] Nur geringe Mengen. 3-cc. die schlafen ein. Keine Krämpfe. Auf Befehl des Standortarztes. (How many?) "Vielleicht drei."

"Not married. Not engaged." "Mein Bekannter ist gestorben an Lungenentzündung in 1940. Zuerst: very depressed. That happened 4 months before I went to Ravensbrück. Had intended to marry him – there was war. Knew him since 1939.

Dr. Victor *Brack*
Born, Nov. 9, 1904, in Haagen, Kreis Aachen. Vater, died at 63 from heart disease (1941). Physician. Mutter died at 65 (42') from Leukemia. Congenial. 2 br., 1 sister. Inf. is oldest. One br., aged 38, l, in Waffen SS, at present interned. One br. killed in actions in 1940 at age 26 yrs; shot down near Aberdeen. 1 sister; aged 39; l & w [living and well].

[85] No neur[ological]. + ment[al] dis[ease] in family: wenigstens keine mir bekannten. Abitur 1923. Then studied agriculture – but because of the loss of his parents' Sanatorium and herd in the palatinate changed to economics: graduated

---

109 Gerda Ganzer (née Quernheim, 1907–1996) was a German political prisoner at Ravensbrück. Quernheim was interned in the camp in November 1940. She had a romantic relationship with Rosenthal, one of the doctors at Ravensbrück. They both performed abortion experiments on inmates. Both Rosenthal and Quernheim were imprisoned by the SS once their relationship was discovered. Quernheim was sent to Auschwitz in April 1944, and then back to Ravensbrück in April 1945. Quernheim was initially sentenced to death at the fourth Ravensbrück trial in 1948 for the mistreatment and killing of Allied women prisoners but her sentence was commuted to life imprisonment. She was released in 1961. The National Archives, London, WO 309/419, "Major Arthur Keith Mant RAMC, Special Medical Section War Crimes Group, H.Q. B.A.O.R, Ravensbrück Concentration Camp. A report on the Medical Services, Experimentation and various other atrocities committed by medical personnel in the camp".

1928, at Technische Hochschule München. Then helped in father's small sanatorium, which he founded near Munich. Inbetween worked as motor cycle racer for the Bavarian Motor Company [Bayerische Motoren Werke, BMW], which supplied most of his income, until 1932. Then was employed in Reichsleitung NSDAP, as section chief under Bouhler,[110] the chief business manager. 1934 he was made chief of the chancellery office of the NSDAP, when he took informant [?] with him. Remained in his position until April 1942, then joined Waffen SS on active duty; SS Division Prinz Eugen, later SS Mountain Corps, as general officer and [quarter]master. Sea Service in the Balkans, Carpathian Mountains.

[86] Oct. 1944 returned to Reichsleiter Bouhler upon the latters' request, for "Durchkämmungsaktion" der Truppe in Denemark; to comb them out. Brack did this job for the Waffen SS and police (as Sturmbannführer).

Married 1934; congenial. 6 children: 3 sons, aged 11, 8, 6; 3 daughters, aged 5, 4, and 1.

Religious; catholic; had left church 1936; recently reentered.

Wie lange [Krieg geglaubt] gewonnen [zu gewinnen]? Bis Stalingrad habe ich die Auffassung gehabt, das[s] der Krieg gewonnen wird. Dann sehr skeptisch (January 1943).

Mother was born in Russia; spent long periods with grandparents, frequently some early childhood in 1914. Nach dem Krieg Verbindungen abgebrochen. Grandmother had been [?] by Bolsheviks, and died of hunger.

Euthanasieprogramm; und Vorschläge zur Sterilisation durch Rö[ntgen] Strahlen.

Ich war der Verbindungsmann des Reichsleiters Bouhler, der den Auftrag des Euth[anasie] program[m]s zusammen mit [87] Dr. Brandt hatte, und der Stelle[,] die er für die Durchführung herangezogen hat. Meine Aufgaben waren administrativer Art.

Sterilisation: Kompliziert. Kein Nationalsozialist wie sich Hitler vorgestellt hat. Ich habe einen Freund gehabt, der ¾ Jude war, den habe ich nicht aufgegeben.

Party member and SS 1929.

Gehört von geplanter Vernichtung des Judentums. Umsiedlung vorgeschlagen, nach Madagaskar (1940/41), Abgelehnt. Anderer Weg, Sterilisation. Teil der Juden vor der Vernichtung zu retten.

Hoven:

Born 10–2–1903.

Vater died 1930, at 60, of cancer of pancreas. Farmer, sind owner of 2 Sanitaria in Freiburg, Mutter l & w [living and well] at 72. Congenial. 2 brothers, one died in 1933 at 37 from cirrhosis of the liver; he was physician, x ray man, who shifted [?] working after he had suffered severe bleeding. One brother l & w [living and well] at 47. [88] No nervous or ment[al] dis[ease] in family, Realgymnasium until 8th grade, at age 14; mother then sent him to a boarding school (Knabeninstitut) at Königsfeld in Baden, near by Herrenhüten Brüdergemeinde (protestant kid). There

---

110 Philipp Bouhler (1899–1945) was a German senior Nazi Party functionary who was a National Leader and Chief of the Chancellory of the Führer of the NSDAP. Bouhler was arrested in May 1945 by American allies and committed suicide shortly afterwards. Schmidt (2004), 213; Burleigh (1994), 123.

til 10th grade. Mother was busy running the sanatorium as a lazarett, while father was in the Army (Warrant officer).

Then stayed at home for a while, then went to Denmark and Sweden with a friend of his father, studied agriculture practically on a farm (19, 18 year of his life). Returned in 1921. Then went to the U.S. with the same friend, who went to the U.S. as an interior decorator. There worked on a farm; then again joined his friend in Minneapolis. Visited him for 23 months. Returned to Germany in 1924; was homesick. Worked on fathers' farm and sanatorium; For K. B. [Karl Brandt?], Minister was in charge, the patients were for the most part Englisch and American. Worked in the office. Sanatorium Hoven, Hovenstraße 9, Freiburg i Br. Worked there til 1931. 1931 went **[89]** to Paris. worked as secretary for a Baron de Meyer, who was a Heimat correspondent and Harper's Bazaar.[111] Worked there til 1933. Returned to Germany then.

(Jam?): "Ich wollte mich umschauen in der Welt."

As early as Königsfeld (1918) wanted to become a physician; but his brother, 7 yrs older than himself, always said it was enough of one son as doctor. He died in 1933. Mein Vater hat sich auch davon beeinflussen lassen. Mein Vater antwortete, sagte, ich sei zu alt. The 5 year older brother was not jealous. No open [...] though.

1934 made up his mind to study medicine. Had to complete Abitur, accomplished in 1935. Then entered medical school in Freiburg i Breisgau; last semester in Munich. Graduated 1939; MD 1943, in Freiburg.

Reason for medical study: "It was my fervent desire to help people." Mein Vater war immer bös mit mir weil ich zu viel heuchelte, **[90]** da sagte er sei pathologisch geworden.

Psychiatric examination; which the SS did but thank that mother could be as I classified them. Hochverrat ich "blutdürstiger Mörder." Untersucht von Prof. Heyde[112] aus Würzburg; he said I should not say too much about this condition, or it would be dangerous to my life. Condition are intolerable for a normal human being, and he made a report in which he closely selected the edge of § 51. Er sagte mir es wundert ihn nicht wenn ein normaler Mensch damit verrückt würde. He gave his report in March 1944. His trial did not come up til Sept. 1944. 12–Sept. 44–15 März 45 in Buchenwald als Häftling.

Der Kampf zwischen Gewissen und Ratio ging auf Leben und Tod.

After graduated immediately called to Waffen SS. Never worked in a civilian hospital.

---

111 Baron Adolph de Meyer (1868–1946) was a prominent photographer of fashionable society in the early twentieth century and the first fashion photographer for the American magazine "Vogue". Harper's Bazaar is an American monthly women's fashion magazine. It was first published 1867 as the weekly "Harper's Bazar".

112 Werner Heyde (1902–1964) was one of the main organisers of the euthanasia programme. After the war, Heyde used the alias of Fritz Sawade to practice medicine in Flensburg, on the north German border with Denmark. After his identity was revealed in 1959, he was put on trial. He hung himself in 1964. Burleigh (1994), 281, 269, 284. See also Godau-Schütte (1998).

[91] Professor Gerhard *Rose*[113]
born 30–11–1896

Vater killed on August 29, 1944, in Stettin, during an air raid. Postal official. Mother died on 28 Dec. 1941, of skull fracture in an accident. Congenial, normal, occassional difficulties. 1 sister, died 1940 from euthanasia – was schizophrenic, aged 45 yrs. Had been in various hospitals for 9 years. Killed in Grafeneck. "Gallenblasenperforation."
   Married 1942 – ... normal marriage. 1 child, aged 1 ½ yrs.
   No other neur. or ment. dis. [neurological or mental disorders] in family.

Abitur March 1914. Studiert Medicine at Univ. Berlin + KW Akademie; after one semester, called into Army, general regiment soldier; captured at the Marne. Spent 4 yrs in captivity, as French PW, in 21 different camps in France and North Africa. Later interned in Switzerland because of malaise with blackwater fever. On 3 Nov. [92] 1918 returned to Germany. Went back to medical school; graduated 15–11–1921. MD 1922. Studied in Bochum and Berlin; graduated at MD in Breslau.
   Ursache: "Interesse für Naturwissenschaften."
   Internal and Resident with Pfeiffer in Hygienische Institut in Breslau – ½ yr; then became Assistant at the Robert Koch Institute[114] until Feb. 1923. Then Assistant of Voers, Hygiene Inst. in Basel, until Sept. 1925; Wintersemester 1925/26 as assistent with Kallus (Anatomy) in Heidelberg. Wanted to become a clinician on the basis of his bacteriologic education; Enderck advised Anatomy: 1926–1929. Surgery, assistant Enderlein, with the intent to become a surgeon. Slowness deterred him of a University career. Applied for posts abroad; received appointmend in China, Hongchow, as Director of the Institute of Public Health. Stayed there til 1936. Then [93] became Klaus Schilling's[115] successor at the Robert Koch Institut. Professor and Abteilungsdirektor der Tropenmedizinischen Abteilung; 1942 Vice president and Professor. Never habilitated.
   In China interested in Parasitology, Malaria and medical entomology.
   Bilharciosis[116] in Aegypten.
   Party member since 1930.

113 Gerhard Rose (1896–1992) was a German *Tropenmediziner* (Tropical Medicine Doctor) complicit in experiments at Dachau and Buchenwald which involved the infection of prisoners with typhus. He was sentenced to life in prison at the Doctors' Trial. He was released in 1953. Schmidt (2004), 143, 260.
114 The Robert Koch institute, founded in 1891, is a German federal government agency and reasearch institute which aims to control and prevent disease. See Hinz-Wessels (2021).
115 Claus Schilling (1871–1946) was a specialist in tropical diseases. He led the Department of Tropical Medicine at the Robert Koch Institute between 1905 to 1936. He researched malaria immunisations; towards the end of the 1930s, he experimented on patients in Italian psychiatric asylums. In 1941 or 1942, Schilling was provided a malaria institute by the Reich Physician SS. He experimented on prisoners at Dachau Concentration Camp towards the end of February 1942, in the attempt to demonstrate the validity of his immunisation theory. He was sentenced to death at the Dachau War Crimes Trials in 1946 and subsequently executed. Ebbinghaus/Roth (2001), 140.
116 Schistosomiasis, also referred to as bilharzia or snail fever, is an acute disease caused by parasitic flatworms (schistosomes or blood flukes). The parasites live in freshwater snails and individuals can contract this disease from contaminated water.

Generalarzt d.R. der Luftwaffe.
Beratender Hygieniker und Tropenmediziner.

"Not religious"; atheist, since the end of the twenties. Formal resigned from the prot. [Protestant] church in 1936.

Deutschland Krieg gewinnen: Am Anfang nicht an die Möglichkeit geglaubt. Nach den Erfolgen 1940 zweifelhaft geworden. Von 1942 ab habe ich mit einem milit. Sieg nicht mehr gerechnet, als es nicht gelang Russland in einem Stoss niederzuwerfen, wie das im Westen geschehen war. Motto 1942: Immer noch [94] mit diplomatische[m] Ausgleich gerechnet. Zurückhaltend ob mündliches Bündnis zwischen Kommunismus u. Kapitalismus.

Exp.: Hepatitis Versuche – vollkommen schleierhaft. Nie etwas damit zu tun.
Typhus: das einzige wovon ich Kenntnis gehabt habe waren die Versuche in Buchenwald. Ich war einmal da und habe die Versuche gesehen. In 1942.
Then lets loose. For one visit he knows a hell of a lot.
5–12–46 *Blome*: Blood coag. [coagulation] Polygal, cancer research, alpine plant (Rascher, Lützelburg)
Biolog. [Biological] Warfare Posen.

born 1894.
Father 1 + w [living and well], at 81, Fabrikant; Mother died March 45 from CA [cancer], at 75.
1 brother, aged 51; l+w [living and well]. Congenial. Married 3x; 2x geschieden. 3rd marriage 1941; congenial. She [95] is a physician, aged 36. 3 chi. [children], sons 7, and 4, daughter aged 2 yrs. 2nd marriage: one daughter aged 10 yrs. Inadaptability; marriage 1935, divorced 1940.
1st marriage 1930. wife committed adultery. No children. Divorced 1934.
Med. Study: 1912–14
Göttingen, then Rostock.
Substit. 1914, soldier, became officer, 2nd Lt., accepted in regular Army.
1919 Med. School Münster, Giessen, Rostock. Grad. in Rostock 1920, MD 1921.
Then 3 years at the university clinic in Rostock under Friebös in Dermatology and Venereal diseases; practiced from 1924–1934.
1934 Adjudant of the German Red Cross; aufpassen, daß es National Sozialistisch wurde und die Reaktionen herauskamen.
Official of the Reichsministerium.
1935 in charge of education of physicians.
Die gesamte ärztliche Fortblg. [Fortbildung] [96] organisiert (German postgraduate education).
1938 held a congress, suggested international academy.
Alt Rhese [Alt Rehse]: Ärztliche Führer gerichliche und standespolitische Frage. Krieg: staatl. Gesundheitswesen, Komplex Naturheilkunde – Schulmedizin, Erbbiologie u. Erbforschung, grundsätzliche Rassenfragen. Weltanschauliche Fäden durchzogen. 3 Wochen für Jungärzte; bis (?) dann 8 or 14 days. Ärztinnen. On a hill near a lake, wonderful forest; modernes Herrenkasino. Gutsarbeiter im Dorf. Built 1933–35. *Reichsgesundheitsführer*

1939: Conti; Leiter des Hauptamts für Volksgesundheit; made Blome his deputy. Stellvertreter Leiter der Reichsärztinnen + Ärzteführer. Could not call himself Stellvertreter. RG Führer; only Stellvertreter des Hauptamtes. Stellv. Leiter des NS Ärztebundes.
1940/41 Fachsprecherleiter im Reichsforschungsrat. Erbbiologie, Volkskrankheiten. Gemeinsam mit Sauerbruch, Fach-sp.-leiter [Fachspartenleiter] Medizin.

[97] 1943: Bevollmächtigter für Kriegsforschung im Reichsforschungsrat. The rest was Sauerbruch.
Geber: Forschung für Abwehr biologischer Kriegsmethoden.

1936: erste Krebskranke – Schicksalsstatistik für Mecklenburg, und Meldezahlen sämtlicher Geschwulstkranker. Führungsdienst. (Md Lasch).
Other counties: Halle, Würzburg, Saacherd, Groß Köln.

Honorarprofessor Med. Fakultät Berlin, 1942.
Not habil. [habitulated]
Stut. u. Dr. No SS Member,
Sanitätsgruppenführer SA (Major General).
Religiös? Ja. Resigned from church, 1934; had been protestant.

(Wie lange gedacht Deutschland Krieg gewinnen wird?) Erster Schock wie Hitler Churchill als Säufer beschimpfte; [98] Roosevelt einen Idioten – wenn man einen anderen [kränkt] das ist der Anfang vom Ende. 1940.

Blood coagulation, Polygal: Wirkung auf Pectin, from apple peelings, and sugar beet.
Ich habe Rascher für tüchtig gehalten, Ehrgeizig, sexuelle Hörigkeit zu seiner Frau.[117]
Aussicht: Idee von Polygal von Herrn Feix,[118] a concern for jelk (opekta).
Rascher: Laborversuche und Bluttropfen. Hat mir einmal gesagt, er hätte gute Wirkung des Polygals am Menschenversuch festgestellt, Oberschenkel blutig gerieben.

Cancer alpine plant: in Heidelberg von jüdischen Ärzten. Dr. Lützelburg[119] heard of them; he was in U.S. at beginning of war. Leitstellung; Sievers; Rascher, Prof. Weltz. Result: Lützelburg should make the sort retract, so that [99] Weltz could test it chemically and physiologically. The study was never completed. Does not know name. F. H. Weltz: vielleicht kommt da ein gutes Abführmittel heraus:

---

117 If Rascher told Blome that he was 'sexually devoted to his wife', then this frank discussion of sex between two men appears to support the view that society was not sexually prudish during Nazism and that heterosexual sex between individuals deemed racially and socially 'valuable' was a topic openly discussed and promoted. The historian Dagmar Herzog has argued there were "injunctions and encouragements to the majority of Germans to seek and experience sexual pleasure." Herzog (2005), 13.
118 Robert Feix (1893-1973) was an Austrian chemist who assisted Rascher as a prisoner in 1943 at Dachau, working on Polygal, a substance to stop bleeding. Weindling (2014), 181.
119 Philipp Xaver von Lützelburg (1880–1948) was a German civil engineer, botanist and explorer.

Biological Warfare Institute in Posen [Poznań]. Not completed, with construction.
Kartoffelkäfer mit Flugzeugen. Kommt lebend an; they eat potatoes. Ungeheurer Schaden, schwer zu bekämpfen.
Does not know of Mustard gas; nor of Lost[120] or Sulfonamide.
Tuberculous Poles: I prevented it. They were not liquidated.
Euthanasia: I was not participant, heard only names.

Dr. S. Ruff: born 19–2–1907, Friemersheim, a. Niederrhein. Father l & w [living and well], electrical engineer, still active at 73; Mother l [living], suffering from pernicious anemia. sister, aged 35 yrs. l & w [living and well], deutsch. Parents harmonious.

[100] No neur. + ment. ailm. [neurological and mental ailments] in family. Realgymnasium Aachen, Gymnasium Bonn; Matura Berlin. Med. Study: Berlin u. Bonn, 1926–32; 32 Staatsexam. und MD.

Then internal; 3 months gynaecology, then 2 yrs internal medicine (under Prof. Buerger) in Bonn. 1934 grad. Versuchsanstalt für Luftfahrt under Hoff; in charge of medical department. At first alone; then he obtained assistant, Romberg in 1936/37, until he had 9 collaborators, of whom 6 were physicians. Had [reverse?] office, Lt., in Luftwaffe, did not bother going on active duty because they merely would learn details known to his own institute. Book and Strughold 1939; second edition 1944. Was interested in aviation since student days, worked with Buerger[121] on neuro-medical problems.

AVL originally private, industry; since 1933 the state. Sold instruments to all the world.

[101] Married 1933; congenial, 2 chi. [children], boy aged 8, girl aged 4 yrs.

Freude an der Medizin: Naturwissenschaft; später an der Medizin. Already in school interested in Biology.

(Wie lange Deutschland Krieg gewinnen wird?) Ernste Skepsis als Gehilfe des Militärattaches in Washington über Rüstungsmöglichkeiten sprach, in kleinen Kreis (Mitte 42). He said it was impossible for Germany to compete and […] with America. The successful landing in Sicily and Italy clinched it.
The front: ¾ yrs after entering of U.S. into the war.

Experiments: "Versuche zur Rettung aus großen Höhen." Vortrag, gehalten in d. Deutschen Akademie der Luftfahrtforschung, 6 Nov. 1942. Jahrbuch 1942/43 **[102]** der Deutschen Akademie der Luftfahrtforschung.

Weltz: machen Sie es doch in Dachau. Sein Mitarbeiter Rascher hatte schon die Genehmigung für Dachau. Die anderen nicht so wichtig u. dringend, die anderen nicht so gut experimentell vorbereitet, die sind doch experimentell vorbereitet.

---

120 A type of gas (mustard gas) that causes large blisters on the skin and was used in warfare.
121 This could be a reference to Max Ferdinand Bürger (1885–1966), a German internist and director of the Medical Clinic at the University of Leipzig. He conducted experiments associated with heart circulatory research at this clinic during the Nazi era. Forsbach/Hofer (2017), 58.

(VP?) Kriminelle, auf keinen Fall politische Gefangene, und die Gefangenen können sich freiwillig melden. Das hat mir Weltz in Buch gesagt. Keine Ausländer.
(Was noch?) ...
Strafnachlass oder Erlass als Belohnung.
Mit Rascher then in Munich. Zunächst soldatischen Eindruck. Übertrieben schneidig.
Inspected experiments at the beginning of April. Allein. In der Zwischenzeit war Differenz mit Weltz u. Rascher.[122]
End of March or beginning of April Romberg told him about the fatal experiments.
Corrects himself, end of [103] April, begin. of May. Did not revisit Dachau after that. Decided to remove the chamber from Dachau.
Later: cold did not change it.
Psychologische Sicherheit: automatic inflation of parachute at 3000 meters (end of war).
Katapults to later, as est. for fast aircraft, in order to relieve the occupant of the labor of stepping out (end of 1943).
Me 163[123] went as high as 16.000 meter.
The 20.000 meter aircraft were never produced: that whole development was stopped in 1943. Göring[124] said let the others fly high, if they want something let them come down. 1944 altitude was again desired, but was not carried out.
Development for long-range purposes.
The mouse experiments we made ourselves. We froze it -40–50°.

[104] Experiments started early in March. Habil., Physiology and Luftfahrtmedizin, 1939 Univ. Berlin. Not promoted to Professor, because of lack of political testimony. Not bad, but lack of interest. Turned down 1942.
Party 1938.
June 1942 Rascher was in Berlin to finish the report.
Zur Rede gestellt: he said that the fact that he knew about it indicated a breach of silence on the part of Romberg. Special orders from Reichsführer SS. Ruff was not present when report on RLM was made. Did never see the film, was promised to see it; one day suddenly Romberg was taken to Führerhauptquartier to show film.
(Höhenkrankheit?) tonisch-klonische Krämpfe; das sah man in dem Film, habe ich gehört. 2 minutes. Hängen im Fallschirmgurt.

[105] 6–12–46 Worked on 'ethical and non-ethical experimentation in human beings'. Corrected biographies; dictated the night before to Miss Ray. Dictated paper in the evening, after sending Walter Reed,[125] etc.

122 It is not clear whether Alexander is referring to differences in scientific or personal opinion.
123 Messerschmitt Me 163 Komet; a rocket-powered aircraft.
124 Hermann Göring (1893–1946) was commander in chief of the Luftwaffe during the Third Reich. In September 1939, Hitler designated Göring as his successor and deputy in his offices. Göring was convicted of war crimes at the Nuremberg trials in 1946, but committed suicide before the sentence was carried out.
125 Walter Reed was a member of the US Army who led research experiments in Cuba in 1900, which entailed the exposure of volunteers to mosquito bites to test the hypothesis that

7-12-46: Re-interview Genzken (see reports sheet appended). Completed ethical and non-ethical exp. on human beings. Corrected General's opening address, as it came off his typeriste. Dinner, went out to Park Hotel.

8-12-46 Worked with General on opening address. He tied in a good deal of my material. Evening: General's party at Villa Schickedanz.[126]

9-12-46: In Court. Opening address. Photographed for the Matiz with Mant, Bayle,[127] Hardy. Interview by Mr. Foss, NY Post. Talked to Mr. Fauber, the painter at Dachau. He certainly has Concentration Camp Neurosis.

[106] 9-12-46 evening: *Lutz*:[128] Saw Rascher once in the Institut in the summer 1941.

Job offer: In the early stages, asked Wendt[129] and Inf. – I still see him ahead of me, we know which things went on – he said – as if he wanted, expected a negative answer. Weltz's Einstellung undurchsichtig.

Weltz wusste, daß Wendt und ich diesen Versuchen ablehnend gegenüberstand.

Vorgestellt: Korrekt zum Tode verurteilte Kriminelle, daß ihnen eine Chance gegeben wird,

(?) „Weil ich nicht die Brutalität hatte."

(?) Wenn man einen Menschen nimmt, der spürt vielleicht Mitleid, es ist sehr schwer, einen Hund umzubringen.

---

mosquitos were carriers of yellow fever. Alexander referred to Reed's experiments in a memo to Telford Taylor in April 1947 entitled 'Ethical and Non-Ethical Experiments on Human Beings' (an earlier version of this memo had been sent to Taylor in December 1946). Alexander stated that it was "ethically permissible for an experimenter to perform experiments involving significant risks only if the solution, after thorough exploration along all other lines of scientific investigation is not accessible by any other means, and if he considers the solution of the problem important enough to risk his own life along with those of his non-scientific colleagues, such as was done in the case of Walter Reed's yellow fever experiments". Gaw (2014), 141; Miller/Moreno (2021), 42.

126 The Schickedanz family founded in 1927 the German catalogue retailer "Quelle Versand". The "Villa Schickedanz" was built in 1875 and is a large living complex in Fuerth (near Nuremberg).

127 François Bayle (d. unknown) was a French naval officer and psychologist who published *Croix Gammé Contre Caducée* (1950), a book based on handwriting samples and physical measurements of the defendants of the Doctors' Trial. Schmidt (2004), 7.

128 Wolfgang Lutz (1913–2010) was a military physician in the airforce. He determined that if pressurised cabins malfunction at high altitude, it is the abrupt drop in pressure that makes pilots lose consciousness. After the war, he served as a witness in the Nuremberg trials. Schmidt (2004), 90.

129 Günter Wendt (1923–2010) worked as a flight engineer for the Luftwaffe during the Second World War. After the war, he emigrated to the United States and worked for NASA. Armstrong et al. (1970), 53.

Fig. 12: Members of the US prosecution team, including Brigadier General Taylor, James McHaney, and Leo Alexander. Nuremberg, Germany, 1946/47 (Source: NARA).

Gutes aufgreifen und propagieren.

Mrs. Lili Lutz, Haag am Hausruck, Ober-Österreich.

[107] 10–12–46 In court, organisation. Completed Thanatology article. Talk with Tauber,[130] and Mr. Foss.

Dr. Hans Rascher, geb. in Fürstenfeldbruck, 20–10–1880, father of Sigmund Rascher, born 28 Feb. 1909.

Son of first marriage, Rose, geb. Klüppel, born 22–10–1882, in Corfu. Raised in Egypt: Very labile, and "maßloser character, in ihrem Ich betont hertzlich. Nich[t] schön, aber interessant. Vater war Nürnberger, Kaul Klüppel; Mutter war keltische Engländerin, Welsh, Helen Witfield, born in Corfu or in the Greek Islands. Karl Klüppel war im Egyptischen Dienst, Polizeipräsident von Alexandria, would have been made Serdar of the Sultan,[131] but did not get it because of fight with Lord Kitchener.[132] High position in Ministry of agriculture, egypt; gambler. Lost all his money in calls. Helen war Engländerin [...] sie nicht geheiratet [...] ihre Kinder [108] und [...] mit der whip zu züchtigen. Die lag immer auf dem Tisch. Beliebte Strafe war das "Hautschabenmüssen" – a form of turture. Remerged Strafe, 9–10 Jahre. Start in Hamburg 1929 or 30.

Met wife when she was 16 yrs old. Married her 1905. 3 children: girl, Sigrid, born 1906; Sigurd, born 1907, is professor of the summer conservatory in Kopenhagen and Malmore, Saxophonist, gave concerts all over the world, include. U.S. Was in Washington at beginning of war. Present whereabouts unknown. Sigmund, born 1909.

Marriage was uncongenial; constant fighting; she was extravagant. Sex relations were allright [alright]. Inf. had not much influence on education of chi[ldren], great [...]; wife stayed most of the time e [with] the chi[ldren] in Ascona, Switzerland. Während des Krieges in Dornach. Wien, das kam später. Lebte mit den Kindern in Stuttgart, da kam es zur Trenung, 1922. Da übernehme [109] ich das Sanatorium in Lugano; das war eine Flucht. Dauernde Diskussionen, bis spät nachts. Differenzen ihres Machtbewußtseins, ihres Versuchs zu dominieren. Ihre Schwester hat meinen Bruder geheiratet; selber character.

---

130 This is a reference to Georg Tauber, a former Dachau prisoner. Tauber was an illustrator who documented the experiments at Dachau. He only drew the experiments twice, saying he was unable to watch anymore. His drawings were used as documents during the Nuremberg Medical Trial. See "Description of two illustrations of freezing experiments", d.1946, held by the Harvard Law School Library Nuremberg Trials Project, Evidence Code: NO–855. For biographical details and further illustrations by Tauber, see Pilzweger-Steiner/Riedle (2018).
131 Serdar (also spelt Sardaar/Sirdar): military officer rank in the Ottoman Empire, associated broadly with the rank of Commander-in-Chief. In the Egyptian context, Sirdar can also refer to a British military rank given the Commander-in-Chief of the British-controlled Egyptian Army in the 19th and 20th centuries, including Lord Kitchener.
132 Lord Kitchener (1850–1916) was a British army officer and colonel administrator. He was the Sirdar from 1886–1892, and Consul-General in Egypt between the years of 1911–1914. He was British Secretary of State for War between 1914–1916. Cassar (2016), vii.

Seit 1911 haben die Kinder in Ascona gelebt. Zu Festzeiten, Ostern, Weihnachten. 5 or 6x annually, apart from 4 weeks furlough. Father-in-law is also divorced, about 1904. Mother-in-law spent long periods of time in Ascona. She liked it better there. Studied singing with Frau Languare, an Austrian; Cloaca maxima von Europa. Divorced 1926. Sie hat Geld verpulvert, Sohn Sigmund hat sie zu sich genommen. Sigmund stayed e [with] mother, until she went to live with Sigurd. „Das hat mich nicht mehr berührt."

Second marriage 1927. Hanna Lampe, born 1905. Very happy marriage, nur getrübt durch schwere Krankheit, die am Anfang der Ehe totkrank war, nicht operabel. Selbst behandelt. One daughter, Brigitte, aged 17. Wife died 17–2–1937. One son, Hans-Michel, aged 15 yrs.

3rd marriage, 29–6–1940, **[110]** Maya Pernat, born 27–11–05. Happy marriage, one girl aged April 10, 1943.

Sigmund from beginning very egotistic. "Ich" was his first word. Sonst fröhliches Kind. More fond of mother. Physically resembles her. Had private tutor in Ascona, then went to school in Munich, while wife lived e [with] inf. for 3 yrs 1918–21; then both went to Stuttgart, where they lived for 1 ¼ yrs, when inf. went to Switzerland, but wife stayed in Stuttgart. In Stuttgart he went to a private progressive school (Freie Waldorfschule). Failed matura, which had to be taken in a state school.

After separation in 1922 wife stayed in Stuttgart.

III At 19 Abitur.

Flunkert the second time again; had trouble with one examiner over a medico-biologic question.

Vater: zunächst aufgeben, praktischen Beruf. Voluntärstellung in einer Großdrogenhandlung. But Sigmund made the Abitur in Constanz, and went to Freiburg **[111]** to Medical School (1930), Forced father through the Vormundschaftsgericht to finance him. Weil er seine Vereinbarung nicht eingehalten hat. "Er schrieb mir dann von sich aus." "Seit dieser Zeit Beziehungen gespannt." "Er hat mich mehrmals pfänden lassen; 1929, 30." Zweite Frau hat ihm in Gewissen geredet, daß ich ihn in München studieren ließ, und ihn dort unterhalten habe. Finished study in Munich; graduated 1936, MD + same year. Then on "Blutforschung", "crystallization sensible"–copper sulfate crystallization figures. If glant juices are added; there is a typical change of crystallization. Sigm. Rascher applied this to blood, working under Prof. Trump; he was given a laboratory in pathology under Borst,[133] with special extension on neoplasmus cases, could diagnose tumors. 97–98% certainty of diagnosis; also in tuberculosis. Left all that work, until under the influence of Diehl[134] he was drawn into other circles.

---

133 See page 68 of the diary for information about Borst.
134 This is a reference to Karoline Diehl, Sigmund Rascher's wife. Rascher publicised the fact that his wife had given birth to three children even after reaching the age of 48 in an attempt to please Himmler. Himmler used a photograph of Rascher's family as propaganda material. However, during her fourth 'pregnancy' she was arrested while attempting to kidnap a baby. It was then discovered that her three other children had either been purchased or kidnapped. She was arrested in April 1944, alongside her husband, and condemned to imprisonment in a concentration camp. They were both eventually hung in the final weeks of the war by the SS. Janze (2020), 8.

Hitler dämonisiert.
Then described Nini's activities in 1938/39.

[112] In 1939, March, arrested by Gestapo as "staats-subversiv". Schwere Krebsbehandlung. One day's leave. 5 days fasting, in order to have a free mind. Laye write of accusation by Mose Diehl and his son.

Anthroposophische Einstellung, die ja nicht abdingbar ist, das ist mir Lebenseinstellung geworden. Released after 5 days. Absolutes Schweigegebot. Visited Hamburg. After return to Munich, on May 1st, 1939, rearrested.

Evening: Blaha[135] – a disappointment. An obvious faker.

11–12–46 Morning: Court and paperwork.
Afternoon:
Dr. Rascher:
So "abgeschaltet", that in 1940 he stood beside his son without recognising him.

Tells of Mrs. Rascher's child abductions. Sehr hübsches Kind, von Frauen sehr verwöhnt, die das schöne Kind bewunderten. Ganze Jugendzeit hindurch, include. puberty.

During gymnasium, about 1919 or 20, he and his brother Sigurd ran away. Did not get back at noon. Heard they had not been to school that morning.

[113] Father remembered that he had asked him about Bavarian topography toward Bodensee, knew "Fluchtrichtung." At 6 PM both returned. Had gone til Ammersee, decided here to go further. Wollten nach Dornach marschieren: das Schweizer Zentrum der Anthroposophy, where both had spent several years, 2 years, during the war.

Wie die Beziehungen gespannt waren, hatte er immer das Bestreben mich auf einer Erinnerungstäuschung festzunageln.

1917. Wife and children came to Munich from Dornach.

Had thrown a snowball (1917) into the General's face, who had been nasty to informant (father). Informant gave him verbal repremend, but S. used to say that he had put him in the cruck and beat him bloody with a saber. He always tried to

---

135 Franz Blaha was a Czech doctor and an inmate of Dachau concentration camp. He was at Dachau from 1941 to April 1945. He produced an affidavit for the Doctors' Trial and was cross-examined on 11 January 1946. He testified on human experimentation which took place at Dachau. For Blaha's cross-examinsation, see "Witness Franz Blaha testifies at Nuremberg Trial", United States Holocaust Memorial Museum Film, Accession Number 2001.358.1. For extracts of Blaha's affidavit, see "Extract from an affidavit concerning the freezing experiments", d.1945, Harvard Law School Library Nuremberg Trials Project, Evidence Code: PS–2428; and "Testimonial exhibits in the report on atrocities committed at Dachau: Report of the Atrocities Committed at the Dachau Concentration Camp Volume II[.] Testimony – Exhibits 3 to 24", d.unknown, Harvard Law School Library Nuremberg Trials Project, Evidence Code: PS–2428.

manoever himself into position against father. Nini Diehl sammelt immer "material." Always considered himself ill treated by father, that he had large sums of money, and would not give him anything. Had friends, in Dornach (1915–17). Wife was anthroposopher, „Schmerzenskind [114] der Gesellschaft. Masslosigkeit". Voher lebten in Ascona. Ging nach Dornach zur Fortsetzung des Gesangsstudiums. Ich bin nur vorübergehend dort gewesen, zu kursen. Blutforschung, Heilmittelforschung. Biologisch-dynamische Wirtschaftsweise. Ich weiß von einer Tierschänderei, eine Katze, mit dem Hansi Großheinz. Sie wollten mit den Katzen daran Versuche machen. Das war in Dornach. Nach dem Krieg sind wir jedes Jahr ein-, 2mal nach Dornach gekommen. Er war 10 oder 12 Jahre alt. Der ging später nach Dupont to USA. Eine Angehörige der Dupont Freundin wollte S. heiraten, wie er 22 oder 23 J. alt war; die hat ihn in Dornach kennen gelernt. Von der Familie sind verschiedene nach Dornach gekommen.

In puberty, not under Father's supervision. Sexuell normal: übliche Erfahrungen mit Frauen, in Konstanz.

Never baptized: weil ich ja keiner Konfession angehörte. Christlicher Religionsunterricht im anthroposophischen Sinne; anthroposophische Richtung [115] des Christentums. In der Waldorfschule, from age 12–19. At home [in] anthroposophischem Sinne erzogen. Gesamte Naturwissenschaft. Sehr intersssante Dinge zu Tage getreten.

Anthrop; Reale Geisteskenntnis ins Leben zu führen. Umbau des gesamten kulturellen Denkens. Jünger, die Perfection der Technik.

Novalis: wer kann sagen, daß er das Blut versteht?

"Die Christenheit oder Europa." Met Mrs. Diehl in 1936, wohnte bei ihr. Brought her to father after February 1937.

Told father that he did not any longer wish to call him father, but just "Hans".

Idee über Blutforschung von Pfeiffer in Dornach. Freier Naturwissenschaftler. Während eines Dornacher Aufenthalts in den Dreissigerjahren.

12–12–46 Trial. Lutz excellent witness. Interrogation *Neff*.
Born.
Todesliste. Irgendeiner bis März nicht gefallen. Todesversuch.
   1) Unterdruckkammer.
[116]   2) Unterkühlungsversuch.
   3) Luftunterkühlungsversuch. Nachts, nackt, bis Körpertemperatur auf 25° gesunken war. Mich belasten: Rascher selbst 11 Versuche. Dabei bestialisch gewesen, geschlagen wenn geschrien, jegliche Narcose verboten.
   4) Gifttabletten hergestellt aus Cyankali, ins Crematorium und den Bunker gegangen. So- und so- viel umgelegt.
   5) Polygal. "Von uns bewußt lanciert." Mit Versäumnis, Jauche und Panzergruben. Von Todesversuchen und schweren Versuchen abbringen. Lured him with money. Took Robert Feix into his laboratory. Hat das Umbringen gelassen, außer den Giftversuchen. Das Umbringen hat er nie ganz sein lassen können.
Erlag in Erschießungen und Erhängungen.
Kartoffelpulver: 3 Teile: Feix, Ahnenerbe, Rascher. R. pocketed it all.
Russische Offiziere. Gemeinsam nackt ins Bassin. Keine Narkose.

[117] 2 Stunden bei vollem Bewußtsein im Wasser gelegen. Asked the officer to take them and and shoot them to end torture. Rascher left, tried narcosis. Tried chloroform. R. entered, steals pistol, threatened collaborators. Since then[,] swore he would kill Rascher. Attempted to kill him, by doping his antineuralgic tablets. After that, less cruel.

October 1942. At that experiment H [Hoven?] & F [Feix?] were not present. Got ideas in Munich:

Schwind, Herbert: born 4 Aug. 1916. 8th grad.

Then ran away from home; father beat him. Then worked on Werft in Hamburg. 1936 went to Spain. Courier, Medical, etc. Unteroffizier; ein Scherler. Flak-Kanonier, hit wine. Never in party. Disapproved of Hitler. Arrested in France by Gestapo, 1940. After the fall of Spain interned for a year. To Dachau 1942 (Jan. 31). Sterilized 16 April 1942. His last commando was a bomb disposal commando.

10 April 1940–31 Oct. 40 in Ravensbrück.

[118] Physical: Tall, well built young man, 185 cm. Ulcerations right leg, involving nerve there the lower half of the leg, with several ulcerations, one open, others recently healed; and induration and black-blue brownish discoloration of the entire anterior half of the leg in front, fourth in the back, and about third on the sides, from the ankle up. Beaten by an SS man with the bult Kolben of a gun. Unusual sterilisation, by cutting the vas deferum immediately above the epithelium scrotum; causing testicles to sag without a day under connective tissue support, of which he complains.

In der Poliklinik in München, Städtisches Krankenhaus.

Reinterrogation Walter Neff, Kufsteinerstraße 2, Dachau.

Gutsverwalter. 22–2–1909, in Westheim, bei Augsburg. Volksschule 14, dann Praktikant in Westheim, Kriegsackerbauschule in

[119] Landshut (3 yrs: 16 yrs – 19 yrs) am Lech. Gutsverwalter in Feldberg Württemberg, 1929–31, bei Herrn Vassen. Dann Schweiz, Markthallen bei Zürich, als Gutsbaumeister bei Kantonsrat Berger: 9 months. Permid expired: then Hungary, 3 months on a farm Dunaföldvor near Budapest. From there to Africa, 4 months on a large farm near Tunis. From there to Austria 1933/34 Apfelmeierhof bei Bruck a.d. Mur, wo ich durch Anzeige eines Bombenattentats, das 2 Nazis ausführen wollten, zum ersten Mal mit Politik in Berührung kam. Had to leave, went to Graz to work for Baron Reininghaus[136] (1934). 1937 returned to Germany, Reichsnährstand in Passau, Oberkontrollassistent. Feb. 1938 arrested by Gestapo, because of Anzeige des Bombenattentats in Österreich (against Gendarmerie).

14 März 1938 to Dachau.

---

136 Peter Edler von Reininghaus: the Reininghaus family from Stryia, Austria. Their family company ran one of the largest breweries in Austria; Brothers Reininghaus AG. Sondhaus (2000), 113.

As male nurse to Revier August 1940.[137] Jan. 1941 Tuberculöss Station, Jan. 42 aufgelösst. 22 Feb. 1942 Rascher began with experiments.
Then chamber end of January, begin of February 1942. 1st experiments

[120] 22 February.
Recognises Romberg, Sievers and Ruff by name.
(Karl Brandt) Den habe ich im Lager gesehen aber als ziemlich hohes Tier.
(Weltz): Den Mann habe ich gesehen aber ich weiß nicht wo. So ist Weltz.
1st deaths begin of March. On one day 16 Russian prisoners of war were killed.
1st fatal experiments 4 days later, in Rombergs' presence. 15.000 meter; then oxygen stopped; observation how long it takes until death. Romberg watched the EKG with those experiments. From then on fatal experiments came after fatal experiment. Die Toten wurden alle seziert. Die Feststellung des noch schlagenden Herzmuskels wurde Anfang Mai festgestellt und durch Rascher u. Romberg am EKG festgehalten. Sektion in der Unterdruckkammer, gegen Mitte Mai. Apparatus sabotaged shortly after this experiment; asked Romberg when those cursed vans would be removed; promised to ask Milch – estimated **[121]** about 3 weeks. That was end of May. After that inf. sabotaged the scale of the meter, which cracked under pressure; Romberg took a trip to Berlin, brought the parts, but too soon, so that 20 more people were dispatched. How many people killed in Romberg's presence? "mindestens 15, bis 25." Sicher bei 15. Im ganzen 60–70 personen getötet.
Wieviel Sektionen bei schlagendem Herzen zugesehen? 3–4.
Middle of July 42; low pressure chamber was removed. Inf. served in 30 experiments, until pain in eyes made it impossible. Romberg stopped it. Steigeversuche: 10–15 personen zusammen, und während des Aufstiegs die Pulsation, sowie Kraftproben an Dynamomotor machen mußten.
Made them because he knew the emergency values. Prevented mass liquidation with the 16 Russians.
Liberated Sept 15, 1942. Written order by the Reichsführer. Released, but made obligation to continue e [with] experiments **[122]** until end of war.
Water experiments started middle or end of August 1942. In excess of 80, probably more, were killed. Completed in May 1943.
Later für Todesversuche bei the political department.
Miss Christine Zamoyska.
Aged 21 yrs. Ex-Polish underground. Interesting life history. Marvellous history on aggression diverted toward the line of least resistance.
13–12–46.
Neff: Only one tub for warming, white enamel, hot water: 45–50°.
Wood tubs: Feix used wooden tubs for his folter for extraction of pectin.
Large tub, 2 meter deep; experiments were not started. Rascher killed large numbers at the Crematorium: "heute sind wieder 6 draufgegangen."

---

137 In many instances, concentration camp hospitals were staffed by male nurses who were prisoners at the camp. Occasionally, men from outside the concentration camp were paid by the SS to work in these hospitals. A nurse named Alfons Kreisel, for example, was employed at Hersbruck, a sub-camp of Flossenbürg, at the end of October 1944. Nursing in concentration camps was sex-segregated; male nurses staffed concentration camps for men, and female nurses staffed the institutions for women. See Betzien (2018), 339.

1st Child: 1938, boy, stolen in Prague.
2nd Child: 1940, boy, stolen in Prague.
Marriage after 2nd child.

[123] 3rd child. end 1942 or early 1943, stolen.
4th child March 1944, stolen at the maison railway station in Munich.
Came into a home (Heim). Mrs. Rascher stole altogether 9 children; re-exchanged them if she did not like them, thus 9 were stolen altogether. Motiv: RF prohibited marriage with the statement that this woman could not give him children. Permission was granted after birth of second child. Brought heart and lungs of 5 victims to Strasbourg in September 1942, to Professor Hirt.[138]

Brief und Karten an Schwester Pia, von Prof. Hirt. "Blutordensträgerin". Bis 1938 Weihnachtspakete. Hat einmal Versuche angesehen, Erwärmung mit animalischer Wärme. Wohnte in Hallaching. Häftlingskommando. Häufig auf den Krankenabteilungen. Kasmirz Washiniak.

Schwester Pia:[139] ugly, bashed-in-nose, about 50 yrs old.

[124] *Rascher*: Graduated 1936. Begining "Blutforschungsarbeit" as a student. Sehr exact gearbeitet, photographien mit polarisiertem Licht aufgenommen. Laboratory in pathological Institute with Trump. Borst thought highly of it. Trump was paediatrician. Did his doctor's thesis on that. Mrs. Diehl caused his break with Trump. She offended the old man concerning his part in the investigation. Trump died in 1943 or 44.

After MD served in the Army, but at the same time had an internship at the Schwabinger Krankenhaus. I had already little interest in him, because of the Diehl; who was very disturbing: "Early in 1938 the thefts in my house began. During vacation (August) 1938, while son took his place, these thefts occured. His patients liked him as a physician, expressed themselves laudatory. He was a musician, able violonist. Also dabbled in sculpturing, in the Waldorfschule. Pedagogic principle, free painting, for psychologic senses. Paint what occurs to you, the same [125] with plastillin. Inf.[ormant] was shocked; it was about puberty, 14 or 15 yrs. It is this characterization of [...], the lost principle (as differentiated from Lucifer). Kept it because it was very interesting. "Um es ihm einmal entgegenhalten zu können," hübsch, aber neuer nach einer Seite.

Weiß nicht, wo er gearbeitet hat, nach 1939. Then recalls: 1938 served in Army with occupation of Austria, later Sudetenland; at that time the Diehl forced him to design with him into the operational room, to get signatures over various documents in folio; had empty folio sheets for which she wanted blanket signatures. Divisional Command Post. Demanded that she telephone from the last CP [Command Post]

---

138 August Hirt (1898–1945) was a Swiss/German anatomist who performed experiments with mustard gas on inmates at the Natzweiler-Struthof concentration camp. He played a key role in the murder of 86 people at Natzweiler-Struthof for a collection of Jewish skeletons. He committed suicide in June 1945. Lachman (1977), 596, 600; Hildebrandt (2014), 77.

139 Eleonore Baur (1885–1981), also known as 'Schwester Pia', commanded and administrated the München-Schwabing Dachau subcamp. She was one of the first Nazi Party members and had close connections to Party officials, after meeting Hitler by chance on a tram in Munich. Despite never formally qualifying as a nurse, she co-founded the National Socialist Order of Sisters in 1934. Schalm (2009), 524.

she went to; succeeded in persuading the General to let her talk to Sigmund by way of Berlin: "Ich hab mich ja blos auf Himmler berufen brauchen." Has a snapshot. March 1939 the Gestapo episode. After beginning of war joined the Luftwaffe, served in Africa and Sicily; later at home.

[126] A niece of Nini lived with the Rascher's, from the beginning. She was in her late thirties. During the war, 1942 or 43, she killed herself by exposure to cold, let herself be frozen on the way to the Kampenwand.[140]

Sigmund had a country house (Blockhaus Rascher) in Gaisach bei Tölz. Knew nothing of the house at the Swiss border.

Name Polygal von Polygala a hectagagum, in der Homeopathie beeinflußt. Drüsen der inneren Sekretion.

Nini never brought the children. 1942 asked Neff's father could forgive him, since he had chi. himself, and knew what it meant. Father said he could forgive, but not forget. (through Mrs. Natheiss, a patient).

The other woman in the Luftschutzraum gave away: contradiction of stating that she had delivered a child a few days ago, and the several months-old look of the child.

[127] *Neff*: Reinterrogation with Mr MacHaney. Rascher's niece was killed between Nov. 43–Jan. 44.

Neff's diary, p. 59. They were to disappear. That, according to SS opinion, was the purpose of our Station. "I asked are we experimental Station, or mass liquidation Station?"

Ask Neff:
    How many hours?
    Experiments daily?
    Which hour of day?
    Who was the Amtschef?

In his diary Neff admits that he po[a]ched [?] subjects for the experiments – sometimes unpopular Capos.
    31 "only in Germany".
    Page 35 "Invalidenaktion". Dr. Brecht select 50 for annihilation
    45 Fatum wife – not much
    46 Birthday – poem
    48 Hoher Besuch. Luftwaffe.
    50 16 Russians – Mities, were German elite.

[128] 50 Enkes brings a tailor, who refused to make him a suit.
    52 Wagner incident "Why don't you take that saw-head?"
There were sure who that a prisoner had no right to condemn another, especially to death, etc. (April 42)
    56: Seenot.

---

140 Kampenwand: a mountain in Bavaria Alps with the tallest summit.

58: Holzlöhner and Finke[141] that they had enough. Rascher denounces them of Humanitätsduselei.

Asks for Todesexperimente. Results 20 Polish priests. [...] him about the Vatican.

59: "15 Jews: Refuses them as this exp. sta. [experimentation station], or mass liquidation station!"

Franz = Franz Jauck (Spanienkämpfer)[142]
Kasimir = Wawrcziniac
Harry = Harry Pichowiak
Boris = Boris Kraine

62 Die Burschen hole ich mir bei der ersten sich bietenden Gelegenheit. Hutterer,[143] the worst. They turn family father in etc.

[129] 63 Then I became hard again. The capos have to get out of reach of our station.

p. 49: Dr. Romberg's presense etc.

14–12–46: *Neff*: Duration of killing in cold water:

Death: 80 minutes to 5 hours; no case longer than 6 hours. In clothes: longer, but none over 7 hours.

Shock and unconsciousness: Shock soon after going in; Kältenarkose at temp. of 32°, time very individuell, after til 60 minutes, some cases over 2 hours.

(Russische Offiziere?) "Viel länger. At least 4 hours that the subject were fully conscious and could talk."

Times: U. Druck K.: 3 or 4, in 20 or 30 daily. Began at 9 AM, Rascher worked on occasion til late at night, shortly before 10 PM, on the last day til midnight.

[130] *Wasser*: höchstens 6, meist 3 daily. Begin at 10 AM; stayed til late at night, 11 or later. The last daily deaths occured at that time. Leichen sofort in die TK [Totenkammer]. Totenkammer was in the Revier. Möglich dass sie im Block liegen geblieben sind, im Waschraum auf einer Bahre.

Amt D chef:[144] – Sievers.

---

141 Erich Finke (1905–1945) was a German doctor who, together with Rascher and Holzlöhner, carried out the freezing experiments at Dachau. Klee (1997), 231.

142 This is probably a reference to Franz Jauk, who served as a witness during the Nuremberg Doctors' Trial. He was a prisoner at Dachau (https://www.kpoe-steiermark.at/franz-jauk-zeuge-der-medizinischen-verbrechen-im-kz-dachau.phtml). He was apparently able to save the lives of the victims of the experiments by manipulating the measuring devices involved in the freezing experiments, and with other prisoners, destroyed the devices, which meant that the experiments had to be terminated. See http://www.stolpersteine-graz.at/stolpersteine/jauk-franz/.

143 Hutterer (Hutterites), also known as Hutterian Brethern, are a branch of Anabaptist Christians that developed out of the Radial Reformation of the sixteenth century.

144 Amt D: Amtsgruppe D SS-WVHA was a unit within the SS Economic-Administration Main Office (WVHA) that co-ordinated the concentration camp network. Lasik (1998), 272.

Dr Rascher, *Hanns* [-August]
München, Franz Josephstraße 191.
Tel. 30758. born 1880.

No nervous + ment. dis. [nervous and mental disorders] in family. Paternal grandfather was physician. father was middle railroad official. Died at 62, pneumonia + pleuritis [?]. Mother, died 10 yrs later, also at 62, from Ca[ncer] of liver. 4 br., 1 sister. One sister died in childhood from diptheria, one br. died in infancy. Romen, oldest, died in 1914 at 46 yrs from bulbar palsy, and symptoms of amyotophic lateral sclerosis, [...] + in syphilitic. Willy, aged 64, farmer **[131]** (Diplomlandwirt) lives in Bethel near Bielefeld, on the Bodelschwingh mission. Is employed by them: Fritz, born 1888, aged 58, physician practicing in Hamburg. Address: Parkallee 78, Hamburg.

Gymnasium Augsburg. 1 Jahr Universität Würzburg, [...] in Munich; graduated 1905, MD 1906, in Munich. Thesis on influence of stillen on health and mortality of suckling; proved that natural "stillen" [breast feeding] is superior. Voluntärassistent [sic] bei Dr. Spohr in Frankfurt, ¾ Jahre, then settled in Elberfeld, practice. There 1 ½ yrs. Did not like the predominantly religious atmosphere. After the riots on City Hall Square, where Social Democrats were mistreated during an election, inf.[ormant] wrote an article against this, was tried and fired. Ugly scenes in court (1907). Left Prussia in disgust, returned to Munich. Practiced there until March 1915, when he was drafted into military Service. Worked in the surgical section of the military hospital. Did not get on too well; did not like the Army; the CO objected **[132]** to his writing and to his long hair. Then transport physician ¾ years; then transferred to Macedonian front, there one year. Constant difficulties ("Krach") with his Major because he treated patients until they were well, did not immediately return them to the front. Nevertheless, received a decoration, because during the retreat he saved the entire hospital equipment. Was Landsturmarzt, equivalent to Oberstabsarzt (Major). Family was in Munich since 1917, up to that in Dornach.

After the war returned to practice in Munich. 1921 moved to Stuttgart in order to enable chi. to go to Waldorfschule.[145] 1923 "fled" to take the position of Chief physician at Monte Bad Hospital in Lugano. After 1 ½ yrs had to leave Switzerland, because German physician[s] could no longer practice there. Lugano Loge wanted to keep him there, wanted to get him approbation; he declined this offer because as anthroposoph[146] he wanted nothing to do with Masonry. To Stuttgart for a few weeks, then to Hamburg, worked together with his brother, 1924–26; **[133]** then returned to Munich in 1927. Did not get along, because brother's wife was his divorced wife sister. Since 1927 practicing in Munich.

---

145 A "Waldorfschule" is a school where teaching is based on the Waldorf education founded by Rudolf Steiner (1861–1925). The pedagogy of these schools aims to develop the intellectual, artistic, and practical skills of pupils in an integrated and holistic manner. The first Waldorf school was founded in 1919 in Stuttgart. Stehlik (2019), 1, 23.

146 Anthroposophy, a movement pioneered by Rudolf Steiner in the early twentieth century, argued the existence of an objective spiritual reality that could be comprehended through intellectual inquiry. Central to Anthroposophy was the belief in the potential for humans to develop awareness with this spiritual realm to achieve both personal and societal transformation. Bamford (2002), 1, 2.

Fig. 13: Herta Oberheuser (left) at the Nuremberg prison, 1946/47. She was tried for her involvement in medical experiments at the Ravensbrück concentration camp (Source: NARA).

Since first meeting Dr Steiner[147] on occasion of Amnie Beseat's[148] speech in 1903; when he went to Elberfeld in 1906, was accepted in anthroposophic circles. Active member since then. Internationale anthroposophische Gesellschaft. Tieferen Einblick in den Zusammenhang des Geistigen, Seelischen und Körperlichen. Verzicht auf stark-wirkende Mittel. Ursprünglich ärztlicher Nihilist; zweifelte an allem. Schlechte Erfahrungen als Patient während Studium; 3 mal schwerst operiert. Gewöhnliche Hernien, wurden von den Chirurgen operiert während sie durch Salvator Starkbier besoffen waren. Unsauber, persistent abscess, Impfcystitis, und Urticaria.

(durch unsauberen Catheterisms) Ostern 1903. Returned fistula. Christmas same year operated for fistula; a large cotton pledget was formed at the bottom. Recurrence of hernia, reoperated Easter 1904. Since then, allright.

[134] Became interested in Naturheilmethoden, Wasser, Licht, Luft, Vegetarismus. For 15 years, 1900–1915, was strict vegetarian. Fastenkuren, in Patienten. Tried at himself once for 10 days to try it. Made a medical experiment with herbs on himself when treated a phlegmon, left his own blister alone to see how far he had schooled his Abwehrkräfte. The little infection took care of himself.

1910 automobile accident; injured forehead; fell into large revine. Ich habe nur kein Tetanus genommen, um zu sehen, ob ich mit dem Tetanus allein fertig werde. Nothing happened; his experiment succeeded. 5 days later resumed his practice, that was the medical sensation of Munich.

Um Seuchenfestigkeit an mir festzustellen, habe ich keinerlei Impfungen während des Krieges vorgenommen. Auch keine Malariaprophylaxe. Manche bekamen schwere Malaria trotz Prophylaxe; chininfeste Stämme gezüchtet.

[135] Practiced homeopathy in anthroposophic sense; apart from small surgery on obvious abscesses.

In der Mittelwahl. Der Steiner hat seine ärztlichen Cyclen gehalten. Typenlehre; Einteilungsprinzip sinnlicher Mensch; Nerven-Sinnes-Mensch, Stoffwechselmensch (pyknisch) und der rhythmische – was mit dem gesamten Rhythmus zusammenhängt – Schlaf, Verdauung. Alkoholanzeige aus Pflanzen, Veleda (anthroposophische Medizin). Joined NSDAP in the fall of 1931, in order to represent anthroposophy in the party, to know what goes on; and in order to modify. But the party became strongly anti-anthroposophic.

Has difficulties reestablishing himself. Other homeopaths, as well as ex-party members, received permission to practice. Was frequently attacked by orthodox medical men.

---

147 Rudolf Steiner (1861–1925) developed a philosophy which came to be known as "Spiritual Science" (Geisteswissenschaft). In 1919, he published a book entitled *The Threefold Social Order*, linking the three parts of the social organism to liberty, equality, and fraternity. He believed that the human being was represented by thinking, feeling and willing. The Steiner Education is based on these principles, understanding the developing child as a trinity of head, heart, and hands. The curriculum at the First Waldorf School was based on Steiner's philosophy. Stehlik (2019), 4, 10 and 13.

148 Amnie Beseat (1847–1933) was an influential British freemason and women's rights activist.

„Ich bin Arzt aus Leidenschaft. Mein Vater wollte nicht, zwang mich erst 2 Semester Chemie zu studieren, aber ich bin dann übergeschwenkt. Gut ausgekommen, (?) Weil sein.

[136] Vater Landarzt war, und er nur nicht das mühselige Leben wollte. Effect, daß 2 Söhne Ärzte geworden sind. Noch etwas: ich war die ersten Jahre meines Arzttums ein Instinktarzt, ich wußte häufig nicht, wie ich die Fälle kuriert habe. Der Maler Stuckgold war ein classischer Jude, der sagte, es ist nicht so wichtig, was für ein Mittel du gibst, aber dass Du es gibst. Mediale Heilfähigkeit; war nur mit der Anthroposophie unangenehm, weil A scharfe Begriffsbildung wollte, um das Bewußtsein zu erreichen. Therap. Stabilität bis ich so weit war, bewußt zu übernehmen. Training mit Tagessehen, Rücksehen, Kontrolle des Tages [...] noch als freier Mensch zu empfinden. Söhne durch Waldorfschule prädestiniert, aber hat es nicht praktiziert. Er konnte nicht verstehen, daß das finanzielle Entgelt mir wurscht war. Inf. hatte Ruf eines Wunderarztes, über 100 Patienten täglich. Successful. Meditationsstoff. Seele formen. Nicht in autonomer Freiheit, sondern Kadavergehorsam. Das kann man ja auch erziehen. Nach dem letzten Krieg wurde Praxis kleiner, aber [137] noch beachtlicher. Die 100-Patienten war in der ersten Münchner Zeit, vor dem Ersten Weltkrieg.

Der Krebsschaden ist die Masse, die hereinspricht [sic]. Es ist fürchterlich, ich möchte das amerikanische Volk warnen.

Originally Protestant. Left Church in 1903. Aus dem Grund, ich hatte Verwandte, die evangelische Geistliche waren, zu starker Widerspruch zwischen Lehre und Praxis. Nicht atheistisch, sondern trägt religiöse Einstellung.

Sigmund's Lehrer sind noch da: Freie Waldorfschule, Kanonenweg, Stuttgart.

S.R. [Rascher] had his laboratory at first in the pathology institute Borst, then in the Schwabinger Krankenhaus. Was highly thought of. His work is being continued by Weleda in Schwäbisch-Gmünd und in Dornach. Er ist über seine Pubertät nicht hinausgekommen – mußte prahlerisch sein, angeben – noch im KZ-Lager, Frau Dr. Heberlein hat mir das gesagt, hat er seine Frau als Filmschauspielerin von großem Ruf ausgegeben. Er wollte eine Rolle [138] spielen. Ein Grund seines Abrutschens war, daß einer ihm eine Professur für Wehrmedizin in Marburg in Aussicht gestellt hatte.

Bruder of inf., in 1945, told him of a psychic collapse; Mrs. Diehl had temporarily estranged us. Visited him in Dachau, asked him to see the records, hat ihm furchtbar die mörderische Gefahr hingestellt. Told him that whole [...]. Rascher stopped the exp. [?], held hands before face; said: „Ich darf nicht dran denken, ich darf nicht dran denken." He [...], which his during [...] a beautiful holy family.

15–12–46 Dr. Rascher: Ambivalence of sign.; arranged for collection [?] of a Jewish prisoner who stood cold exp. 3x, and that of a catholic priest. Tauber knows about that case, and brother (Fritz) in Hamburg. Brother told that to inf. in summer of 1945.

Re. Tauber: He loves much in Munich; all the KZ comrades come to see him. Starvation to the [...].: Tauber can [...] a witness who has [139] been through the cold experiments three times.

Fig. 14: Victims of Ravensbrück medical experiments arriving at Nuremberg. From left to right: French navy specialist, Françoise Bayle (French trial observer); Leo Alexander; Jadwiga Dzido, Maria Broel-Plater, Maria Kuśmierczuik, and Władisława Karołewska. The women were operated on while prisoners at Ravensbrück concentration camp. Nuremberg, Germany, 15 December 1946 (Source: NARA).

16-12-46 Wladislawa Karolewska. born 15 March 1909, Polish, Grade school teacher, Warsaw, Inzigerska 7.

Jadwiga Dzido, Polish, Student of Pharmacy, born 26 January 1918, Warsaw, Geywoslauska 14

Maria Kusmierczuk Polish, Student of Medicine, born 1 January 1920, Gdansk, Retiborska II.

Maria Broch-Plater, Polish, Chemist and Bacteriologist, born 18–12–1913, Warsaw, Grobowska 171.

Miss Jadwiga Dzido: (Father died when inf. was 3 yrs old; farmer) Mother killed during German air bombardment at Lukow = Lukúw in 1944. Only child. Born in Suchowah.

Grammar school. high school (gymnasium) Maturum 1937. Then began the study of chemistry and pharmacy at the University of Warsaw. Did not graduate because of the war. During summer holidays 1939 worked in a pharmacy in Lukúw, when war began [140] continued that work, until arrested by Gestapo 28 March 1941. Was a member of the resistance movement known as conspiracy since Nov. 1940; worked as a messenger. Imprisoned, finally taken to Ravensbrück 23 September 1941. At first farm work, in winter sewing boots for Army. On 22 November 1942 taken to sick quarter with 9 other Polish girls; an SS woman took her there; she was washed and prepared for operation; legs were shaved: 2 days later, 24 Nov. 1942, was operated. Was asleep. Did not see the man who operated on her.

Picture: recognised Oberheuser. Cold, uninterested, but did not beat her, Morphine was given by SS sister[149] prior to operation. After operation pain control was inadequate, suspects that only water was given instead of morphine.

Has seen Fischer passing by. He is Fischer, is he? He meant nothing to me then. Never saw Gebhardt. However, recognises his picture. He was known to a friend of hers.

After operation very sick for 5 weeks. Could not eat, had high fever, was delirious, unconscious for 5 weeks, [141] adequate recollection except for the pain and for the fact that she was sleepless and restless. Does not recall changes of dressings, except for one in January 1943. Always put sheets over head. Dressings were changed by Oberheuser, Schidlausky or Rosenthal. Suffered a great deal. Wound was very pussy, and it had a bad smell. Was in sick quarters until Feb. 1943; returned to block, was given bed rest privileges. Broke out with blisters over the leg, returned to Revier 2 weeks later, in March 1943. Then 2 weeks there. Returned to block, but could not walk. Had to use crutches. May 25, 1943, called all the operated ones to the Revier. They were told that they must work. Could not work, but was bedingt tauglich. Had to knit stockings. Had to use crutches until late in June 1942. Pain and walking difficulties continued, until now. Evacuated April 29, 1945; after 2 days liberated by the Red Army.

---

149 Nurses were not involved in conducting human experiments. They assisted in pre-operation preparations and provided 'care' for the victims. For example, Erna Böhmer, stated that she bandaged patients who were subjected to bone transplantation experiments some months after she came to work at Ravensbrück in October 1943. See TNA, WO 309/416, "Deposition of Erna Boehmer", 18 April 1946.

[142] *Neurologicals.*
Miss Broel Plater:[150]
Atrophy of peroneal musculatur and of lateral part of right calf adjacent to a disfiguering retracted scar, 6 inches long, over the lateral part of the right culf, half inch wide. Another large scar, 4 ½ : ½ inch, lateral to at slimbones.

Neurological exam: Foot drop, and inner rotation of right foot, which interferes with gait, and e [with] stance knee.

K) and A) active and equal.

Domination of [...], pain and temperature sense in the distribution of N. cruris lateralis of the right leg.

No program and signs. Additional note: Received tablets by mouth after operation.

2. Miss Karolewska:
2) Other additional disfiguring scars; one over the anterior [...] of the right lower leg. Both are anterior [...] scars, over either leg, are deep, retracted and involve the bone, which feels regged. Both these scars feel hot to the palpating hand of the examiner, indicating inflammation underneath.

[143] The scar over the left leg, involving the medical part of the tibia, measures 5 ½ inches and is obviously the residual of a bone experiment. The one over the right leg measures 5: 3/8 inch. Several smaller scars are laterally adjacent to the leg. The main scar on the right is symetric to the one on the left. Likewise involves the medial part of the tibia. Also[,] this scar is obviously the [residual?] of a bone experiment. The lower end of the tibia scar on the left is 5 inches, than on the right 4 ½ inches above the ankle.

1) Deep retracted scar over lateral part of right musculus solens, the lower and terminating 3 ½ inches above the ankle, measuring 3 ½ inch; (infection experiment). This patient rec. [received] no tablets at any time after her operation.
17–12–46 Succeeded getting court transcripts.

---

150 Maria Janina Broel-Plater (1913–2005) was a Polish bacteriologist. She was a member of the Polish resistance movement, working as a messenger. The Gestapo arrested her in June 1941, and she was sent to Ravensbrück. In November 1942, she was assigned by Herta Oberheuser to be experimented on. Broel-Plater was forced to undergo two operations in November. After the procedures – which left her with swollen, discoloured legs and a high temperature – she only received care from other prisoners. Schmidt (2004), 182. Broel-Plater served as a witness at the Nuremberg Medical Trial. See Direct Examination of Maria Janina Broel-Plater by the President, 19 December 1946, Harvard Law School Library Nuremberg Trials Project. After Broel-Plater testified, Leo Alexander was called to the stand to give his expert medical report on the scars she sustained on her legs as a result of the experimental operation. He remarked upon Broel-Plater's 'two deep scars' and the 'thickening and irregularity of the middle third shaft of the fibula', which had 'the appearance as a result of direct trauma to this area without fracture, including removal of muscular attachments'. Alexander commented on how Broel-Plater's injuries impaired her 'function of gait and stance, especially, she cannot stand and maintain herself on her toes'. He concluded that injury to the bone, to the muscles and to the nerve had been sustained. See Direct Examinaton of Leo Alexander by Mr. McHaney, 20 December 1946, Harvard Law School Library Nuremberg Trials Project.

Miss Dzido:[151] Was told by sister from Revier to come. There Dr Oberhauser [sic] told her to disrobe. SS sister put her to bed. After 2 days was given Morphine and operated. It was impossible to say anything. Physically was healthy. The girls operated on before her protested, but they were beaten.

[144] ½ year later Binz[152] called 10 of her friends to be operated on; on 15 August 1943. When they refused[,] they were taken to Bunker, and the rest of the block was locked in without light, air and food, the shutters were closed, and no food was allowed for 3 days. Binz came with the Commandant, and the latter said they were rebels, that thing was impossible, that we must behave and be obedient, that if we would be obedient, he would be good to us; otherwise[,] mad SS with carabiners would shoot them down. One girl said the political prisoners all preferred execution to operation; he said there shall be no more operation in the camp. Binz smiled and said death was victory, but that we must suffer first and then die. Karolewska[153] was in the bunker at that time.

Examination:
Severe atrophy at rt. calf, mit smashed M. biceps of rt thigh, especially of the lateral flexor group, whose functions, which normally should insert at the lateral epicondylus of the tibia, are absent.

[145] The lower half of the leg and the [...] and malleolean region of the foot show bluish discoloration indicating circulatory interference. Skin and musculatur of the right foot are atrophic. Right K) diminished, A) absent.

The right leg is disfigured by 2 ugly scars; the lateral one beginning 3 inches above the knee above the lateral epicondylus, 16 inches long, running over the lateral part of the calf 2 inches above the lateral malleolus. The width of the scar varies from ⅛ to ½ inch. The lower part of this scar still shows inflammation (sew-purulent).

2 ⅛ inch medial to this scar, and parallel to it, is another equally ugly one, measuring 7 ½ : ¾ inches.

There are 4 small, neat scars, indicating heating, by first intention, to transplantation of tender to connect foot drop, on 25 Sept 1945, by Dr. Grucz, Warsaw. He also [146] improved the plastic appearance of the upper end of the main scar; which was badly disfigured by fraction of connective tissue scar. The main scars were not touched.

---

151 See page 139 of the diary for more information about Jadwigo Dzido, a victim of the human experiments at Ravensbrück.

152 This is likely a reference to Dorothea Binz, a guard at Ravensbrück. She behaved incredibly brutally towards prisoners at the camp, and was executed at the first Ravensbrück concentration camp trial for her crimes. Schwartz (2018), 371.

153 Leo Michalowski (1908–unknown) was a Polish Catholic priest interned at Dachau concentration camp from December 1940 until the liberation of the camp. He was subjected to malaria and freezing water experiments at Dachau. See Testimonial exhibits in the report on atrocities given at Dachau, Leo Michalowski, 13 May 1945.

Fig. 15: During his testimony at the Nuremberg Doctors' Trial, Leo Alexander, medical expert for the US Prosecution, points to the scars on the leg of Jadwiga Dzido. Nuremburg, Germany, 20 December 1946 (Source: NARA).

Dorsiflexion of right foot abolished although foot disp in sitting position abolished. Gait disturbed by loss of dousflexion of right foot. Lateral rotators likewise abolished. Severe personal palsy.

18,19–12–46: Worked on the four Polish witnesses. Race against time.

20–12–46: Presented the Ravensbrück victims in Court.

21–12–46 Father Michalowski's testimony in court.[154] Deeply impressive.

Address: At present: Chaplain, Polish Military Mission to HQ British Army of the Rhine Raderhorst, Kreis Minden, Westphalen.

[147] Expects to be transferred to: Reckenfeld bei Münster Westphalen.
On October 7, 1942, was used for one severe chilling experiment.

Recognizes *Neff's pictures*[155] as authentic; Tauber's pictures are not authentic. There was no prodding device.

Recognizes Holzlöhner[156] and Rascher and the 2 Luftwaffe officers. However, knew only Brachtl's[157] name.

Bas[s]in voll mit Eisschollen: 4:4, square, there the 2 officers and Dr. Brachtl. Was wired with electro wires; between shoulders, and rectum. Then dressed in aviation uniform. Mac West. "I looked like the man in the picture, except for the cap."

Lükeln [?] Tabletten, weiß der Kuckuck was die machen.

Brachtl remained present throuhout the entire experiment.

From 2 PM til 9PM.

Füße und Hände steif wie Eisen.

Mühsames Atmen wie ein Hund. Kalter Schweiß.

Gelb-grüne Tropfen, 4–4. Süsser

[148] Geschmack.

(Stimulol, by injection, instead of pyrifer).

Warmed by Lichtbügel (light cradle).

Heard, on cooling, 34° clearly, aslo still 33, 30 vaguely, while passing out. The feeling of warmth on awakening was a happy one; inspite of exhaustion and a severe hunger. Was given a piece of bread and some potato[e]s, which to him was a rich gift, by a fellow prisoner who worked there. After the chilling experiment: For a number of days, about 14, had needed oscillations of temperature, spikes up to 38,

---

154 Leo Michalowski was a prisoner at Dachau. He was a Catholic priest. Leo Michalowski, 'Testimonial exhibits in the report on the atrocities committed at Dachau', 13 May 1945 (https://nuremberg.law.harvard.edu/documents/2585-testimonial-exhibits-in-the-report?q=michalowski#p.1).

155 Originally underlined.

156 See p. 27 of the diary for info on Holzlöhner.

157 Rudolf Brachtel (1909–1988) was a camp doctor in Dachau. He worked at the camp between April 1941 and February 1943. In November 1947 he was accused in the main Dachau concentration camp trial of deliberately infecting patients with malaria when he worked as an assistant to Claus Schilling but was acquitted. He then worked as a doctor in Giessen. Weindling (2017), 327.

lows down to 36, gradually decreasing. Different from malaria chills. May have had several per day, but does not remember whether it may have been only one oscillation per day.
Inspiring story of the liberation.
Dachau Report: Wm. W. Quim, Colonel, G.S.C. AC of S, G2, 7th U.S. Army
[Marginalia]: Write to USTET

[149] Letter to third Army G2 Section, Ac of S G2 APO 403, 3rd U.S. Army.
Mr. Manfred Wolfson, OCC WC, Berlin Branch.

Sterilisation most severe 1942, and shortly before the end.

Das ist etwas Kriminelles, Kriminelles darf man nicht verstecken, man muß doch die Welt vor diesen Sachen warnen.
Conversation with Father Michalowski, continued in the evening, most inspiring.
His strong fascination about the Dachau report.

Erst kam die Wehrmacht; they shot 192 priests of his diocese. Forced one priest to have intercourse with his housekeeper, pelted him e [with] bottles, and cut a swastika in his forehead. Then came Arbeitsdienst, then the SA, then the SS. They took them to Dachau.
Michalowsky was arrested. 11 Sept. 1939, first prison, 2 months later into a Sammellager for priests, an old monastery; in prison on one occasion 38 prisoners were taken out and shot **[150]** on a Jewish Cementry. They were members (many of them) of the Westmarkenverein. Inf.'s name was not on the list: they are the ones whose turn will come tomorrow. The priests had to clean the toilets and messes on Sunday.
Purpose of the camp brothel: the bill was sent to the wife, the idea was to make wives divorce their husbands who were in KZ's. The prisoners resented it and staged a demonstation against it. Still sees it in front of him, how they whistled and howled when it was announced.
The sermon for the dead priest on the line-up square (Appellplatz). Perfid-sadistische Tendenz.
To Stutthof early in February 1940. From there on 10 April 1940 to Sachsenhausen. From there on 13 December 1940 to Dachau. There til liberation. 5 ½ years in Dachau.
Altogether 40 survived out of 140–200 arrested in his diocese. 180 removed. The total was 570 or 670 in his diocese before the war.

[151]
Total	570
Shot	192
Removed	180
Arrested	198

Camp number: 22769.

Chaplain to a Polish DP Camp. Domherr (Monsignor) 2 Oct. 1946. Was in charge of religious teaching in 2 schools in Sweecie, near Chulm on the Vistula, between Thorn and Gdansk. Rapportführer Boettcher killed 92 Russian officers, and many thousands of prisoners brought to death by chicanes.

Affidavit: The photographs are authentic and real.
The sharings and the water cibor are not representative of condition in his time. There was no such pully; there was no big tables and no gloss wood; there was only one or two small tables; entering 2 box like pieces of apparatus; painted white, like a radio; one was an EKG with a [...] suggest for photo [...]. This apparatus was tried out on him before out the water. Another small table contained a type- [152] writer, where notes were made immediately under constant dictation, also his statements, for instance after request of schnaps were taken down. There were 8 prisoner assistants, and 3 doctors, incl. Brachtl [Brachtel]. The basin was square and deep; inf. was maintained by the Navy West, could not reach bottom e [with] his feet.

Herrenvolk is the key idea.

Hegel (Himself later an insane invalid). Gesund, stark, jede Schwäche müsste beseitigt werden. So die Häftlinge behandelt. Stark – schwach.

23-12-46 Interview with Gebhardt. Miss Shelly heard from Horving: Miss Wegner, later Miss Punzengruber, worked at 6 Bauerstrasse in Munich.

24-12-46 Talk with Mr. Ervin re morale. Talk with Gebhardt & Fischer. Another difficulty re permission to talk with defendants. Pictorial atlas arranged.

[153] 25-12-46 Xmas day. Rewrote the transcript of my testimony.
26-12-46 Showdown re Bayle; talks with Erwin, the General, Rapp. The better the power behind the throne.
27-12-46: Mac Haney's return. Interrogations resumed.
Expense account submitted:
Nov. 19-30th.

Rose: Die beiden Impfstoffe der Behringwerke konnten nicht den Tod verhindern. Der Kopenhagener impfstoff hat nicht beschützt. Die starben dran. Eidotter und Läuse-Impfstoff waren gleichwertig, der Eidotter war etwas besser. (Otto und Wollrab, Gildemeister und Hagen), Gemisch von Rickettsia [...] und Provazeki [prowazekii]. Die Kaninchen- und Mäuselunge hat sich auch bewährt.

Does not speak Chinese. Record kept separately. Engländer erfolgreich als Eroberer eines grossen Teils der Erde, quantitativ ihr Beitrag zur Kultur nicht so groß wie der anderer Völker.

[154] Politisch überlegen. Durchschnittliches Bildungsniveau gesunken als civilisatorisches Niveau.
America: drüben gewesen, aber mich nicht wohl gefühlt. Not consistent, sometimes they laugh over something tragic, sometimes they don't.
Die Japaner haben den Chinesen Patriotismus beigebracht.
40 Gründe des Protests instinktmässiger, gefühlsmässiger. George I [...] Vorurteil, ein Henker zu sein. Unerwünschter, skrupelloser Typ[,] würde diese wichtigen

Entscheidungen in die Hände fallen, verstandesmässig ja, wenn eine Führung sich dafür entscheidet.

28-12-46: Gebhardt, Fischer & Oberheuser: Started working on cases.

Dr. Oberheuser: 15-5-11.
No disciplinery difficulties. Political interest since – 1931 Schule verlassen, Spannungen von Jahr zu Jahr größer. Interest: Mathem., Physik, Chemie, Biologie.
8) Ordnungswütend. No disciplinary action ever, until now.
[155] 9) Sport, swimming, riding horseback, gymnastics, since age 7.
10) Dogs, since age 7 or 8 yrs. Until study (at age 19) always had her own dog.
10) [sic] Krankheit. "The suffering, which the animal cannot express.["] Recalls one incident at 10 or 11 yrs. In summer in the country.
11) No Youth group activity, until BDM as a physician in 1935, at age 24 yrs. No Wandervögel, no Pfadfinder. Nicht sehr viele Freunde, einige. „Die eine hat Jura studiert, eine Theologie, 2 Theologie . . . und eine Bibliothekarin. Knew them since age 14 yrs. Ziemlich nahe Freundinnen. Das hat sich dann geschieden, weil ich auf die Studienanstalt ging.
Rothligne [?]: Immune to typhus – Moabit prison.

29-12-46: Sunday. First day of rest.

30-12-46: Re-interviewed Fischer and Gebhard. Completed the writings of their experiments. Evening: Conversation with Mr. Punger, who had been at Buchenwald and who took an important part in its **[156]** Liberation.

31-12-46: Dr. Weltz re-interrogated. His amazing suggestion of geno-suicide for Germany.

1-1-47: Generals reception; reading.

2-1-47: Court reopened. Photographic record insisted.

3-1-47 Photographs progressing. Witness Hall. Conversation e [with] Seidl and Hardy.

4-1-47 Dr. Jan Ochozki, witness. Wilhelm Tellstraße 1, München, 2Std. UNRRa Team 108, Deutsches Museum. 9-12, 2-4 ½. Ext.11.
Meyer came back e [with] Polygal and Dr R.'s affidavit.

Fischer: Kalchizin. Lettre a Brodersen. Rudolf Virchow Krankenhaus 1937. Im Mittelalter bekannt, im 15 Jahrhundert Miton-hemmende Wirkung. Jontophorese. 34.000 Molekulargewicht. Brodersen's Habilitationsschrift (Zbl. f.d. ges. Röntgenologie u. Radiologie).

Fig. 16: Entrance to the gate of the Nuremberg courthouse. Nuremberg, Germany, 1946/47 (Source: NARA).

Haber[158] war Chemiker bei Sauerbruch.[159] Nebennierenmittel für die Bluterkrankheit AT10. Hört mit Aeridin: Himmler war Anthroposoph. Reincarnation Heinrich's des Städtebauers. Ohlendorf told him about anthroposophy, Lebenscyklus, die Möglichkeit sich höher zu entwickeln. Lebensweg wiederholt sich, nach Maßgabe seiner vorhergehenden Leistung. Rudolf Brandt sollte auch Inkarnation aus dem Lebens **[157]** kreis Heinrich des Städtebauers sein.

In the afternoon, interrogation of Miss Schmidt's, Haagen's technician, and pharmacist Hirtz. Then studied Col. Andrews' report on Polygal, freezing, high altitude, poison and other Rascher work. Dr. Singer's autopsy reports.

On leaving, discovery of curious caricature under my door sign: [rudimentary sketch of a hand]. Must get in touch with CID [Combined Intelligence Directorate]

In the evening reception for Lord Wright,[160] the chairman of the War Crimes Commission. Good floor show.

5-1-47 up late. At breakfast conversation with Mac Kove, the IG men. Afternoon: some more of Col. Andrew's report, then a long nap. The General plans to go to Paris with me.

In the evening saw "The Stranger". At the same time similar event right here in the Hotel, where Miss Shelley entertained Miss Schmidt and Hirtz. Lu [?] Schmidt recognized on having been with Haagen to Natzweiler on 6 occasions, including visits to the Crematorium.

Talk with Mac Kove and Mrs Virginia Miller. What a potential Nazi the latter would have made!

[158] 6-1-47 Sent Shelley off after Punzengruber.

7-1-47 Kogon's[161] magnificent testimony. 2 letters from Phyllis.

8-1-47 Kogon on cross examination. Magnificent. Respected as real authority.

---

158 Fritz Haber biographical reference, p. 156 of the diary: Fritz Haber (1868–1934) was a German chemist who received the Nobel Prize in Chemistry in 1918 for inventing the Haber-Bosch process, an industrial method which synthesises ammonia from nitrogen gas and hydrogen gas. The process is important for producing fertilisers and explosives. Stoltzenberg (2004), 100. Haber developed the first chemical weapon. Schmidt (2024), 2.

159 Ferdinand Sauerbruch (1875–1951) was a surgeon and university professor. He is deemed to have been the founder of modern thoracic surgery. From 1927 to 1949, he was Director of the Surgical Clinic at the Charité hospital in Berlin. Sauerbruch led the Medical Science Department of the Reich Research Council during the war. Sauerbruch advised the health board in Berlin after 1945, but he was dismissed during the Doctors' Trial proceedings and underwent a 'denazification' process after authorities obtained knowledge of his wartime role. Ebbinghaus/Roth (2001), 135.

160 Robert Wright (1869–1964) was a British judge who led the United Nations War Crimes Commission between 1945 and 1948. Madajczyk (2024), 16.

161 Eugen Kogon (1903–1987) was a political prisoner at Buchenwald concentration camp between 1939 and 1945. From 1943 onwards, he worked as a clerk for the camp doctor Erwin Ding-Schuler, who was in charge of the typhus experimentation which took place at the camp. He published a book in 1946 entitled *The SS State. The System of the German Concentration Camps*. Ebbinghaus/Roth (2001), 110. He testified extensively during the Doctors' Trial on 6, 7 and 8 January 1947. He was examined by McHaney and various defence lawyers. See Harvard Law School Library Nuremberg Medical Trial Project, Direct Examination of Eugen Kogon by Mr. McHaney, 6 January 1947, and Cross Examination of Eugen Kogon by Dr. Nelte, 7 January 1947.

Dr. Maczka: 1) Special operations. 2) Lethal injections. 3) Child murders.
Dinner with Kogon and Kirchheimer, and Miss Bontecomp.
  9–1–47 Dr. Maczka's pre-trial interrogation continued.
Lunch with Kogon and Kirchheimer. Discussion with them and Kove.
Dr. Bruno Fialkowski,
Destouchestrasse 36,
München.
  Plantage: Roltenbuch b. Schöngau, Oberbayern. „Biozane K.G." Früher Kräuter gepflanzt. Durch die Plantage viel zugelernt.
  Zwiebeln und Vitaminversuche.

Mr Haremza, Ignatz: aged 26.
  Was used in an altitude experiment. Was saved by a capo. Chamber: 2x2 meter. Unconscious. Later confused.
  1945: Dr Phoetus preferred a blood coagulation experiment. Fasting, got injection. Then [159] every time blood was taken from ears and vain, and tested e [with] various glosses, for 7 hours. That happened 2 times. Was very weak. Nobody died.
  Once, in 1942, while on Rascher's station for 2 weeks, happened into a room where Dr. Rascher did something with 2 naked corpses, Dr. Rascher and an assistant were there. Dr. Rascher yelled at him and said "if you come in again, I'll do the same to you." What scared him was that he was taken to the lung station. Neff made papers of people to be gassed disappear.

Invitation to the Paris meeting by Dr. Bayle.

10–1–47 Dr. Maczka's testimony. Afternoon: BBC broadcast. Miss Shelley's new assignment. Euthanasia started.

11–1–47 Weltz re-interrogated. Fischer re-interrogated, Sievers re-interrogated.
  Talk with General Taylor, re Paris meeting.

[160] Dr. Karl *Dirr*, born 27–10–94
  Rieden a.d. Kötz, Bayern. Gräfelfing b. München, Reginpertstrasse 1A. tel. Munich 89–127. Knew Rascher 1935 or 36, while he did his doctor's thesis. Had to control his work, on his pregnancy test, and early cancer diagnosis. Had a meeting with Prof. Trump and him. Disappeared the paper. Prof. Schütterhelm[162] rejected the paper. Was in charge of clinical laboratory.
  Saw him again in 1942. Asked to teach methods of blood examination to some of his coworkers.
  1925 – Nov. 1946 Assistent at Medizinische Universitätsklinik und Leiter des Klinisch-Chemischen Laboratoriums, Privat Dozent seit 1940. Now in practice.
  Taught Punzengruber, who was always accompanied by an SS man in civilian clothes: „einer von den wilden Typen." Usually came every 8 days, then once in a month.

---

162 Alfred Schittenhelm (1874–1954) was an internist during the Nazi regime. Kater (1989), 130.

„Die SS waren bekannt als gefährliche Unternehmen, und Dachau war uns **[161]** natürlich bekannt als das Konzentrationslager wo es nicht einwandfrei herging mit den Häftlingen." „Das war schon vor dem Krieg bekannt."
Ich habe gesagt: Ich will von Dachau nichts wissen.
(Jemand zeigt in Dachau schön [?]) Dann will er sich irgendwie ausreden oder einen helfen, überzeugt kann er nicht sein."
„Dann hat ers nicht angesehen." Dann muß ich mir alles ansehen, dann ist er ein Schwindler. Oder er hat gesoffen, und es sich nicht angesehen. Inspizieren heisst alles ansehen, jeden Keller und jeden Häftling."
Punzengruber[163] wurde Ende 1943, Anfang 44 entlassen. Dann Beziehungen abgebrochen. Rascher has been in the African campaign, and that went on his nerves: desire not to return to the front.
Was often to see Prof. Schittenhelm.[164]

Mrs. Punzengruber
Gisa Punzengruber, geb. Wagner.
born: 3–5–17.
KZ „ordentlich" [?]
Erfahrungstatsache: man hat gelacht darüber, man hat gewußt man kriegt das **[162]** Wirkliche doch nicht zu sehen.
Former prisoners said they saw Rascher [...] in Dachau.
but first time Sept. 1942. Had come to Dachau in June 1942. Came to research station August 1942. Hat mit Aussuchen der Häftlinge nichts zu tun gehabt.
After liberation took over the supervisory position of the chemical industry in Bavaria.
Thinks that all the trouble started when the Betreuungsstelle refused to do things for the greens and the blacks. Thus the struggle between reds and greens was continued after liberation. The criminals then opened their own Betreuungsstelle and information Buro.
Der Rascher wollte nicht mehr hinaus an die Front. Sich unentbehrlich zu machen. Maßlos ehrgeizig. Dr. Punzengruber was locked up in September 1946. Seinen Familienbesitz hat der Tote, sein Vermögen die SS.
Rascher: Ab und zu soll man einen entlassen, das hebt die Stimmung, aber er wünscht daß der Häftling dann sofort auto- **[163]** matisch auf der Station dienstverpflichtet wird, damit er sich die billige Arbeitskraft erhalten kann.
Vater hat von Anfang an geahnt [?] daß der Krieg nicht gewonnen werden kann.

13–1–47 Preparations. Dictated brief for Leibbrand. Dr. Ivy's arrival.

---

163 This is probably a reference to Dr. Punzengruber who was an inmate at Dachau. From 1942–1943 he was assigned to Rascher's station as a chemist. See c. Selections from the Argumentation of the Defence. Extracts from the Closing Brief for Defendant Sievers. The Freezing Experiments, in Trials of War Criminals before the Nuernberg Military Tribunals Under Control Council Law No. 10, Volume 1, Nuernberg October 1946–April 1949, p. 208.
164 Alfred Schittenhelm, who worked at the University of Munich as a professor of internal medicine. He was quite heavily involved with Nazism.

Frl. Anneliese Frick, born 1920. Daughter of Wilhelm Frick, who was divorced from mother since 1935. 2 brothers, one killed in action (born 1914), one committed suicide on May 2, 1945.

Inf.[ant] lives with mother.

At present jobless. Never party member, never in BDM.[165]

Abitur 1939, in Munich. ½ yr labor service, then commercial school, in 1940 (April) trained for technician, graduated 1942. Went to work for Dr. Weltz on April 15, 1942. Animal experiments, cold experiments in guinea pigs and rabbits. Spleen and stomach [...]-less [?] in Unterkühlung. Did also secretarial work. Fliegeruntersuchungen in der Unterdruckkammer. Stayed e [with] Wendt in Munich until Dec 1944; the others went to Weihen- [164] stefan [Weihenstephan] a year earlier. Met Dr. Rascher once at the Institute in the spring of 1942. He had a conference with Dr. Weltz; they had disagreement. After that he did not come again to the Institute. "I started in April; that must have been May or June." Nicht am Institut gearbeitet, hat nur „planstellenmäßig" dazugehört.

Weltz: kurz. zurückhaltend, manchmal grantig. Hat geschimpft, wenn man manchmal etwas nicht so machte wie er wollte. Sachen angeordnet die man nicht so machen konnte, ungern Widerspruch vertragen. Ausgesprochen unfreundlich. Rascher erinnert sich daran, da er sich von Frl. Frick ihre Uhr erbeten hatte, so daß er ihn bald loswird.

Weltz came to the Institute at 10 in the morning; dropped in for an hour in the afternoon, because he was still carrying on his practice on the side. Mostly wore uniform; sometimes civilian clothes.

Thought that Germany would win the war until the first winter in Russia (1941/42)

Soldaten auf Urlaub haben von Aus- [165] rottungskommandos (Dörfer ausrotten, und die Judengeschichte) erzählt, man hat das mit Entsetzen gehört, aber nicht geglaubt (Polen „minderwertig") Nein. (Juden?) „Persönlich nicht sympat[h]isch. Aber meine beste Freundin ist Halbjüdin. Man soll niemanden ausrotten. Schließlich hat jeder sein Recht zu leben. (Zigeuner?) „Ich kenne keine Zigeuner." Vater war Beamter (Polizeiverwaltungsbeamter), nach 1923 ist er beim Reichstag Fraktionsführer der Partei geworden.

(Persönlich?) „Immer in seine Akten vertieft. Mir war er immer persönlich fremd. Selten zuhause gewesen. Mit meinem Bruder hat er mehr Ausflüge u. Bergtouren gemacht."

14-1-47 To Paris in Genl. Taylor's plane. At Pierre I, Roi de Serbre. In the evening saw Martin Roumaguec, a combination of Carmen & Madame Bovary, but superb.

15-1-47 Meeting at the Institut Pasteur: Lord Moran,[166] Legrove, Lépine, Genl. Taylor, Mant, John Thompson,[167] Bayle, etc. American participation, publiccations, etc.

---

165 League of German Girls, or Band of German Maidens (*Bund Deutscher Mädel*, BDM).
166 Lord Charles Moran (1882–1977) was Winston Churchill's doctor from 1940 until 1965. He was appointed by Clement Attlee to head the delegation of British medical scientists examining human experimentation in Nazi Germany. See Lovell (1992), and Weindling (2001), 54.
167 John Thompson was a doctor who investigated medical war crimes ahead of the Nuremberg Doctors' Trial. Further Reading: Weindling (2010).

[166] Lunch at British Officers Club, the former Palais Rothschild. Afternoon: [...] slide demonstration by me; saw Molharet, then Pasteur's tomb. Evening: Samson & Delila[h] at the Opera. Magnificent. Went with Thompson, got tickets; afterwards conversation re actual purposes of Commission.

16-1-47 Breakfast with Genl. Taylor. Clarification of practical and immediate objectives of the Commission. Then to Institut Pasteur, interesting demonstrations by Lépine. Greek dictionary in the library of the Pasteur Institute: Androktonology or Androktenology, or Androkteinology.[168]

17-1-47 To the Clinique Charcot at the Salpêtiere. Taken around by Mrs. Malleret, Dr. Pluvinage and Dr. Bausch. Dr. Guillein's assistant, somewhat reminiscent of Charlie Kubic. Dr. Agmon's assistant: the old psychiatric ward, only partly shown, because "trop degoutant"[169] in the doctor's wards. The old single cells with the seats in front. The salle Pinel.[170] Charcot's library, and the Charcot Museum,[171] deeply impressive, [167] the latter with the moulage of the old woman with the Charcot joints. Dr. Alajoneusne's lecture, and Dr. Bourgignon's laboratory.

Lunch in the French restaurant, with Lapin sauté and vin rosé.

Afternoon: conference with John Thompson and Group Capt. Somerhough.[172] Obtained full address of members, and the minutes.

Miss Shelley's report on the victim with cancer.

Evening: with Major Mant and Miss Shelley – Oysters with Spanish wine (Anguls), then to the Opera for the ballet: [La Fille aux Yeux d'Émail, Coppélia]. Old Dr. Copplius [...] [sinister?], with his transplantation of the soul into Coppelia; her gradually coming to full human life is a masterpiece of the dance.

18-1-47 With Mant to see at the Hospital Necker.

[168] 20-1-47 Dr. Beiglböck, with Dr. Ivy. 18 out of 44 [...].

21-1-47 Conversation with Dr. Ivy. Corrected aggressive behaviour paper. Dictated document analysis re sea water experiments.

Afternoon: Interrogated Sievers and Schröder. Dictated letters. Telegrams Ktenology.

---

168 Here Alexander is experimenting with the Ancient Greek roots of 'andro-' and 'kteino' to explore different forms to describe a 'study of killing men.' The prefix 'andro-' is derived from the word 'andros', meaning 'man', while 'kteino' means 'to kill'. The terms Androktonology, Androktenology, or Androkteinology are attempts by Alexander to evoke in a single word the concept of a 'study' or 'discipline' dedicated to murder, with similar connotations to Thanatology.
169 "Very disgusting".
170 Philippe Pinel (1745–1826) was a French physician and important precursor in the development French psychiatry. Alexander visited his rooms at the Hospice de la Salpêtrière, one of the most important teaching hospitals of the Sorbonne University.
171 Jean-Martin Charcot (1825–1893) was a French neurologist and anatomist. The library and museum Alexander visted were made from Charcot's clinic and teaching rooms. The library and museum are a short walk from the Salpêtrière along the river Seine.
172 Somerhough was Group Captain of the British War Crimes Group. Weindling (2004), 108.

22–1–47 Discussion re Ktenology with Dr. Ivy; he considered *Busche's* speech important, and my formulation re fundamental purposes.
Interrogation Schäfer.
Afternoon: rewrote sea water part.

Ruff: Congenial childhood. Folgsam, child, ruhiges Kind in früher Kindheit. Obedient, quiet child in early childhood. Later revenge. Average student. More fond of father. No disciplinary action in school. Early childhood in the country, many animals. Always had dogs, since 3yrs of age, had a Dachshund then, with whom he grew up. No unpleasend incidents. Boy scout from 1919 or 20 til 1925. In school much sport activity, successful as a soccer player [169] and swimmer; also Stabhochsprung [pole vault] and rowing, sports of endurance. Began to fly in 1926. Limited to [...] periods. Took part in hiking. No leadership position. Hiking during free time & vacations. times: accomplishment. Money plays a role. Several money: money in life insurance, the remainder savings account. No industrial investments: for that the war not enough. Religion: protestant. Not very active. Never left church. Party member since 1938.

At 13 or 14 had artricular rheumatism. Lost much time from school, about 3 months. Appendectomy. Otherwise never significantly ill. No nervous breakdown. Personal grievouses when got along well with people. Recreation: sport, flying: later reading, mostly natural sources, but also classic literature. Travel[...] Music interested, but not active. Used to take in concerts.

No suicide thoughts.

Travel: before the war: Switzerland & Holland; during the war France and Hungary. Gave lectures in Budapest & Debreczen. In France Luftwaffe duty.

[170] No friends abroad. "I have them now, with all the Heidelberg men going to the U.S." Feels the trial is necessary.

Defence: Weltz [Walter] Reed's[173] first studies. Doll [?] and Forbes Am. J. Physiology [American Journal of Physiology].

23–1–147 (Unjustly treated?) During the war, my scientific work did not found [find] the appreciation which it deserved. 1941 the RLM requested that he be made professor. 3 professors were asked. Prof.'s Rein, Strughold and Knote. Rein gave a very good approach. But he did not receive the professorship. In 1944 he was told that his political background "uninterested and inactive" caused the rejection. Jan.[uary] 1945 another request was made, which did not bring results.

(After 1945?) No, apart from the fact that I don't think it is very beautiful that I am accused. Insufficient cause. Nazi physician and SS physician. Objectively, if I were representative of the prosecution, I would probably do the same. Confidence in justice.

No phobias.

German people have shown that in certain fields accomplished more: memory, literature, science, belongs to those nations who are on the top.

[171] Jews, Poles, Gypsies inferior? The Poles, for example, are in many fields of very high value. Poles and Czechs during the occupation showed that they have

---

173 See footnote on Reed; page 105 of the diary.

extraordenary people in people & country, and on the whole behaved so that one must respect them. Literature, music.

With the Jews it is so that I never identified myself e [with] the Nazi ideas. Justifications deemed, I had close contact, teachers, friends. Never found anything inferior about them.

Gypsies – the answer is more difficult. Their whole mode of life, their frequent petty breaches of the law – a not small percentage are ascocial, and therefore inferior.

French? Little opportunity for personal contact. English? I take them for extraordinarily clever and especially successful in practical life. (Americans?) Ja – as far as I know them it is a people of many component parts, immigrants from many peoples, certainly did not come from the worst components. Successes in all fields in the last 40–50 yrs show that also scientifically they keep pace e [with] the average other country and because of their superior means will surpass them. (Japs?) difficult.

[172] (Italiens?) After the experience we made e [with] them during this war, are a dying people, who really for hundred years have not accomplished great things.

(Spanish?) Similar.

(Chinese?) Ja, Chinese – thats for us difficult to see them.

(Negroes?) also diff. [difficult] to judge for us.

(Treatment of Jews?) Many reasons that one needed a propaganda means, a scapegoat.

Not justified.

(Gypsies?) No acceptable excuse. Even if one considers them selfish, one does not have the right to wipe them out.

(Poles?) No excuse, that is a crime of worst kind.

(Oath of Hippocrates?) Important.

(No damage?) important principle.

(few for many?) Under certain conditions yes. To clear a disease which kills thousands. Under such conditions the researcher should have opportunity to do experiments on all problems to fight the disease, [173] such as was always done practically in medicine.

(Volunteers?) If necessary and practicable, if the subject does not have to cooperate, under certain conditions also involuntary. Criminals condemned to death should be abgestellt to those experiments. Like Georg I did for the first vaccination, when he ordered 6 condemned criminals. He then ordered to take orphans; that I would not consider justified. Georg I is the first who [...] human experiments. I would consider it allright eventually to put criminals condemned to death at disposal.[174]

---

174 Karl Gebhardt also believed that individuals condemned to death could be experimented on. He remarked in an examination conducted during the Doctors Trial that he had insisted on the procurement of men from Sachsenhausen who had a death sentence to undergo the first series of sulfonamide experiments. See Nuremberg Medical Trial, Microfiche number 38, Resumed cross-examination of Karl Gebhardt by Mr McHaney, 7 March 1947. This statement needs to be treated with caution, since Gebhardt may have deliberately been trying to rationalise in court why the experiments were performed on human subjects as a way of exonerating himself.

In the last ten yrs the number of malpractice suits increased, but the judgements decreased.

Quackery was done away with, which is a must of National Socialists, in Dr. Ruff's opinion.

Then came the bombshell: Ruff feels it would have been Morell's[175] duty to do away with the Fuehrer as soon as he found that he had become mentally incompetent (in 1942!).

In the afternoon, Genzken re-interrogated.

[174] 24–1–47 Sent of Ktenology article. Finished the additions to the article re *ethical and unethical experimentation*.

Halder's diary: „Sondergruppen für Blutübertragung und Seuchenbekämpfung", reported on by *Handloser*. General Wagner (Mrs. Punzengruber's father!): Verhalten gegen Insassen von Irrenanstalten bei Mord [?]: „Russen sehen Geistesschwäche als heilig an. Trotzdem Tötung notwendig" (page 100).

The document concerning the whipping order in concentration camps signed by Glücks and Liebehenschel.

25–1–47 Worked on Ethics article, drew up Affidavit. Letters to Abi, Gehren, etc.

[175] 28–1–47 Dr. Edwin Katzen/Ellenbogen.
Born May 22, 1882.

Arrested in Paris, 19–2–1943; 5 months in Fréjus, from there to Buchenwald where he stayed 19 months until liberation. Never in Dachau. Worked as Psychiatrist in the hospital.

Overcrowded mental ward on the "invalid block." Pole with homocidal tendencies.

Worked with Münsterberg[176] at Harvard. Later assistant physician at *Dauvers*. Later worked in New Jersey, State Colony for epileptics; then Trentor State Hospital. In last war, did Red Cross work in Poland and Russia. Married Judge Pierre's daughter. Deranged, after their only son died in an accident. Since 1918 wandering about Europe, doing some scientific work, practicing, etc. After 1933 went to Prague. Couched physicians for State Boards and English in America.

Buchenwald? really enjoyed – helping a lot of people who otherwise would not be helped. Did not know Hoven himself. Never gave lethal injections. Head of hospital was Capo-Busse. Selections of mentally ill patients for extermination was

---

175 Theodor Morell (1886–1948) was Hitler's personal physician. Brandt, and other German doctors, believed that Morell did not know much about medical science or medical practice; according to Brandt, he was a 'businessman', not a doctor. Brandt and his colleagues attempted to remove Morell from his position in 1944 but the plan failed, and Brandt was expelled instead. Morell surrendered himself to American military authorities in 1945. He was interned and then released. Morell died in 1948. Schmidt (2008), 85, 86. Ebbinghaus/Roth (2001), 120. Stackelberg (2007), 187.

176 Hugo Münsterberg (1863–1916) was a German-American psychologist. He pioneered the areas of forensic psychology, business and industrial psychology, and film criticism. He was a subject of German sentiment two years before his death due to his support of the German standpoint in the First World War. Moskowitz (1977), 824.

done by SS physicians, [176] on the basis of *Arbeitsstatistik* compiled by German red prisoners of communistic leaning. They were asked 1000 man for example. So they sent about 1500, of those the 1000 were selected. Mentally and physically ill. A patient who said he felt ill, was referred to the specialist in the field. The ill ones stayed. „Arbeitsfähig, leichte Arbeit, Lagerarbeiter." Saw one death transport; 1200 French officers were selected and sent to "Dora".[177] They were picked at random. 6 weeks later 97 came back in wretched condition. Only 23 later survived. They died from pure exhaustion. The "Dora" were tunnels where V2s were later manufactured. It was Pohl's idea. When one set of 1200 was finished, they sent the next group. It was a plan to get rid of the young French reserve officers (Genocidal!). Dr. Rogge supervised these actions. Dr. Katzen Ellenbogen refused one instance of euthanasia (genuine in that case!) because it would be wrong, especially in the KZ.

Judge Morgen knows his case. He knows more about Hoven than [177] anyone else. He should be called as a prosecution witness.

Ferdinand Roemhold was inf. pal. Feels Roemhold is 100% truthful. Claims that the Buchenwald insane were not sent to Bernburg for annihilation. Only healthy people were sent. There were 4 blocks with invalids including insane, but they were never sent on death transports.[178] Knew that experiments with lethal results were done in Ward 46. But does not know of lethal injections. The prisoners were in deadly street of block 46. Never believed that Germany would win the war. In November 1941 German officer told him that too.

"Oath of Hippocrates: sufficient." I was very near one to give a lethal injection. That was that Polish homocidal patient. What to do e [with] him? The German suggested lethal injection, because he was dangerous to the community. I wavered, asked the Polish Committee. If all 8 were of the opinion, I would do it. 7 were, one not, so I did not do it. He [178] survived.

(Kill 5 to save 500?) This hypothetic question is very difficult. Supposing I were sane – if 5 men were infected with [...], for instance, and you could not return them.

(In an experiment?) No. No such exp. is possible for a physician. Even if the men would be for it, I would abstain. The only way is to experiment on ourself.

(Right to decide over the right to live?) "Not one physician. May be a medical court. Like the sterilisation law. But not to kill, except maybe save man from pain who is dying from cancer, anyway. While it is forbidden, I could satisfy my own

---

177 The Dora camp was established in summer 1943 in the Nordhausen area from a system of Buchenwald subcamps. The Mittelbau camp was established in autumn 1944 and became a site for rocket production. The Dora camp later became the main camp of Mittelbau. The name 'Mittelbau-Dora' refers to both the Dora subcamp and the independent Mittelbau concentration camp. In April 1945, the Mittelbau camp with its 40 subcamps interned over 40,000 people. Over 20,000 prisoners died at Mittelbau. Wagner (2009), 972, 973; Neufeld (2009), 970.

178 Individuals classed as 'mentally insane' by the Nazi regime were frequently sent on death transports. They were also sterilised and subjected to the 'euthanasia' programme. Torrey/Yolken (2010), 28.

consience, if there is no hope to save the man. Like in the book." Sorrel and his son.[179]

Evening: discussion with Mitscherlich,[180] later with Wing Commander Thompson. Führer-Selbstauslese. Ward-worshippers.

[179] 29–1–47 Generalarzt Prof. Dr. Erich *Hippke*. Born 7–3–1888.

Father: farmer, alter Forestry employer. Died at 70, from heart disease. Mother: daughter of a physician. Died at 70 from heart disease. Congenial.

1 sister, died in Danzig in 1945. Single, teacher.

Married 1920; 2 sons, aged 25 and 20; divorced 1940, uncongenial; remarried 1941, one son aged 2 yrs. Congenial.

Gymnasium, Abitur 1907. then University of Berlin, KW Academy, graduated 1913, MD 1920. Kreisarzt 1924

1913 Unterarzt, 1914 Assistenzarzt; Saw service at Eastern Front, Russia til Turkey; remained in Army; special training as hygienist 1919–22, served in that special capacity; consistently promoted; 1933 became CO of the military hospital. However, with the rank of Lt. Col., 1935 placed in charge of medical service of Luftwaffe. Did that til end of 1943, when he was removed and pensioned, because of political and organisational differences.

[180] Became industrial physician for AEG. 1945 to Hamburg as physician for the elevated. After capitulation went to physician chamber Hamburg, worked out their system of distribution. Then practiced. Arrested, December 14, 1946. One month later here.

Rascher was Captain of the Luftwaffe. May 1941 he came and asked for participation in altitude experiments, saying he wanted habilitation and therefore scientific work. He had taken a course in Munich; thus he became interested. He proposed to perform Fremdversuche in criminals condemned to death, whom one could utilize, with the chance of pardon. Inf. took the view that exp. in non-physicians should not be made; no binding agreement was made. Hippke himself had been trained as stunt flier and passed then all hints of experiments. Thus May 1941. Then there was a discussion in Munich, which Rascher did not attend, with Prof. Weltz. That was also in May 1941. Kameradschaftsabend im Behring Palais. „Mir waren Versuche an anderen als an Aerzten unsympat[h]isch, ich habe mich [181] ausgedrückt

---

179 'Sorrell and Son' was a novel by the British writer George Warwick Deeping, published in 1925. The novel gave a sympathetic view on euthanasia. The plot centers on the relationship between a Father, Sorrell, and his Son, Kit, highlighting the sacrifices Sorrell makes so that his son may one day become a doctor. At the novel's end, Kit euthanises his suffering father with an overdose of morphine. The novel was a popular success, adapted as a silent film in 1927 and again in 1934. In 1984 the novel was adapted again into a television miniseries by ITV.

180 Alexander Mitscherlich (1908–1982) was a German psychologist who published the book *Das Diktat der Menschenverachtung* in 1949 and *Medizin ohne Menschlichkeit* in 1960 with Fred Mielke. Mitscherlich and Mielke had been posted to Nuremberg (together with Alice von Platen-Hallermund) to report on the trial by the German medical profession. Their aim was to report in medical journals about the extent to which medical malpractice was conducted in the Third Reich. Schmidt (2004), 7, 194.

„amoralisch". Kottenhof disagreed, said in the international literature experiments in murders condemned to death are accepted. I mentioned they were „unsympat[h]isch", but admitted one could do it, if with greatest care and simultaneously with doctors, mit der Pflicht sich selbst einzusetzen. Weltz, accepting inf.'s view, delayed the begin of the experiments. Soldiers could not be taken. Civilian volunteers could have been obtained. He did not consider the experiments dangerous, with care and proper selection ("fainting types"). Possibility to save lives rather than endanger lives, if condemned men are used. Weltz then tried to pass the buck – contacted Ruff and Romberg. They had more experience, so he showed good judgement. But Weltz had the orders from inf., in May 1941, orally. In February 1942 Ruff asked inf. whether he should be in charge instead of Weltz. Inf. agreed that he could collaborate, but reminded him of his special conditions, that is combined with self-experiments, and only on volunteers condemned to death. Rascher also should be subject, and go thru equally difficult experiments, as an example **[182]** for the others. The experiments were running then – all he heard was a prolongation of Rascher's orders beyond April 15. This request came through SS channels, Wolff.[181] The orders were prolonged, through Luftgau. Does not know whether the orders were over Weltz, or z.b.V. [zur besonderen Verfügung] of Luftgau mit Abstellung nach Dachau. Middle of May 42 Ruff came to see inf. and told him he had given orders to withdraw the low pressure chamber; told him that exp.'s were completed, and second he had the impression that Rascher did some secret personal experiments for which he was not authorised, and that he suspected that one case of death had occured. I thought Forscherehrgeiz. Chamber was withdrawn. The SS tried to get the chamber again over Staatssecretär Milch.

In the middle of June 42 Rascher came and asked – did not give details, asked did anything happen, said everything was in order. „Hab mich sehr gefreut über den Bericht." Asked for participation in experiments on shock-from exposure to cold. Demanded some condition, plus analysis. Leadership again thru an **[183]** experienced physician, who had worked in this field. That of Professor Weltz, because he had done the animal experiments on Unterkühlung. Then also Prof. Holzlöhner's name was mentioned, who had a research commission on protective suits. He was stationed at the channel coast, in rescue service. Also Singer's name came up, and Janosch in Innsbruck. „Wenn Todesfälle eintreten könnten, wäre es doch sehr wichtig diese noch unerforschten Fragen erkunden zu lassen." With the possibility of death had to be counted more than with the altitude experiments, because in practice in the Navy it was known that people even after rescue still die. Commission was arranged e [with] Holzlöhner as leader, his assistant Finler, and Rascher as collaborator. Experiments in September & October 1942. "Weltz may have taken part, I don't know. My job was at the front". "I was mostly on the way on trips, only gave general directions".

Straff und stramm, forsch und energisch, einsatz[...] und einsatzfröhlich.
Nur 3x gesehen. Das dritte Mal bei seiner Entlassung.
Gegen Forschung als Selbstzweck.

---

181 Karl Wolff (1900–1984) was a German SS functionary who served as Chief of Personal Staff Reichsführer-SS (Heinrich Himmler) and as a liaison to Hitler during the Second World War. Schmidt (2004), 292.

[184] (Win the war?) Until the beginning of the war with Russia.

(Oath of Hippocrates?) fundamental idea, physician is there to help and heal.

(5 for 500 or 5000) No, that's not "ohne werte" [sic] his job. Religious faith add to the ethical. I am a positive protestant, even during the war. Durchstehen des Lebens als Schicksalsaufgabe. Lebenserhaltung.

Is religious. Every quarter to church. Church wedding 1941. Never Nazi party member.

(Vernichtung lebensunwertigen [sic] Lebens?) Difficult question. Even in cancer one cannot predict. Decision has to be, the same applies to mental diseases. Remissions. (Minderwertig?) Abwegiger Standpunkt. Dilettantinc standpoint. Only heard internment of Jews.

30–1–47 In court. Opening statements.

31–1–47 Robert *Feix* worked with Rascher – like living in the cage with a tiger or jaguar. Rascher once posed [?] up a cancerous gland, in order to inject it into a prisoner.

Re-inter. Mrugowski.

[185] *Hippke*: *Jews*: Ungeheuer braun durchgest[...] Ablehnend zum Nationalsozialismus. Himmler hat mich herausmanouvriert. Wolff und der SS im Wege. Immer die U. Kammer verweigert. Tötungen: Ruff, shortly before May 20, 1942, said I have taken off the altitude experiments in Dachau, because the exp. [experiments] are completed, and because he had the "suspicion" that Rascher had begun to make experiments secretly, and that he had the impression that one case of death had occured: Not the certainty, otherwise would have taken other measures. I would have requested an immediate report. (Any reports from Weltz?) No. My impression was that Weltz supervised everything. Weltz never complained about Rascher; I have placed Rascher under Weltz's order. (When was Rascher ordered away from Weltz?) I received a request from Wolff to prolong Rascher's orders to Weltz, on 16–4–42, was prolonged until 15 May 1942. That was about the time Ruff came to me.

Rascher came before the 15–6–42.

[186] Holzlöhner was then added as investigator. Rascher was placed under Weltz about end of 1941 or beginning of 1942, until May 15, 1942. Weltz never complained about Rascher, especially that he did not carry out his duties correctly. First information that Rascher was not allright was when Ruff came to see him about May 20, 1942. Until then no report or complaints that R [Rascher] was not perfectly allright. The chamber was not there to get Rascher a professorship.

Die Anwälte überfallen einen mit Akten.

Hoven (personality inventory)

Evening: conversation with John Thompson, re "punishment". Catalysmic crime requires actually divine action, or action on celestial proportions – everything else inadequate. If one thinks of Gersteins's[182] affidavit, or of Himmler's speeches, one

---

182 Kurt Gerstein (1905–1945) was a member of the Hygiene Institute of the SS from June 1941.

feels that only punishment on the level of a last judgement is actually adequate. German inability to even explain the word clairty. We thought **[187]** that it would be interesting to write "conversations in Germany", because after leaving here, all this madness might again fade into unreality, where it belongs.

The appalling mysticism, the belief that dead matters or abstract things are enriched by deaths that have merged into it – that anything is better or stronger by blood spilled into it – that human bodies enrich steel, that the Luftwaffe is stronger with every dead German pilot (Goering) and the probability that Pohl could claim the V1's were stronger by the fact that successive waves of young Frenchmen of military age worked themselves to death in the cove underground factory (see Katzen-Ellenbogen's interrogation).

1–2–47 Becker-Freyseng personality inventory.

2–2–47 Report on Hippke.

3–2–47 Karl Brandt testimony: Man kann es nicht vom tatsächlichen aus betrachten Regime – Oath of Hippocrates. Made Blitzableiter out of Blitzarbeiter.

4–2–47 Testimony continued. Mac Haney really shook him to his foundations, when he began the cross examination today. (see attached news).

[188] 6–2–47 Dr. Singer from Munich. The Luftwaffe brought him the first corpse. Labelled "Odysseus." "I said what is that? They said I was supposed to do autopsies and not to ask questions."

Karl Brandt testimony continued: the first criterion for the permissibility of the freezing experiments was their importance. Judge Sebring's[183] question: Brandt's reply was a clear profession of totalitarian faith. The doctor like an officer leading his men into a fatal mission, or rather sending his men onto a mission involving certain deaths.

An 800 Fällen von Malaria in Amerika mit Todesfällen zu rechnen.

738 or 812 would indicate voluntary character; 800 suggests involuntary.

Tries to fog the issue.

There was an order that an officer did not need to carry out an order if he recognizes it is a crime.

"The State must assume the responsibility." In the KZ's the only responsible person was Himmler himself.

McHaney continued: dramatic introduction of Brandt's order to abolish medical secrecy. Hitler: "I don't care how I win the war, for me it is decisive that I win the war."

[189] 7–2–47 conversation with Steinbauer, re Ladell's letter. Cross examination Brandt continued. The Grawitz letter.

He established the Sanitary Engineering Department, developing delousing and water tanker trains for the SS. Gerstein was implicated in the killing of Jews in the camps through Zyklon B, which he partly obtained through manufacturers and commercial firms. He was captured by French authorities after the war. Gerstein wrote a report while imprisoned about the murder of Jews with Zyklon B for the French investigating authorities. He committed suicide while in custody. Ebbinghaus/Roth (2001), 92.

183 Harold Sebring (1898-1968) was a judge in the Supreme Court in Florida. He served as a judge in the Doctors' Trial. Schmidt (2004), 144.

Lammers: Beschwerden der Angehörigen, die wichtigeren Beschwerden aber von kirchlicher Seite. Immer politische aussenpolitische, kirchenpolitische Bedenken.

As to Brandt's other functions, Lammers describes them as essentially as those of a police man (right to direct whenever he chose).

Paper by:
Dill, D. B., and Forbes, W. H.: Respiratory and metabolic affects of hypothermia. Amer.J. Physiol., 142, 685–697, 1941.

Talbott, J. H., and Tillatson, K. J.: An experimental hypothemia treatment of schizophrenic patients, N. E. J. Med. (in press).

Smith, L.W., and Fey, J.: Am. J. Clin. Path., 10:1, 1940.

Instituted at Mc Leran Hosp., Waverly, Mass. 9 cases: T: 25.5, 26.7, 28, 25.6, 32.8, 35, 32.3, 30, 32.2.

Duration: 21, 29, 48, 9, 24, 23, 28, 28, 32. Times of lowest temp.: 13, 24, 24, 9, 24, 23, 28, 11, 23.

[190] The naked and lightly anesthetized patient was placed between rubberized blankets. These contained rubber coils through which a refrigerated fluid circulated.

Lammers: unpublished decree not a law.

Gutzeit: Magen-Darm, Stoffwechsel, Leberkrankheiten. Dr. Dohmen found the virus responsible for epidemic hepatitis cultures. Jaundice played a tremendous role in Germany, in civ. pop., armed forces, refugee camps, children's camps & concentration camps. Dohnmen rejected Grawitz' request. „Gewisser wissenschaftlicher Besitz". Wanted to keep control over the cultures and their use. Vaccination non-dangerous.

Leif. Stockton, Nati and Reinhardt: J.A.M.A [Journal of the American Medical Association], 1945.

Experimental paper on infectious jaundice, in conscientious objectors.

8-2-47 *Dr. Singer*: doubts the intravital volume of the air embolism. Autopsy method, with punctury of right ateries with continued action article [?], led to [...] air embolism. In favor of **[191]** this is the great amount of air, especially in the liver and in the vessels of the heart itself. The part-hypoxemia disturbances must have been purely functional since there was no time for organic changes yet. Büchner has shown that conclusively. Rascher's conclusions are therefore wrong. This is also proven by the fact that on those who were allowed to survive no lasting changes occured. Dilettantism.

Knew Rascher first as a student. Nothing unusual was noted. 1940 he became a voluntary assistant at Schwabing, did some tests with cristallization figures pleueral results, which caused him to become the laughing stock of everybody, and was more or less asked to leave:

Summer 1941 he returned, asked inf. to take part in experiments on shock from exposure to cold. Answered that he was under consulting pathologist Dr. Büchner, and that he declined. Did not see him again. Reasons for declining were "instinctive", knew he was a person tied up with the SS, which was common knowledge among students and younger staff assistants, all of whom knew that he was close to Himmler. Inf. always had an aversion to the SS.

[192] He even declined to appoint the daughter of a Sturmbannführer as a technician. It was an antipathy. (If told about Dachau, would you have gone?) No. (If invited to visit?) I would not have gone. I would have been afraid to see something that went against my [...]. I did not want to have anything to do with these people. I never even went to see Weltz's institut. The people ceased to appreciate me too. Recalls a discussion e [with] Weltz at invasion of Austria. Yelled at him the Führer won't do that. (Evil in the KZs) always antipathy. Always had a horror of the SS, since their uniform first appeared. The reality of their dealing with the Jews first repelled him.

Autopsies: Odysseus: 2 Oct. 1942
    Sch.: 21 Oct 1942
    Bl.: 21 Oct 1942
    G., 1.9 yrs 19 Oct 1942
    K 33 yrs 19 Oct 1942
    Circulatory collapse. Burn reactions are frozen reaction.

When asked about the first of the five corpses, was told that his job was to do autopsies, and not to ask questions. Had this conversation with Stabsarzt Ouken, the **[193]** Adjutant of Medical Department of Luftgau 7.

When he first refused Raschers request for collaboration, he threatened to tell it to the Reichsführer SS. Dr. Singer replied: „Tun Sie das" („Go ahead"). Rascher then came to attention, turned around and strolled out. Never heard of him again. Did not know that the 5 corpses had anything to do e [with] Rascher.

Learned in 1945 that Rascher concluded from the fact of a reduction of fluorescense that neutrons migrated out of the hypophysis during Unterkühlung. That was done at Hirth's institute. Was shown photographs by 2 naval officers (Andrews, Jaque). Major Limic arranged this interview.

10–2–47 Cross examination Gutzeit continued. Writes out questions.
    Gave report on high altitude to Mr Denny. Gutzeit: incubation period: if I find a louse in a typhus epidemic, I can safely assume that the louse has transmitted infection.
    11–2–47 Handloser on the stand. Paper completed and sent off.
    12–2–47 Worked on Singer report ("Odysseus"). Jeep approved.

[194] 13–2–47 Punzengruber, Rudolf Emanuel,
    Dr. chem., 19–2–1900, Schwerinbach, Unterkärnten.
    Sievers got original protocols. Warned Sievers of Rascher.
    At 30° insulin (10 units) raises the body temperature.
    Potassium in Hypophysis and heart. Dr. Blaha and Schneeweiss did autopsies in the „Totenkammer" (behind „block 3"). Tells of vivisection in a dysentery patient; Rascher started it. Left the guy bleeding. Ali could not do it. Then saw to the death chamber, tried to get Blaha, who was ready to come, but the men died before Blaha got around to it.

Was with Rascher from August 1942 til Sept. 43 as prisoner then til June 44 as pardee, but came only 2 or 3 times to the Station.

Blome or Gebhard came and made him work on a poison gas in 1943; they wanted one that works "partially", causing paralysis. They wanted to put a cyanide molecule into diphenylchlorexine, or an organic acid, such as chromium gas.

[195] German poison gases: TABUN, SARIN, SOMAN.[184]

Blome wanted to develop a Nerve-gas, of which several existed already at that time. Claims to have reported it.

Potassium-Sachium cyanide. Hot water of 45–47°. After 8–10' recovery/ Dilatation of the right chamber. Far more than 100 experiments. 80 of them were saved by hot baths. Remained until they were completely warm and clear, naturally ¾ hours.

Blood sugar above 180 strengt[h]es [?] danger to life.

Rascher in der Mausmühle bei Passau.

14–2–47: Testimony in the Milch[185] case.

16–22 Feb. 1947: Garmisch,[186] with the Wallaces.

23–Feb. 47: caught up on Milch trial and correspondence.

Mrs. Ruth Mc Kelway Scithers, born, Aug. 16 1901. Married to Col. George R. Scithers, born 1900. One son, aged 17 yrs, at West Point.

Husband went overseas Jan. 1945, to Germany, as executive officer 71st Div. Art. [illery].

[196] Wife stayed in Dallas, Texas. Husband came home July 1946, for 6 weeks. Found him changed. Consulted psychiatrist, Dr. Daniels in N.Y., in Nov, 1946. Saw him 3 times. Left for Europe Nov. 18, 1946, or Nov. 24; arrived Dec 4. Consulted Capt. Harris one week after arrival; saw him 4 times, for the last time 4 weeks ago; wrote Dr. Daniels, who advised to see Dr. Levi here; wired later, that Dr. Levi advised to see Dr. Leo Alexander.

Lost about 10 lbs in wt.

Sleep is disturbed by lightness of sleep, with frequent walking at night, early waking in the morning, "ever since my husband came home." Appetite is allright, "but I am not very interested."

Husband: "Strange ideas in her head." Thinks he keeps an other apartment in town. Operation (hystorectomy) in 1938. Suspects that husband has several apartments in Munich, for purposes of illicit love affairs.

---

184 For further information on the history of chemical and biological warfare, and human experiments, see Schmidt (2015).
185 Erhard Milch (1892–1972) was a German field marshal general who oversaw the development of the Luftwaffe as part of the re-armament of Germany following the First World War. He was State Secretary in the Reich Ministry of Aviation. He was in charge of all aircraft production and supply during most of the Second World War. He was tried in 1947; his trial was named the 'Milch Trial' and it was the second of the twelve Nuremberg trials. Milch was sentenced to life imprisonment, but his sentence was commuted to fifteen years of imprisonment in 1951 and he was released in 1954. See Opitz/Frewer (1999).
186 Garmisch-Partenkirchen, a Bavarian ski resort town.

Wife: "Someone said, casting off at a party, that feeding and billetting Germans was the lowest sort of business everyone thought of George." "A small boy casting off as [197] [...] at each other." "Some of it hooks off with things I love dearest."

Merely tumors of uterus was removed, not entire uterus. Lost menstruation 3 months ago. Regularly every 28 days until then.

"From the remark she made I thought she wanted me to think that she was George's mistress."

Dx.: PN, react.depn, with paranoid features

? Psychosis, paranoid type, involutional. Munich Psychiatrist: Capt. Wm. Harris, 98th General Hospital, APO 407A, Munich. One night woke up, feared she had gonorrhea or cancer of the womb, or might be pregnant.

Pulse 72 BP 120/70

Skin dry, with tissue paper winkling at [...] aspects of legs.

Absent ankle jerks.

Dx's Psychosis, alcoholic, paranoid.

24–2–47 Rostock. Preparation of glossry (Schiller) and of seawater questionnaire.

25–2–47 Completion of seawater questionnaire.

26–2–47 Beiglböck. NP appraisals: the counters, her illegitimate child, blandly admitted, as proof of NS indoctrination. The German "confessional" minister as proof for Schröder. Schröder himself. Interview by Miss Dubrow, clear formulation of propesterous manoevers of [198] defence: comparison with bank robber, treatise on money. Argument against work. She promised to submit manuscript.

27–2–47 The incident with the prowler ("you are on the list"), at 5.49 AM. Miss Shelley's Hitler book, conversation with Judge Bayle re Thompson.

The Dutch report: (Auschwitz) Michel J. M. Steyns, M.D., aged 55, 14 Malibaan, Utrecht.

Dr. Eliazar de Wind, M.D., 128 Rijusburgenwey, Leyden. (author of a book). (Auschwitz)

Johannes Drost, M. D., 21 Kralingssche plasloow, (born 28 March 1905), Rotterdam. (Dachau).

E. de Wind, Medical Practioner at Doorn. Report of Gynaecological experiments in Auschwitz. – Evening: Pokorny, Romberg.

28–2–47 Mrs Scithers: Looks & feels better, has been abstinent. Still has delusions of jealousy.

Col. George R.S., 3rd Army Liason Office, APO 407A, Munich. Office: Possartstr. 9 [Bogenhausen]. Tel. 2979 or 2460

Home: Hofbrunnstrasse 11. Tel.: Civ. 794727 (München-Solln).

Husband: she claimed he mentioned the name Rose in his sleep. She also heard [199] him say "Katuck" in his sleep; a girl named Katy, whom her friends call Katusch.

1 March 47: Karl Brandt. His mistress: Sister Elisabeth Joerdens.

SS: "To spill blood in order to know oneself, on every battle field."

Goering said the German airforce became stronger with every pilot killed. *Thanatolotry*.

March 4–7: Gebhardt testimony
March 9: Gebhardt-Speer problem, Hoven-like behaviour.
March 10: Conversation with Dr. von Bayer-Pokorny [...] Thanatolotry, "Oblique plans."
March 11: Continuation direct exam. Fischer, Memo to Mr. Hardy.
Mrs. Scithers: Better, is able to put her thoughts re husband out of her mind.
Referring Dr.: Dr. George Eaton Daniels, 129 East 69th–Street, New York City.

Nutrition problem in KZ, memo to Mr. Hart, suggestion for pictorial demonstration with the aid of Mrs Robbins.

Thanatolotry – the idolatrous (fiendish) delight in death.[187]

[200] 13-3-47 Arrived Rotterdam. Prof. Z. Sneller:[188] Evidence is in Amsterdam and the Hague.

J.C. Dosterewyk. Donkerslootstraat 41 A. Rotterdam-Holland.

Mr. Gerrit Hendrik Nales. (Natzweiler)

Brandt/Schröder: Gas experiments: small ampoules of varying sizes. Came from University Strassburg: „Wehrtechnisches Laboratorium der Deutschen Luftwaffe." (Prof. Haagen). Hoher Besuch, langer hagerer Mann, speziell für Fleckfieberproben interniert. Kam 2x. Could recognize him. Never heard the name Schroeder. He was in Luftwaffe Uniform. Kleiner Degen. regular Army Medical Officer. Wore white coat in the ward. Karl Brandt was there too, but did not see him. Nobody was allowed to leave the block. But heard the name twice, summer 1943, and early summer 1944. Once high visit of 7 members came, some times (summer 1943 and summer 1944).

---

187 Here Alexander explores a further elaboration of his concept of 'Thanatology'; placing it within the theological frame of idolatry. For Alexander, at this date, his thoughts seem to be moving away from understanding the actions of the Nazi doctors as a "science of death" – thanatology – towards an idolatrous relationship with death; that death had taken on metaphysical proportions for the doctors as a thing to be worshipped and pursued for its own sake. His thought on the theological and metaphysical relationship towards death appears to show that he was exploring the idea that these doctors had become part of a death cult; that their actions went beyond any scientific rationale and could thus be better described as "Thanatolotry". This may have been based on an apprehension about the close etymological link to reason and truth (*logos*) within "Thanatology" and was an attempt to further the actions of the doctors away from any argument that they had acted in the interests of medical science.

188 Zeger Willem Sneller (1882-1950) was a Dutch economic historian at the Handels-Hoogeschool in Rotterdam, Erasmus University of Rotterdam. Following the end of the war, he was part of the directorate of the National Institute for War Documentation (*Rijksinstituut voor Oorlogsdocumentatie*). In 2002 the institute was renamed as the NIOD Institute for War, Holocaust, and Genocide Studies (*NIOD Instituut voor Oorlogs-, Holocaust- en Genocidestudies*).

Fig. 17: Fritz Fischer, defendant at the Nuremberg Doctors' Trial being cross-examined. Nuremberg, Germany, 1946/47 (Source: NARA).

[201] In Dachau from Sept. 6, 1944 til liberation. Brandt visited Dachau that winter. Nurses got orders to clear Revier for Karl Brandt's visit, but he did not come through; saw only 1st élite barrack, accompanied by SS Hauptsturmführer Hintermeyer.[189] He went thru the camp accompanied by the elite.

Has a complete record of all people killed, in two books (2500 people).

Would be an excellent witness. (Average earnings 65 Gulden per week).

Saw 80 Nacht u. Nebel prisoners murdered (English and French parachutists, young men and women).

Numerous nameless gypsies, pulled out of the Wehrmacht, still in uniform, used for experiments. „Karl Brandt sah wie ein Gott aus. (Die sahen wie Götter aus) mehr Uniform als Seele. Seelen haben die nie gehabt, die Deutschen."

Has heard that Gebhardt and Blome visited the camp, but does not remember particulars.

„Der Gebhardt gehörte zum Stab von Himmler. Hat das Lager 2x besucht. War in Dachau, about the turn 1944/45. Was introduced [to] prisoners near the entrance, handpicked well fed one of [202] all categories. Did not enter the camp proper.

Is decorator in a clothing store. Address: 87a Slagekstraat, Rotterdam.

Experimented killings marked with V.

Rotblonde Assistentin mit Hakennase, Elsässerin; (Frll. Schmidt?); saw her 100–150x; never knew a male nurse named Hirtz. Frl. Schmidt has sich immer gefreut, wenn was Gemeines vorging, nicht das mindeste Mitgefühl; unfreundlich; hat sich gefreut, „typisch deutsch", Leute nicht für die Giftgasversuche zu sehen. Haagen ist ein „ganz gemeines Luder", saw him often.

Ampoules came in coal dust in plain tin containers.

Might recognise Haagen's quest, Rose. Remembers the "skeleton collection." Photographed, came from Auschwitz.

Book kept according to Nationalities, date of birth and month of death.

„Sie haben ein gutes Gesicht u. ein Böses; das Gute hat nach dem Roten Kreuz geguckt, u. das Schlechte war die Wirklichkeit, ihre Seele, wie sie wirklich waren."

[203] SAW (Sonderabteilung Wehrmacht), § 175, a special book on Russians and Poles.

Women were shot before evacuation of Natzweiler, shot into the neck by officers.

Br.- [brother] in law of Mr Dosterewyk: Mr. Henrik de Zeeuw, Beyerlandschelagaan 174 B, Rotterdam – (Zuid),

Wife: Edith (Klaber), father was Felix Klaber of Vienna, mother Relly Weissmann. Uncle: Dr. Isidor Klaber, now in Tel Aviv.

14–3–47 Dr. Drost: 7th–9: Tel. 25035. 12'clock Parkhotel Westersingel [Rotterdam]

---

[189] Fritz Hintermayer (1911-1946) was the camp doctor at Dachau from 1944 until the liberation of the camp. He participated in the malaria experiments conducted by Schilling. During the Dachau concentration camp trial in 1946, it transpired that Hintermayer had been involved in the execution of 90 Russian prisoners of war and had murdered two pregnant Russian women by lethal injection. He sentenced to death as a result of the trial and hanged in April 1946. Hipp (2020), 69.

Met Phyllis at the boat, the Noordam. Bert and Lene. Wonderful to see her again. To Utrechte Bert and Leny. Steffen and Irene.

15–3–47 Walk thru Utrecht. History of underground. Afternoon: drove to Nieuw Port on the Dyke; visited Dr. Wim van Straaten; who had been hiding in a room for 2 ½ years – Dr. Jan Cornelis.

[204] 16–3–47: To Amsterdam. Rijks-Museum. Tea with Prof. Dr. *Heringer* and Dr. Brutel de la Rivère, the leader of the Dutch Medical Resistance. History of Dutch Medical Resistance.

17–3–47: To Amsterdam, U.S. Consul. Visited Jewish District: Portuguese Jewish Synagogue, preserved through the help of monument protection. The Thornes. The Shammes hid for 1 ½ yrs under a roof; his son jumped off a train to Auschwitz. His story of the Aharamos [?], Prayer for the Queen in Spanish. Dr. Sillevis-Smit, the Professor of Neurology. Dr. Cornels came and brought manuscripts.

18–3–47 To Amsterdam, obtained permit. Then to the Hague, e [with] Lene. Rijkstafel. Peare Palace, Parliament, Queen's white house. Home by way of Leiden University, City Hall – pure renaissance. Tea at delightful baroque teashop across the way. Return, talked of old days with Leny.

19–3–47 Shopping tour, bought silver keepsakes and presents for Abe, etc.

$2–2.^{45}$: Lecture on: "The social-psychological structure of the SS", at the Medical School of the Rijks University of Utrecht, at the [205] invitation of Prof. Sillevis-Smitt (Maliesingle 59, Utrecht), the neurologist, who invited me to give this as a clinic at the University Hospital. Evening: Bert's father (Mr. Steffen Hulst, his brother-in law, Mr. Christian Singelenberg, and his wife, Anne.) Later: Dr. Johannes Zoon & wife, Mr. Dirk Boschloo and wife (smiles) at the Jaarbeurs Restaurant.

20–3–47 Shopping for tiles and toys, and for ticket. Found that central train goes on 22–3. Visit by a student who had been at the lecture: Mr. Franz G. Wyslicks, C.V. Dissel Straat 31, Breda, Netherlands. He was formerly e [with] JAWCB 7th Army (28–2–45 – 11–11–45), Sgt. Dutch Army, attached; ASN 102800, Interpreter, Research Analyst. Investigated the Gardelegen Crime (burning & machine gunning of 1200 KZ prisoners, on 14 April 1945).[190]

Met, after the lecture, Dr. Bernhard Pfältzer, who had been an inmate at Buchenwald, Vright, Mühlheim, Neu-Brandenburg, Ravensbrück, 31–1–41 til 6–6–45. Is convinced that Gernan civilians knew all about atrocities; heard and saw following poem in *March 1941*: „Gott im Himmel, mach mich blind, Damit ich alles prächtig find; GiH [Gott im Himmel] mach mich taub, damit ich immer alles glaub; GiH mach mich stumm, daß ich nicht in [nach] Dachau kumm; GiH mach mich blind, stumm, taub zugleich, Damit ich pass ins dritte Reich."

---

190 Members of the German local population – the Volkssturm (the national militia established by Nazi Germany), Hitler Youth, and other civilians – forced over 1,000 slave labourers who had been evacuated from Mittelbau-Dora and Hannover-Stöcken concentration camps into a barn near the town of Gardelegen in northern Germany. The barn was then set on fire, and most of the prisoners burned alive or were shot while trying to escape. The massacre occured after an order came from Gerhard Thiele to liquidate the prisoners who had newly arrived in the town. Gerhard Thiele was never brought to justice for his actions. Blatman (2011), 293–366.

[206] Dr. Michel Jean Emile Marie Steijns, 14 Maletaan, Utrecht. (200200).

Arrested 13 Juliet 1942, hostage; Haaren, Vught, Sachsenhausen Sept 44, Oranienburg (11 Sept.44 – 22Nov.) (Heinkel), Auschwitz (23 Nov.1944 – 16 Jan. 1945), then Mauthausen (28 Jan. 45 – 28 April 45).

The German people knew what was going on in KZ's, because many free laborers worked there.

Day and night the furnaces burnt, always this terrible odor.

Pregnant women were allowed to rest to deliver, but killed with their child the next day.

Movies, theater, jazzband and brothel.

Experiments by Gobel [Goebel] & Clauberg:[191] substance to replace lipiodol,[192] caused terrible pain, inflammation, peritonitis; 40 % mortality. Kept 150 women at a time, the dead being replaced; it [marginalia: Secret the Polichinelle] was common knowledge in the camp that they had been bought by the IG Farben as guinea pigs. Were fed better than rest of the camp. Young women from 16–30 years.

Mr Nat, v st. Merchlean 5, Zeist has seen children being thrown alive [207] into a fiery pit, specially dug for that purpose, because the gas chambers were overcrowded.

Knows a Miss Michielsen, who has been an experimented subject, and who has married since. She lives somewhere in Holland.

Dr. Walters at Vught, was decent to prisoners, closed eyes to all kinds of rescue actions, one (smuggling a condemned men out of Holland in a Red Cross Car) brought inf. into Bunker, and got Walters transferred. Walters then became a biest at his next station. Bunker attendant at Vught: "FatherXmas" who had killed hundred with his own hands, became decent after talking to prisoners one Xmas about his youth and his mother. Then got up at 2 AM, to let prisoners go to toilet, who had only 1 minute to do their business during day time.

At Auschwitz, Ukrainian doctor who worked with Gobel [Goebel], and killed hundreds. Polish doctor Wasileaski, who had killed thousands by lethal injections.

Knew that cancers were transplanted in Auschwitz, and heard the name Blome.

[208] 21-3-47 Ima Spanjaard van Esso, born 9-10-1920, in Amsterdam. [marginalia: 42646 (the triangle means that she is Jewish and should not leave the camp alive; should be gassed)] HBS 1937. Then studied music, played the flute, conservatory. After Germans came, worked for a dentist. Parents were arrested Oct 1942; Westerburg, Bergen-Belsen; exchanged with Palestine Germans in 1944

---

191 Carl Clauberg (1898–1957) was a gynecologist who conducted sterilisation experiments at Auschwitz concentration camp, who conducted sterilisation experiments at Auschwitz concentration camp from 1942 to 1944, and at Ravensbrück concentration camp in February 1945. After the war, he was sentenced to twenty-five years in prison in the Soviet Union, but returned to West Germany in 1955 due to a repatriation agreement of German prisoners. Preliminary legal proceedings took place against him in West Germany, and Clauberg died in a Kiel prison before his trial was due to begin in August 1957. Benedict/Georges (2006), 283. Ebbinghaus/Roth (2001), 83.

192 "Lipiodol", also known as ethiodized oil, is a poppyseed oil used by injection as a radio-opaque contrast that is used to outline structures in radiological investigations.

(December). Inf. hid at first, was tricked into one of the Gestapo underground railways in Belgium, arrested Nov. 1942. Imprisoned, then to Auschwitz April 1943, until evacuation 18 January 1945; to Ravensbrück, Malchow, Tauche; freed by the Americans in April 1946 [1945]. Returned Nov. 1946; husband had been in Westerburg.

Two-facedness of the Germans in musical, Haessler, camp commander, came to the cabaret, spoke gently, but then arranged public hangings in which he himself hanged the women, saying this is the nicest thing to show that "sabbateans" are being killed. And he himself went to witness gassings, after selecting the victims himself.

Inf. was assigned as a nurse to Clauberg and Goebel's[193] Block 10, under Wirtz,[194] who had a section in the same block.

Researches: Wirtz: 1) portio amputations in 300–400 women, in order to look for early signs of cancer. Operated virgins as well as married women. Asepsis was bad, wooden floor, instruments sterilised only for a few **[209]** minutes. Infections were numerous. After Wirtz had the portio, he was no longer interested in them, sent them quickly to Birkenau to work before they had recovered, where most of them died quickly. There are a few survivors. They were all Czech and Belgian Jewish girls. Does not know any survivors. These experiments ran from April 1943–April 1944. Most of the operations were made by Samuel[195] under Wirtz; he also did colposcopic photographs. He was shot in July 1944. He was a frightened man, afraid for his own life. Finished the experiments and a book, "knew too much". Wirtz did 2 operations a day, and he did 4. The partio were sent "to Berlin". Nobody knew who the party in Berlin was.

2) Twin research, in Birkenau. Separated, one worked hard on starvation rations, the other fed well. Wirtz did that too.

3) Schumann's[196] sterilisation experiments. Many died of X-rays, 14 young women; chose the youngest and the most beautiful, all Greek women. Would have almost chosen informant, but was told she was a nurse. April 1943 – began, they all developed awful burns. 2 months later ovaries were removed; 2 had died 2 weeks after the xrays. No sterilisation was used in removing the ovaries. Those who did

---

193 Johannes Goebel (1891–1952) was a chemist who was an employee of the Schering Works. He worked as an assistant to Clauberg at Auschwitz, obtaining material for Clauberg's injections associated with sterilisation. He was involved in the mass sterilisation of Jews. Weindling (2014), 151.

194 Eduard Wirths (1909–1945) was the chief SS doctor at Auschwitz between September 1942 and January 1945. Lifton (1988), 453.

195 Maximilian Samuel (1880–1943) was a German-Jewish obstetrician-gynaecologist. He was deported to Auschwitz in August 1942. The extent to which he collaborated with SS doctors in the medical experiments which took place in Block 10 at Auschwitz has been a contentious issue amongst Holocaust survivors and historians. He served as a doctor under Horst Schumann and Eduard Wirths. Samuel was murdered at Auschwitz in 1943. Siegel (2014), 454, 450.

196 Horst Schumann (1906–1983) was a doctor at Auschwitz concentration camp. He was director of the Sonnenstein 'euthanasia' institute from June 1940, and selected concentration camp inmates to be killed. In the autumn of 1942, he came to Auschwitz where he conducted medical experiments involving castration by X-Ray radiation. He was arrested by American authorities in January 1945 but was quickly released. Schumann fled to Egypt in 1951. He was arrested in Ghana in 1966. Legal proceedings started against him in 1970. He was found not fit to stand trial and released in 1972. Ebbinghaus/Roth (2001), 143.

not die from sepsis were sent to Birkenau for gassing. **[210]** Birkenau meant work without food, sleeping 8 in a bed, before gassing. Birkenau was Hell on Earth.

4) In Birkenau a Polish SS men Niemrecki gave lethal injections into the heart, likewise selecting the most beautiful girls.

5) Clauberg's and Go[e]bel's experiments. Feb. 1943, chose 6 or 8 women; in April they came to block 10, the exp. block. 500 nothing(?) 2 years. He injected various solutions into uterus and tubes, altogether 10 or 20 mixtures. Started with Jodipin (brown) then a white mess (probably barium). The solution was sterilising, painful; 10 died immediately and directly from it. After being "finished", the women were sent to Birkenau (after injecting them twice, he could see whether the injection had "done something"). When the experiment worked, they were kept in the block; re-injections were made every 2 or 3 months, 5 or 6 times. The first injection was brown or white; the following were done with other substances. Survivors are: Mrs. F. Koster, Minervaplein 8, Amsterdam. Xray photos were taken. The procedure was extremely painful. Inflamations followed, e [with] fever, peritonitis, illnesses of 6–8 weeks duration. Nursery care was inadequate. **[211]** The substance was supposedly sterilized, but Clauberg's "nurse", a Czech peasant woman, contaminated it due to clumsiness. Goebel was worse; his word could not be trusted; was nice to a nurse one day, sent her to Birkenau the next. Commandeered inmates to sexual intercourse. Clauberg paid for the women "to Berlin". He told them that they were his property because he had bought them. When "Berlin" wanted to send the women to the gas chambers, Clauberg said "no, they are mine." Himmler inspected twice; inf. saw him. Gebhardt may have been with him; inf. believes she remembers the name. Inspections were terrible: a bit of dust under the bed, an ill-fitting number over the arm, may send one to the gas chamber. A few months later the IG Farben paid for the women; Goebel said that; he himself was paid by the IG too. He said the IG Farben had paid several hundred Mark for every woman.

6) Münch used 50 women to test a new anti-tetanus vaccine, over their breast.

7) Münh and Weber drew large amounts of blood for unknown reasons.

8) Münch u. Weber did some unknown work on typhus.

[212] 9) A "racial" study was done under Weber; measurements were taken and 30 women were sent to Germany, presumably to a "special" hospital, actually to be made into mummies. They were Polish, Belgian and German Jewesses.

10) Pregnant women were "aborted" in the 5th to 7th month. One recent admission was in the 8th month. She was allowed to deliver. Next evening SS came took mother & child to be gassed.

11) A block was prepared for impregnation experiments under Goebel, e [with] the aid of 100 men; but that was stopped from "Berlin".

12) No mutation experiments. One woman was operated in the 5th month, and something done to the uterus; baby was removed; she was then sent to Birkenau.

He was an IG Farben tributary among the Auschwitz work shop, on a Buna plant.

Husband at present serving e [with] Dutch Army, psychologist.

Dr. Erwin Valentin was an imprisoned doctor who taught gynecology to Scharführer Bühning, and knows all about the experiments. The women's camp was in Birkenau; only the experimental block was at Auschwitz. Later there **[213]** were 5 women's blocks in Auschwitz, among the SS blocks, where 300 women were kept. Feels main motivation for experiments was to stay away from frontline service.

Address: Pausdam 3, Utrecht, Holland.

The last ½ year people were burned alive in pits; mostly Hungarian Jews, hundred thousands of them. They had no food for them. They were given flowers, coffee, were made to write a cheerful letter home, and then killed. The clothes and jewels were sent to Germany. Brought their best things with them, because they had heard how nice things were. The smell of burning nails and hair was over the camp. They came in such numbers, there were no crematoriums enough. That was in the second half of 1944. Every day 2000 were killed. The Hungarians came latest, and they were the richest. Phantastic amounts of food, jewels, clothes. they worked day & night to get all that to Germany, 60 wagons each day. They brought them for their possessions. there was no work further to do. Those who were brought in s [without] planned annhilation were treated well that last year, so they would not say it was bad; cabaret, etc. A few Italien women [214] succeeded in killing an occasional SS men; but thousands were gassed for punishment. The workers there were gassed every 2 months. To be human e [with] the Germans, means not to understand the German soul.

Nab, Jan; born 25-7-1915. Butcher. (71954)
    Arrested for killing German Army cows; to Auschwitz Sept 1941–Jan 1945.
    Transported corpses to the crematorium; later (1943) transferred to butcher's department.
    Experiments in Block 10; many had fever, many died. Every month 30–200 were killed; sometimes the whole block was gassed. Knows about artificial insemination; some Jews were caught, taken to Block 27 (spender Block), forced to masturbate, and semen collected in vials for artificial insemination. Prof. Goebel did that, e [with] a Dutch assistant Dr. Frank, and his wife; 2 dutch SS women guarded the block. Mrs. Frank was Goebel's assistant. He was accused in Belgium. Dr. & Mrs. Frank were hated a great deal.
    Wasilewski did hundreds of Abspritzungen in Block 28.
    Unterscharführer Kaduk, Klause & Hedweg [215] took the sick to gassing. They were thrown on a truck like animals, dead and alive, and then they sent on top. Were always drunk when they did that.
    In Block II people were killed by Genickschuß.
    One day went to Birkenau. Every day 6-7-8 transports of 2000 Jews each arrived, which overturned the crematorium. 100 people per car, frequently 80 dead on arrival. Women e [with] children were immediately taken to the gas chamber, s [without] registration. One could be happy if one got a small number; Jews were sometimes numbered on the penis, or got huge numbers burned in.
    Selection by Unterscharführer Kaduk ("Volksdeutscher"), who spoke prime polish, selected those who looked thin(?) for transport to the gas chamber. SS men got a day furlough for every man shot.
    Poles, Jews & Russians were treated worst. One day went to Birkenau to bring offal from the daughters house. Saw Jews digging 2 deep holes, of the size of a

house, 8 meter, or rather 15–20 meter deep, 50–60 meters, 20 : 40 or 50 meters. A transport of Hungarian children had arrived. Saw them debark: **[216]** the SS men took the chn [children]; then he heard the children shriek; people heard them shriek for kilometers; saw Haessle grab a 3 months old child from a woman and smash it on the floor. At least 40.000 chn. were killed in those pits, were not taken to the crematorium.

Once a transport of Italian Jews defended themselves to the last man; killed 6 or 7 SS men, 2 Arbeitsdienstführer. 80 or 90 butchers were in his commando; once in a while 6 or 7 were called out and shot without cause. All cruelty took place e [with] music, all National music of Europe was played. Défilé before the eviscerated corpses of 3 men who fled.

Industries: *D*eutsche *A*uto *W*erke; Union; Bauhoft (Steine, Klinker); *Buna* Aussenkommando; Strassenkommando; Stahlwerke; Schuhfabrik.

Size: 1 m 88 cm; 110 chest meas. [measurement] *Address*: Van der Merschlaan 5, Zeist.

Dr. Frankje Caroline de Leeuw-Bernard. Gerard Don Straat 23, Utrecht.

Taken to Auschwitz 26 August 1943. Had been taken on August 10 in Amsterdam.

[217] Assigned to experimental block, worked with 2 other physicians, Aline Brarde, Sheve Klein from Paris. Had the Dutch ward, take care of incidental illnesses of the experimented persons. Experiments were performed by Dr. Wirths, Prof. Samuel, Prof. Clauberg, and Dr. Goebel. Ovaries were removed by Prof. Schumann.

Himmler came twice, but not into inf.'s block.

1) *Carcinoma experiments.* Colposkopy, leukoplaky was found, some were initially positive, some negative; then piece of portio was removed and studied microscopically. Those who were "uninteresting" were killed in Birkenau.

On arrival, they asked "Frau or Fräulein", and the first 44 were taken for the experimental block. In the beginning, those who refused were sent to Birkenau. Later no refused was accepted.

Mrs. Brouco van Tyn, Dr. pharmacy, told Dr Steynes that intraperitoneal implantations of cancer were made.

2) *Sterilization experiments.* Clauberg and Goebel used a contrast fluid, which was injected into uterus and tubes, under X-ray control. Very painful. Infiltrations and inflammations were produced.

[218] July 1944 they were moved to another new barracks, with new beds, blue and pink silk covens; and the toilets in those blocks were divided. Everyone said that men would come to test sterility. But "Berlin" forbade it.

3) Rassenforschung. Wirtz selected prototypes of Dutch Jewesse.

4) Twin research; one fed well, the other underfed.

It was told that Prof. Clauberg had paid for the women in his experiments, and that therefore they did not have to go to Birkenau. Later they went just the same. Man [hat] gesagt that Clauberg for IG Farben arbeite.

5) Prof. Schumann's Xray experiments. Greek Jewesses had their ovaries irradiated; many developed ulcers; later a great number of them went to *Birkenau*; a few weeks later 10 returned, in the afternoon one or both ovaries were removed; Schumann did them all within 2 hours; they cried and prayed all afternoon. One died the next day, from peritonitis.[197] The other 9 had festering wound for months; it was terrible, done s [without] decent [219] asepsis.

Olbricht, a Pole, had orders to do autopsies as soon after death as possible; found that heart always stopped in distole, systole being due to rigor mortis. Block 28, together e [with] Dr. Steijns. Always refused experiments.

Wasilewski gave lethal injections. Poles (politicals) and Jews.

Theater, good Jazzband, Film. 6 PU + Grauen, Panic, Unruhe. Bombed Rotterdam, because the 6 PU had locked up the people of Rotterdam, bombed to free them.

Bordell: one daughter of 13 of a Vienna lawyer: ich will leben. Were told that after 6 months they would be free. Reklame-Rundgang durchs Lager. 28 girls, in well furnished rooms. Had to be examined daily, blood once a week; those infected were taken to the hospital. In pregnancies, abortions were done.

Dr. Steijn: delivered many women, who were gassed the next day. They knew it, begged for an injection. That is one of his most painful memories. Never gave one.

Intravenous injection of tubercular sputum, daily, for 1 month. A nurse did that. (Zweiren, a mass murderer, disposed of that way).

3 children in the block: Frau Dr. Seemann, [220] and Mrs. Umschweif invented a serum against typhus; were permitted to keep their hair and their children. "Ehrenhäftlinge." Worked in the bacteriologic Institute Reisko near Auschwitz. A third women from Berlin, also had a 3 yr old boy; Wirths saw the boy at the station, took her as a nurse to Block 10. "Sentimentality."

Dr. Willem Hop, Malibaan 47, Utrecht.

Imprisoned Nov. 1944 until liberation of Neuengamme; on May 2 was taken to Sweden by Swedish Red Cross, after prison ships were bombed on Lübeck Harbor. Was in Neuengamme from Jan 31 til April 20, 1945; brought to Lübeck, put in ships s [without] food and water; Red Cross tried to liberate the Dutch, Belgian and French and brought them to Sweden the day before the bombing. Next day the ships were bombed.

Does not know much about the medical experiments in Neuengamme. Heard about the "experimental blocks".

Was in an Aussenkommando near Lüneburg.

"Its their nature; only few Dutchmen [221] could do what the Germans did. I hated them since my youth; saw them as physicians in the Indies. "Prevent that they come to might again". "If you let them free, there is a new Army in one year; and a good one too." "Of course[,] there are nice Germans, I met some, but not many." "Always trouble e [with] the nurses, downstairs; upstairs never troubles." "Always commanding." "It is difficult what to do; I am happy I don't have to decide that."

---

197 Inflammation and swelling of the belly/abdomen.

Knows a Mrs. Leib-Cohen in Utrecht, who was a patient in the experimental block in Auschwitz. Was in Sweden for mild Tbc [tuberculosis]. Was injected. Was questioned regarding menstruation. Was injected e [with] sex hormones.

23–3–47 With Phyllis through Frankfurt.

24–3–47 The use of poisonous substances for the combatting of plant and animal "Schädlinge" is subject to restrictions (Verordnng der Reichsregierung, 29–1–1919. RGBl No. 31, 1919). The use of hydrocyanide and cyanide is prohibited in every form. However, this prohibition does not apply to Army and Navy, and the technical committee for combatting "Schädlinge." This was essentially reaffirmed with further exceptions applying to Ministries on 22–8–1927. There is also

[222] an order requiring addition or *stornutant,* but this order has not been found. The canister in Poland (Auschwitz) carried the legend "Achtung Vorsicht – ohne Reizstoff". Further elaboration on 30 March 1931. (RGBl. 1931).

Censorships' report on Gebhardt: Prof. Wachsmuth,[198] in a letter to Handloser, called Gebhardt *"the criminal and un-scientific* (unwissenschaftlicher) *Landsknecht."*[199]

April 4–7: Heidelberg. 7th: Opening of Rhein bridge, followed by celebration with champagne and concert by Algerian guards. Luncheon with Col. Twichell; loss of Phyllis's luggage.
    April 13th Bamberg
    April 15th: Worked on medical experimentation aspects [?]. Answer to Danish doctor's letter. Sievers submitted witnesses' name re-turning of live prisoners to Pohl team. Yesterday (April 14) attended Pohl case, after interview of witness from Auschwitz, who had brought out the first court evidence (see Pohl case, testimony of April 14th).
    April 16th Teletype from Washington!
    April 17th Interview with Blome. Nazi's merely insisted [223] the Jewish proportion-lessness.
    Apr. 18 Rose on the stand. General Clay's visit. Talk with Servatius, on "Einsatzbereitschaft", Principles, and yet unprincipled activity (Prinzipienmensch, der einfach tut, aber doch gestohlene Bilder sammelt). Unecht. According to S, all the Nazis were that way: Hitler, on the one hand, praising Sauckel[200] for his 10

---

198 Werner Wachsmuth (1900-1990) was Consulting Surgeon at the Medical Inspectorate of the German Army Berlin from 1939. After 1942, he headed a surgeon's group of the Supreme Command of the German Army. In 1946, he held a chair position at the University of Würzburg Surgical Clinic, where he remained until retirement. Ebbinghaus/Roth (2001), 149.
199 *Landsknecht* (literally: land knight): generic term for German mercenaries, particularly pikemen, active in many European armies from the late fifteenth century through to the early seventeenth century.
200 Fritz Sauckel (1894–1946) was the General Plenipotentiary for Labour Deployment from March 1942. He recruited Soviet workers on a mass scale. He was tried at the International Military Tribunal at Nuremberg in 1945 and sentenced to death. Herbert (2000), 195, 196. Lehnstaedt/Lehnstaedt (2009), 120.

children, that he wished all Nazis were that way, and then turns around telling Brandt that in these dynamic times people just have to grow out of their philistine limitation and must have outlets away from bourgeois restrictions.

April 24 Cross examination Rose. (MacHaney used submitted by me).

Witness Walter Jahn, Dresden A 21, Scariastrasse 14.

Oberheuser was Lagerschreck. A Dr. Ritter[201] performed operations in July 42, cesarean section without anesthesia; had rubber sheet over face, just one baby produced thru one asterol. Yelled for 3 minutes, then fainted from pain and [224] died in the course of operation. That was the object to be proven. Oberheuser assisted. Jewesses were used.
    Pohl personally beat him on one occassion.
    Oberheuser attended beatings regularly; there was never one case in which she called a stop. If they vomited or defecated from pain, they were forced by women guards to eat it or drink it respectively. Men did the beating. Saw her 20 x.

Colonel Leroy D. Saper. 98th Gen. Hosp. Schwabinger Krankenhaus. Friday afternoon. Tel: 2078, Munich Military.

Trip to *Austria*.
    Hans *Queck*.
    Homunculus Verlag
    Bregenz.[202]

May 6, 47/ Willy de las Heras, aged 34, Wien XIV, Pierrongasse 10. Professional photographer. 54 photos given for reproduction. Will have enlargements made of cold pictures. [225] Has an interesting collection of murders and suicides in Dachau; with […] and […] of legs of victims.
    One SS man, ran amok, killed 4 or 5 other SS men; they shot out of the bunker window. The SS then threw a brand grenade into his cell, which did not kill him; then they hanged him.
    Has all the facts with the names and the dates of birth!

Evening of May 6, 47 Visit with Mrs. Lederer. Jewish home, Seegasse 9 (Joint Distrb.)
4 May 1947: Left for Vienne. Thru Salzburg (mural with houses left great impressions); at night to Wels. Supper at Youth Club. Overnight at the Gzef.
    5 May 1947: To Emms; turned back from border for proper grey passes. 5 hours delay, our driver Matti Rumbahn got his civilian eldersome before we did. Easy entry with proper papers. How will this exit be? Arrival in Vienna at dark. Only me

---

201 Robert Ritter (1901–1951) was a German medical anthropologist at the Reich Health Office. He was a racial scientist and was chosen to lead the classification of the Gypsies. His team registered and racially assessed every Gypsy and half-Gypsy in Germany. By March 1944, the project was completed; 23,822 Gypsies were assessed in total. Weindling (2010), 322; Friedländer (2000), 249; Evans (2008), 530.
202 This address was specially marked with three lines at the left side and four at the right.

billetted at Hotel Josephstadt, of all places. Sgt. Bill Porter put up Phyllis and driver as a favor. Dr. Klingshand, will see him Wednesday.

6 May 1947: To USFA Headquarters. The old "runaround" at first, later some action. Lt. Col. Goodhart [226] called up an arranged for Rumbaler's messing facilities.

Then saw Lt. Shopinsky (for Russian liason) and Capt. Rockwell. The latter very delightful. Saw him at lunch again. Mr Mondschein (Room 19, Allianz Bldg., G2, Travel Control).

Then to see Mr. Peltibone, War Crimes Representative, 14 Schmidtgasse (the former Sanatorium Fürth), B–47037.

Then saw Mr Karl Roeder, at 8 Brahmsplatz, his home tel. A–13404. With him to see Mr de las Heras, the photographer (see p.224).

Then saw Neurological Institute, studying Physiology – all the same, but as of a cloud of dust had descended on it, shabby, down at the heels.

Supper at the Goldener Hirsch. Then to see Mrs. Lederer.

7 May 1947: To Vorbicek, found him not at home. Arived Pötzlinsdorf to Phyllis. Then visited fathers and grave. It was recently taken care of, at Lene's suggestion, via Mr Hubert Fritz. Took pictures. Then to Mr Schwarz, left message. Volksgarten e [with] Phyllis. Lunch. Brought presents to Mrs. Lederer. Then to Mr Fritz, who [227] is still an unreconstructed Nazi. Then moving visit with Mr. Schwarz. Valerie Meckauf's sad father. He managed to escape annhilation twice. Strong personality. I shall help him. Then via Demben canal, Kriegsministerium (gory, practically unchanged), visit Konzerthaus, to KZ Verband.

[Insert]: Bund der politisch Verfolgten, Landesverein Wien, ehem. politisch verfolgter Antifaschisten (KZ-Verband, Häftlingsverband, Verband der Abstammungsverfolgten) Wien III, Lothringerstrasse 14, tel. U 16–4–56; Wilhelm *Wichtl* (Amtsrichter im Innenministerium) A–18540, Klappe 108, 1Teinfaltstraße 4 (iV).

[228] 8 May 1945 [1947] sent Dr. Paul Reisinger. In the evening conference with Dr. Klinghand. Joseph Vorbicek, aged 35 yrs. (5 yrs impris.) Assistant nurse on Dr. Beiglböck's experimental ward. After the incident with the wet cleaning rag, when get's stated how they got the water, Dr B threatened V. that if it happened again, he would take V. as a "guinea pig" (Versuchkaninchen). The patients became very weak, immediately after the exp. they were discharged. During the exp. one man was transfered to the typhus block. After the experiment the guniea pigs were immediately transferred to the overcrowded labor blocks, some to Aussenkommando. The promise of a period of recuperation was not kept. He lost contact with them immediately. 3 or 4 months later he met one in the camp, a gypsy from Munich; and he said that one died, he even said the name, but V. forgot it. They were sent to Aussenkommandos, so that if they died, nobody would know it. They were members of all nations; Czechs, Austrians, Germans, Hungarians, Poles. No Jews. They had volunteered at Ausschwitz for a "good Kommando"; but they were not told what commando, they were ashamed after they found it [229] was experiments, but they were forced, and if they showed signs of rebellion, were threatened. "It is in your interest to refuse because if everything goes well, you get a great commando". The alternative was obvious. He also threatened informant

sharply, inf. knew that he meant it. One Czech gypsy was a barber and informant became friendly with him; had written down his address.

Then: to parents grave, flowers on VE [Victory in Europe] day. To Klinghand, who gave lead for more witnesses.

Alfred Kollmann, aged 50 yrs. Wien XIX (Zentrale: A32–0–57 (8–10, 1–3) Ludwig Schmidt, Wien I, Felix Mottlstraße 22, Salzgries 6: tel. U 22–4–46 (1–5) Home tel. A 16–2–24 (afterwards) He will undertake the mission to the Burgenland for us. Buch: Meter für Meter, by Haydn.

To Bank; got a resounding no; moral bankruptcy. To Kultus generale, there the sad news of Uncle Gustav's transport to Poland, and the Thiemann's transport to Minsk.

Then to University; Cafe Sibattutos; in the evening opera (Barbier [von Sevilla]), then Hotel […].

[230] 9 May 47: Vorbicek Affidavit. Then to Ministerialrat Dr. Franz Sobek, Schlösselgassel, tel. 252552, Bundeskanzleramt, Bullhausplatz U24–5–20. Contacted Mr Otto Wessely, KZ–Vertand, Wien I, Stubenring 20, (R 27–2–65) or R 23–2–27. He is investigating.

Feels that Punzengruber was objectionable and "unheimlich".

Would like material on Capo Josef Haydn. Stöhr, Heinrich würde ich Bezeichnung eines Heiligen geben.

Vienna War Crimes: B 47–0–37 (Seilern, Teresita).

Mr Robert W. Mapes. Judge Advocate Section. War Crimes Branch. XPO 777 US Army.

B'in law: August Gstettenbauer, 24 Geymüllergasse, Wien XVIII.

Lt. W. Shoopinsky, Capt. A. Rockwell, Liaison Section.

[231] In the evening talk with Mr Wessely: Excellent suggestion:
Which gypsies died in Dachau and when? Aussenkommandos were numbered in the Dachau list. Call: International Information Office, (13b) Dachau, Schleissheimer Straße 90.

Wessely war im Arbeitseinsatz, früher Kapo der Kommandantenvereinigung. Saw letter by Piodrowski: "vom Freiwilligenprinzip will ich absehen, weil es die Häftlinge mir verderben würde".

Evening: went to visit the Horst's: Mrs Robert Horst, 9 Dreihufeisengasse, Vienna VI, and their daughter Erika, relatives of the Hirschs. Appalling lack of understanding of the real situation.

10 May 47: To get authorized affidavit. Then Natural Hist. Museum, Px, USFA;[203] Russian clearance held up. After lunch Skodagasse 15; before lunch conference with Mr Röder, who re-urges Queck as a witness. Mrs Feketh Oliver thru Prater. Back to USFA. Still no Russian clearence. Supper, then to Kohlendey and Leopoldsberg.

[232] 11 May 47 Breakfast at RC Club, Chem-Galles [?]. Then to USFA, still no Russian clearance. Then to Belvedere; the incident with the two armed Russian soldiers. Then to central Friedhof, found grandfather's and grandmother's grave unchanged. Cleared the shrubs; laid down flowers; Phyllis planted begonius. After lunch to Policlinic, saw father's bust. Mr Fischer.

Then to Schonbrunn castle. In the evening ballet at the opera (Theater a.d. Wien); this we'end [weekend] as well in Vienna, and the peasant wedding. Superb performance, especially of Miss Julia, as Anne, with the most stressing scene at the Wine harvest festival dance. Thus change the times in Vienna, and to whom did it any good?

12 May 1947 The hunt for witnesses resumed. Kollmen has something from his weekend trip to the Burgenland; Wessely is to start this afternoon.
    To university, after Lebensdorfer. Not in lists.
    UNNRA Jewish Camp.
    Met English director, and doctor,

[233] Dr. [?] Georg Kollmann, Rothschildhospital, Vienna.
Mr. Fred Sillett, Director,
UNRRa[204] [sic] Team 350, Vienna.

    Then to UNRRA camp mit [art.] [?]
Alsenbach camp (AJDC[205] camp).
Mrs. Linden, Mr. Rosenzweig (23 Alsenbachstrasse).
Mr. Kollmann:
    Dr. von Papelka, Wärter im Revier.
    Bundesministerium für Inneres,
    Department Teinfaltstraße
    Already released before summer 1944.
    Burgenland: Die Zigeuner vom Burgenland sind in Wien, in Floridsdorf.[206]

    Olah, [Insertion:] B 39–5–90, Löwel [deleted: straße] bastei 18, Generalsekretariat,

Skrtek [?] (Socialdemokratische Partei)
A–13–5–60, Klappe 13

203 USFA: United States Forces in Austria, in Allied-occupied Austria, 1945–1955.
204 United Nations Relief and Rehabilitation Administration.
205 American Joint Distribution Committee.
206 21st district of Vienna, located in the northern part of the city and comprising seven formerly independent communities.

Book: Greiner, das Ende des Hitlermythos[207]

Advice: Inserat in allen Zeitungen
[inserted with lead pencil:] Olah Russ.[ian] Pris.[oner of] War
Wessely: Lebersdorfer [Lebensdorfer?], Josef, Medizinstudent,
Geb. 2. VII. 1912, in St. Valentin, O[ber]-Österreich
Wien IX. [Bezirk], Strudelhofgasse [Strudlhofstiege?] 14, Tür 12, bei Frau Alice Beck
   19[.] April 1941 verhaftet, 5. Juni 1941 Dachau. Keine Spur.

[234] Telephone: Mr Franz Olah, Schotterfeltgasse 21, B 39–5–90.
   Anfang 1944 auf Hallenstelten [?] bei Augsburg, dann Dorne (Strafweise [?], hat Versuchsstation Münstergraben [?] [genannt]).
   Will search, gave new lead: Dr Franz Buchta, Alpine Montangesellschaft; B 29–5–20.

Back to War Crimes, left instructions re contact with Wessely.
   No Russian clearance.
   Back to Wessely: 44 gypsies. Collected names of members of KZ organizations. Will contact Buchta and Skritek. Found one tribe mother.
   Mr. Rosner from Dachau worked with Wessely. Also Mr Kirschbaumer.

Back to Wessely after supper, e [with] 5 gallons of gas. Found there: Wessely, Pillwein, Vorbicek and Gstettenbauer. Pillwein stated that he had a bad concsience about the affidavit he had signed for Steinbauer, that he had to fight with Steinbauer about every point, but that Steinbauer succeeded against his will to talk him in to it. After all, he had not seen the birth certificates, so he could not well say there were foreigners, although [235] he had thought there were Czechs, Poles and Hungarians among the experimental persons. Also[,] Steinbauer had insisted that 3 Dachau gypsies were added to the group, although he had known of only 2; but Steinbauer convinced him. Still, he felt badly about having signed it. He would like to make a supplement to it. In the meantime, 3 names were recalled (of gypsies): Teubmann, Herzberger and Papei. Wessely seems to be alright.
   To Döbling to see Kollmann. (presents) Clock "collector?" Talk with Kirschbaumer from the Buchenwald team: a witness against Hoven may be Dr Roman Hadelmeyer (In 1926 HJ, friend of Horst Wessel), Wien XIX, Kobenzlstrasse 54 (Bunker Kalfactor unter Sommer).
   Pillwein also admitted that patients were sent to their regular blocks immediately (one to 2 days) after termination of the experiments; "Schonung" up to 8 or 10 days was recommended there, in some case no "Schonung" at all was recommended. Dr Steinbauer did not want anything about the weightloss said in the affidavit, although that was severe. 1 lb per day, which even in the Schäfer-starvation group amounted to a lot; they were carried much longer. Pillwein very much on the defensive, said after all that was something [236] many comrades had done of their own free will during protest actions.

---

207 Josef Greiner (1947): *Das Ende des Hitler-Mythos*, mit 8 Bildern. Amalthea-Verlag, Zürich, Leipzig, Wien. 342 pages

13 May 1947 No Russ. clearance, so by way of Linz to Mösterberg [Österberg] in the Tauern by way of the Pyhn pass [Pyhrnpass].
14 May 1947 To Klagenfurt. Reported to Major R.R. Cooke, M.C. JAG[208] Branch, War Crimes Section, BTA[209] Klagenfurt (BTA 198).

Mr Josef Tschofenig, aged 34, 23 Miesstalerstraße, Klagenfurt. Klagenfurt 1928 (Landtag member, Landtag and party office) Affidavit. Further investigation: Josef Pirker, Secretär, KZ-Verband, Klagenfurt, Sponheimerstrasse. Tel. 1217.

In the blockstreet between 3 and 5 in the revier, in the back, near the wall in the little garden lots, 10 or 15 meter away from the end of the block, 2 bottles are buried ½ metter deep, with names and dates of people killed by Rascher. Poles buried it, and Russians; Tschofenig heard about it.

[237] 15 May 1947 To Lienz, Gerl had gone to Vienna.
16 May 1947 Back to Nuremberg. Party (with gypsies); an excellent success, apart for Phyllis' attitude about it.
17 May 1947 Interview with Dr Karl Tauböck. Worked for I.G. [Farben] was given assignment to prepare Caladium seguinum[210] for experiments in human beings in the Fall of 1942 (on 2 November), by Dr Müller-Conradi, who was contacted by "Forschungsinstitut Grunewald", an SS Front organization.
Was also given "Anabasin" to test (extract of the plant anabasis aphylla), toward the end of 1943. Did do nothing about either, prepared invisible inkes for Himmler instead.
Pharmakologist: Prof. Laves, Erlangen, Pharmakologisches Institut, Maximilian[s]platz, 2660.
Zitrullin, an amino acid-against epilepsy, was given in tablets of 1 g each, 3 t.i.d. [times a day]. Was initiated by Gustav Klein, formerly Molisch's successor in Vienna, who went to work for IG Farben in Oppen. He was transferred because of the fraudulent failure of the Kaminer-reaction (Freund-Kaminer-reaction).
Was with IG from 1.1.30 to 31.12.45.

[238] *Ultraschall* to influence mood. In Berlin.
Physiker Fuchs (Major work in Gmünden, Austria, Intelligence section).
Dipl. Ing. Otto Paul Fuchs, Kitzbühl, Tirol. Landhaus Seerose. Tel. 167, Austria.
Back: Reko, Magische Gifte. Stuttgart, 1936.
Aphrodiziacre.
Haagen: *Gelbfieberimpfstoff.* Vaccine production. Immunität by mouse protection test. Order from the Navy, taken over by Luftwaffe. Similar tests also in other diseases.
Gelbsucht. Collected patients material. Meeting: Büchner, Kalk and others were present. No experiments in human beings.

208 JAG: The Judge Advocate General's Office at the War Office.
209 BTA: HQ British Troops Austria.
210 Caladium seguinum, English Dieffenbachia seguine etc. The plant is used as remedy in homeopathy.

Typhus: in Robert Koch Institute prepared vaccines. Had antitoxic, but not anti-infectious affect. Therefore[,] attempted to produce vaccine from medified or attenuated virus. 1943 started vaccinating with it. March 1944 typhus epidemic broke out in Natzweiler; also[,] in Merkirch and Wesseling, in Neckar-Eck, Neckar-Gernech, Kochem a.d. Mosel and others.

[239] Came from Ausschwitz, Buchenwald & Dachau. Vaccinated 100 people. No influence on selection. Rejected them because of poor physical condition. Then inoculated another 100, who had more severe reaction than expected. After 4 weeks gave them living virus, which, however, was also attenuated, by scarisfication. None died. Fieber, Kopfschmerzen, unpleasant, but no other after-effects.

Impfstoff – getrocknet
Teststoff – ungetrocknet
Virus bred in egg jolg sac.
Getrocknet: zur besseren Conservierung.
Ungetrocknet: also to get a more definite reaction.
No deaths: "Die hätten wir ja vermisst, die beiden Leute!"

20 May 1947
Dr. Tauböck: Liebe im Orient, Anaugarauga, die Bühne des Liebesgottes, edited by Dr. Ferdinand Leiter und Dr. Hans H. Hal, with introduction by H.H. Ewers and Dr. Magnus Hirschfeld, Verlag für Sexualwissenschaft Schneider & und Co., Leipzig und Wien, 1929.

Citrullin, and Citrullin vulgers (Wassermelone) für epilepsy.
Mimosa, the same in tea.

[240] Mr Mapes: Gerl was found. TWX requesting Albert Gerl as a witness.

Prof. Forst In Munich, Pharmacologist. Of 90 Pharmacologists in Germany, about all were with the SS.

Dr. phil. Karl Tauboeck, Wien V, 55, Schoenbrunnenstraße 36, Tür 14, at present: Rückert Strasse 21, Nürnberg.

Office of Military Government for Germany (US), Field Information Agency, Technical, Pucher/g2, Mail Address, Industry Branch, 7748 FIAT,[211] EUCOM,[212] Frankfurt, APO 757, US Army. Dr. R. Pucher. Coordinator, Pharmaceutical, Medical – and Food Unit FIAT (US).

[241] Most interesting Report, War Crimes Group, US FET,[213] vol. 191–195, File No.12-2847.
1) Letter by Rascher to Pfannenstiel, 18–11–43, implicating Blome as collaborator (800)
2) Formulation of plans (610)

---

211 FIAT: Field Information Agencies Technical, Office of the Military Government for Germany.
212 EUCOM: European Command.
213 USFET: United States Forces European Theatre.

3) Participants at Nuremberg meeting, includg. Büchner (113)
4) Letter by Sievers to Wüst.
5) Most interesting letter by Rascher to a "Herr Professor" (dated 8 June 1939), in which he relates accusations of communism made in Febr. 1938, from which he had been cleared by Himmler himself, and because of which Geheimrat Borst had forbidden him to enter his institute. (489–2). States that he had known Dr. Hirner (who sided with his accusers) on May 22, the Reichführer letter of 19 May 1939.
6) Letter by Nini to Sievers, of 1–9–39: "If there should be war, it can't take very long" (457).
7) Rascher to Himmler, on 2 May 1939, offering to make cristallographic studies on human blood, would like to begin with serial examinations at the KZ as soon as he gets clearance (216).

[242] 8) Letter to Romberg. Film given to Oberst Vorwald, but took it back again.

23–6–1947 Ohlendorf, E.A. Otto, 40 yrs. Gruppenführer: Einsatzgruppe: "die waren entsetzt." Den menschlichen Jammer sowohl der zu exekutierenden, als auch der exekutierenden [sic].
31: studied Fascism, because antifascist. National socialist since 1925.
1933: Referendar am Amtsgericht und Landgericht, Institut für Weltwirtschaft Kiel. Eingesperrt [?] 1935. Wirtschaftshochschule Berlin. 1936 Wirtschaftsreferent im SD, unter Prof. Jessen. "Politisch angestossen". Sprechverbot. Kritisch darstellen und sie den Führungsorganen zuzuleiten. 1937 Differenzen mit Himmler. 1938 "hauptamtlich" ausgeschieden aus SD, Geschäftsführer der Reichsgruppe Handel. 1939 Differenzen mit Heydrich's Gestapo, RSHA gegründet. Reorganisationsplan. Amt 3, Inland, SD. Auf einer Reise nach Polen, Himmler kritisierte ihn, nach Minderheitsstatut-Vorlage (October 1939). Einzelne Willkürmassnahmen, Krystalltag [Kristallnacht, Novemberpogrome] 1938, dagegen. Reichsführer verlangte Ausscheiden, Heydrich hat es nicht genehmigt. 1936 höher into SS als Hauptsturmführer. 1939 Obersturmbannführer. SD, begleitete Reichsführer als Heydrich's Stellvertreter: 1940 allgemeine Spannungen. Standartenführer.

[243] 1940/41 Höhepunkt; nach Hess's Flucht. Bormann ließ Sitzung bei Heydrich abhalten, gegen Anthroposophen. Für die Organisation eingesetzt. Bormann verlangte Entfernung aus Berlin, mit Heydrich. wollte ihn aus der Reichsgruppe Handel des Wirtschaftsministerium's herausbringen. Heydrich gab ihm Einsatzgruppe, bat ihn 2x, ihm das nicht zu geben, befohlen June 1941. Standartenführer. In Russland befördert, wegen volksdeutscher Arbeit in Treuindustrien. Oberführer. Im Einsatz bis Weihnachten 1941; aus Amt entfernt, zurück zu Einsatz, Sah Heydrich März 1942 in Prag. Nach dem Fall Heydrich's. Himmler schlug andere Politik ein, übernahm das Hauptamt selbst. Juni 1942 nach Berlin zurückbefohlen. Von da an in Berlin; wenn er sich meldete, Brigadeführer. Verlangte wieder daß er aus dem Amt Handel ausscheidet. Sept 42 – Oct 43 Brigadeführer und Generalmajor der Polizei. Differenzen über Ostpolitik, SD Inland. 1943 wurde Ministerialdirektor im Wirtschaftsministerium. Gruppenführer Nov. 1944.

1941 Gestapo Untersuchung gegen ihn geführt. 1934 im Zusammenhang mit schwarzer Front verhaftet.

[244] 24–6–47 Karl F.O. Wolff, Obergruppenführer und General der Waffen-SS. entered Oct. 31, SS man, born 13 May 1900, Darmstadt. Abitur, 1917. Fahnenjunker, Lt. Hessische Leibgarde, 1918. Aktiv until May 1920. Banklehrling, Bankbeamter Sek, Bertelmann in FfM bis 1922; kaufmänn. Angestellter Zellstoff 1923/24, Deutsche Bank, Annoncenexpedition Wal[th]er [von] Dan[c]kelmann, 1925–33 Inhaber der Annoncenexpedition Karl Wolff von Roemheld (maiden name of wife). 1933, Machtübernahme, Adjutant to von Epp, rellieved May 1933, and an Adjutant to Himmler. 1933–36 Adjutant and Chef Adjutant to Himmler, 1936 Hauptamtschef des persönlichen Stabes RFSS,[214] 1–9–39 – 18–2–43 Verbindungsoffizier für die Waffen-SS in Führer-Hq. Nebenher an kriegsbedingter Not umfang [?] die Geschäfte des RFSS weiter geführt. 18–2–43 Nierenstein operation. Kuren in Karlsbad und Gastein. Führerreserve, 9–9–43 als Höchster SS und Polizeiführer in Italien bis Kriegsende. Ab 26–7–44 zusätzlich Militärbefehlshaber in Italien. Mitte Sept. 43 bis Kriegsende Sonderbeamter des Duce in polizeilichen Angelegenheiten.

[245] Globocnik: Gauleiter von Wien, Standartenführer allg. SS failure, disappearred them, because a scruple SS man; was broken because he had troubles with the old fighters of the Ostmarck, then was made SS and police leader of Lublin; he was something of a bear. Hatte nicht die Qualitäten für einen Gauleiter. Wolff got him in Oct. 1943 in the four provinces about Triest, with the rank of Gruppenführer und Generalleutnant der Polizei. Sehr fleissig, tatkräftig, zu viel selbst machen wollte, mangels solider Entwicklungszwischenstufe von SS Untersturmführer zu General der Polizei. Polenfeldzug als SS man or Unterscharführer, wurde Untersturmführer. Dann grosser Sprung zum SS und Polizeiführer für eine ganze Provinz, Generalmajor der Polizei (SS Brigadeführer). Alter Kämpfer, der in Wöllensdorf gesessen hat, durch Intrigieren gestürzt, dem man eine Rehabilitierungschance geben wollte.

Ohlendorf: immer ein besonders anständiger Mann, Idealist, nach Auspruch des Reichsführers "klagend durch die Gegend lief', als einziger den Gral in seinen Händen unbeschmutzt trug. Gemüt eher weich, was RF beanstandete und [...] geändert haben wollte. Tadellose Vergangenheit, ohne dunklen Punkt, so daß man ihn nicht unter Druck setzten konnte. RF wollte [246] diese hinter allen Menschen horten.

RF hat sein 2tes Gesicht erst zum Schluss enthüllt. Entzustand.

Hauptsturmführer, "ohne Gewinnbeteiligung". Auf Treu und Glauben gedient. Am 3 Mai 1940, als Generalleutnant der Waffen-SS, erst versorgungsberechtigt geworden.

"Die über Nacht wie von einem Taschenspieler, aus einer Garde zu einer negativen Auslese geworden ist". Festgefügter Block durch die Not zusammengefügt, in den Konzentrationslagern wie auf einer Hochschule zusammengeschmiedet worden ist. Die sich am heiligen Feuer der Nation ihr Süppchen kochen wollten. kleine Minderzahl Schreckliches angerichtet.

RFSS ein gemütsvoller, weicher Mensch, sein altes Kindermädchen, Therese Hinterarches, brachte ihr selbst einen Korb. Jedem, herzlichst Ihr H. Himmler. Mit unendlicher Liebe an seine erste Frau an dem Kind aus der ersten Ehe gehängt.

---

214 RFSS: Reichsführer-SS.

Neben sich Heydrich: klar. messerscharfer Verstand. Wir nannten ihn den Oberverdachtschöpfer; hart, Schutz des Reiches nach innen, unbelehrbahre unbekehrbare Staatsfeinde. Verschärfender Einfluss. Ich nebem ihm als Protokollchef, social, kulturell, schöne, positive Seiten. Heydrich nach den scharfen, ich nach der begütigenden Seite. Ermordung von Gusthoff in der Schweiz, Legationsrat [247] von Rath in Paris. Im Krieg wuch die Stellung des Reichsführers. Endmacht gipfelte November 1944. Im Krieg Machtstellung. Vergötzung des Machts[-] und Erfolgsstandpunkts. Grundgesetze der SS. Ausgeschlossen der eine Cigarette verschwand. Schutz der Waffen- u. wehrbaren. RF hoffte nur, seinen Machtkomplex zu erweitern. Untierwerden der anständigen Ziele der SS. Oben begann das Untierwerden. Erfolg haben wollen. Recht ist was meinem Volk nützt. Nicht wie in England gewachsen und ausgewogen, Preis abgewogen; sondern masslos. Politik um jeden Preis. Damit er dem Führer alles abnehmen wollte, ihm die Aufgabe, den Osten keimfrei zu machen, sich eines kleinen Kreises bedient, unter Drohung, auch der Sippenhaft, die nicht die Kraft gehabt haben, sich zu widersetzen. Das ging hinter der Mauer vor. Führer hat es niemals bei seinen Tischreden erwähnt; König Arthus Tafel.

(Nach welchen Gesichtspunkten der "kleine Kreis" ausgewählt?) Dienststellenmässig gegeben. Eichmann war schon Sachbearbeiter. War vorhanden als der Entschluss kam, auszurotten. Hoess war auch schon da. Eines Tages ist in seinem Gehirn der Entschluss gereift, wie kann ich es beschränken auf einen kleinen Kreis von Mitwissern. Globocnik der geeignetste für einen so brutalen Auftrag. Wächter stammte aus so einer anderen Mentalität. (Gruppenführende nicht gehört).

[248] (Eichmann geweigert hätte?) Er wäre mundtot gemacht worden. Er hätte ihn nicht leben lassen. Er hätte ihn auf irgendeine Art illegal liquidieren lassen. Aus der Überzeugung, einer muss es machen, wenn es für die Wohlfahrt von 85 Millionen notwendig ist, da muss einer sein Seelenheil aufopfern und es machen, oder sein Leben lassen." "Ich muss es, muß mich aufopfern, mein Seelenheil, meine Ehre, oder mein Leben, um diesen neuen Lebensraum keimfrei zu machen." Hat den Gedanken des Führers erraten. Niemand aus unserem Kreis in Erinnerung, der verschwunden wäre. Muß bedenken grosser Gewissenshörigkeit, nach Erziehung zur Treue und absolutem Gehorsam. "Ich muss sein, wir müssen dieses Opfer bringen."

Bach-Zelewski ist ein sehr unklarer und undurchsichtiger Charakter, charakterlich gemischt wie er aussieht, ostisch unterwandert. Zeifellos tapferer Soldat. Kriegsfreiwilliger. Hatte den Mut 1935 oder 36 – hatte Schacht eine Rede gehalten, cynisch, Ehre, Blut, Fahne, aber Gold ist eine Realität. Hat den Mut u. die Entschlossenheit gehabt, mit der SS abzurücken. Hätte um ein Haar seinen Kopf verloren. Er ist so ein bischen ein Typ Globocnik. Er ist ein Büffel.

[249] Ich habe für ihn interveniert. Hat aber nie gesagt daß 2 seiner Schwestern mit Juden verheiratet sind. Etwas hinterlistig. Beruft sich erst jetzt darauf. Auf der Marrenburg hat uns mit Stolz auf das Wappen Zelewskis geführt. Im Krieg hat er den Zelewski abgelegt, wir haben ihn nur als von dem Bach gekannt. Jetzt im

Gefängniss hat er sich wieder den Zelewski zugelegt. Wenn es die Endauseinandersetzung mit dem Bolschewismus gibt, wird er wieder die Kurve schneiden wollen, wenngleich mit dem Dienstgrad des SS-Obergruppenführers.

Ohlendorf Opfer der unverantwortlichen Führung und Aufgabenstellung. Ich war entsetzt daß der 80–90 tausend Männer, auch Kinder u. Frauen ausgerottet haben soll. Das ist nicht in ihm drin. Mutig, wie er sich zu seiner Tat vor dem grossen Gerichtshof bekannt hat.

Im Russlandfeldzug 3 HöSSPF.[215] Bach einer der wenigen die als Majore in der Wehrmacht gedient haben. Lassen Sie das nicht in der roten Feder hineinpressen, er war auch ein Fehler des Reichsführers. Weiss nichts von Criticism re Warschau. Ich musste auf den Duce aufpassen, Italien das klassische Land der Verräter. Chef der Bandenkampfverbände.

Er hatte Ritterkreuzschmerzen, hat Zahlen übertrieben. Heute hängt er drin. Wie ich ein paar **[250]** Tage wegkam, kam er zu Hobocud, hat dann die Zahlen für sich und seine Tasche mitgezählt (May, June 1944). Für Warschau hat er dann das Ritterkreuz bekommen.

Russland: Unterkühlung des Westens. Militärische Auseinandersetzung, wenn Russland nicht politisch zurückweicht. Die Aktivsten, die tragenden, die charactervollen, Russische u. Amerika besteht Kluft. Hoffe, daß er nicht Deutschland auf die falsche Seite zwingt. Ende und Schrecken lieber als Schrecken ohne Ende.

5 children, 7 stepchildren, (4 of 1st marriage, 1 of second): 1st marriage 1923, divorced 6 March 1943; remarried 9 March 1943. 4 are with ü1st [sic] wife in Egene [Egern] at Tegernsee, 2nd wife lives in Strabl on Wolfgangsee. Kein Geldüberhang wie bei uns.

Ages of children: 21 to 9 yrs; Auslösung einer alten Ehrenangelegenheit: Ergebnis der Himmlerschen Ideenwelt[.] Versuch, sich von einer hochwertigen Frau ein anderes Kind schenken zu lassen. Durchführung hat mich die Gunst und Gnade Himmler's gekostet. Himmler wollte, daß ich es nur tue, wenn ich die Operation überlebe; ich wollte es vorher tuen. Himmler konnte gerade noch meine optische Erscheinung neben sich ertragen. Himmler fühlte sich überspielt. Hätte selbst nicht den Mut gehabt. So fiel ich, der rechte Flügel, aus und **[251]** die anderen drängten hinein, Fegelein, der illegale Schwager; Kaltenbrunner, und dann kam der Reichsführer. So hatten die die überflügelt und in den Schatten gedrängt.

Vom Treuhänder zum Eigentümer, der zu entscheiden hatte, ob das deutsche Volk mit ihm untergehen soll oder nicht. 50% der Lebensborngeburten waren ehelich. Die diskreten Fälle der hohen Führerschaft.

---

215 HöSSPF: Höchster SS- und Polizeiführer (Supreme SS and Police Leader).

Fig. 18: The judges of Nuremberg Doctors' Trial. Left to right: Harold L. Sebring, Walter B. Beals, Johnson T. Crawford, Victor C. Swearingen. Nuremberg, Germany, 1946/47 (Source: NARA).

6

LEO ALEXANDER – SELECTED EXPERT TESTIMONY[1]

[Page 800]

Official transcript of the American Military Tribunal in the matter of the United States of America, against Karl Brandt, et al., defendants, sitting at Nurnberg, Germany, 20 December 1946, 0930-0945, Justice Beals, presiding.

THE MARSHAL: The Honorable Judges of Military Tribunal 1.

Military Tribunal 1 is now in session.

God save the United States of America and this Honorable Tribunal.

There will be order in the courtroom.

THE PRESIDENT: The Marshal will ascertain that the defendants are present.

THE MARSHAL: May it please Your Honor, all the defendants are present.

THE PRESIDENT: The Secretary-General will note for the record the presence of all the defendants in the courtroom.

MR. HARDY: May it please the Tribunal, due to some unforeseen circumstances the arrival of the witnesses has been delayed. If it would be possible to recess for ten or fifteen minutes pending the arrival of the witnesses it would be very much appreciated.

THE PRESIDENT: The Tribunal will be in recess until we are notified of the arrival of the necessary witnesses.

(A recess was taken.)

THE PRESIDENT: The witness having arrived, the Tribunal will proceed.

[Case of MARIA BROEL-PLATER]

[…] [Page 804]

BY THE PRESIDENT:

Q. The witness will state his name?

Q. Lee [Leo] Alexander.

Q. Will you repeat this oath after me:

---

[1] Nuremberg Military Tribunal 1. "Transcript for NMT 1: Medical Case," 20 December 1946, page 800–855. Harvard Law School Library. Nuremberg Trials Project. https://nuremberg.law.harvard. edu/transcripts/1-transcript-for-nmt-1-medical-case?seq=817& q=dzido. Accessed 20 August 2024. Minor errors have been silently corrected, including pagination [in square brackets].

I swear that the evidence I shall give shall be the truth, the whole truth and nothing but the truth, so help no God.

(The witness repeated the oath.)

[Page 805]

THE PRESIDENT: You may sit down.

DIRECT EXAMINATION BY MR. McHANEY:

A. Your name is Lee [Leo] Alexander?

A. Yes.

Q. When and where were you burn?

A. I was born October 11th, 1905, in Vienna, Austria.

Q. Are you a citizen of the United States?

A. I have been a citizen of the United States since 1938.

Q. Have you studied and practiced medicine?

A. I Have studied and practiced medicine from 1922 to 1934 and practiced since then.

Q. What is your present occupation?

A. My present occupation is that of consulting Neurologist and Psychiatrist in the city of Boston. At the same time I am practising as a research specialist in Boston State hospital. I am also on the staff of various other private and public hospitals in Boston and its vicinity.

Q. Are you new acting as a special consultant to the Secretary of War?

A. I have new been appointed special expert consultant to the Secretary of War.

Q. Doctor, in answering my questions, will you please pause for a few moments so that the interpreter can interpret the answers into German?

A. Yes sir.

Q. I would like to put a series of questions to you concerning your education and medical experience. Did you receive your A.B. degree in Vienna, Austria in June of 1923?

A. Yes sir.

Q. And from 1923 to 1929 did you study medicine at one University of Vienna medicine School at Vienna, Austria?

A. Yes, sir.

[Page 806]

Q. And from 1927 to 1928 did you intern in the Second Department of Medicine at the University of Vienna Hospitals.

A. Yes sir.

[Page 807]

Q. Did you receive your M.D. degree from the University of Vienna Medical School in July, 1929?

A. Yes sir.

Q. And from 1929 to 1931 did you intern in neuropsychiatry at the Neuropsychiatric Department of the University Hospital, Frankfurt?

A. Yes sir.

Q. And from 1931 to 1932 were you a resident in neuropsychiatry, the Neuropsychiatric Department of the University Hospital in Frankfurt?

A. Yes sir.

Q. Were you a lecturer in psychiatry and neurology at Peiping Union Medical Hospital, Peiping, China in 1933?

A. Yes sir.

Q. And from January, 1934 to October, 1934, a clinical assistant at the Worcester State Hospital, Worcester, Massachusetts?

A. Yes sir.

Q. And from 1934 to 1941 an instructor in neurology at the Harvard Medical School?

A. Yes sir.

Q. And over the same period were you a neuro-pathologist at the Boston City Hospital?

A. Yes sir.

Q. From 1935 to 1941 a research associate at the Boston State Hospital, Boston, Massachusetts?

A. Yes sir.

Q. And have you also practiced in other hospitals in Boston?

A. Yes sir.

Q. Are you non a member of the editorial board of the Journal of Neuropathology and Experimental Neurology?

[Page 808]

A. Yes sir.

Q. And were you, from 1941 to 1942, an associate professor of neuropsychiatry at Duke University Medical School, Durham, North Carolina?

A. Yes sir.

Q. Have you boon [been] on leave of absence from Duke since that time?

A. Until my resignation in January, '46.

Q. Were you, from July 1942 to January, 1946, in the Medical Corps of the United States Army?

A. Yes sir.

Q. What rank did you attain, Doctor?

A. Major, and later appointed Lieutenant Colonel in the Officers Reserve Corps, United States Army.

Q. Did you serve as chief of the section of neuropsyc[h]iatry, 65th General Hospital from July, 1942 until May, 1945?

A. Yes sir.

Q. And that was the United States Army General Hospital which served the Eighth Air Force in England?

A. Yes sir.

Q. And were you on detached service with a G-2 Specialist Task Force, Sixth Army Group, in the American occupied zones of Germany on special orders from Supreme Headquarters, Allied Expeditionary Forces from May, 1945 until September, 1945?

A. Yes sir.

Q. You state you. resigned from Duke University in January, 1946?

A. Yes sir.

Q. What have you done since that date?

A. I have returned to practice of neurology and psychiatry in Boston, and I have taken over the positions mentioned at the outset of my testimony; namely, those of Associate Director of Research at the Boston State hospital; Consulting Neurologist and Psychiatrist to to Washingtonian Hospital, and various other public and private hospitals in Boston and vicinity.

[Page 809]

Q. Now, Doctor, are you a member of a number of medical associations?

A. Yes sir. I am also a Diplomate and former Examiner on the American Board of Psychiatry and Neurology.

Q. Could you name just a few of those medical societies of which you are a member?

A. American medical Association, American Neurological association, American association of Neuropathologists, American Association of Psychopathologists, Association for Research in Nervous and Mental Disease, Harvey Cushing Society, American Association of Pathologists and Bacteriologists, Boston Society of Psychiatry and Neurology, Now England Psychiatric Association, and a number of others.

Q. Thank you. Now, Doctor, what experience have you had with medical legal work, if any?

A. Considerable, both in civilian practice, in university teaching, and in military practice.

Q. Could you describe that experience in just a bit more detail?

A. It consists in serving as an export to courts, both civilian courts and military courts and teaching methods and principles of examination and testimony to medical students.

Q. What experience have you had with cases of trauma or injury with or without subsequent infection?

A. Considerable, especially during my time at the Boston City Hospital and in the Army.

Q. What experience have you had with the reading of X-rays?

[Page 810]

A. Likewise a great deal. I served among others as examiner in X-rays of the skull, spine and nervous system on the American Board of Neurology and Psychiatry.

[…]

[Continued from page 848]

THE MARSHAL: The Tribunal is again in session.

MR. HARDY: If there is no cross examination of this witness by the defense counsel, I propose now to call Dr. Alexander to the witness stand.

THE PRESIDENT: I understood before we recessed there was no cross examination of this witness by defense counsel. Is that correct? Proceed.

DR. LEO ALEXANDER, a witness, was recalled to the stand and testified as follows:

THE PRESIDENT: Dr. Alexander is reminded that he is still under oath as a witness in this Court.

DR. ALEXANDER: (Addressing Jadwiga Dzido). Please take off both shoes and both stockings, if you will.

(The witness removed her shoes and stockings.)

DIRECT EXAMINATION – Continued BY MR. HARDY:

Q. Dr. Alexander, have you examined Miss Dzido before today?

A. Yes, sir, I did, on several occasions and during the last three days.

Q. During your examination, did you have x-rays made of the patient's legs?

A. I did, sir.

MR. HARDY: At this time I will introduce document No. nO-1091 which is the x-ray of one witness, Miss Dzido. We will pass two copies to the Tribunal and one copy for the Secretary General.

BY MR. HARDY:

Q. Dr. Alexander, in the course of your diagnosis of these x-rays, will you kindly diagnose this x-ray in English and then repeat in German for the benefit of the defendant?

A. Yes, sir.

Q. Doctor, will you identify that x-ray which carried No. NO-1091?

A. Yes. This is the x-ray which included the lower two-thirds of the thigh bone, the femur and the knee joint, and –

MR. HARDY: I offer this x-ray as Prosecution Exhibit No. 215.

[Page 849]

BY MR. HARDY:

Q. Do you have any further explanation of this x-ray, Doctor?

A. Yes, sir. I would like to tie it in, if it is agreeable to you, with the chemical examination.

Q. All right, Doctor.

A. The most remarkable finding in Miss Dzido's case is at first marked atrophy of the right leg, including thigh, leg and foot. Will you please stand up, Miss Dzido. (The witness stood). And will you gradually slowly turn around? You can compare here the two legs and you notice the marked atrophy. You see the femur of this bone, of this leg, as compared to the other. This atrophy is predominantly on the calf but also includes the lower part of the thigh. Here, the thigh (indicating) as compared with the other side. The atrophy of the thigh is due to the fact that the lateral flexor group, including the musculus biceps, is absent which leaves the lateral epicondylus and the lateral prominence of the tibia without the tendinous insertion. You see this tendon here, strong tendon is absent on this side. The lower part of the leg, including the malleolar region and the dorsum of the foot show bluish discoloration, indicating interference with the circulation of the leg, probably due to loss of blood vessels. (The witness now faced the judges). Skin and musculature of the right foot, including the toes, are likewise atrophic. The right leg is furthermore disfigured by two ugly scars, one here and one here.

THE PRESIDENT: One where, Doctor, for the sake of the record.

DR. ALEXANDER: Here. (Indicating).

THE PRESIDENT: I know, but it must go into the record.

DR. ALEXANDER: Take the lateral one and the medial one. The lateral one begins three inches above the knee, above the lateral epicondylus of the femur running down over the lateral part of the calf until two inches above the lateral malleolus. This scar is sixteen inches long. The width of this scar varies from one-eight inch to one-half inch. The lower part of this scar still snows inflammation and oozes sero-purulent discharge, indicating the presence of a sinus. Two and one-half inches medially to this scar and parallel to it is an equally disfiguring one measuring seven inches in length and partly three-quarters of an inch in width.

[Page 850]

There are four small recent neat scars indicative of having healed by first intension over the right foot and ankle These are incidental to transplantation of tendons to correct a foot drop. It is referred to as phalphesus (?) which was carried out by Dr. Gruca. There are a number of neurological disturbances in this location. The dorsiflexion of the foot is abolished.

(Addressing Miss Dzido). Would you try to life up your foot like this. (Indicating). Although they are present, in view of the tendon repair, there is no longer any foot drop but the patient cannot lift the foot off the ground to any significant extent. The gait is disturbed by this loss of dorsiflexion of the right foot and lateral rotation of the right foot is likewise abolished.

(Addressing Miss Dzido). Will you please try to do this, put the foot inward and outward. There is very little lateral rotation possible.

(Addressing Miss Dzido). Would you like to walk first? Would it be desire to have the patient walk?

You notice that during the gait the toes of the right foot remain planted to the ground because of the inadequacy of the lifting movement of the foot which is accomplished by the perineal nerves. These findings indicate paralysis, or loss rather, in this case of the perineal nerve. The right knee joint is diminished and the right ankle jerk is absent. Here you get a very good knee jerk and on this side a less active one. You see here very marked atrophy because of the loss of the whole flexor musculature. There is a good ankle jerk here. I never was able to retain one on the right. Sensory examination showed an anesthesia for fine touch on the dorsum of the right foot, which means the back of the foot. The pressure is felt. The lower two-thirds of the antero-lateral aspect of the right leg, as well as that part of the lateral and posterior aspect of the leg which is lateral to and between the two scars – this part and thus, which shows hyperesthesia for touch and not complete loss. All these areas show marked hyperesthesia for pain. In the medial part of the calf here sensation to touch is normal Thank you very much.

[Page 851]

Q. Now, Doctor, I will give you all these x-rays together. There will be an addition to the one that he has, No. 1092, No. 1093 and No. 1094. Would you kindly identify these three x-rays first, Doctor, so that we can offer them as exhibits?

A. Yes. In 1092 is the x-ray of the leg, including the tibia and fibula.

MR. HARDY: That is offered at this time as Prosecution Exhibit No. 216.

DR. ALEXANDER: In 1093 is an x-ray of the right feet.

MR. HARDY: That is offered as Prosecution Exhibit No. 217.

DR. ALEXANDER: And in 1094 is another x-ray of the right foot, with particular attention to the metatarsal bones.

MR. HARDY: Document No. 1094 is offered as Prosecution Exhibit No. 218.

BY MR. HARDY:

Q. Proceed, Doctor.

A. The first of the x-rays, the picture of the femur, shows marked osteoporosis of the lateral epicondylus. This is due to the fact of the removal of muscle and tendon attachments. It is an osteo-porosis of disuse because the normal pull of the tendon has been removed from this epicondylus. The epicondylus is the big prominence of the thigh bone adjacent to the knee joint where the large flexor muscles insert normally. Where that insertion has been abolished here, leaving the epicondylus without soft major tendons. This osteo-porosis is the obvious result of that, and marked osteo-porotic prominence with an arrow in this picture.

[Page 852]

Q. Doctor, this x-ray you are referring to now is No. 1092?

A. This is No. 1091. The arrow points to the osteoporotic atrophy of the tibia. Number 1092 is the x-ray of the leg. It shows the fibula which is the smaller of the two Larger banes of the leg, about in the middle between the area just mentioned under the bracket called "B". On the side, looking toward the tibia is the osteoperiostitis of the periosteum. This group of marks are particularly severe in the smaller area which I have marked with the bracket "A" indicates a smaller area of the shaft of the tibia within the larger area of the disturbance marked as "B". This alteration is indicating and consists of an ordinary inactive Coxa, which in view of the osteoperiostitis of the periosteum was probably an osteomyelitis process. However, there is no active osteomyelitis at the present examination of the right foot, In pictures 1093 and 1094, it shows arthritic changes of the cuniform navicula joints with narrowing of the joint spaces and increased marginal sclerosis. This has been marked in the x-ray with an arrow pointing to the joint. The other prints are the same. The prints have come out too dark, but it shows the condition clearly in the film.

This arthritis is due to the immobilization of the right foot. Secondary to the muscles and especially the paralysis of the perineal nerve. It is evidentally arthritis of an immobilization nature which one sees also by inspection of the patients foot.

Q. Doctor, can you determine from your examination –

A. (Interposing) 1094, have I mentioned it shows the same as 1093 in a slightly different exposure. The marks are the same pointing to the most marked arthritis between the cuniform navicular joints.

Q. Doctor, in your opinion, from your examination of this patient can you determine what was the purpose of the experiment?

A. It appears that in this experiment a highly infectious agent was implanted, probably without the addition of a bacteria static agent such as sulfanilaide, and for that reason the infection got out of hand and became very extensive.

Q. Do you mean, Doctor, it is highly possible this patient could have been considered as one of the control groups?

[Page 853]

A. Yes, probably one of the control group. The two previous patients both mentioned white powder which has been used in their wounds, which was probably one of the sulfanilaides, and while this patient as well as the subsequent patient, knew of no use of the white powder. Therefore, I assume that they may be of the control group. They have been injected or implanted with the bacteria culture without the subsequent use of sulfanilaide. From the general appearance, it is suggestive of a Streptococcus in this case. The way it is spread makes it likely, and the fact that the spread is mostly lengthwise.

Q. Could you say, Doctor, the reason for the spread in this case was because of the lack of treatment, where as the other patients had been treated after being operated on, is that correct?

A. Presumably. The other patients were given sulfanilaide in the wounds sometime after the wounds were made; presumably to test the efficiency of the use of sulfanilaide on the battle field such as we started to do it in the United States Army.

Q. Now, Doctor, you, as a psychiatrist, can you say what psychological effect these operations had on the patients?

A. I think that it was that of deep humiliation which was the most remarkable reaction in all these women. I would say it was rather a resentment against humiliation. The use of the name "guinea pig" – they are all high spirited girls. They were all soldiers. This girl is of a superior intelligent a student of pharmacy, a woman of culture, and speaks very good English which she feels is not good enough to testify in it. This whole treatment caused a deep humiliation, and. on the other hand, it also aroused a fighting spirit, and the remarkable thing is that this prisoner showed how she rebelled against this treatment. She was one of a group which was forcibly operated on. Here is a woman who fought like a wild cat in a concentration camp against this treatment, and who had to be held down by to or more SS men.

Q. Thank you Doctor.

MR. HARDY: I have no further questions to put to Doctor Alexander, at this time, Your Honor.

[Page 854]

THE PRESIDENT: Do any of the defense counsel desire to cross examine Doctor Alexander?

CROSS-EXAMINATION BY DR. SEIDL:

Q. Only a few questions, Doctor Alexander. Are you able to state exactly which scars came from the, transplantation in 1945 in Warsaw?

A. Yes. In 1945, the operation involved two things: Transplantation of the tendons. You can still recognize those wounds because the tissues still show. That was done to lift the foot up. This girl has a marked loot drop, more marked than the first witness and these tendons lift the foot up, and fixed it in that position (indicating). In addition, the witness told me that the upper end of the scar here was treated cosmetically. The main scar from the knee down to here, was not touched, and specifically the open side was not touched.

Q. Is it possible that to biceps is lacking because it was used in this transplantation in Warsaw?

A. I did not obtain that history. I can ask here through the interpreter.

DR. ALEXANDER: Will you please ask the patient these questions:

DR. ALEXANDER: Do you feel this tendon here, the big tendon on the side?

MISS DZIDO: No.

DR. ALEXANDER: Here.

MISS DZIDO: Yes.

DR. ALEXANDER: Now, on this side, do you remember whether you still had this tendon when Doctor Gruzer operated on you in Warsaw?

MISS DZIDO: No.

DR. ALEXANDER: It is very unlikely that one would use a bicep tendon for transplantation. It is more likely that the tendon was snipped off during the acute state of the infection.

Q. That is your assumption?

A. Yes.

Q. Now something else, you are of the opinion apparently that this big scar on the back of the calf was necessary in order to combat the gangrene surgically? -854

[Page 855]

A. I do not know. The case looks to me like streptococcus. The way it is distributed – for gasbrand it as not complete enough. Of course it is difficult to distinguish that but the next patient you see a typical gas bacillus scar and it looks different than this one. This looks like streptococcus, but it is probable that one or two cuts were made in order to control the infection surgically.

Q. Do you know Doctor whether the patient was treated with sulfanilaide?

A. No, the only thing is she is one of two patients who did not mention white powder. That is all I know.

DR. SEIDL: I have no further questions.

THE PRESIDENT: Any further questions by the counsel for the defense?

(Apparently none)

[…]

THE PRESIDENT: The witness may be excused and the Polish witness is also excused. I think counsel for both parties understand that some time ago the Tribunal announced that it would, tomorrow at 12:30 o'clock, adjourn until the morning of Thursday, January 2. I suppose you can use the morning, Mr. McHaney, in reading records from the book?

MR. MCHANEY: Yes indeed, sir.

THE PRESIDENT: The Tribunal will now recess until 9:30 o'clock tomorrow morning.

(The Tribunal adjourned until 21 December 1946 at 0930 hours.)

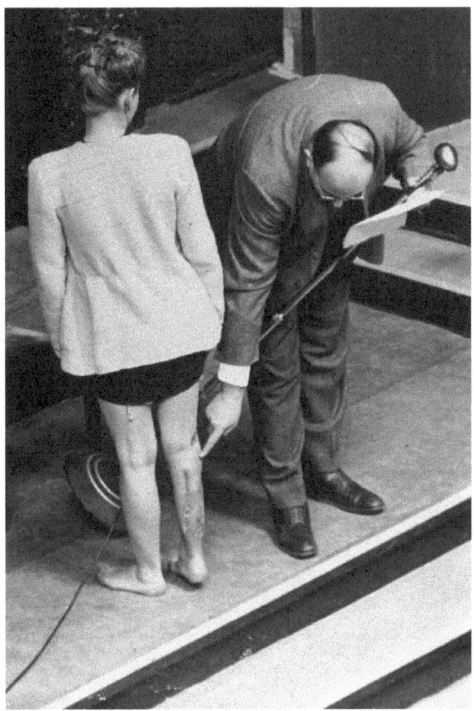

Fig. 19: Jadwiga Dzido alongside Leo Alexander giving his expert testimony about the Ravensbrück experiments at the Nuremberg Doctors' Trial on 20 December 1946 (Source: NARA).

7

WAR CRIMES AND THEIR MOTIVATION – THE SOCIO-PSYCHOLOGICAL STRUCTURE OF THE SS AND THE CRIMINALIZATION OF A SOCIETY[1]

Leo Alexander[2]

INTRODUCTION

War Crimes are crimes committed with group approval. In this way they are similar to gang crimes, and different from crimes committed by single individuals in ordinary society. The main approving and instigating group in Germany during the Nazi regime was the SS which was the most important political organization in Nazi Germany.

SS stands for Schutz-Staffel, which, translated, means "protective squadron." No totalitarian state can function without an SS-like organization. It is therefore important for us to know all we can about the SS, to understand its motivation and how it worked, what its strength was and what its weaknesses were; and it is the duty of sociologists, psychologists, and psychiatrists to study these facts and to make them generally understood.

The Office of the Chief of Counsel for War Crimes in Nurnberg [sic], founded by Justice Robert H. Jackson and continued and developed further by General Telford Taylor, has provided many new and challenging opportunities. Among these opportunities, unique in history, is the opportunity for a scientific postmortem of the body politic of the defeated enemy. The material is enormous. Documents abound in the archives, significant books in the libraries. Vast numbers of the participants, active and passive, in the life of this totalitarian state are available for

---

1   This article originally appeared in Leo Alexander, "War Crimes and their Motivation: The Socio-Psychological Structure of the SS and the Criminalization of a Society," *Journal of Criminal Law & Criminology*, Volume 39, Issue 3, pp. 298-326 (1948). Copyright 1948 by Northwestern University. Reprinted by special permission of Northwestern University Pritzker School of Law and the *Journal of Criminal Law and Criminology*, Chicago, Illinois, USA.
2   The author was consultant to the Secretary of War of the United States, on duty with the Office of the Chief of Counsel for War Crimes in Nurnberg [sic], U.S. Zone of Germany, 1946–1947; Lieutenant Colonel, ORC, MC, USA; Associate Director of Research, Boston State Hospital; Instructor in Psychiatry, Tufts College Medical School, Boston, Massachusetts. The following article was read in part at the 75th anniversary meeting of the *Nederlandsche Vereiniging voor Psychiatrie en Neurologie*, in Amsterdam, The Netherlands, on 12 June 1947, at the meeting of the Boston Society of Psychiatry and Neurology on 16 October 1947, at the First American Medicolegal Congress, in St. Louis, Missouri, on 20 January 1948, and at the meeting of the Massachusetts Psychiatric Society, in Boston, on 29th January 1948. – Editor.

examination in the prison, the witness house, and on the streets, railroad trains and farms of Germany.

A number of studies concerning the leading participants, especially the 22 men who stood trial before the International Military Tribunal, have already appeared in print, notably the books by Kelley and Gilbert. But before the International Military Tribunal not only specific individuals were tried, but also organizations composed of large groups of partly nameless men, notably the SS. In the subsequent trials before the Nurnberg [sic] Military Tribunals composed entirely of American judges, the emphasis has shifted even more to the investigation and trial of members of organizations declared criminal by the International Tribunal, of which the most important, far-flung, and powerful was the SS.

In its days of power and activity the Nazi State liked to compare itself with a racing train in motion. While men stood at the throttle, the engine which drove Nazi Germany was the SS. It is therefore important to understand the SS and the socio-logic and psychologic forces which created it, held it together, and made possible its defeat. This is not only of historical and academic interest. Totalitarianism has not been eliminated as a threat, external and internal, with the defeat of Nazi Germany. By understanding the SS in the socio-psychologic setting of Germany we may be able to draw general conclusions in regard to the dynamics of totalitarian rule anywhere, and in regard to the socio-psychologic structure of any country under such rule. More specifically, it will aid us in the re-education, the socio-psychologic rehabilitation of defeated and occupied Germany.

THE SS AS A CRIMINAL ORGANIZATION

The SS was found to be a criminal organization by the International Military Tribunal in Nurnberg [sic]. In order to understand the SS[,] it is necessary to realize thoroughly and to understand the meaning of this finding, and not merely to accept the dictum of the Military Tribunal. This organization was criminal not only because its members actually committed crimes but also because the essential mode of its thinking and its group behavior was that prevalent in criminal organizations. The individual criminal as well as the criminal organization commits crimes for the purpose of gaining selfish ends by criminal means. But in addition[,] the criminal organization also commits crimes for the purpose of maintaining and enforcing the continued adherence and group loyalty of its members since it is vital to the criminal organization to insure against desertion by its members. This additional purpose becomes increasingly important as the organization increases in numbers. It is achieved by involving all members in sufficient criminal activity to cut off their return to normal society.

In addition, such criminal societies will continuously search for and recruit outside accomplices in order to enlarge the circle of people that will stand together, part-time members as it were, who are tied to the organization by being allowed to profit from the society's crimes, without being completely involved. Such accomplices are chosen particularly among people of political, civic, social, or other public influence, so-called "front" men, who are corrupted and made agreeable to the ends of the criminal organization, but who are pushed into complete or overt participation only if and when their loyalty is questioned for some reason or other. This is the basic pattern of all criminal organizations such as the Maffia and Camorra in Italy and the well-known criminal gangs of outlaws which have cropped up time and again in the United States but which have been successfully held down by the constructive forces of society. Germany was not so fortunate, and a criminal gang actually gained power over essential phases of government. This gang constituted the SS. Its nondrafted members were held together by the same sort of ties that bind together members of criminal gangs. In the SS as in all criminal organizations there existed that inclined plane where nobody could stay at the brink for long, but all had to roll down into more crime, or be killed or eliminated. We understand these ties very well because we have studied them and legally dissected them, as it were, in many gang trials in the United States, and we are now continuing the same process in studying the SS.

We know that in the SS, as in any other criminal organization, if a man did anything which put his loyalty to that organization into a questionable light, he was either liquidated – that means killed – or he had to undertake a criminal act which would definitely and irrevocably tie him to that criminal organization. We say in such a case the man was put "on the spot." Such an act must include murder, according to the age-old custom of criminal gangs. In the SS this was specifically called blutkitt (blood cement). I first learned of the existence of this special German term from Dr. Wanda von Baeyer, a German psychologist, who also told me that Hitler himself introduced the idea and the word blutkitt, which he had discovered in a book about Genghis Khan in which it was emphasized that the crimes which the Khan's hordes committed served as "blood cement" ("blutkitt"), holding the organization together. He was supposed to have read that book as early as his Landsberg Prison days.

The concentration camps were the main places within the confines of Germany where SS members were expected to acquire blood cement, until they were considered reliable enough to be sent abroad into the occupied countries where they could thebe relied upon to perform similar crimes inside and outside the confines of specific camp areas. The peculiar process of indoctrination in crime and cruelty which young men went through in concentration camps after they had joined the SS constituted the "hardening process," the "brutalization course" which the SS organization regarded as essential for transforming its personnel into willing and reliable tools for its criminal purposes. While many joined willingly, no doubt others were seduced by a double appeal-one in the form of a rationalization that this was for the best interests of Germany (actually for the interests of the SS), and the other in terms of a far more sinister and direct process of seduction, that of letting the novices taste the satisfactions obtained from release of repressed destructive primitive and sadistic drives.

The similarity of the SS to the classical criminal organizations is also expressed in other circumstances. As in all criminal societies there were "front" men, "inner circle" men, and "behind the scenes" men. The SS, like a really large-scale criminal gang, ran, as it were, on several tracks which sometimes were shielded from each other by tunnels. One has to understand the SS running on at least three tracks beside and around each other. The men recently on trial were mostly the "inner circle" men. The "front" men were sometimes not pushed into actual criminal activity unless they had come under suspicion of disloyalty in word or deed as in the case of Dr. Karl Gebhardt, one of those convicted in the medical case, in the matter of Heydrich's death, or if they had shown an inclination to dissociate themselves from the group or to sever ties with the SS. Gebhardt was a well-known specialist in bone and joint surgery, Professor of Surgery at the University of Berlin, and Surgeon-in-Chief of the noted and renowned Hohenlychen Hospital, which had been the official hospital designated for the treatment of injuries sustained during the Olympic Games in Berlin in 1936. He held general's rank in the SS.

Gebhardt was in just such a spot, as he himself said on the stand (p. 4051 of the German transcript). Gebhardt was suspected of having contributed to the death of Heydrich, who was under his care after his injury, by failing to treat his wound infection with sulfonamides, and this omission could definitely be interpreted as an act which would make him politically suspect in SS circles. Gebhardt was then expected, and was ready, to commit a criminal act which would definitely tie him into deeper union with the criminal organization, namely the SS. This act, in his case, was the criminal experiments which he then carried out on young girls captured from the Polish resistance movement, in whom he produced wounds complicated by tissue destruction which he subsequently infected with gas gangrene bacilli, and then demonstrated that a number of these victims died in spite of sulfonamide treatment. Thus he proved that Heydrich's death was "fate determined" (a favorite SS phrase), and that he was not guilty of causing Heydrich's death. He went one step further by involving the entire German medical profession in "SS blood cement," by presenting his report before a national medical meeting without objection being aroused by any of its members.

The same motivation can also be recognized in the progressive criminal involvement of members of the inner circle. An example of this type is that of Viktor Hermann Brack, member of the Nazi Party and the SS since 1929, who held the rather low serial number of 901 in the SS. Having been Bouhler's personal assistant since 1932, he became in 1934 Bouhler's Chief of Staff at the Chancellory Office of the National Socialist Party. In this capacity he participated in three major crimes: 1) the killing of "useless eaters," including patients suffering from nervous or mental diseases in German state hospitals; 2) the experimental, administrative, and technical preparations for mass sterilizations of unwanted national and racial groups; and 3) the administrative and technical arrangements for the mass killing of unwanted national and racial groups, for which he suggested and introduced the use of camouflaged gas chambers, which became known as "Brack's remedy." This program was to begin with the extermination of seven to eight million Jews. The killing of the Jews was to be the preliminary phase to the killing of 30 million Slavs, in just the same way as the killing of the insane was the preliminary phase to the killing of the Jews. The personality and motivations of this man who held the position of key executive in the main genocidal crime of the German State are of great interest in connection with our subject. It was surprising to find that he was a rather meek and polite, decidedly unimpressive individual who claimed that he had been living in mortal fear of Reinhard ("The Hangman") Heydrich for several years, ever since he first started having difficulties with him in 1937. These difficulties arose from the fact that Brack, in his capacity as Chief of the Chancellory Office, handled many petitions addressed to Hitler and took particular pains in investigating petitions appealing for discharge from concentration camps. Brack's interest in such petitions was considered inordinate and an interference in their spheres and policies by Heydrich, Bormann, and Himmler.

In the following two years this matter came to a head, the culminating point being an incident in the course of which Heydrich accused Brack of divulging the contents of secret Gestapo (SD) files to the relatives of a petitioner who was in a concentration camp. Himmler and Bormann complained to Bouhler about Brack, demanded Brack's removal from office; and Heydrich, by whom Brack had felt personally threatened for some time, openly threatened him with arrest. It was at that point that Brack was picked by his chief Bouhler, also an old SS member, to take charge of the technical preparations for the extermination program of the insane which got underway in the latter part of 1939, and it was Brack who was taken by Bouhler, Conti, and Brandt to the first demonstration of a group killing of mental patients in December 1939. His, later, was the duty to make repeated checks at the various killing centers where he had to witness these killings in order to report on the efficacy of the various types of poison gas used. The choice at that time fell upon carbon monoxide which was later to be replaced by "Cyclone B."

Early in 1941, however, Brack once more roused some displeasure in high SS circles by again taking up occasional cases of political persecutees. In that period he had intervened, notably and unsuccessfully, in the case of a Dr. Ludwig Schmitt who had given assistance to various persecuted socialists as well as to Otto Strasser and his group, and who was at that time imprisoned in a concentration camp, and also in the case of a highranking racial persecutee, Professor Otto Warburg the Nobel Prize winner, who was threatened with dismissal from the Kaiser-Wilhelm Institute and whose dismissal Brack prevented. Furthermore, Brack had been critical of certain aspects of the "winter catastrophe" in Russia, especially of the fact that the armed forces had not coped with the problem of adequate care for the sick and the wounded particularly the sick and wounded SS men in that campaign. Chiefly because of his activity in behalf of Schmitt and Warburg, Brack was called to Gestapo headquarters where Heydrich gave him a stern warning. Again shortly after that, in March 1941, it happened that Himmler entrusted him first with working out plans for mass sterilization of conquered peoples, and subsequently, in September 1941 with the preparations for the mass extermination of the Jews.

Brack's involvement is of great interest and I have the impression that Brack himself was quite unaware of this blood-cement connection in the setting of the conversation in which Himmler first informed Brack of his plans and of the role he, Brack, was to play in the extermination of the Jews. Brack told the story on the stand (pp. 7507 and 7508 of the English transcript). He stated that he had gone to Himmler to tell him about the shortcomings of the motor transport problem and how it affected the care of the sick and the wounded and what catastrophes had resulted from the lack of motor vehicles. He continued:

> "I reported these matters to Himmler but subsequently, I don't know why, I voiced my criticism about other matters within the SS. Himmler quietly listened to me but then tried to convince me in his way about the correctness of what he was doing. He admitted that some things in the SS were not as he would like them to be, and that some of the men in the SS did not quite fit into the organization. But, he said, at this critical point he needed every single one of the old SS members. He said, essentially, that only if the old comrades would stand by him faithfully could the SS cleanse itself of these people who did not fit into it. He could only expect the most heavy tasks to be carried out by the old SS members. Then he suddenly stopped and told me that Hitler had sometime ago given him the order for the extermination of the Jews. He said that the preparations were already in progress, and I think that he used the expression that for reasons of camouflage one would have to work as quickly as possible."

Thus a man such as Brack, who was not quite enough of a conformist, somewhat too troublesome and too critical of his organization than was considered desirable, although there must have pre-existed an essential willingness on his part, was made into a fully cooperative tool of the criminal organization by becoming involved as an active participant in one of his organization's greatest crimes.

It is characteristic of the peculiar schematized thinking which was fostered in SS circles that Brack defended himself with the most peculiar sophistry against having been a member of a criminal organization. His defense counsel asked Brack whether on the basis of his personal conferences with Himmler in 1941 and 1942 he could tell that Himmler wanted to use the SS for the execution of plans which were judged as criminal by the International Military Tribunal. Brack replied that he could not arrive at that conclusion because he assumed that

> "Himmler was planning these things as chief of the German police in which capacity, of course, the RSHA (Reich Security Main Office) was subordinate to him. I could not assume that the SS was to be used for such purposes," (p. 7549 of the German transcript, p. 7455 of the English transcript).

And Brack kept a perfectly straight face when he said that in his capacity as an SS man he had never received any criminal orders. He admitted that Himmler gave criminal orders and that he himself received criminal orders and requests. He admitted that the acts of genocide which were instigated and carried out were a crime. Brack, however, had no realization of the fact that he slid into this criminal activity in his capacity as a member of the SS and that the SS was the main source from which this criminal activity originated, although this criminal activity did not remain restricted to the SS itself.

Large elements of the Wehrmacht were integrated into the criminal group, frequently under the motivational influence of attached SS personnel but with the connivance of key personnel in the army high command, Keitel for instance. The manner in which army people were drawn into criminal activity was similar to the way in which this was done with SS personnel. Thus, individuals were frequently picked for the commission of certain crimes of which these people themselves had been vocal in disapproving. This is vividly shown in the case of Colonel Karl von Bothmer, a commander of German armed forces in Yugoslavia. In the files of the supreme command of the Wehrmacht we found a letter from this officer, dated August 6, 1941 (Doc. No. NOKW 1011) in which he had protested against an order for the indiscriminate shooting of arrested Yugoslav civilians who had not been specifically taken as hostages for specific crimes, without due process of martial law. Von Bothmer concluded his letter as follows: "Any request to have people shot to death who were not involved in the matter I cannot fulfill, particularly since one may assume in most cases that it will not touch the culprits at all." We do not know exactly what type of pressure was exerted on this man. But we know that this was the very same Colonel Karl von Bothmer who later became notorious as the mass murderer of Nish, Yugoslavia, where he committed the very same crime of which his letter of August 6, 1941, had so eloquently disapproved. He has since, namely in February and March of 1947, been tried for the murder of 700 civilians in February 1942, and he has been executed as a war criminal.

One of the men sentenced to life imprisonment in the Medical Case, Professor Dr. Gerhard A. H. Rose, vice president of the Robert Koch Institute in Berlin, was on trial for participation in a crime of which he had originally disapproved. This crime consisted of typhus experiments in the Buchenwald concentration camp, during which 290 people were killed by inoculation with live typhus virus, and of similar experiments at the Natzweiler concentration camp, where about 50 people were killed in the same manner. Prior to his own participation Rose had made a personal protest against these experiments to the president of the Robert Koch Institute, Professor Gildemeister, who had organized the experiments; and later, after he had already participated, he again expressed himself as opposed to these experiments on scientific and moral grounds, in an open meeting of the third conference of consulting physicians in May 1943 in Berlin, at which Dr. Ding-Schuler, who carried out the Buchenwald experiments, presented his first scientific results. Nevertheless, Rose soon resumed his participation.

It is obvious that group pressure, although no overt threats or coercion, was brought to bear on von Bothmer, on Rose, and on the others who committed crimes in violation of their own principles. This illustrates that an important fact concerning motivation and with which we are so familiar in ordinary crime applies also to war crimes and to these ideologically conditioned crimes against humanity – namely, that fear and cowardice, especially fear of ostracism by the group, are in a number of cases more important motives than simple ferocity or aggressiveness. Another example is that of Otto Ohlendorf, Gruppenfuehrer (lieutenant general) of the Waffen SS, whose ghastly testimony before the International Military Tribunal in Nurnberg will be remembered by all who know the record of the case. He was the chief of the dreaded Einsatzgruppe D, one of the four special task forces which operated in the conquered eastern territories. His testimony of January 3, 1946, covers pages 2001 to 2055 of the transcript. Ohlendorf admitted on the stand responsibility for the killing of 90,000 unarmed men, women, and children (p. 2010 of the record). He admitted that he was present at these mass executions. The question by a member of the tribunal, "Were all Jewish children murdered?", was answered by Ohlendorf with "Yes," (p. 2037 of the record). Ohlendorf carried out his ghastly work in the East from July 1941 till June 1942. Prior to this assignment he held a position under the Economics Ministry and at the same time acted as part-time chief of Office III of the RSHA (SD) of the SS.

Upon meeting this confessed mass murderer I was rather surprised to find him to be a mild-mannered man of slight build and of a deliberate, hesitant, even diffident, manner of speech. He stated that he had been a loyal Party member and a member of the SS since 1925. His first difficulties with the Party hierarchy occurred in 1933 after the rise to power of National Socialism because he had opposed a trend toward what he called "National Bolshevism" within the Party. He was imprisoned for a short time in Kiel but was soon released and promoted. He again had serious difficulties with Himmler in 1939 because of his disagreement with Himmler's anti-Jewish policy. He had submitted a plan to give the Jews a minority status shortly after the beginning of the Polish campaign, in October 1939, which was violently disapproved of by Heydrich and Himmler. At that time Himmler demanded Ohlendorf's dismissal from the government service and from the SS, but Heydrich smoothed things out because he preferred to have subordinates who were not on too good terms with Himmler and whose contacts with Himmler would therefore have to go through him alone. Ohlendorf again got into difficulties in 1941 when he attempted to protect the adherents of the anthroposophic movement[3] who were then beginning to be persecuted by the Nazi government. It was shortly after that that he received his orders to head one of the dreaded "*Einsatzgruppen*" (special task forces) in the East. These *Einsatzgruppen* consisted of 500 enlisted men, 150 officers, and one commanding officer. Their sole purpose was to kill large groups of unarmed, defenseless men, women, and children who had been registered and collected for the ostensible purpose of being re-settled in another locality. In reality they were transported in trucks to lonely places in the country where they were murdered. Ohlendorf was slated to be the commanding officer of one of these *Einsatzgruppen*. He stated that he had refused this assignment twice but had accepted when he was ordered the third time. I asked him why he had refused. He replied that he had no inclination for this task, saying,

> "I never have been friendly toward the State police and I never wanted to have anything to do with this matter, but I was ordered by Heydrich because I must express it the way I know it – for one thing, he wanted to have me removed from Berlin because Bormann demanded it. I had come into disrepute as a protector of the anthroposophers. I had first supported them in opposition to policy in May, 1941 after they had been forbidden and locked up by Bormann. And furthermore, Heydrich wanted to take away my liberty which consisted of the fact that I was not financially dependent upon the SS but that my official assignment was under the Economics Ministry. These two motives were the reasons he wanted to get me away from Berlin; and that he gave me this assignment was probably caused by the fact that he wanted to demoralize me because already then and later I was against his SD[4] activity ... And that not only came from Heydrich but especially from Himmler."

---

3   The adherents of an esoteric sect similar to one known in the United States as the theosophic movement.
4   SD, or Sicherheits-Dienst (Security Service), is the SS equivalent of the Gastapo, which in view of the fact that Himmler, the chief of the SS, was at the same time chief of the German police, was actually the controlling and policy-making element of the Gestapo.

Ohlendorf then continued that he had refused the assignment at first because the manner of killing these people was disagreeable to him. What "manner" I asked.

He replied, "The shooting of defenseless human beings." I then asked him: "When did you know for the first time that this was not merely a disagreeable assignment, but that it was a crime? When were you for the first time conscious of that fact?" He replied,

> "When I first heard that these things happened." "When was that?"
> "That I cannot exactly say; but whether I already had heard of it before I received the order or afterwards, that I can no longer say. At any rate this order was a subject which was difficult to take from the human standpoint."

I then asked Ohlendorf what he meant by the term, "to demoralize me." Did he mean that because he had shown some opposition in the question of treatment of the Jews and the anthroposophers, he was subsequently deliberately put into a position where he not only had to accept decisions which went against his grain but where he himself actually had to act against his own convictions? Ohlendorf replied that this was the general policy in dealing with such people who, like himself, dared to disagree, in order "to corrupt us morally" (*um uns moralisch kaputt zu machen*).

Ohlendorf went on to say that in this system of controlling people by corrupting them morally various methods were used. He stated that he did not know for sure to what extent Hitler used this technique, but Himmler and Heydrich always tried to corrupt people whom they wanted to use in order to have them completely in hand. This was not always done by involving them in capital crimes; in some cases lesser, compromising situations sufficed. Heydrich established a special brothel in Berlin for that purpose. He would invite people there, put them into a compromising situation – in some cases by using a quite primitive system of seduction – and then suddenly Heydrich appeared on the scene and it was made clear to the person involved that Heydrich had been a spectator. Heydrich used this special brothel as a means of blackmail. An SS general who had a mentally ill brother was occasionally reminded of that fact as a means of blackmail by a no lesser personage than Himmler himself. Other people were bribed, such as the field marshals, or were involved in financial corruption as were many people in the Speer ministry. The Speer ministry was just one hotbed of corruption – everybody was doubly paid and more than that. Other people who could not be bribed by Hitler, Himmler, and Speer or compromised by means of seduction to sex escapades by Heydrich were involved in more sinister ways. All knowledge of a man's weak points was used against him.

Ohlendorf continued,

> "Since I was in disrepute as an unsoldierly type who had previously declined to become a soldier, they hoped in this way to influence my character, which they knew was predominantly sensitive, in order to make me transgress and thus to force me into their pattern."

The type of blood cement outlined above played a role even in the case of Dr. Sigmund Rascher, the notorious vivisectionist of Dachau concentration camp. Prior to making application to Himmler and the SS to permit him to make experiments on inmates of Dachau concentration camp in May 1939, he had been forbidden to use the facilities of the Pathological Institute of the University of Munich because he was suspected of having communist sympathies (Doc. No. NO – 3679). A very important case in this connection is that of Erich von dem Bach-Zelewski, SS Obergruppenfuehrer and General of the Waffen SS and police. Von dem Bach was in charge of all so-called antipartisan activities in the eastern territories. He commanded troops which roamed all over the vast conquered eastern territories behind the German fighting fronts in Poland and Russia, whose record of looting, arson, and mass murder is equaled only by that of the Huns and Mongols of days past. General von dem Bach was the deputy Genghis Khan of this horde which was composed of SS and police troops and attached Wehrmacht formations. The number of these troops was greater than that of the Einsatz groups. Von dem Bach had up to two divisions at his disposal, although the number of troops which were assigned to him varied during various phases of the war. The troops which he commanded included the notorious Dirlewanger Brigade which was composed of habitual criminals including poachers, robbers, murderers, men condemned because of sex crimes, and those political prisoners who had been members of the Nazi Party prior to the commission of their political offense. Its commanding officer, Oskar Dirlewanger, had himself been in prison for sex crimes. The number of people who were murdered in cold blood by Von [sic] dem Bach's forces is likewise much greater than the victims of any one Einsatz group. While Ohlendorf, head of Einsatz Group D, admitted the killing of 90,000 men, women and children in the space of one year, merely one single report of antipartisan activities (Report No. 51, of 29 December 1942 applying to the months of August to November 1942) shows that among others 363,211 Jews were executed by these formations.

The exact records of infamy which these culprits kept is a novel feature in crime, which is quite characteristic of the SS as a whole, with only a few cagey exceptions. It is obviously the result of indoctrination. Non-SS Nazis, when involved in similar crimes, usually tried to cover up at the same time.

The case of Von dem Bach is interesting because he not only admitted the fact that crimes were committed but he also showed a certain amount of insight into how they came about. All the while he was of course trying to minimize his personal participation and responsibility, more so than Ohlendorf. But he showed greater insight in regard to the fact that the Nazi ideology and the basic structure of Nazism and the SS were the cause of these crimes, while Ohlendorf and others held not National Socialism itself responsible for these crimes but rather what they called the "dark side" of Hitler's and Himmler's personalities.

Von dem Bach testified before the International Military Tribunal on January 7, 1946 (pp. 2219–2244 of the record). He stated that he enlisted in the German army in 1914 at the age of 15 years, that he served from 1914 to 1918 and was wounded and decorated twice. He remained as an officer in the peacetime army after the last war, was discharged in 1924, and then transferred as battalion commander to an unofficial border defense formation but continued to remain a reserve officer in the army. He joined the Nazi Party and the SS in 1930, and in 1932 he was elected as a National Socialist representative of the German Reichstag. In 1934 he became superior SS and police leader for East Prussia and in 1936 for Silesia. At the beginning of the war against Russia he was sent to the Russian front with the rank of *Gruppenfuehrer* and lieutenant general of the Waffen SS and police. He saw frontline service before Moscow and near Veliky Luky. He was subsequently appointed as higher SS and police leader for the rear zone of the central army group under General Von Schenkendorff with the principal assignment of fighting partisans in the rear of the German central army group. Formations of the Waffen SS, of the border police, and of the Wehrmacht were put at his disposal for these activities. At the end of 1942 he was appointed chief of all antipartisan units for the entire eastern territories, in which capacity he was subordinate only to Heinrich Himmler.

Von dem Bach admitted that these antipartisan operations were carried out in such a way as to result in the unnecessary killing of large numbers of the civilian population (p. 2225 of the record). He claimed that he and General Von Schenkendorff were powerless to stop these excesses because of an order issued by the highest Wehrmacht authorities that German soldiers who committed offenses against the civilian population were not to be punished. "This order was an obstacle to correcting the excesses of the troops," and "prevented the only proper way of fighting" (p. 2225 of the record). Von dem Bach was then asked, "Do you know anything about the existence of a special brigade which was formed from contrabandists, poachers, and people released from prison?" He replied:

> One battalion under the command of Dirlewanger was put in as an antipartisan unit in the central army group. This battalion was gradually enlarged by some reserves, actually reaching the size of a regiment and later of a brigade. This was the Brigade Dirlewanger, and it consisted for the most part of criminal elements. officially of poachers, but there were real criminals among them who bad committed robbery and even murder.

He was then asked why the German army used forces recruited from the ranks of criminals especially in the war against the partisans. He replied:

> I am of the opinion that there was a close connection with the speech made by Heinrich Himmler at the beginning of 1941 before the campaign against Russia, when he spoke of the purpose of the Russian campaign, which was to decimate the Slav population by 30 million, and in order to be active in this direction, a troop of low characters would have to be formed, (p. 2228 of the record.).

Von dem Bach then admitted that the type of troops used and the instructions given were aimed at the direct destruction of the population. He stated that official reports had to be made as to how many partisans had been killed in battle, how many partisans had been executed, how many people suspected to be partisans had been executed, and how many losses the troops themselves had sustained; from these reports the highest authorities could see exactly what went on.

Individual commanders were empowered to decide for themselves whom they wanted to suspect as a partisan and to kill him (p. 2230 of the record). Von dem Bach admitted that the fighting against partisan movements was designed for the deconstruction of the Slav and Jewish people in the eastern conquered territories. He stated that the Wehrmacht was aware of this aim that the methods of antipartisan warfare were designed for the destruction of the Slavic and Jewish races – that is for the complete destruction of the Jewish race and the reduction of the Slavic race by 30 millions (p. 2231 of the record). Upon repeated questioning, he reiterated that the Slavic population was to be reduced by 30 millions. He stated that Himmler had mentioned this in his speech-prior to the Russian campaign.

Von dem Bach claimed that he had made many proposals to change this policy and to limit the use of antipartisan forces strictly to real antipartisan activity; but he petitioned unsuccessfully because, as he found out, such a change was not desired by Himmler (p. 2232 of the record). At Himmler's Wewelsburg speech in 1941 twelve of the leading Gruppenfuehrers of the SS, including von dem Bach, had been present. In the cross-examination by Rosenberg's defense counsel, Dr. Thoma, Von dem Bach again confirmed the fact that many innocent people were killed in the so-called antipartisan activities. He was then asked by the defense counsel (p. 2241 of the record): "How did you reconcile it with your conscience to be an inspector general and to remain an inspector general with the antipartisan forces?"

> A. I did not reconcile that with my conscience.
> Q. Do you believe that Himmler's order in which he demanded that 30 million Slavs should be exterminated – do you believe that was his opinion or was it a part of the whole National Socialistic attitude toward life?
> A. I am today of the mind that the logical consequences of that attitude was such an order.
> Q. Today – what was your opinion at that time?
> A. It is difficult for a German to make this confession and it took me a long while.
> Q. How does it happen that a few days ago a witness appeared before this tribunal, namely Ohlendorf, who admitted that under his command of Einsatz groups, 90,000 people were killed, and informed the court that this did not correspond to National Socialist ideology?
> A. I am of the opinion that when for years, for decades, the doctrine is preached that the Slav race is an inferior race and Jews not even human, then such an outcome is inevitable.
> Q. Nevertheless, the fact remains, along with the attitude that you may have had at that time, you also had a conscience?
> A. Today also, and that is the reason I am here.

In a preceding interrogation which took place on October 19, 1945, Von dem Bach had stated that he was relieved from his position in Silesia and sent to the Russian front because he had refused to put the Jews in his area into ghetto camps and, especially, to arrange pogroms in which 5,000 were supposed to be shot. In other interrogations Von dem Bach had made the same and similar statements and had also made the statement that as early as 1935 he had difficulties with Himmler. At one time in 1935 he had been arrested by order of Goering and Himmler and was supposed to be executed, but his life was then saved by the intervention of Darre. I therefore decided to re-interrogate Von dem Bach and to obtain some more data about the socio-psychological setting in which he had committed his crimes.

I found Von dem Bach to be a well-built man of athletic physique who gave the impression of a man of hard-driving energy and of a great deal of ambition. He spoke with clarity and vigor. He showed definite eagerness to make a good impression and to minimize his own participation, and yet it appeared that he had given a good deal of thought to what he and others about him had done during the last 13 years. All leading questions were avoided and he was allowed to express himself and to state his case quite freely. It is interesting that in this connection he formulated, without the slightest suggestion on my part, a very clear conception of the blood cement theory outlined above. His statements of facts were later checked with others, especially Ohlendorf and Wolff.

As to his arrest and threatened execution in 1935, he stated that he had, in his capacity as superior SS leader for East Prussia, objected to the corrupt financial practices of the Gauleiter Koch; and for this reason during a speech which Finance Minister Schacht gave in Koenigsberg in which he endorsed Koch's policies, Von dem Bach demonstratively walked out of the hall and took his entire SS detachment with him. (Karl Wolff, Himmler's former chief of staff, confirmed this incident: He recalled that Schacht had said in his speech that honor, blood, and flag were all right, but gold also was a reality to be reckoned with. Wolff stated that he approved of Von dem Bach's courage and determination to march out with the entire SS at this point. He added that Von dem Bach missed being executed by a hair's breadth because of Goering's and Himmler's resentment of this action.)

After his rehabilitation on Darre's intervention, Von dem Bach was not sent back to East Prussia but was given all equivalent assignment in Silesia to which certain provinces taken from Poland were later added. In 1940 he again incurred Himmler's displeasure by not cooperating in the establishment of ghetto camps for Jews and later by his failure to arrange pogroms in his territory.

About his subsequent activities in Russia and in the parts of Poland taken from Russia after the beginning of the Russian campaign, he of course tried to incriminate himself as little as possible, as he had done on previous interrogations. In an interrogation on January 15, 1947, when he was shown the above cited report on the execution of 366,211 Jews by antipartisan forces during August to November 1942, he merely stated that this was the sort of camouflage which he had always disapproved of because execution of Jews is certainly not antipartisan warfare. These mass executions were usually carried out in lonely places in the country before deep gullies or large anti-tank ditches into which the bodies fell or were dumped and covered with dirt.

It is obvious, however, from the documentary evidence that Von dem Bach himself included such and similar executions in his reports on antipartisan warfare, for instance in his report dated Minsk, 23 June 1943 (Doc. No. NO–2608) in which the ratio of casualties (600 on the German side versus 10,000 partisans) and the small number of weapons captured (900 rifles) indicated that the majority of partisans listed as "killed in action" in the report were actually rounded up and massacred. (Obergruppenfuehrer Wolff stated that Von dem Bach was always intent on giving large figures because he wanted to get the Knight's Cross very badly and that one time he had criticized him because in a report covering May and June 1944, Von dem Bach had taken credit for people, by including them in his own report, who had actually been killed by SS *Gruppenfuehrer* (Lieutenant General) Globocnik's outfit in the southeastern theatre of war in northern Italy and Yugoslavia when Von dem Bach inspected Globocnik's operations in that theatre during May and June 1944.)

Von dem Bach expressed great pride over the fact that he had once preferred court martial charges against some of his men who killed a group of four or five civilian suspects in a particularly cruel manner by pouring gasoline over them and setting them on fire while they were still alive; this was done in the courtyard of a building amidst shouts of approval from a great crowd of soldiers. The court martial sentences which included death and prison sentences were, however, disapproved by higher authority and the culprits were freed (Interrogation No. 633 of 17 January 1947). In a similar incident when the entire male population of a village was executed and fire was set to the village after the women, children, and cattle had been driven away, he decided after consultation with higher authority not to prefer charges against the perpetrators under his command because a conviction was considered unlikely (Interrogation No. 633A of 20 January 1947). There is, however, documentary evidence to prove that Von dem Bach by no means condemned such outrages prior to German's defeat, but on the contrary recommended to higher authority the court martial of one of his subordinate SS Sturmbannfuehrers who had made an official complaint about such atrocities in 1944 (Doc. No. NO–2530).

Von dem Bach told me and previous interrogators that on three occasions in 1941 he had warned the Jews of Bialystok, Mogilev, and Baranowicze respectively of the fact that his forces were approaching and of what was in store for them, by sending ward ahead to the chief rabbi of each of these three towns. His motive for doing this was that one of his sisters who had emigrated to Brazil was married to a Jewish musician who had been born in Bialystok and whose relatives still lived there. He knew this brother-in-law well and had been rather fond of him before this brother-in-law and his sister were forced to emigrate from Germany after the Nazis came to power. For that reason he sent the warning. He stated, however, that his warning was not taken seriously enough. After hiding a few days and when they thought "that the German civilian administration was there" the Jews returned from the woods and walked in to their own destruction. (Obviously these rabbis and their country flocks did not understand the complexity and the characteristic "dual-track thinking" of this high-ranking SS man who had seemed to be friendly by warning them; on the other hand, it is much more likely that they returned because they ran out of food in the woods).

> "Thus the misfortune came about. They did not believe ... I am the only living witness but I must say the truth. Contrary to the opinion of the National Socialists that the Jews were a highly organized group, the appalling fact was that they had no organization whatsoever. The mass of the Jewish people were completely taken by surprise. They did not know at all what to do; they had no directives or slogan as to how they should act. That is the greatest proof of the lie of anti-Semitism because it gives the lie to the old slogan that the Jews are conspiring to dominate the world and that they are so highly organized. In reality they had no organization of their own at all, not even an information service. If they had some sort of organization, these people could have been saved by the millions; but instead they were taken completely by surprise. Never before has a people gone as unsuspectingly to its disaster. Nothing was prepared. Absolutely nothing. It is not so, as the anti-Semites say, that they were friendly to the Soviets. That is the most appalling misconception of all. The Jews in the old Poland, who were never communistic in their sympathies, were, throughout the area from the river Bug eastward, more afraid of Bolshevism than of the Nazis. This was insanity. They could have been saved. There were people among them who had much to lose, business people; they didn't want to leave. In addition there was the love of home and their old experiences with the pogroms in Russia. After the first anti-Jewish actions of the Germans they thought now the wave was over and so they walked back to their undoing."

In August 1944 Von dem Bach was put in charge of the suppression of the Warsaw revolt which was led on the Polish side by General Bor-Komorowski. This military action, with its resulting sacking and razing of Warsaw and the wanton murder of a large part of its civilian population, is one of the worst crimes committed by the German armed forces. Von dem Bach admitted that even before the defeat of Germany he had disapproved of the conduct of that operation. He stated that he was given the singular honor of having a medal strack in commemoration of this action and to be in sole charge of its award to meritorious participants in this operation; but because of the type of operation it had been he never made use of this privilege and did not award this medal to anyone. However, he admitted that he himself received the coveted Knight's Cross after the successful suppression of the Warsaw revolt. He credits himself with two acts of chivalry-one, that he court martialed one of his subordinate SS Gruppenfuehrers, Kaminski, and had him executed unofficially because of his excesses in looting, without waiting for approval by higher authorities; and secondly, for the fact that he took his military opponents as prisoners of war contrary to Hitler's and Himmler's orders – according to which they should all have been killed by execution upon capture. Contrary to these orders he brought the revolt to an end by giving General Bor-Komorowski and the remainder of his forces the status of prisoners of war as terms for their surrender. For this purpose he had to countermand Hitler's and Himmler's order which explicitly stated, "Everyone is to be killed. No prisoners are to be taken. Warsaw is to be razed to the ground and an example is to be made for all of Europe." He stated that he incurred both Hitler's and Himmler's wrath by disregarding that order and for taking General Bor-Komorowski and the remainder of his forces prisoners on 28 September 1944. He was ordered to report personally to Hitler's headquarters and to explain his action.

The way in which Hitler handled the situation was very characteristic of our theory outlined above and entirely in conformity with it. He immediately gave Von dem Bach a new and still more criminal assignment as plenipotentiary to carry out the coup d'etat in Hungary. In the course of this coup d'etat on October 14, 1944, the regent of that country was imprisoned, his son kidnapped, the entire country taken under German control, and 60,000 Jews were arrested immediately for purposes of extermination and deportation, of which 25,000 were killed outright or perished on the subsequent eight-day death march which began on October 15, 1944. Von dem Bach described this interesting interview with Hitler, which took place early in October, 1944, immediately prior to his assignment to Hungary, as follows:

> "Hitler told me, 'Actually you have forfeited your head because you have acted against my orders. But since your method has been successful and the battle is won after all, I have accepted it.' That was typically Hitler. But I still felt uneasy because I could name innumerable examples of people to whom he gave a decoration and then had them hanged. He continued: 'The success was decisive. I have approved of it now. You were lucky. Maybe you will be lucky again the next time too. You seem to have a streak of luck now.' Everybody was there, Keitel, Himmler, Goering, all prominent people. I said, 'I have held out and been successful only because I kept up negotiations with the partisans.' Hitler then said, 'Hungary threatens to secede. I shall send you now to Hungary to prevent the secession of Hungary and I will give

you plenipotentiary power. You have to prevent Horthy from jumping off the running train, if need be by armed force. The moment of action I will determine myself. I shall send you word by courier. You will have to arrest the entire Hungarian government and to take care that the Hungarians will not fight against Germany as the Roumanians did.'"

Himmler's reaction on the same occasion was in the form of a bit of not too subtle blackmail. He congratulated Von dem Bach on his victory over Warsaw and at the same time gave him a notarized certificate that his brother Viktor Von dem Bach had died insane in a sanitarium near Bielefeld. This was obvious blackmail because of what it meant to an SS officer to be "hereditarily tainted" in any form.

In Hungary, after Regent Horthy's son was kidnapped by Von dem Bach's subordinate, SS Lieutenant Colonel Skorzeny, Von dem Bach received word from Hitler to take over as pleni-potentiary, to deliver an ultimatum to Horthy, and to bring about his capitulation on October 14, 1944. Von dem Bach was still rather proud of the trick which he played on Horthy by bluffing him with a large number of heavy tanks for which no ammunition had yet arrived. As soon as Von dem Bach took over the control of Hungary, on October 14, 1944, Heinrich Himmler immediately telephoned him long distance, offered his congratulations, and urged him not to delay and make difficulties with the immediate deportation and extermination of the Jews of Budapest. There is no doubt that these measures were carried out immediately, namely on October 15, 1944, but Von dem Bach went through a great deal of explanations that this was actually Winkelmann's and Veesenmeyer's responsibility. Although Von dem Bach was the plenipotentiary he insisted that Veesenmeyer could have prevented the action against the Jews but that he would have been dismissed from office had he done so (Interrogation Summary No. 1875 of 14 April 1947).

Von dem Bach revealed the first evidence of real insight into the social-psychological role which involvement in crime played in Nazi Germany in a rather surprising connection when he discussed the fact that the Allied countries had not utilized with sufficient determination the antagonisms which existed in pre-war Germany between the army on the one hand and the SS and Party on the other. He said:

> "There were opposition groups in existence. Think of the enormous animosity which existed between army and Party. Then, compelled by the war and by their bad conscience they were brought together. Hitler let them all become guilty. I am firmly convinced that his great crimes had only that one motive: 'I will let them all become guilty. They must never be allowed to jump off the running train.' If one sees it that way, you see how one becomes guilty, if you take Field Marshal von Weichs for instance as an example. This man, who throughout the entire army not only in Hitler's time but even before was called 'the pious general,' this man, who as a devout Catholic never missed a religious service, who still in this war in Belgrade had his own private chaplain who held masses especially for him – this man will be tried here and it will be proven that he is guilty, that he has really backed up pure terror orders which were entirely inhuman, the hostage orders, that he in any case passed them on."

I then asked General Von dem Bach, "Did you hear in this connection the word 'blood cement'?" He answered: That is quite clear. That is the same as what I mean.

Q. Did you hear that expression?
A. I don't recall that expression. Is that supposed to be a Hitler expression?
Q. Yes. Hitler was supposed to have obtained that from a book on Genghis Khan.
A. I received this book. I can testify that it was officially sent out by Hermann Goering with Himmler's approval. At Christmas in 1938 it was sent to everyone in the Party down to county leader (Kreisleiter). There were two volumes and a supplement. Therefore I became convinced that one wanted to solve this question of the excess birthrate in the East, which was bound to crush Germany some day, in this war once and for all in the manner of a Genghis Khan. I therefore was not surprised when already during the war against Poland ghettos were established, but the main danger I found in the East was the annihilation of the Slavs.

He went on to say that in 1943 preparations for the systematic mass extermination of the Slavs were made in the neighborhood of Smolensk, near Mogilev. In this region which was under the control of Von dem Bach, the erection of large gas chambers and crematoria was planned by a commission which arrived from Hamburg, Germany, and looked over various sites including an armament factory which was to be transformed into an extermination center which would dwarf the gas chambers and crematoria at Auschwitz. After the complete occupation of Russia the "problem of the Slavs" was to be solved by large-scale exterminations. The enforced retreat of the German army, however, foiled this plan.

Von dem Bach stated that in the system of letting people become guilty in order to control them with which the Nazis operated, presents of money and the encouragement of financial corruption were also used. He said:

General Brauchitsch let Hitler pay for his second wife. Hitler paid the settlement to Brauchitsch's first wife and in that way Brauchitsch became Hitler's bound serf. If I accept 100,000 marks I am no longer a free man. Guderian allowed Himmler, on Hitler's order, to give him a baronial estate in Posen. The old Field Marshal Hindenburg allowed Hitler to give him the Prussian Forest in East Prussia as a present. Mackensen let Hitler give him an estate near Stettin which once belonged to his ancestors. I saw already in these early days how Hitler bought these people. All these people thus became accomplices.

The talk which I had with Karl Wolff, SS *Obergruppenfuehrer* and general of the Waffen SS, who had been chief of Himmler's personal staff from 1933 until 1943, was likewise very revealing. Obergruppenfuehrer Wolff was expected to be thoroughly familiar with all personnel problems concerning Himmler's staff until September, 1943, when he was transferred as supreme SS and police leader to the Italian theatre of war where he was taken prisoner of war by the Allies after Germany's defeat.

Obergruppenfuehrer Wolff is a tall slender man of good appearance and manners, who is exteriorly smart, suave, and smooth. He is somewhat overpolite, indicating a marked eagerness to please and to make a good impression. He is the type of man whom the Germans call Streber, by which they mean an effectively ambitious person, a place hunter.

Wolff was very much on the defensive about his personal participation in crimes. He claimed that as chief of Himmler's protocol he was merely in charge of the social, the cultural, the beautiful, and the positive aspects of Himmler's activities; while for all matters which had to do with what he called Himmler's *"second face,"* Heydrich exclusively was in charge. I did not want to disturb the interview by pointing out the fact that on a captured film record of one of Himmler's visits to a death camp in Minsk in 1941 the striking figure of *Obergruppenfuehrer* Wolff can be seen walking immediately behind and to the right of Himmler amid the scenes of horror, walking along the barbed-wire enclosure in which huddled masses of emaciated humanity look on in mute fear and despair while the hangmen strut by. This film which shows the visit of Himmler and his staff to the extermination camp in Minsk in 1941 is included in the documentary film "The Nazi Rise to Power" which is a document of the International Military Tribunal (Doc. No. USA 167).

Subsequent conversation likewise brought out the fact that Wolff knew far more about Himmler's activities than he was willing to admit under direct questioning. He said that the beginning of the development of what he called the "second face" of Himmler was his deification of power and success which caused him to become unfaithful to the decent goals of the SS. By his infidelity he involved others in that same infidelity to the old, decent SS ideals:

> This unfaithfulness began at the top. He wanted to have success at any price. He thought that "Right is what is useful to my nation." This concept has not grown up gradually as it had in England where it was balanced by a careful weighing of the price, but with him became boundless without weight and measure of the cost. It became the enforcement of policy at any price. In carrying out the task set by the Fuehrer to render the eastern territories free of all contamination by non-Germans he used a small circle of people as principal aides. Himmler rendered those people whom he intended to use powerless to resist his commands by implied and open threats, including the threat of holding their families responsible if they did not cooperate (Sippenhaft). All this recruitment and these pressures went on behind closed doors. At the time the decision was made to carry out the planned exterminations, principally the extermination of the Jews, the matter had already been prepared by a few collaborators, especially Eichmann and Hoess. They were already there when the decision came to exterminate. When that decision had ripened in Himmler's brain one day he also decided to entrust the execution of the plan to a small group of close associates which he picked himself. Globocnik[5] appeared the most suitable for such a brutal task. He was always considered a ruthless person. Also, Von dem Bach was somewhat similar. Others were of a different type of mentality and were chosen for other reasons. Ohlendorf was always an especially decent fellow. He was an idealist who, as Reichsfuehrer Himmler used to say, "always ran about lamenting and deploring, and acted as if he were the only one who carried the Grail in his hands unsullied." Ohlendorf was rather soft by nature, to which the Reichsfuehrer objected and which he wanted to see changed by education. He had a blameless past without dark points so that he could not be put under pressure. The Reichsfuehrer wanted to harden this valuable man.

I then asked Wolff to tell me more about Globocnik. He replied that Globocnik was an old Nazi Party member from Austria who had been imprisoned there in Woellersdorf prior to the Anschluss because of his Nazi Party membership. After the conquest of Austria, he was made Gauleiter of Vienna with the rank of colonel in the SS. However, he failed in this position because of his difficulty in getting along with other old Party members there. He was subsequently deprived of his

---

5   SS Gruppenfuehrer Odilo Globocnik was the man in charge of the extermination center in Lublin, Poland, where the first mass executions of Jews by means of gas were carried out in specially built gas chambers.

rank and reduced to a simple enlisted SS man. He served in the Polish campaign as an enlisted man and later became a sergeant, finally being promoted to second lieutenant. Then suddenly, after the extermination program had been decided upon, he was put in charge of the exterminations of Jews by gas and for that purpose was made superior SS and police leader of Lublin with the rank of Major General of Police, which was quite a jump in rank; this was done because after all he was an old fighter. He had been imprisoned in Woellersdorf and the view was taken that he had been overthrown by intrigues and so Himmler wanted to give him a chance to rehabilitate himself by this assignment to Lublin.

In October, 1943, Globocnik was transferred and promoted to the rank of SS Gruppenfuehrer and Lieutenant General of Police, in which capacity he was placed in charge of five northern-Italian and Yugoslav provinces, obviously in recognition of his participation in the organization of the extermination program of the Jews in gas chambers, which he instituted in Poland with the advice and expert guidance of Brack who had placed experience and personnel from the extermination program of ["]the insane["] at his disposal for the genocidal program in the East. According to a report received on 2 June 1945, Globocnik committed suicide by poison after his arrest by Allied forces.

I then asked Obergruppenfuehrer Wolff what would have happened if Ohlendorf, for instance, had refused to carry out his assignment. Wolff replied:

> He would have been silenced. He (Himmler) would not have let him live. He would have liquidated him in some illegal way. Himmler would have done so from his conviction that someone must do it if it is necessary for the welfare of 85 million Germans. Then one must sacrifice the salvation of one's soul, or one must give up one's life. Wolff added that the view which an SS member had to take in this matter was like this: "I must do it. In order to clear this new living space I must sacrifice myself, the salvation of my soul, and my honor, or else give up my life."

The fact that the blood-cement theory was applied on a much larger scale than merely in individual cases is nowhere more clearly expressed than in Gottlob Berger's reaction to reports on SS crimes, particularly crimes committed by Von dem Bach and Von Gottberg and their units in Russia, which he received in July 1943. It is interesting to realize at this point that the German army at times prepared extensive reports on atrocities committed by the SS in various theatres of war. Usually the SS countered this by compiling a still larger number of reports on atrocities committed by the army in the same theatre of war, according to Kogon.[6] Kogon states in his book that this went so far that once the army compiled an entire volume containing evidence on atrocities committed by the SS. The SS parried this move by compiling two volumes of evidence on atrocities committed by the army in the same theatres of war.

It is very interesting and revealing to go through some of these original reports. One of the earliest is a transcript of an oral report by an army commander to Lieutenant General von Bomhard and General of the Police Daluege on 6 February 1940 (Doc. No. NO–3011). In this report the German commander expressed the opinion

---

6   Kogon, Engen. Der SS Staat. Munich (Karl Alber), 1946, I–XXITI, 1–339.

that the official policy of persecution of Jews and Poles, acts of violence against the Jews, and in the first place the atrocities committed by SS and police personnel were doing great harm to the German cause.

The report went on:

> It is bad policy to slaughter, as is happening now, some tens of thousands of Jews and Poles. This does neither kill the idea of the Polish state in the eyes of the masses nor does it dispose of the Jews; on the contrary, as this slaughter is being done it does the greatest harm, complicates the problems and makes them much more dangerous than they would have been if we had acted in a considered and practical way. These are the effects of the present policy:
> a) Enemy propaganda is furnished with the most effective material that could possibly be thought of. What foreign radio stations have reported so far was only a tiny fraction of what actually happened. We must be prepared for an increase of foreign propaganda which will do extreme political damage since those disgusting atrocities actually happened and cannot be denied by any means.
>
> [...]
>
> d) The greatest harm, however, which will be suffered by the German people itself owing to present conditions, is the extreme brutalization and moral degeneracy which will spread among valuable German human material like pestilence in a very short time.
>
> There is only one chance to stop this plague: to subject those criminals and their following instantly to military command and military jurisdiction.

The report then quoted a statement by General Ulex, commander of Grenzabschnitt Sued, addressed to the supreme commander of the army in the East and dated 6 February 1940. General Ulex also condemned the atrocities committed by police forces passionately and in addition believed that the superiors of those who committed the crimes tacitly approved their misdeeds and just did not want to interfere. He added that the atrocities which came to his knowledge were most likely only a small fraction of the total number of atrocities actually committed. He recommended that all police forces including their higher leaders and all commanders attached to the organizations of the Government General be dismissed quite abruptly, that all those units be inactivated and "replaced with morally intact and honorable units." Finally the report quoted a statement on the same subject by Major von Tschammer und Osten, liaison officer at the Government General. This statement emphasized that in addition to atrocities against the population the SS and police also committed acts of robbery and looting whenever they carried out searches. Officially seized goods of all sorts were distributed among the police and SS forces or sold at a nominal price. At a conference at the Government General, held on 23 January 1940, Major General Buehrmann, commissioner for the four-year plan, reported that Rittmeister Schuh, the exceptionally efficient chief of one of the four-year-plan offices, managed to have the SS give up large quantities of watches and gold. With regard to such conditions, von Tschammer und Osten went on, one could not be surprised to see that everybody made use of every chance to get rich. It could be done without any danger, for when stealing is committed by the whole organization the individual thief has no reason to be afraid of punishment. The Polish population who were defenseless in the face of these crimes and were driven to despair by such acts would, of course, fanatically support every movement aiming at revolt and revenge. "It is only natural that their feelings are increased to boundless hatred when they see, every time a transport arrives, the many corpses of child[r]en who died of hunger and the trucks full of human beings frozen to death."

The main report contained an enclosure listing and describing 33 specific instances of the most revolting acts of atrocity committed by SS and police personnel. In most of these cases the names of the SS and police personnel who committed these crimes and the number and denomination of their units were given.

On 1 November 1941, Wilhelm Kube, General Commissioner for White Ruthenia, sent a letter of complaint to Heinrich Lohse, Reich Commissioner for the eastern territories, in which he complained "about the manner in which the *Judenaktion* (the extermination of the Jews) in Sluzk was handled.["] He declared the officers of the Police Battalion No. 11 from Kauen to be responsible for the "insufficient and uncoordinated execution of this action, where the injured were buried together with the dead, only to work their way out of the graves again." He declared this to be highly detrimental to the reputation of the German administration and demanded that the responsible officers be prosecuted (Doc. No. NO–2456). The most condemning document is a group of six reports (Doc. No. NO–3028) with a letter of transmittal dated 10 July 1943 from Dr. Braeutigam, the Reichs Minister of Occupied Eastern Territories, to SS *Obergruppenfuehrer* Berger, the Chief of the SS Hauptampt which was responsible for the recruitment of SS personnel. These reports included a report dated 2 July 1943 by Propaganda Leader Lauch, obviously a representative of the Propaganda Ministry who was sent to the East to spread National Socialist propaganda among the population; reports by the Reichs Commissioner Wilhelm Kube of 3 June 1943, by the General Commissioner of Minsk and others. Lauch's report gives a day by day description of antipartisan activities near Minsk, which started on 16 May 1943. Characteristic is his entry for the 24th of May 1943, describing what he found at Nebyschino:

> There were two barns filled with the corpses of partisans or those suspected set to the barns, the corpses had not been burned completely. In one of the barns four pigs were feeding from six charred bodies ... The whole picture was one of senseless devastation and made a very bad impression on the remaining population ...

Lauch stated in his report that on the 27th of May 1943 he discontinued his propaganda campaign. He obviously compiled his report as an explanation of why he did so. He concluded that he considered propaganda ineffective in the face of an obvious policy of burning villages down and shooting the people. Lauch's report was forwarded to Braeutigam by Wilhelm Kube, to whom it had been sent by the General Commissioner of Minsk who included also his own observations and other adverse reports concerning the large antipartisan operations of the SS and police under the leadership of Von dem Bach and Von Gottberg.

An event very similar to that observed by Lauch was also described by Langer, a member of the staff of the General Commissioner of Minsk. Langer tells of incidents which occurred in Witonitsch near Borrisow, which is in the vicinity of Minsk. He states: "Inhabitants were driven into a barn, shot down and the buildings set afire. Since the corpses did not burn completely, the pigs are carrying parts of the charred bodies into the villages where they lie about."

In his forwarding letter to Kube the General Commissioner of Minsk closes by saying, "Particularly the Regiment Dirlewanger excels in actions of that sort. It consists almost entirely of convicts from Germany."

Another report by Langer, from the Office of the General Commissioner of Minsk, contains the following information:

> On the 27th of May at 1400 hours, the inhabitants of Krjwsk were herded into two houses by the SS and Ukrainians and fire was set to the houses so that they burned to death. The same happened in another village, Kraschynn.

Berger's reaction, in his one-page letter addressed to Braeutigam of the East Ministry, is very revealing. He stated that he regretted deeply that such reports were sent on without further investigation and thus caused a great stir and above all hampered close cooperation. In Berger's opinion, Generalkommissar Kube should have investigated these cases immediately and then contacted Von Gottberg and Von dem Bach. Berger closed:

> We cannot change anything from where we are anyhow, for it is not possible to give orders to troops without thorough knowledge of the situation. Moreover, Herr Kube's attention might be directed to the fact that these criminals are primarily former Party members, previously convicted for poaching or some other slight offense. They are now given an opportunity to prove themselves and do so in spite of bloody losses and with great ardor.

In other words, this assignment was a means of blood cement by which offenders and recalcitrants could gain readmission into the good graces of the SS.

A revealing additional sidelight was provided by Walther Eppehauer, Berger's adjutant, who stated in an interrogation Summary (No. 314 of 17 October 1946) that SS officers whom Berger disliked were usually transferred to the Dirlewanger Brigade. This was obviously a move to make them acquire blood cement and thus to become acceptable to him as firmly welded to the organization.

Of the "behind the scenes" men we have not caught all because some were not known as SS members. Accessories to SS crimes were to be found everywhere in Germany and especially in the vicinity of the concentration camps. The merchants who profited from deliveries of merchandise to concentration camps and who saw to it that the major portion of the delivered material reached the SS administrators in the form of graft were accomplices. And the civilian employe[r]s who calmly worked in the sight of abject misery on the concentration camp grounds – they also were accomplices. We have not caught them all, and we have not made a point of catching them all and especially in the recent trial we limited ourselves to the "inner circle" alone because they were beyond doubt the moving powers in this nasty business and were the main triggermen of the gang.

The master crime to which the SS was committed was the genocide of non-German peoples and the elimination by killing, in groups or singly, of Germans who were considered useless or disloyal. In effecting the two parts of this program Himmler demanded and received the cooperation of physicians and of German medical science. For this trend of research in Nazi Germany – namely, that toward developing scientific methods of destroying and preventing life – I have proposed the term "ktenology," the science of killing.

In the course of this ktenological research, methods of mass killing and mass sterilization were investigated and developed as well as methods for rapid and inconspicuous individual execution. Among the studies on mass sterilization some rather fantastic methods were proposed; for instance, Brack suggested non-conspicuous x-ray sterilization of conquered populations by building high-powered x-ray machinery into desks at which inhabitants of conquered nations would have to sit for five or ten minutes while filling out questionnaires. In this process they would all be sterilized. Research carried out on young male prisoners at Auschwitz concentration camp by Dr. Horst Schumann showed that this method was far from inconspicuous because of the intense burns and tissue necrosis produced in the genital regions. At the same camp, with equally callous use of young female prisoners, sterilizing intrauterine injections were developed by Dr. Clauberg, with the assistance of Dr. Goebel, a pharmacologist, with the intention of having them administered during the course of a regular health inspection in conquered territories.

A committee of physicians and medical experts headed by Dr. Karl Brandt developed various methods of extermination by gas. At first carbon monoxide was used, later cyanide gas ("cyclon B") with occasional use of warfare gases for which this program supplied human experimental material. Of the individual methods of inconspicuous execution, which were usually carried out in camp hospitals by medical personnel, the most widely used method was the intravenous injection of phenol or gasoline. This, however, left a tell-tale odor with the corpse which made it an undesirable means of executing prominent prisoners or high-ranking Nazi Party personnel where secrecy was essential.

The triumph of that part of ktenological research aimed at finding a method of inconspicuous execution which would produce autopsy findings indicative of death from natural causes was the development of intravenous injections of a suspension of live tubercle bacilli which brought on acute miliary tuberculosis within a few weeks. This method was produced by Dr. Heissmeyer, who was one of Dr. Gebhardt's associates at the SS hospital of Hohenlychen.

As a means of further camouflage so that the SS at large would not suspect the purpose of these experiments, the preliminary tests for the efficacy of this method were performed exclusively on children imprisoned in the Natzweiler concentration camp.

This perversion of the role of the physician in Nazi Germany extended beyond the SS. Dr. James C. White told me that on German submarines it was the physician's duty to execute trouble makers among the crew by lethal injections. The pattern of this activity, however, was set by the SS and flourished in no other organization of the Third Reich as generally and in as high echelons as in the SS.

8

MEDICAL SCIENCE UNDER DICTATORSHIP

Leo Alexander, M.D. *[1]

Science under dictatorship becomes subordinated to the guiding philosophy of the dictatorship. Irrespective of other ideologic trappings, the guiding philosophic principle of recent dictatorships, including that of the Nazis, has been Hegelian in that what has been considered "rational utility" and corresponding doctrine and planning has replaced moral, ethical and religious values. Nazi propaganda was highly effective in perverting public opinion and public conscience, in a remarkably short time. In the medical profession this expressed itself in a rapid decline in standards of professional ethics. Medical science in Nazi Germany collaborated with this Hegelian trend particularly in the following enterprises: the mass extermination of the chronically sick in the interest of saving "useless" expenses to the community as a whole; the mass extermination of those considered socially disturbing or racially and ideologically unwanted; the individual, inconspicuous extermination of those considered disloyal within the ruling group; and the ruthless use of "human experimental material for medico-military research.

This paper discusses the origins of these activities, as well as their consequences upon the body social, and the motivation of those participating in them.

PREPARATORY PROPAGANDA

Even before the Nazis took open charge in Germany, a propaganda barrage was directed against the traditional compassionate nineteenth-century attitudes toward the chronically ill, and for the adoption of a utilitarian, Hegelian point of view. Sterilization and euthanasia of persons with chronic mental illnesses was discussed at a meeting of Bavarian psychiatrists in 1931.[1] By 1936 extermination of the physically or socially unfit was so openly accepted that its practice was mentioned incidentally in an article published in an official German medical journal.[2]

---

* Instructor in psychiatry, Tufts College Medical School; director, Neurobiologic Unit, Division of Psychiatric Research, Boston State Hospital; formerly, consultant to the Secretary of War, on duty with the Office of the Chief of Counsel for War Crimes, Nuremberg, United States Zone of Germany, 1946–1947.
1 This article has been adapted from *The New England Journal of Medicine* 241 (1949), pp. 39–47. We are grateful to the Massachusetts Medical Society for granting permission to reprint an edited version of the article.

Lay opinion was not neglected in this campaign. Adults were propagandized by motion pictures, one of which, entitled "I Accuse," deals entirely with euthanasia. This film depicts the life history of a woman suffering from multiple sclerosis; in it her husband, a doctor, finally kills her to the accompaniment of soft piano music rendered by a sympathetic colleague in an adjoining room. Acceptance of this ideology was implanted even in the children. A widely used high-school mathematics text, "Mathematics in the Service of National Political Education,"[3] includes problems stated in distorted terms of the cost of caring for and rehabilitating the chronically sick and crippled, the criminal and the insane."

EUTHANASIA

The first direct order for euthanasia was issued by Hitler on September 1, 1939, and an organization was set up to execute the program. Dr. Karl Brandt headed the medical section, and Phillip Bouhler the administrative section. All state institutions were required to report on patients who had been ill five years or more and who were unable to work, by filling out questionnaires giving name, race, marital status, nationality, next of kin, whether regularly visited and by whom, who bore financial responsibility and so forth. The decision regarding which patients should be killed was made entirely on the basis of this brief information by expert consultants, most of whom were professors of psychiatry in the key universities. These consultants never saw the patients themselves. The thoroughness of their scrutiny can be appraised by the work of on expert, who between November 14 and December 1, 1940, evaluated 2109 questionnaires.

These questionnaires were collected by a "Realm's Work Committee of Institutions for Cure and Care."[4] A parallel organization devoted exclusively to the killing of children was known by the similarly euphemistic name of "Realm's Committee for Scientific Approach to Severe Illness Due to Heredity and Constitution." The "Charitable Transport Company for the Sick" transported patients to the killing centers, and the "Charitable Foundation for Institutional Care" was in charge of collecting the cost of the killings from the relatives, without, however, informing them what the charges were for; in the death certificates the cause of death was falsified.

What these activities meant to the population at large was well expressed by a few hardy souls who dared to protest. A member of the court of appeals at Frankfurt-am-Main wrote in December, 1939:

> There is constant discussion of the question of the destruction of socially unfit life – in the places where there are mental institutions, in neighboring towns, sometimes over a large area, throughout the Rhineland, for example. The people have come to recognize the vehicles in which the patients are taken from their original institution to the intermediate institution and from there to the liquidation institution. I am told that when they see these buses even the children call out: "They're taking some more people to be gassed." From Limburg it is reported that every day from one to three buses which shades drawn pass through on the way from Weilmunster to Had[a]mar, delivering inmates to the liquidation institution there. According to the stories the arrivals are immediately stripped to the skin, dressed in paper shirts, and forthwith taken to a gas chamber, where they are liquidated with hydro-cyanic acid gas and an added anesthetic. The bodies are reported to be moved to a combustion chamber by means of a conveyor belt, six bodies to a furnace. The resulting ashes are then distributed into six urns which are shipped to the families. The heavy smoke from the crematory building is said to be

visible over Hadamar every day. There is talk, furthermore, that in some cases heads and other portions of the body are removed for anatomical examination. The people working at this liquidation job in the institutions are said to be assigned from other areas and are shunned completely by the populace. This personnel is described as frequenting the bars at night and drinking heavily. Quite apart from these overt incidents that exercise the imagination of the people, the[y] are disquieted by the question of whether old folk who have worked hard all their lives and may merely have come into their dotage are also being liquidated. There is talk that the homes for the aged are to be cleaned out too. The people are said to be waiting for legislative regulation providing some orderly method that will insure especially that the aged feeble-minded are not included in the program.

Here one sees what "euthanasia" means in actual practice. According to the records, 275,000 people were put to death in these killing centers. Ghastly as this seems, it should be realized that this program was merely the entering wedge for exterminations for far greater scope in the political program for genocide of conquered nations and the racially unwanted. The methods used and personnel trained in the killing centers for the chronically sick became the nucleus of the much larger centers on the East, where the plan was to kill all Jews and Poles and to cut down the Russian population by 30,000,000.

The original program developed by Nazi hot-heads included also the genocide of the English, with the provision that the English males were to be used as laborers in the vacated territories in the East, there to be worked to death, whereas the English females were to be brought into Germany to improve the qualities of the German race. (This was indeed a peculiar admission of the part of the German eugenists.)

In Germany the exterminations included the mentally defective, psychotics (particularly schizophrenics), epileptics and patients suffering from infirmities of old age and from various organic neurologic disorders such as infantile paralysis, Parkinsonism, multiple sclerosis and brain tumors. The technical arrangements, methods and training of the killer personnel were under the direction of a committee of physicians and other experts headed by Dr. Karl Brandt. The mass killings were first carried out with carbon monoxide gas, but later cyanide gas ("cyclon B") was found to be more effective. The idea of camouflaging the gas chambers as shower baths was developed by Brack, who testified before Judge Sebring that the patients walked in calmly, deposited their towels and stood with their little pieces of soap under the shower outlets, waiting for the water to start running. This statement was ample rebuttal of his claim that only the most severely regressed patients among the mentally sick and only the moribund ones among the physically sick were exterminated. In truth, all those unable to work and considered nonrehabilitable were killed.

All but their squeal was utilized. However, the program grew so big that even scientists who hoped to benefit from the treasure of material supplied by this totalitarian method were disappointed. A neuropathologist, Dr. Hallervorden, who had obtained 500 brains from the killing centers for the insane, gave me a vivid first-hand account.[5] The Charitable Transport Company for the Sick brought the brains in batches of 150 to 250 at a time. Hallervorden stated:

> There was wonderful material among those brains, beautiful mental defectives, malformations and early infantile diseases. I accepted those brains of course. Where they came from and how they came to me was really none of my business.

In addition to the material he wanted, all kinds of other cases were mixed in, such as patients suffering from various types of Parkinsonism, simple depressions, involutional depressions and brain tumors, and all kinds of other illnesses, including psychopathy that had been difficult to handle:

These were selected from the various wards of the institutions according to an excessively simple and quick method. Most institutions did not have enough physicians, and what physicians there were either too busy or did not care, and they delegated the selection to the nurses and attendants. Whoever looked sick or was otherwise a problem was put on a list and was transported to the killing center. The worst thing about this business was that it produced a certain brutalization of the nursing personnel. They got to simply picking out those whom they did not like, and the doctors had so many patients that they did not even know them, and put their names on the list.

Of the patients thus killed, only the brains were sent to Dr. Hallervorden; they were killed in such large numbers that autopsies of the bodies were not feasible. That, in Dr. Hallervorden's opinion, greatly reduced the scientific value of the material. The brains, however, were always well fixed and suspended in formalin, exactly according to his instructions. He thinks that the cause of psychiatry was permanently injured by these activities, and that psychiatrists have lost the respect of the German people forever. Dr. Hallervorden concluded: "Still, there were interesting cases in this material."

In general only previously hospitalized patients were exterminated for reasons of illness. An exception is a program carried out in a northwestern district of Poland, the "Warthegau", where a health survey of the entire population was made by an "S.S. X-Ray Battalion" headed by Professor Hohlfelder, radiologist of the University of Frankfurt-am-main [sic]. Persons found to be infected with tuberculosis were carted off to special extermination centers.

It is rather significant that the German people were considered by their Nazi leaders more ready to accept the exterminations of the sick than those for political reasons. It was for that reason that the first exterminations of the latter group were carried out under the guise of sickness. So-called "psychiatric experts" were dispatched to survey the inmates of camps with the specific order to pick out members of racial minorities and political offenders from occupied territories and to dispatch them to killing centers with specially made diagnoses such as that of "inveterate German hater" applied to a number of prisoners who had been active in the Czech underground.

Certain classes of patients with mental diseases who were capable of performing labor, particularly members of the armed forces suffering from psychopathy or neurosis, were sent to concentration camps to be worked to death, or to be reassigned to punishment battalions and to be exterminated in the process of removal of mine fields.[6]

A large number of those marked for death for political or racial reasons were made available for "medical" experiments involving the use of involuntary human subjects. From 1942 on, such experiments carried out in concentration camps were openly presented at medical meetings. This program included "terminal human experiments," a term introduced by Dr. Rascher to denote an experiment so designed that its successful conclusion depended upon the test person's being put to death.

THE SCIENCE OF ANNIHILATION

A large part of this research was devoted to the science of destroying and preventing life, for which I have proposed the term "ktenology," the science of killing.[7–9] In the course of this ktenologic research, methods of mass killing and mass sterilization were investigated and developed for use against non-German peoples or Germans who were considered useless.

Sterilization methods were widely investigated, but proved impractical in experiments conducted in concentration camps. A rapid method developed for sterilization of females, which could be accomplished in the course of a regular health examination, was the intra-uterine injection of various chemicals. Numerous mixtures were tried, some with iodopine and others containing barium; another was most likely silver nitrate with iodized oil, because the result could be ascertained by x-ray examination. The injections were extremely painful, and a number of women died in the course of the experiments. Professor Karl Clauberg reported that he had developed a method at the Auschwitz concentration camp by which he could sterilize 1000 women in one day.

Another method of sterilization, or rather castration, was proposed by Viktor Brack especially for conquered populations. His idea was that x-ray machinery could be built into desks at which the people would have to sit, ostensibly to fill out a questionnaire requiring five minutes; they would be sterilized without being aware of it. This method failed because experiments carried out on 100 male prisoners brought out the fact that severe x-ray burns were produced on all subjects. In the course of this research, which was carried out by Dr. Horst Schuman, the testicles of the victims were removed for histologic examination two weeks later. I myself examined 4 castrated survivors of this ghastly experiment. Three had extensive necrosis of the skin near the genitalia, and the other an extensive necrosis of the urethra. Other experiments in sterilization used an extract of the plant caladium seguinum, which had been shown in animal studies by Madaus and his co-workers [10,11] to cause selective necrosis of the germinal cells of the testicles as well as the ovary.

The development of methods for rapid and inconspicuous individual execution was the objective of another large part of the ktenologic research. These methods were to be applied to members of the ruling group, including the SS itself, who were suspected of disloyalty. This, of course, is an essential requirement in a dictatorship, in which "cut-throat competition" becomes a grim reality, and any hint of faintheartedness or lack of enthusiasm for the methods of totalitarian rule is considered a threat to the entire group.

Poisons were the subject of many of these experiments. A research team at the Buchenwald concentration camp, consisting of Drs. Joachim Mrugowsky, Erwin Ding-Schuler and Waldemar Hoven, developed the most widely used means of individual execution under the guise of medical treatment – namely, the intravenous injection of phenol or gasoline. Several alkaloids were also investigated, among them aconitine, which was used by Dr. Hoven to kill several imprisoned former fellow SS men who were potential witnesses against the camp commander, Koch, then under investigation by the SS. At the Dachau concentration camp Dr. Rascher developed the standard cyanide capsules, which could be easily bitten through, either deliberately or accidentally, if mixed with certain foods, and which, ironically enough, later became the means with which Himmler and Goering killed themselves. In connection with these poison experiments there is an interesting incident of characteristic sociologic significance. When Dr. Hoven was under trial by the SS the investigating SS judge, Dr. Morgen, proved Hoven's guilt by feeding the poison found in Dr. Hoven's possession to a number of Russian prisoners of war; these men died with the same symptoms as the SS men murdered by Dr. Hoven. This worthy judge was rather proud of this efficient method of proving Dr. Hoven's guilt and appeared entirely unaware of the fact that in the process he had committed murder himself.

Poisons, however, proved too obvious or detectable to be used for the elimination of high-ranking Nazi party personnel who had come into disfavor, or of prominent prisoners whose deaths should appear to stem from natural causes. Phenol or gasoline, for instance, left a telltale odor with the corpses. For this reason a number of more subtle methods were devised. One of these was artificial production of septicemia. An intramuscular injection of 1 cc. of pus, containing numerous chains of streptococci, was the first step. The site of injection was usually the inside of the thigh, close to the adductor canal. When an abscess formed it was tapped, and 3 cc. of the creamey pus removed was injected intravenously into the patient's opposite arm. If the patient then died from septicemia, the autopsy proved that death was caused by the same organism that had caused the abscess. These experiments were carried out in many concentration camps. At Dachau camp the subjects were almost exclusively Polish Catholic priests. However, since this method did not always cause death, sometimes resulting merely in a local abscess, it was considered inefficient, and research was continued with other means but along the same lines.

The final triumph of the part of ktenologic research aimed at finding a method of inconspicuous execution that would produce autopsy findings indicative of death from natural causes was the development of repeated intravenous injections of suspensions of live tubercle bacilli, which brought on acute miliary tuberculosis within a few weeks. This method was produced by Professor Dr. Heissmeyer, who was one of Dr. Gebhardt's associates at the SS hospital of Hohenlychen. As a means of further camouflage, so that the SS at large would not suspect the purpose of these experiments, the preliminary tests for the efficacy of this method were performed exclusively on children imprisoned in the Neuengamme concentration camp.

For use in "medical" executions of prisoners and of members of the SS and other branches of the German armed forces the use of simple lethal injections, particularly phenol injections, remained the instrument of choice. Whatever methods he used, the physician gradually became the unofficial executioner, for the sake of convenience, informality and relative secrecy. Even on German submarines it was the physician's duty to execute the troublemakers among the crew by lethal injections.

Medical science has for some time been an instrument of military power in that it preserved the health and fighting efficiency of troops. This essentially defensive purpose is not inconsistent with the ethical principles of medicine. In World War I the German empire had enlisted medical science as an instrument of aggressive military power by putting it to use in the development of gas warfare. It was left to the Nazi dictatorship to make medical science into an instrument of political power – a formidable, essential tool in the complete and effective manipulation of totalitarian control. This should be a warning to all civilized nations, and particularly to individuals who are blinded by the "efficiency" of a totalitarian rule, under whatever name.

This entire body of research as reported so far served the master crime to which the Nazi dictatorship was committed – namely, the genocide of non-German peoples and the elimination by killing, in groups or singly, of Germans who were considered useless or disloyal. In effecting the two parts of this program, Himmler demanded and received the co-operation of physicians and of German medical science. The result was a significant advance in the science of killing, or ktenology.

MEDICO-MILITARY RESEARCH

Another chapter in Nazi scientific research was that aimed to aid the military forces. Many of these ideas originated with Himmler, who fancied himself a scientist.

When Himmler learned that the cause of death of most SS men on the battlefield was hemorrhage, he instructed Dr. Sigmund Rascher to search for a blood coagulant that might be given before the men went into action. Rascher tested this coagulant when it was developed by clocking the number of drops emanating from freshly cut amputation stumps of living and conscious prisoners at the crematorium of Dachau concentration camp and by shooting Russian prisoners of war through the spleen.

Live dissections were a feature of another experimental study designed to show the effects of explosive decompression.[12–14] A mobile decompression chamber was used. It was found that when subjects were made to descend from altitudes of 40,000 to 60,000 feet without oxygen, severe symptoms of cerebral dysfunction occurred – at first convulsions, then unconsciousness in which the body was hanging limp and later, after wakening, temporary blindness, paralysis or severe confusional twilight states. Rascher, who wanted to find out whether these symptoms were due to anoxic changes or to other causes, did what appeared to him the most simple thing: he placed the subjects of the experiment under water and dissected them while the heart was still beating, demonstrating air embolism in the blood vessels of the heart, liver, chest wall and brain.

Another part of Dr. Rascher's research, carried out in collaboration with Holzloehner and Finke, concerned shock from exposure to cold.[15] It was known that military personnel generally did not survive immersion in the North Sea for more than sixty to a hundred minutes. Rascher therefore attempted to duplicate these conditions at Dachau concentration camp and used about 300 prisoners in experiments on shock from exposure to cold; of these 80 or 90 were killed. (The figures do not include persons killed during mass experiments on exposure to cold outdoors.) In one report on this work Rascher asked permission to shift these experiments from Dachau to Auschwitz, a larger camp where they might cause less disturbance because the subjects shrieked from pain when their extremities froze white. The results, like so many of those obtained in the Nazi research program, are not dependable. In his report Rascher stated that it took from fifty-three to a hundred minutes to kill a human being by immersion in ice water – a time closely in agreement with the known survival period in the North Sea. Inspection of his own experimental records and statements made to me by his close associates showed that it actually took from eighty minutes to five or six hours to kill an undressed person in such a manner, whereas a man in full aviators dress took six or seven hours to kill. Obviously, Rascher dressed up his findings to forestall criticism, although any scientific man should have known that during actual exposure many other factors, including greater convection of heat due to the motion of water, would affect the time of survival.

Another series of experiments gave results that might have been an important medical contribution if an important lead had not been ignored. The efficacy of various vaccines and drugs against typhus was tested at the Buchenwald and Natzweiler concentration camps. Prevaccinated persons and nonvaccinated controls were injected with live typhus rickettsias, and the death rates of the two series compared. After a certain number of passages, the Matelska strain of typhus rickettsia proved to become avirulent for man. Instead of seizing upon this as a possibility to develop a live vaccine, the experimenters, including the chief consultant, Professor Gerhard Rose, who should have known better, were merely annoyed at the fact that the controls did not die either, discarded this strain and continued testing their relatively ineffective dead vaccines against a new virulent strain. This incident shows that the basic unconscious motivation and attitude has a great influence in determining the scientist's awareness of the phenomena that pass through his vision.

Sometimes human subjects were used for tests that were totally unnecessary, or whose results could have been predicted by simple chemical experiments. For example, 90 gypsies were given unaltered sea water and sea water whose taste was camouflaged as their sole source of fluid, apparently to test the well known fact that such hypertonic saline solutions given as the only source of supply of fluid will cause severe physical disturbance or death within six to twelve days. These persons were subjected to the tortures of the damned, with death resulting in at least 2 cases. Heteroplastic transplantation experiments were carried out by Professor Dr. Karl Gebhardt at Himmler's suggestion. Whole limbs – shoulder, arm or leg – were amputated from live prisoners at Ravensbrueck concentration camp, wrapped in sterile moist dressings and sent by automobile to the SS hospital at Hohenlychen, where Professor Gebhardt busied himself with a futile attempt at heteroplastic transplantation. In the meantime the prisoners deprived of limb were usually killed by lethal injection.

One would not be dealing with German science if one did not run into manifestations of the collector's spirit. By February, 1942, it was assumed in German scientific circles that the Jewish race was about to be completely exterminated, and alarm was expressed over the fact that only very few specimens of skulls and skeletons of Jews were at the disposal of science. It was therefore proposed that a collection 150 body casts and skeletons of Jews be preserved for perusal by future students of anthropology. Dr. August Hirt, professor of anatomy at the University of Strassburg, declared himself interested in establishing such a collection at his anatomic institute. He suggested that captured Jewish officers of the Russian armed forces by included, as well as females from Auschwitz concentration camp; that they be brought alive to Natzweiler concentration camp near Strassburg; and that after "their subsequently induced death – care should be taken that the heads not be damaged" the bodies be turned over to him at the anatomic institute of the University of Strassburg. This was done. The entire collection of bodies and the correspondence pertaining to it fell into the hands of the United States Army.

One of the most revolting experiments was the testing of sulfonamides against gas gangrene by Professor Gebhardt and his collaborators, for which young women captured from the Polish Resistance Movement served as subjects. Necrosis was produced in a muscle of the leg by ligation and the wound was infected with various types of gas-gangrene bacilli; frequently, dirt, pieces of wood and glass splinters were added to the wound. Some of these victims died, and others sustained severe mutilating deformities of the leg.

MOTIVATION

An important feature of the experiments performed in concentration camps is the fact that they not only represented a ruthless and callous pursuit of legitimate scientific goals but also were motivated by rather sinister practical ulterior political and personal purposes, arising out of the requirements and problems of the administration of totalitarian rule.

Why did men like Professor Gebhardt lend themselves to such experiments? The reasons are fairly simple and practical, no surprise to anyone familiar with the evidence of fear, hostility, suspicion, rivalry and intrigue, the fratricidal struggle euphemistically termed the "self-selection of leaders," that went on within the ranks of the ruling Nazi party and the SS. The answer was fairly simple and logical. Dr. Gebhardt performed these experiments to clear himself of the suspicion that he had been contributing to the death of SS General Reinhard ("The Hangman") Heydrich, either negligently or deliberately, by failing to treat his wound infection with sulfonamides. After Heydrich died from gas gangrene, Himmler himself told Dr. Gebhardt that the only way in which he could prove that Heydrich's death was "fate-determined" was by carrying out a "large-scale experiment" in prisoners, which would prove or disprove that people died from gas gangrene irrespective of whether they were treated sulfonamides or not.

Dr. Sigmund Rascher did not become the notorious vivisectionist of Dachau concentration camp and the willing tool of Himmler's research interests until he had been forbidden to use the facilities of the Pathological Institute of the University of Munich because he was suspected of having Communist sympathies. Then he was ready to go all out and to do anything merely to regain acceptance by the Nazi party and the SS.

These cases illustrate a method consciously and methodically used in the SS, an age-old method used by criminal gangs everywhere: that of making suspects of disloyalty clear themselves by participation in a crime that would definitely and irrevocably tie them to the organization. In the SS this process of reinforcement of group cohesion was called "Blukitt" (blood-cement), a term that Hitler himself is said to have obtained from a book on Genghis Khan in which this technic was emphasized.

The important lesson here is that this motivation, with which one is familiar in ordinary crimes, applies also to war crimes and to ideologically conditioned crimes against humanity – namely, that fear and cowardice, especially fear of punishment or of ostracism by the group, are often more important motives than simple ferocity or aggressiveness.

[…]²

THE EXAMPLE OF SUCCESSFUL RESISTANCE BY THE PHYSICIANS OF THE NETHERLANDS

There is no[doubt that in Germany itself the first and most effective step of propaganda within the medical profession was the propaganda barrage against the useless, incurably sick described above. Similar, even more subtle efforts were made in some of the occupied countries. It is to the everlasting honor of the medical profession of Holland that they recognized the earliest and most subtle phases of this attempt and rejected it. When Seiss-Inquart, Reich Commissar for the Occupied Netherlands Territories, wanted to draw the Dutch physicians into the orbit of the activities of the German medical profession, he did not tell them "You must send your chronic patients to death factories" or "You must give lethal injections at Government request in your offices," but he couched his order in most careful and superficially acceptable terms. One of the paragraphs in the order of the Reich Commissar of the Netherlands Territories concerning the Netherlands doctors of 19 December 1941 reads as follows:

> "It is the duty of the doctor, through advice and effort, conscientiously and to his best ability, to assist as helper the person entrusted to his care in the maintenance, improvement and reestablishment of his vitality, physical efficiency and health. The accomplishment of this duty is a public task."[16]

The physicians of Holland rejected this order unanimously because they saw what it actually meant – namely, the concentration of their efforts on mere rehabilitation of the sick for useful labor, and abolition of medical secrecy. Although on the surface the new order appeared not too grossly unacceptable, the Dutch physicians decided that it is the first, although slight, step away from principle that is the most important one. The Dutch physicians declared that they would not obey this order. When Seiss-Inquart threatened them with revocation of their licenses, they returned their licenses, removed their shingles and, while seeing their own patients secretly, no longer wrote death or birth certificates. Seiss-Inquart retraced his steps and tried to cajole them – still to no effect. Then he arrested 100 Dutch physicians and sent them to concentration camps. The medical profession remained adamant and quietly took care of their widows and orphans, but would not give in. Thus it came about that not a single euthanasia or non-therapeutic sterilization was recommended or participated in by any Dutch physician. They had the foresight to resist before the first step was taken, and they acted unanimously and won out in the end. It is obvious that if the medical profession of a small nation under the conqueror's heel could resist so effectively the German medical profession could likewise have resisted had they not taken the fatal first step. It is the first seemingly innocent step away from principle that frequently decides a career of crime. Corrosion begins in microscopic proportions.

---

2   The Section on "The Early Change in Medical Attitudes" has been omitted from this edited version of Alexander's article.

THE SITUATION IN THE UNITED STATES

The question that this fact prompts is whether there are any danger signs that American physicians have also been infected with Hegelian, cold-blooded, utilitarian philosophy and whether early traces of it can be detected in their medical thinking that may make them vulnerable to departures of the type that occurred in Germany. Basic attitudes must be examined dispassionately. The original concept of medicine and nursing was not based on any rational or feasible likelihood that they could actually cure and restore but rather on an essentially maternal or religious idea. The Good Samaritan had no thought of nor did he actually care whether he could restore working capacity. He was merely motivated by the compassion in alleviating suffering. Bernal[17] states that prior to the advent of scientific medicine, the physician's main function was to give hope to the patient and to relieve his relatives of responsibility. Gradually, in all civilized countries, medicine has moved away from this position, strangely enough in direct proportion to man's actual ability to perform feats that would have been plain miracles in days of old. However, with this increased efficiency based on scientific development went a subtle change in attitude. Physicians have become dangerously close to being mere technicians of rehabilitation. This essentially Hegelian rational attitude has led them to make certain distinctions in the handling of acute and chronic diseases. The patient with the latter carries an obvious stigma as the one less likely to be fully rehabilitable for social usefulness. In an increasingly utilitarian society these patients are being looked down upon with increasing definiteness as unwanted ballast. A certain amount of rather open contempt for the people who cannot be rehabilitated with present knowledge has developed. This is probably due to a good deal of unconscious hostility, because these people for whom there seem to be no effective remedies have become a threat to newly acquired delusions of omnipotence.

Hospitals like to limit themselves to the care of patients who can be fully rehabilitated, and the patient whose full rehabilitation is unlikely finds himself, at least in the best and most advanced centers of healing, as a second-class patient faced with a reluctance on the part of both the visiting and the house staff to suggest and apply therapeutic procedures that are not likely to bring about immediately striking results in terms of recovery. I wish to emphasize that this point of view did not arise primarily within the medical profession, which has always been outstanding in a highly competitive economic society for giving freely and unstintingly of its time and efforts, but was imposed by the shortage of funds available, both private and public. From the attitude of easing patients with chronic diseases away from the doors of the best types of treatment facilities available to the actual dispatching of such patients to killing centers is a long but nevertheless logical step. Resources for the so-called incurable patient have recently become practically unavailable.

There has never in history been a shortage of money for the development and manufacture of weapons of war; there is and should be none now. The disproportion of monetary support for war and that available for healing and care is an anachronism in an era that has been described as the "enlightened age of the common man" by some observers. The comparable cost of jet planes and hospital beds is too obvious for any excuse to be found for a shortage of the latter. I trust that these remarks will not be misunderstood. I believe that armament, including jet planes, is vital for the security of the republic, but adequate maintenance of standards of health and alleviation of suffering are equally vital, both from a practical point of view and from that of morale. All who took part in induction-board examinations during the war realize that the maintenance and development of national health is of as vital importance as the maintenance and development of armament.

The trend of development in the facilities available for the chronically ill outlined above will not necessarily be altered by public or state medicine. With provision of public funds in any setting of public activity the question is bound to come up, "Is it worth while to spend a certain amount of effort to restore a certain type of patient?" This rationalistic point of view has insidiously crept into the motivation of medical effort, supplanting the old Hippocratic point of view. In emergency situations, military or otherwise, such grading of effort may be pardonable. But doctors must beware lest such attitudes creep into the civilian public administration of medicine entirely outside emergency situations, because once such considerations are at all admitted, the more often and the more definitely the question is going to be asked, "Is it worth while to do this or that for this type of patient?" Evidence of the existence of such an attitude stared at me from a report on the activities of a leading public hospital unit, which stated rather proudly that certain treatments were given only when they appeared promising:

> "Our facilities are such that a case load of 20 patients is regularly carried ... in selecting cases for treatment careful consideration is given to the prognostic criteria, and in no instance have we instituted treatment merely to satisfy relatives or our own consciences."

If only those whose treatment is worth while in terms of prognosis are to be treated, what about the other ones? The doubtful patients are the ones whose recovery appears unlikely, but frequently if treated energetically, they surprise the best prognosticators. And what shall be done during that long time lag after the disease has been called incurable and the time of death and autopsy? It is that period during which it is most difficult to find hospitals and other therapeutic organizations for the welfare and alleviation of suffering of the patient.

Under all forms of dictatorship the dictating bodies or individuals claim that all that is done is being done for the best of the people as a whole, and that for that reason they look at health merely in terms of utility, efficiency and productivity. It is natural in such a setting that eventually Hegel's principle that "what is useful is good" wins out completely. The killing center is the reductio ad absurdum of all health planning based only on rational principles and economy and not on humane compassion and divine law. To be sure, American physicians are still far from the point of thinking of killing centers, but they have arrived at a danger point in thinking, at which likelihood of full rehabilitation is considered a factor that should determine the amount of time, effort and cost to be devoted to a particular type of patient on the part of the social body upon which this decision rests. At this point Americans should remember that the enormity of a euthanasia movement is present in their own midst. To the psychiatrist it is obvious that this represents the eruption of unconscious aggression on the part of certain administrators alluded to above, as well as on the part of relatives who have been understandably frustrated by the tragedy of illness in its close interaction upon their own lives. The hostility of a father erupting against his feebleminded son is understandable and should be considered from the psychiatric point of view, but it certainly should not influence social thinking. The development of effective analgesics and pain-relieving operations has taken even the last rationalization away from the supporters of euthanasia.

The case, therefore, that I should like to make is that American medicine must realize where it stands in its fundamental premises. There can be no doubt that in a subtle way the Hegelian premise of "what is useful is right" has infected society, including the medical portion. Physicians must return to the older premises, which were the emotional foundation and driving force of an amazingly successful quest to increase powers of healing if they are not held down to earth by the pernicious attitudes of an overdone practical realism.

What occurred in Germany may have been the inexorable historic progression that the Greek historians have described as the law of the fall of civilizations and that Toynbee[18] has convincingly confirmed – namely, that there is a logical sequence from Koros to Hybris to Atc, which means from surfeit to disdainful arrogance to disaster, the surfeit being increased scientific and practical accomplishments, which, however, brought about an inclination to throw away the old motivations and values by disdainful arrogant pride in practical efficiency. Moral and physical disaster is the inevitable consequence.

Fortunately, there are developments in this democratic society that counteract these trends. Notable among them are the societies of patients afflicted with various chronic diseases that have sprung up and are dedicating themselves to guidance and information for their fellow sufferers and for the support and stimulation of medical research. Among the earliest was the mental-hygiene movement, founded by a former patient with mental disease. Then came the National Foundation for Infantile Paralysis, the tuberculosis societies, the American Epilepsy League, the National Association to Control Epilepsy, the American Cancer Society, The American Heart Association, "Alcoholics Anonymous" and, most recently the National Multiple Sclerosis Society. All these societies, which are coordinated with special medical societies and which received inspiration and guidance from outstanding physicians, are having an extremely wholesome effect in introducing fresh motivating power into the ivory towers of academic medicine. It is indeed interesting and an assertion of democratic vitality that these societies are activated by and for people suffering from illnesses who, under certain dictatorships, would have been slated for euthanasia.

It is thus that these new societies have taken over one of the ancient functions of medicine – namely, to give hope to the patient and to relieve his relatives. These societies need the whole-hearted support of the medical profession. Unfortunately, this support is by no means yet unanimous. A distinguished physician, investigator and teacher at an outstanding university recently told me that he was opposed to these special societies and clinics because they had nothing to offer to the patient. It would be better to wait until someone made a discovery accidentally and then start clinics. It is my opinion, however, that one cannot wait for that. The stimulus supplied by these societies is necessary to give stimulus both to public demand and to academic medicine, which at times grows stale and unproductive even in its most outstanding centers, and whose existence did nothing to prevent the executioner from having logic on his side in Germany.

Another element of this free democratic society and enterprise that has been a stimulus to new developments is the pharmaceutical industry, which, with great vision, has invested considerable effort in the sponsorship of new research.

Dictatorships can be indeed defined as systems in which there is a prevalence of thinking in destructive rather than in ameliorative terms in dealing with social problems. The ease with which destruction of life is advocated for those considered either socially useless or socially disturbing instead of educational or ameliorative measures may be the first danger sign of loss of creative liberty in thinking, which is the hallmark of democratic society. All destructiveness ultimately leads to self-destruction; the fate of the SS and of Nazi Germany is an eloquent example. The destructive principle, once unleased, is bound to engulf the whole personality and to occupy all its relationships. Destructive urges and destructive concepts arising therefrom cannot remain limited or focused upon one subject or several subjects alone, but must inevitable spread and be directed against one's entire surrounding world, including one's own group and ultimately the self. The ameliorative point of view maintained in relation to all others is the only real means of self-preservation.

A most important need in this country is for the development of active and alert hospital centers for the treatment of chronic illnesses. They must have active staffs similar to those of the hospitals for acute illnesses, and these hospitals must be fundamentally different from the custodial repositories for derelicts, of which there are too many in existence today. Only thus can one give the right answer to divine scrutiny: Yes, we are our brothers' keepers.

Endnotes

1. Bumke, O. Discussion of Faltlhauser, K. Zur Frage der Sterilisierung geistig Abnormer, Allg. Z[e]i[t]schr. J. [f.] Psychiat., 96:372, 1932.

2. Dierichs, R. Beitrag zur psychischen Anstaltsbehandlung Tuberkuloser [sic], Z[e]i[t]schr. f. Tuberk., 74:24–28, 1936.

3. Dorner, A. Mathematik in dienste [im Dienste] der Nationalpolitischen Erziehung: Ein Handbuch fur [für] Lehrer, herausgegeben in [im] Auftrage des Reichsverbandes Deut[s]cher mathematischer Gesellschaften und Vereine. Second edition. (revised). Frankfurt: Moritz Diesterweg, 1935. Pp. 1–118. Third edition (revised), 1936. Pp. 1–118.

4. Alexander, L. Public mental health practices in Germany, sterilization and execution of patients suffering from nervous or mental disease. Combined Intelligence Objectives Subcommittee, Item No. 24. File, No. XXVIII–50. Pp. 1–173 (August), 1945.

5. Idem. Neuropathology and neurophysiology, including electro-encephalography in wartime Germany. Combined Intelligence Objectives Subcommittee, Item No. 24. File, No. XXVII–1. Pp. 1–65 (July), 1945.

6. Idem. German military neuropsychiatry and neurosurgery. Combined Intelligence Objectives Subcommittee, Item No. 24. File, No. XXVIII-49. Pp. 1–138 (August), 1945.

7. Idem. Sociopsychologic structure of SS: psychiatric report of Nurnberg trials for war crimes. Arch. Neurol. & Psychiat. 59:622–634, 1948.

8. Idem. War crimes: their social-psychological aspects. Am. J. Psychiat. 105:170–177, 1948.

9. Idem. War crimes and their motivation: socio-psychological structure of SS and criminalization of society. J. Crim. Law & Criminol. 39:298–326, 1948.

10. Idem. Madaus, G., and Koch, F.E., Tierexperimentelle Studien zur Frage der medikamentosen Sterilisierung (durch Caladium seguinum ([sic] Dieffenbachia sequina). Z[e]i[t]schr. f. d. ges. exper. Med. 109:68–87, 1941.

11. Madaus, G. Zauberpflanzen im Lichte experimenteller Forschung. Das Schweigrohr – Caladium seguinum. Umschau 24:600–602.

12. Alexander, L. Treatment of shock from prolonged exposure to cold, especially in water. Combined Intelligence Objectives Subcommittee, Item No. 24. File, No. XXIX–24. Pp. 1–163 (August), 1945.

13. Document 1971 a PS.

14. Document NO 220.

15. Alexander, L. Treatment of shock from prolonged exposure to cold, especially in water. Combined Intelligence Objectives Subcommittee, Item No. 24. File, No. XXVI–37. Pp. 1–228 (July), 1945.

16. Seiss-Inquart. Order of the Reich Commissar for the Occupied Netherlands Territories Concerning the Netherlands Doctors. (Gazette containing the orders for the Occupied Netherlands Territories), pp. 1001–1026, December, 1941.

17. Bernal, J. D. The Social Function of Science. Sixth edition. 482 pp. London: George Routledge & Sons, 1946.

18. Toynbee, A. J. A Study of History. Abridgement of Vol. I–VI. By D. C. Somervell. 617 pp. New York and London: Oxford University Press, 1947.

9

INTERVIEW WITH CECILY KATE ALEXANDER-GRABLE

Ulf Schmidt

The following interview with Cecily K. Alexander-Grable ("A") (23 November 1938–7 January 2024) was conducted by Ulf Schmidt ("Q") at Cape Cod, Massachusetts, United States, May 1999, as part of research for the book *Justice at Nuremberg* (2004). In this transcript, we have endeavoured to retain the original manner of speech of the interviewee as much as possible.

[…]

A: On that particular subject, I do know when I was grown up, he told me that after the war and after Nuremberg, he could never not be a Jew. He would never consider converting to any other religion, even though he didn't agree with all of the principles, because he felt that since Jews had suffered that it would be, it would show, first of all lack of courage, but also that he felt strongly he needed to be identified – since other people especially identified him as Jewish – that he needed to be identified. And he was always, never in the, he never belonged to a synagogue, but he was very much a prominent person in Boston, a member of the Jewish community, charitable organisations and so forth, then many years later he travelled a number of times to Israel, also, the first time, being invited after the six day [war], I think the first time, being invited after the six day war to talk to people about battle fatigue and stress syndrome and that sort of thing. I guess because he was known to have done some research on that.

Q: Do you think he became more Jewish?

A: As time went on no question.

Q: Through the trial?

A: Through the Nuremberg trial, that I have no direct knowledge of. I don't recall. We always celebrated through and a few Jewish holidays. On Rosh Hashanah he would go to, go to a synagogue, a different one, depends, often his friends would invite him, somebody that he knew. He would say "Oh you are going to a synagogue, why don't you come to my synagogue. Often, I went with him when I was in high school anyway, but he and my mother evidently felt very strongly that the children should learn about religion, but not belong to a church. So, they sent us to Sunday school, they never went, but to the Unitarian church which is a, I think, is a particular New England church. Its full of converts, and there are many jokes about it, but, its, they celebrate all holidays and all sorts of dogma, they sort of work it to a, to a rather practical sort of a religion. They do communion, they celebrate Jewish New Year, they celebrate Passover, they, uh, peace, love, God.

Q: What family did he come from. Was it a very religious family?

A: No, they were not religious, but his grandmother was religious. He told us that he had a bar mitzvah but that in those days it was not a very big celebration, that he had learned to read some Hebrew and that he took part in services, but it wasn't as much of the American-Jewish culture to make a tremendous celebration – this was. He never told me about his brothers or sisters doing that. He said that he felt very close to his grandmother who was very observant. I don't recall that he said that he went to synagogue, but she, she was, she kept a kosher home and tried to honour the Sabbath and that they, they celebrated on Friday evenings a special welcoming of the Sabbath and he always enjoyed that – that was his favourite grandparent. But I think his parents were very assimilated, they were very social and I don't think religion was very much an act or part of their [life].

Q: Did he talk with you about the family home, how they lived life at the time in the 1920s?

A: Yes. Father had his offices, his medical office in the household, I think it was on the first floor, but I'm not, I'm not sure. The children helped out when he was seeing patients, in his, I think they called it a clinic, I think. He often had students there, or fellows, people who were studying with him. He also taught in the university and I think he didn't do much of that at home. So when father was seeing patients they were definitely not around. They didn't see much of their parents during the week, only in the weekends, and father, their father was very very strict. They had to behave in a certain way, they had to do very well in school, they had maids, nannies and people like that, they had a nursery. They ate their dinner in the nursery during the week, it was almost like the British Royal family apparently, this was, there were many servants in the house. And I thought, I was under the impression that they had a summer place or a weekend place that belonged to them; I understand from my cousins that it was something that belonged to the family and it wasn't just exclusively theirs, but I am not sure about that. It was in Baden, and he said there were peacocks on the lawn that spread their feathers and that, that it was very beautiful, very elegant, beautiful lawns, they, they lived a very aristocratic life, did a lot of entertaining and travelling.

Q: What was the profession of the father?

A: He was an ear-nose and throat surgeon. He was very well known in his day, and he had, many of his patients were very well connected, they were artists, they were opera singers, theatrical people, people who were well-known and recognised, maybe the equivalent of celebrities.

Q: When did he go to Germany? Do you remember that, did he talk with you about that experience as a student?

A: I don't remember very much of that. I believe when he went to Germany, he had already had his residency, and he was already a neurologist, is what I believe, and when he went to Frankfurt. I had been under the impression that he was doing neurological research. You [are] telling me that he was actually learning and practising psychiatry, that I really hadn't known).

During that time, I believe that when he was in Frankfurt when his father died, when his father was killed, and that he came home because of that and stayed home for a while, a short while, and there was a lot of concern whether he should move home because his mother wasn't well, and there was turmoil in the family and he felt very, very responsible. His father was, was young and there was no, no expectation of his death, since he was assassinated, he was shot in the street and – what was he 52 or something – in that period of time, so there was, there must have been, I am guessing, but a lot of family reorganisation. There were, I do, I have seen some of the letters back and forth, mundane decisions he was participating in and felt responsible for.

Q: Was he in charge of the family at that time?

A: I don't think he really was. I think, I think probably he was starting to be, I suspect that, that he learned more about the family situation whatever it was, than, than he had ever known before. He probably hadn't been at all consulted or, or responsible. He was the student and away from home. So, but I don't really remember him talking to me about that.

Q: But at the same time, there was a period where he went to China?

A: He told me that that was, that the opportunity was presented to him and appealed to him, that, he, he didn't expect to make his career there. But it was exotic and exciting and he wanted to get away. One can imagine: "Did he want to get away from Frankfurt, did he want to get away from family responsibilities?" But he had throughout his life, things like he. It wasn't that he was impulsive but travel, doing something exotic and exciting that would definitely appeal to him, especially since it was just six months and, and, he was interested in art, antiquities, travel, it was a beautiful trip, they stopped at many many places on the way. He wanted to see the world. He was a young man, he wanted to see the world, why not.

I don't think he, I don't know, I asked him, I had understood that he had stayed a couple of years, but that's probably my impression. It was a glorious time for him. He talked about it a lot. Social mileage, perhaps, you know, he learned a lot about exotic foods and people.

Q: He changed, he sort of changed that kind of perception, but at the same time, it looks as if it was also a very difficult time because he realised that he could not return – did he talk about that?

A: He talked about that. That he talked about a lot. He expected to go back and continue his research. This was just a little, an extended vacation, a tour, and when he wrote to his, and I think, my impression was that he kept close contact with the laboratories there because there was [were] ongoing projects, so he tells about, he told many times a story about writing to his boss Dr. Kleist and fixing the date or something and that Kleist sent him a telegram. I believe that I have seen that telegram, but I don't know whether you've found it, I, where it said, according to him "Recommend continued appointment in Peiping – Letter follows". Leo talked many times that that telegram saved his life. He said many times that it was a great disappointment. He knew it was a great shock to him that this telegram came. He felt that he was safe. He knew that there were things going on in Germany, but he felt he was above all of that, he was a physician and well connected and so on, that he would be safe. In the letter Dr Kleist told him that it was unsafe for Austrians, that Austrians could not work at the university any more and that he didn't think that Leo should return to Germany whatsoever and that in America would be a better place. This was apparently a new idea for my father. And the grant, the people that supplied the money for him to go to China, was a Cana[dian]-American grant, I believe, and so it was also suggested that through his connections that he already had, that he might, might be able to come to America. From what I understand, I don't know whether if it was a suggestion of Kleist, Kleister to, for him to come to Worcester.

Q: Did he talk with you about his war crime investigations later?

A: Yes, oh well, a little bit. He talked about the investigations a lot with other people, but not so much with, with us, as children. I mean if we were present at the dinner table when he was speaking to visitors, we saw in later years, he had, there was the book *Doctors of Infamy* which had a lot of pictures, particularly of those, of experiments in there, and he did explain to us somewhat about that and that's why he was gone so long. He told us that at the end of the war, he went to Europe, that he was sent over there to investigate war crimes, and that he went to some of the concentration camps very early on. He was not with the first people, but with investigating people. He said that he was in a unique position because some of the people, people he knew or had friends in common, or could make small talk about the old days or professors and so forth. And that, that he was a good interviewer, just because of that experience. He told us that he met many of the famous war criminals, and I think some of the generals also that he interviewed – but only that he worked on the doctor trials [doctors' trial], and that it was a very hectic but a very exciting, very exciting time for him.

Q: What did your mother say about that, that he did there?

A: She went over there. I remember that. I can remember when, when he left to go to Nuremberg my parents had a party and they, there were farewell dinners for him and we were very sad to see him go, but thought that it was something very important that he had to go. I think he didn't know how long he would be gone and I don't remember how long in advance I knew that my mother was going to go over there. But she explained it to us that it was, it was her opportunity to be with daddy, but also that she would be able to meet with some of our relatives that were in Europe and that she would help him find some things that belonged to the family or family members that might be in Vienna and so forth. It was, I'm sure, a wonderful but frightening opportunity. Things were very difficult over there, there were a lot of shortages and it was, travelling was apparently quite difficult. And there was a lot of damage. You couldn't just take a train from one place to another place. They used jeeps and had to arrange transportation and so forth. Other than that, I really don't know much about it.

Q: And the investigations, the first investigations, did he do them alone, or had he help, did he, I mean was he part of a group?

A: Yes, but I'm sure of that. He spoke a lot about a driver whose name I don't remember but maybe in some of those pictures. He had one person that drove him I think, there was either the two or maybe there were more of them that travelled, and what created the schedule I don't, I have no idea.

I know from letters that I've read that during that time of the investigations that he was working very very hard, that my mother evidently wrote to him angry, because she wasn't hearing any information. She was frightened, she didn't know where he was, and all of that was very secret.

I can also remember in advance, [this] was the first time that I remember seeing my mother cry and that's when Roosevelt died, and at that time she hadn't, the war was very bad, and she hadn't heard from him for a long time, and so everything was, she was most, most concerned and upset. Other than that, I don't think she confided very much in us at the time but that event I remember. So, if we could figure out what day, what date that was, then that probably could have been during that time.

Mail was very difficult. That I also remember. That we would get no letters for a long time and then we would get five, six or seven and a little package or something so, and I don't know what caused that, but everything was rationed and the children in school were saving stamps and we were saving string and fat and so forth to help the soldiers and so we always imagined that we were helping our father in particular.

Q: So, then he came back, and was he here, how long was he here before he left Germany?

A: Yes, he came back, I associate it with VJ-Day, which is in August, August 1 or something. The three of us, my brothers and I were at a camp in Maine, and sometime associated with that, I remember seeing him, although the dates don't really, really figure on that but that's what I associate with that, maybe, maybe that we celebrated the victory over Japan and figured all the soldiers would be coming home soon. I think he actually came home in September. And, maybe we stayed in that camp extra-long because [of that].

Q: September 45?

A: Right when we came back from that camp, we were moved into a new house, and he stayed till the next autumn, I believe.

Q: Being still a soldier?

A: No, no, no, he was working in Boston. He was, as far as I knew, I was very surprised when he went back overseas, he went in uniform, and I thought he was out of the army, actually he was in the reserve. So, they, they reactivated him. He told me that when they asked him to come to Nuremberg, that he knew he was going to Nuremberg, if the trials were going to take place; there was, after his investigations apparently he was told that there was a plan to do some kind of trials for the war crimes and that if all of this took place they wanted him to be there to help them and the story that he told me was that he felt that was unfair; he felt he had already been overseas for a long time and he had left his family and now the war was over and it was time to earn a living as a physician and be the head of his family again, but he said, if he was forced to do it, if he was ordered to do it, he would do it – because he felt that was also his duty. That way there wouldn't be a choice for him. So, maybe that was one way of dealing with my mother, I, I don't really know, but so the way it worked was that when he left the Army, he was put into the Army reserve and then when the trials took place he was re, he was activated in the Army reserve, so while he was in Nuremberg he was always in uniform. I don't know if everybody was.

Q: And was he approached by the Army beforehand, or did people, who selected him?

A: I have no idea, absolutely no idea. I don't know if there's any data about that. And I don't know who asked him to write those reports after, why he was, they relieved of his duties in East Anglia and sent, I have no idea, I mean obviously he was ordered to do so, but.

Q: What you're implying is that he was relieved, happy to go to Nuremberg?

A: No, I think, I didn't mean to imply that. I think he felt that it was a momentous and very important event and that it would be a great privilege to be there and to take part in that, but that it was selfish on his part, that it would, it would satisfy him, maybe getting even, even with the aggressors, perhaps because of his Jewishness, perhaps because he, like, like many Europeans, was, his family after all was spread out all over the world and destroyed, and things weren't, nothing was left of the family estate, so there must have been some personal, personal feelings. But, in fact, I seem, I seem to recall the selfish, selfish is the word, it would be selfish for him to be there, to give into that. But he definitely wanted to be there, and definitely, we had letters that show, he wrote a letter to my older brother showing that, that he felt this was something extremely important, that it would change the world and that he was a part of that, he was very proud. He was proud of what he did there, his whole life. And he got some fame for that, I mean, for the things that he wrote about it and the fact that he had participated in that event.

Q: Did he talk with you or mention anything about the chaos at Nuremberg, how everything was improvised, how they didn't really know how to produce an indictment, how Telford Taylor was struggling with the actual wording of the opening statement, how Leo was asked to draft the opening statement, did he mention anything?

A: That it was very exciting, very chaotic, that nobody got any sleep, that there was often confusion, red tape, interruptions, and tremendous pressure. I never understood why there was so much pressure until recently when I looked at these, these letters again that they, they felt that they had a certain window of time, and also he spoke about that there was confusion and difficulty in finding witnesses so he used people that he knew, connections, that and perhaps that's why he invited my mother to come over, perhaps when he realised that he would be able to go to Holland because he had reason to consult with his relatives there, that things, that it would be more possible for her to be there. Perhaps that, that wasn't in the original plan, because their living accommodations were also very, they were make-shift and it wasn't very comfortable, it was cold, sometimes there wasn't enough food and people were rushing around. And he did speak about, he used to sometimes make jokes that the Germans kept so many records that they had every day there would be new things coming in and there was nobody there that had enough time to read it all and that this, sometimes they would, apparently the Germans when they left the camp they would burn data and so forth but other stuff was forgotten; so you've been reading through and you would find that you had names and places and then the other stuff was gone; it was very spotty and difficult; but became an other thing, he could read German and it maybe a lot of those people that were there couldn't or couldn't be trusted – but they must have hired a lot of local people, I don't know.

But yes, it was very chaotic. But also a lot of fun. I think they, they had social, social occasions, people, important people from America and England would be there, generals, whatever, and would come in and would have to be entertained, press people possibly.

Q: Was he interviewed?

A: That I don't know. I understand, I mean I read recently but I haven't been able to, it's one of the things we thought we'd be able to go to the library and see if we could find, Life magazine, was he interviewed later on in America, yes. He was invited many times to speak about Nuremberg.

Q: And did he interrogate the defendants?

A: Yes, he told me about that, yes. That he interrogated not just doctors, but other defendants, but I really don't remember any specific things. They were, his opinion was most of them were pretty evil, I mean he had, he had things to say about the various ones, there wasn't any of them he thought was innocent, or that they were unfairly being tried. And I also know that on occasion he was consulted about what he knew or didn't know about people who turned up in American Universities. There was talk on several occasions that sometimes someone that worked in Germany who was never put on trial would become, would publish a paper or get, get an appointment and he would work with, with other people to either discredit them or reaccommodate them.

Q: Did he ever mention the word Hubertus Strugold?

A: I don't remember.

Q: He was one of the men who was assigned to "paperclip" who came over to the United States to work with [Wernher von] Braun, who made the rocket.

A: Yeah, yeah.

Q: He was also a medical scientist who in part collaborated with the Nazis in their experiments who was not tried at Nuremberg.

A: Apparently quite a few of them, there was somebody that had an appointment in New Orleans that, I just have a vague recollection of a group of doctors sitting who were very angry, I think he was, somebody came to, whether he was an appointment of an international organisation, they didn't like that.

Q: You mentioned that it was all very secretive.

A: In Nuremberg?

Q: And before?

A: Yes. Yes, he told us that it was all secret, that, that he, that he was, that it was very confidential material, things that were not made public, and that that's why he couldn't write about it at the time, but that later my impression was that, that this, that after Nuremberg that anything that he knew was made public although no, yeah we had documents upstairs that he said were a secret, that he, that we weren't supposed to look in those, in that room where he had those things, but I'm sure he didn't, it was just a whole lot of papers, wasn't of interest to us.

Q: Do you think he was impartial at Nuremberg?

A: I think that he felt that he was an American. Impartial. I really couldn't make a judgement on that. I think, I know that he felt that experiments that were done by Nazi doctors with the prisoners were evil, that they should never have been done, so in that sense, no not impartial, he was definitely on the, on the prosecutors' side. That these things were evil and inhuman right from get go, that the people, that these people shouldn't have even been imprisoned or in the camps, much less experiments of that nature, experiments where people were killed.

Q: What view did he take on medical experiments on humans? Did he agree?

A: Did he, did he agree that … [?].

Q: Medical experiments on humans in general?

A: He was a physician and interested in, in progress. And that if the patients' safety could be protected, that, that new therapies could be tried, I know that he, that he tried new treatments for mental disease, you know, that but if, but when new medications came out for people who were mentally ill, he was certainly interested in that and in very carefully helping the people of that nature yeah so. He felt that rules should be followed and that there should be a reason to give a new therapy to a patient. He was, he considered his, he considered himself a physician, and a researcher and a teacher. So, so it's a little bit hard to answer that question.

He was, he told me that he had worked on the creation of the Nuremberg Code for human experimentation and that, while there were still discussion to be brought up about how to implement these rules in the Code, but that these were the basis, and that there had to be a lot of development and that people needed to really pay attention to that, that these, these things should never ever ever happen again, that's why he was at Nuremberg to see to it.

Q: But the Code was developed during the trial, isn't that right?

A: That's what I understood, yes, then they call that the Nuremberg Code. By lawyers, and doctors tried to work that out based on the philosophies of experimentation in the past. So, let's see, how would I say that. He felt that he had sacrificed a year, really, of his, of his career to help bring about these changes and that it was very important to protect that, and he gave lectures on this matter often, and when issues came up in the press he would asked years and years until he couldn't give interviews any more what his opinions were about governmental issues, or you know, I remember interviews when there was quite a scandal about Thalidomide, was a new medication that the American FDA hadn't, hadn't released yet but it had, had been released in Europe and there were tremendous birth defects and so on, but at the same time there continues to be a debate in this country about bringing in new medications for AIDS and so forth, people go to Europe for treatments, and so this was a continuing matter of, of learning and discussion on his part.

Q: And do you think he created the Nuremberg Code?

A: Well, we discussed that. He never told me that he wrote it alone. He never said that. As I told you earlier this week, I think if he had sat down and wrote it himself, and presented it to [a] committee and that they approved it, he would have said so. He was not a man to, to hide his accomplishments whatsoever. He gave me the impression that it was a matter of hours of work and discussion, that there was, that there were many people involved. He, he had an ability with language. He may very well have formulated the final sentences or, or something like that, but my impression was that it was, it was something that they worked on under great pressure, that they needed this, I don't know, was it ever presented in court, I don't know, but they needed to create this thing, and that it was more important, he felt, than the guilt or innocence of a few evil doctors. He felt that it was, when he looked back on it, that that was the whole point, was to create a new standard, not just to convict these people. He also told me that he wasn't sure that the right people were, were put in the dock necessarily, that there were others, people who either had killed themselves or escaped or had been protected and couldn't be in reach. So that was another problem about the evidence. There was evidence sometimes of people that they didn't have, but again I, I don't know any specifics on that matter. They weren't the worst ones, he said.

Q: I perfectly agree with what you're saying, not something I had the impression from what I had read, just have to check this. Did he ever say if something like this ever happened again, he would do the job again or if he would have to be called again to a trial like that?

A: I can't remember a particular time when he said that but I think it's implicit yes. It was a real high point in his life. He was very glad that he did it. That story that I mentioned before, you know that I'll go if you order me, that was, that was something he said with a twinkle in his eye, I think it was, you know, it was probably just a way of justifying being away from home, and you know, I don't know anything about whether it was a financial sacrifice, maybe that's why he did [...] the idea, why he came home, during that year there must have been a lot of preparations for the trial, the year between 45 and 46, but he was already here, he'd come back and established his office in Boston and his practice, so that's perhaps why maybe, he felt that he couldn't spend the whole two years, it wouldn't be enough money.

Q: Did he stay in contact with some of the prosecution staff?

A: Yes, yes, there was a lot of correspondence and he travelled a lot. My father [was] organised in psychiatric associations and there were reunions of doctors and so forth, so I'm sure he did, he did continue to have contact with these people. I know he saw Telford Taylor and I think he communicated with Dr Ivy and probably a lot of other people whose names I don't know.

Q: What relations did the two have, Dr Ivy and Taylor?

A: I don't really know, except for when I asked him about Dr Ivy when I was in college, on another issue which had to do with [...] he thought, he told me then, or told me then, he knew Ivy and could introduce me to him, I wanted to meet him, but that, that he was a person that went along with fads sometimes, he liked publicity, he liked being in charge of things, so on this particular occasion and on other occasions he had, he was gone off, half [...], half informed, but very eager for, for publicity and to be in charge, and he thought he had lost, that Dr. Ivy had lost some of his ability to discriminate good information from bad information, so he felt quite superior on that particular issue, then he managed to know that this was not a worthwhile thing.

Q: You mentioned also that he stayed in contact with witnesses, the Ravensbrück witnesses.

A: Oh yes, yes.

Q: What was that?

A: There was a time, and I think it went on for a while, when these, these witnesses, it was a group of, of women who had been operated on in a camp, and they were all young and healthy women, but rather disastrous, outrageous operations had been done to them, in particular of course I have the image in my mind from the video, of, of the damage had been done to the legs, but I think there were other, there were operations that were done, but there was, actually some money was provided by a publisher named Norman Cousins, who was again a friend of a friend. He contacted a group of people who were connected with the medical community and particularly I'm sure my father, since he had interviewed and had managed testimony of these people. So some of the operations, I believe some of surgery was dominated by certain hospitals, some in New York, some in Boston, and one lady in particular was operated on at Beth Israel in Boston and stayed in our house in between restorative reconstruction. Now I don't know if she has complications from the reconstruction or whether it just involved several stages but she did stay in our house and she, she helped my mother do a lot, well she was a seamstress at home, and they made draperies and the dress and became quite good friends. And I know that when we were instructed not to try to understand her when she spoke in her language or in, you know the game charades when she tries to act in, that we as children were supposed to insist that she say the words in English. She wanted to learn English but she, like all of us, was a little bit lazy about that, so we were supposed to help in that way. She was a very nice person, and we, we really enjoyed her visit and I don't even know how long it was, but I think of it as a long time, but it might not have been.

Q: Do you remember her name?

A: No. Maria or now just as I was talking, I was thinking Jadwiga [Dzido]. I have a feeling it was Jadwiga and I don't know what happened to her but I think my parents, my mother used to write, she was quite a correspondent and, but my impression is that she might have stayed in the United States, but I don't know.

Q: Was this a time in the McCarthy era?

A: Yes, whatever year that was, maybe 51, they, the two of them would watch those hearings on TV, she, she was supposed to being learning English for the trial. But it was a time of great fascination in the United States watching those trials. People were quite appalled.
    [See that over there, the guy in the kayak?]

Q: Is it possible to position Leo politically?

A: Democrat. Always voted democrat. He was very much a Roosevelt man. He was definitely a liberal, and, but I don't think he ever became actively involved in any political campaigns but he was very much in favour of Adlai Stevenson, very upset but not surprised. He said, about Adlai Stevenson, he said that he couldn't be elected President because during that campaign Adlai Stevenson's divorced wife published a very negative book about him. She apparently was a woman who had had some emotional problems and continued to be angry with him so I guess these things were reported in the press and Leo said that the Americans will never elect a President who can't control his wife even if it's an ex wife. So that happened to be true, but whether it was for that reason or not I don't know.

Q: Could he control his wife?

A: Apparently, apparently. His first wife, anyway. Not the second, but his first wife pretty much.

Q: Do you think he was a family man or was it part of his upbringing that one had to have a family, had to be head of the family, or was it in his heart that he was a scientist?

A: This is an interesting question. Well, that, that's probably true to a point. He certainly wanted a family and children to reflect honourably on him, yes, that he needed a house and a nice home, and that sort of thing, but I think he loved my mother very much. But he was quite self-centred. At the same time, he patterned family life on what he remembered of his own life, of his upbringing, which was much more formal than by American standards. Children should be seen, and not heard, and well-behaved. And when they entertained, that we would be introduced and shake hands and have good manners, and if we were asked to do something to play the piano or do a little concert for the guests, we were expected to do that. He and his siblings were expected to perform for guests and they had a formal Sunday dinner every week at which father was present and he would ask questions about what you learned in school during the week, quite formal. He wasn't home much during the week. It's a little different today than people pattern their households. I can remember being very jealous that my friends' fathers came home by train from the city, from their work, but he was, he worked into the evening almost every day. Of course if you look back, if you look at that, it was, nowadays psychiatrists have offices in their homes in the suburbs, and they're able to, able to take part in their family life, in those days all doctors had their offices in certain neighbourhoods in the city otherwise you weren't, you weren't a good doctor and you know if you went to see a psychiatrist every week, you couldn't take time off from work in those days to do that, to see a doctor, he was busy as death till 5 o'clock.

So, my mother used to eat dinner with us, with the children and then prepare dinner for him and when we were older, we would say hello in the evening, but when we were small, we would be in bed by then, by the time he came home. Also, he, he had, had meetings of the medical society or he gave a lecture or something like that.

Q: In his later years, you showed me this one article, he was on several occasions criticised of being in favour of or adopting certain measures like electro-shock to patients. How did he, did he ever reflect on the problems, having written basically the medical ethics standards, standards in the world, of being part of that on the one hand and suddenly coming into a sea of criticism of violating those standards? Was that a problem for him?

A: He was, he didn't have any self-doubt about that. He, he felt that at that time, the types of patients he was treating in that way could only be treated in that, in that fashion, and he felt that those who accused him of, of being cruel to patients should, should walk in his shoes for a day or two and he would, he would invite them. There was, there was I don't know, a movie that depicted an electric shock as a very cruel thing to do and it showed awful pictures of the kinds of spasms that patients would go through and he was quite incensed and very defensive and wrote letters and gave an interview about that.

Q: Is it *One Flew Over A Cuckoo's Nest*?
[1975 US drama film directed by Miloš Forman, based on a novel by Ken Kesey]

A: Yes that one, yes for example. I was thinking of a movie called Snakebit which was much earlier. But these were patients that were really, as he called in the back wards of lunatic asylums, who had to be restrained because they would injure themselves and so, so he felt that they needed to have this kind of treatment in order to have a, an acceptable normal, some kind of normal life where they could live in a household with a family, was the justification for that.

He continued to do electro-shock therapy but it was less, as time went on it was less and less of his practices as drug therapy and, and other interventions. He was thrilled to see the movement at least in the United States in being able to close some of these state mental hospitals, that people could live in society without those kind[s] of treatments.

Q: How would you describe him if you had to, how would you describe his identity in a few words? What kind of man was he?

A: Intellectual, brilliant, sophisticated, fascinating, distant, he had very little time for self, what's the word, [Schmidt, injection – 'introspection?'], introspection, thank you. He had a great deal of insight into the problems of other people, but not into those that, that he was close to. When, when people that were close to him were ill or in trouble, it took, took a long time for him to realise it.

He was, it's not that he was cruel, I don't mean that, but concerned mostly for, for himself, for his research, for his schedule, rather than fitting with anybody else. Didn't require much sleep. He loved. He lived a good life, he loved to travel, he loved to dance, he loved art, he loved parties, he loved women. He wasn't too much concerned with money. On occasion he didn't quite have enough, but he managed to carry on and he felt that it would always come, there's always another day. Also, he did, I do know of one occasion when he was really quite depressed for a while. It was usually some life occurrence. In this particular case he had been sued, he felt unfairly because of his [Schmidt, interjection – newspaper article] and it cost him a lot, a lot of energy, and a lot of money and a lot of time which he felt took his, took him away from things that were much more important to do and he really felt persecuted. Ultimately triumphant, although he would have liked, he would have liked to go to a trial, but the various insurance companies and lawyers urged him to settle the case, but he felt that would give that organisation money, but he ran out of energy and he was depressed at that time. Some rest and a vacation, probably a little medication and he got over it.

THE NUREMBERG CODE OF MEDICAL ETHICS

PERMISSIBLE MEDICAL EXPERIMENTS

1. The voluntary consent of the human subject is absolutely essential. This means that the person involved should have legal capacity to give consent; should be so situated as to be able to exercise free power of choice, without the intervention of any element of force, fraud, deceit, duress, over-reaching, or other ulterior form of constraint or coercion; and should have sufficient knowledge and comprehension of the elements of the subject matter involved, as to enable him to make an understanding and enlightened decision. This latter element requires that, before the acceptance of an affirmative decision by the experimental subject, there should be made known to him the nature, duration, and purpose of the experiment; the method and means by which it is to be conducted; all inconveniences and hazards reasonably to be expected; and the effects upon his health or person, which may possibly come from his participation in the experiment. The duty and responsibility for ascertaining the quality of the consent rests upon each individual who initiates, directs or engages in the experiment. It is a personal duty and responsibility which may not be delegated to another with impunity.

2. The experiment should be such as to yield fruitful results for the good of society, unprocurable by other methods or means of study, and not random and unnecessary in nature.

3. The experiment should be so designed and based on the results of animal experimentation and a knowledge of the natural history of the disease or other problem under study, that the anticipated results will justify the performance of the experiment.

4. The experiment should be so conducted as to avoid all unnecessary physical and mental suffering and injury.

5. No experiment should be conducted, where there is an a priori reason to believe that death or disabling injury will occur; except, perhaps, in those experiments where the experimental physicians also serve as subjects.

6. The degree of risk to be taken should never exceed that determined by the humanitarian importance of the problem to be solved by the experiment.

7. Proper preparations should be made and adequate facilities provided to protect the experimental subject against even remote possibilities of injury, disability, or death.

8. The experiment should be conducted only by scientifically qualified persons. The highest degree of skill and care should be required through all stages of the experiment of those who conduct or engage in the experiment.

9. During the course of the experiment, the human subject should be at liberty to bring the experiment to an end, if he has reached the physical or mental state, where continuation of the experiment seemed to him to be impossible.

10. During the course of the experiment, the scientist in charge must be prepared to terminate the experiment at any stage, if he has probable cause to believe, in the exercise of the good faith, superior skill and careful judgement required of him, that a continuation of the experiment is likely to result in injury, disability, or death to the experimental subject.

Source: Trials of War Criminals before the Nuremberg Military Tribunals under Control Council Law No. 10, Vol. 2, pp. 181–182. Washington, D.C.: U.S. Government Printing Office, 1949.

Fig. 20: Work of civil and military experts at the Nuremberg Doctors' Trial. Leo Alexander (first from left) and colleagues 1946/47 (Source: NARA).

BIBLIOGRAPHY

ARCHIVAL SOURCES

Alexander Papers, Boston (in possession of Cecily K. Alexander-Grable's estate)
  Personal correspondence, 1946–1947
Duke University Medical Centre Library and Archive, Durham NC
  Alexander papers (Alexander's record ledger book of activities and notes, 1946–1947)
Harvard Law School Library Nuremberg Trials Project
  "Description of two illustrations of freezing experiments", 1946, Evidence Code: NO–855.
  "Extract from an affidavit concerning the freezing experiments", 1945, Evidence Code: PS–2428
  "Testimonial exhibits in the report on atrocities committed at Dachau: Report of the Atrocities Committed at the Dachau Concentration Camp Volume II[.] Testimony – Exhibits 3 to 24", date unknown, Evidence Code: PS–2428
  Direct Examination of Maria Janina Broel-Plater by the President, 19 December 1946
  Direct Examination of Leo Alexander by Mr. McHaney, 20 December 1946
  Direct Examination of Eugen Kogon by Mr. McHaney, 6 January 1947, and Cross Examination of Eugen Kogon by Dr. Nelte, 7 January 1947
International Physicians for the Prevention of Nuclear War Nuremberg, Fürth, Erlangen
  Photographs by Ray D'Addario
Landesarchiv Schleswig-Holstein
  Abt. 352 Kiel, Nr. 1141, "Auf Vorladung erscheint als Beschuldigte Ärztin Dr. med. Oberheuser aus Stocksee", 5 December 1956
National Archives, London
  WO 235/313, "Deposition of Dr. Gerhard Schiedlausky", 22 November 1946
  WO 235/317, "Deposition of Dr. Rolf Rosenthal", 19 August 1946. Nuremberg Medical Trial, Microfiche number 131, "Affidavit of Herta Oberheuser", 2 November 1946
  WO 309/419, Major Arthur Keith Mant RAMC, Special Medical Section War Crimes Group B.A.O.R, Ravensbrück Camp. "A report on the Medical Services, Human Experimentation and various other atrocities committed by medical personnel in the camp"
  WO 309/416, "Deposition of Erna Boehmer", 18 April 1946
National Archives and Record Administration, Washington DC
Tape recorded interviews with:
  Cecily K. Alexander-Grable, Marion, Cape Cod
United States Holocaust Memorial Museum
  "Witness Franz Blaha testifies at Nuremberg Trial", Film, Accession Number 2001.358.1.
  Selections from the Argumentation of the Defence. "Extracts from the Closing Brief for Defendant Sievers. The Freezing Experiments", in Trials of War Criminals before the Nuernberg Military Tribunals Under Control Council Law No. 10, Volume 1, Nuernberg October 1946–April 1949, p. 208
  Nuremberg Medical Trial, Microfiche number 38, "Resumed cross-examination of Karl Gebhardt by Mr McHaney", 7 March 1947
University of Erlangen-Nuremberg, Institute for the History of Medicine and Medical Ethics, Werner Leibbrand Papers

LITERATURE

Alexander, Leo (1948): War Crimes and Their Motivation. The Socio-Psychological Structure of the SS and the Criminalisation of a Society. In: Journal of Law and Criminology 39, 3, pp. 298–326.

Alexander, Leo (1949): Medical Science under Dictatorship. In: The New England Journal of Medicine 241, pp. 39–47.

Allex, Anne/Kalkan, Dietrich (eds.) (2009): Ausgesteuert – ausgegrenzt – angeblich asozial. Neu-Ulm.

Annas, George/Grodin, Michael (eds.) (1992): The Nazi Doctors and the Nuremberg Code. Human Rights in Human Experimentation. New York.

Annas, George/Grodin, Michael (2018): Reflections on the 70th Anniversary of the Nuremberg Doctors' Trial. In: American Journal of Public Health 108, 1, pp. 10–12.

Arendt, Hannah (1951): The Origins of Totalitarianism. New York.

Armstrong, Niel/Collins, Michael/Aldrin, Edwin (1970): First on the Moon: A Voyage with Neil Armstrong, Michael Collins, Edwin E. Aldrin Jr. Boston.

Bamford, Christopher (ed.) (2002): What Is Anthroposophy? Great Barrington.

Bayle, François (1950): Croix Gammée Contre Caducée. Les Expériences Humaines en Allemagne pendant la Deuxième Guerre Mondiale. Neustadt/Pfalz.

Benedict, Susan/Georges, Jane (2006): Nurses and the Sterilization Experiments of Auschwitz: A Postmodernist Perspective. In: Nursing Inquiry 13, 4, pp. 277–288.

Benedict, Susan/Shields, Linda (2014): Nurses and Midwives in Nazi Germany: The "Euthanasia Programs". Abingdon.

Betzien, Petra (2018): Krankenschwestern im System der nationalsozialistischen Konzentrationslager. Frankfurt/M.

Blatman, Daniel (2011): The Death Marches. Cambridge.

Bock, Gisela (1986): Zwangssterilisation im Nationalsozialisums. Opladen.

Bogue, Nicole (2016): The Concentration Camp Brothels in Memory. In: Holocaust Studies 22, 2–3, pp. 208–227.

Browning, Christopher (1992): Ordinary Men: Reserve Police Battalion 101 and the Final Solution in Poland. New York.

Bruns, Florian (2009): Medizinethik im Nationalsozialismus. Entwicklungen und Protagonisten in Berlin (1939–1945). Geschichte und Philosophie der Medizin, Band 7. Stuttgart.

Burger, Oswald (2009): Überlingen. In: Megargee, Geoffrey P. (ed.) The United States Holocaust Memorial Museum Encyclopaedia of Camps and Ghettos, 1933–1945, Volume 1: Early Camps, Youth Camps, and Concentration Camps and Subcamps under the SS-Business Administration Main Office. Translated by Stephen Pallavicini. Indiana, pp. 554–555.

Burleigh, Michael (1994): Death and Deliverance. Cambridge.

Caplan, Arthur (ed.) (1992): When Medicine Went Mad: Bioethics and the Holocaust. Totowa, NJ.

Cassar, George (2016): Kitchener as Proconsul of Egypt, 1911–1914. Basingstoke.

Century, Rachel (2017): Female Administrators in the Third Reich. Basingstoke.

Cocks, Geoffrey (1985): Psychotherapy in the Third Reich: The Goring Institute. Oxford.

Cooper, John (2008): Raphael Lemkin and the Struggle for the Genocide Convention. Basingstoke.

Dillon, Christopher (2017): Dachau and the SS: A Schooling in Violence. Cambridge.

Distel, Barbara (2009): Dachau Main Camp. In: Megargee, Geoffrey P. (ed.), The United States Holocaust Memorial Museum Encyclopedia of Camps and Ghettos, 1933–1945, Volume I: Early Camps, Youth Camps, and Concentration Camps and Subcamps under the SS-Business Administration Main Office (WVHA). Indiana, pp. 441–447.

Docking, Kate (2021): Gender, Recruitment and Medicine at Ravensbrück Concentration Camp, 1939-1942. In: German History 39, 3, pp. 419–441.

Docking, Kate (2021): Reframing Gender: The Experiences of the Female Medical Personnel of Ravensbrück Concentration Camp, 1933–1949 (unpublished PhD thesis, University of Kent, Canterbury).

Dörner, Bernward (2009): Oranienburg. In: Megargee, Geoffrey P. (ed.), The United States Holocaust Memorial Museum Encyclopedia of Camps and Ghettos, 1933–1945, Volume I: Early Camps, Youth Camps, and Concentration Camps and Subcamps under the SS-Business Administration Main Office (WVHA). Translated by Stephen Pallavicini. Indiana, pp. 147–149.

Dörner, Klaus/Ebbinghaus, Angelika/Linne, Karsten (eds.) (1999): Der Nürnberger Ärzteprozeß 1946/47. Wortprotokolle, Anklage- und Verteidigungsmaterial, Quellen zum Umfeld. Deutsche Ausgabe, im Auftrag der Stiftung für Sozialgeschichte des 20. Jahrhunderts herausgegeben von Klaus Dörner, Angelika Ebbinghaus und Karsten Linne; in Zusammenarbeit mit Karl-Heinz Roth und Paul Weindling. Bearbeitet von Karsten Linne. Einleitung von Angelika Ebbinghaus, Mikrofiche-Edition. München.

Dreyfus, Jean-Marc (2009): Natzweiler-Struthof [aka Natzweiler, Struthof]. In: Megargee, Geoffrey P. (ed.) The United States Holocaust Memorial Museum Encyclopedia of Camps and Ghettos, 1933-1945, Volume I: Early Camps, Youth Camps, and Concentration Camps and Subcamps under the SS-Business Administration Main Office (WVHA). Translated by Gina Cooke. Indiana, pp. 1003–1008.

Ebbinghaus, Angelika/Roth, Karl Heinz (2001): Short Biographies of the 545 Persons Involved in the Trial. In: The Nuremberg Medical Trial 1946/47. Guide to the Microfiche Edition. Eltzschig/Walter (2001), pp. 67–157.

Eltzschig, Johannes/Walter, Michael (eds.) (2001): The Nuremberg Medical Trial 1946/47. Guide to the Microfiche Edition. Munich.

Engelhardt, Thomas/Frewer, Andreas (eds.) (2023): NS-"Euthanasie" in Erlangen: Tatorte – Hungerkost – Opfer. Neustadt a.d.A.

Evans, Richard (2008): The Third Reich at War, 1939–1945. London.

Forsbach, Ralf/Hofer, Hans-Georg (2017): Der Versuch einer großen Integration: Paul Martini und der erste Nachkriegskongress der Deutschen Gesellschaft für Innere Medizin. In: NTM Zeitschrift für Geschichte der Wissenschaften, Technik und Medizin 25, pp. 35–68.

Frewer, Andreas/Eickhoff, Clemens (eds.) (2000): "Euthanasie" und die aktuelle Sterbehilfe-Debatte. Die historischen Hintergründe medizinischer Ethik. Frankfurt/M., New York.

Frewer, Andreas (ed.) (2020): Psychiatrie und "Euthanasie" in der HuPfla: Debatten zu Werner Leibbrands Buch "Um die Menschenrechte der Geisteskranken". Nürnberg.

Frewer, Andreas (2021): Werner Leibbrand: Leben – Weiterleben – Überleben. Geschichte und Philosophie der Medizin, Band 16. Stuttgart.

Frewer, Andreas (2023): Werner Leibbrand und die "Euthanasie" in Erlangen. Seine besondere Rolle bei der Aufarbeitung von NS-Verbrechen. In: Engelhardt/Frewer (eds.), pp. 239–294.

Frewer, Andreas/Neumann, Josef N. (eds.) (2001): Medizingeschichte und Medizinethik. Kontroversen und Begründungsansätze 1900–1950. Frankfurt/M., New York.

Frewer, Andreas/Oppitz, Ulrich-Dieter et al. (eds.) (1999): Medizinverbrechen vor Gericht. Das Urteil im Nürnberger Ärzteprozeß gegen Karl Brandt und andere sowie aus dem Prozeß gegen Generalfeldmarschall Erhard Milch. Erlanger Studien zur Ethik in der Medizin, Band 7. Erlangen, Jena.

Freyhofer, Horst (2004): The Nuremberg Medical Trial. The Holocaust and the Origin of the Nuremberg Medical Code. New York.

Friedlander, Henry (1995): The Origins of Nazi Genocide. From Euthanasia to the Final Solution. Chapel Hill.

Friedländer, Saul (2000): The Years of Extermination. Nazi Germany and the Jews, 1939–1945. New York.

Gaw, Allan (2014): Reality and revisionism: new evidence for Andrew C. Ivy's claim to authorship of the Nuremberg Code. In: Journal of the Royal Society of Medicine 107, 4, pp. 138–143.

Godau-Schütte, Klaus-Detlev (1998): Die Heyde/Sawade-Affäre. Wie Juristen und Mediziner den NS-Euthanasieprofessor Heyde nach 1945 deckten und straflos blieben. Baden-Baden.

Greiner, Josef (1947): Das Ende des Hitler-Mythos. Zürich.

Grossmann, Atina (2007): Jews, Germans and Allies: Close Encounters in Occupied Germany. New Jersey.

Haag, John (1976): Othmar Spann and the Quest for the "True State". In: Austrian History Yearbook 12, 1, pp. 227–250.

Harkness, Jon (1996): Nuremberg and the Issue of Wartime Experiments on US Prisoners. The Green Committee. In: JAMA 276, 20, pp. 1672–1675.

Hehemann, Rainer (1987): Die "Bekämpfung des Zigeunerunwesens" im wilhelminischen Deutschland und in der Weimarer Republik 1871–1933. Frankfurt/M.

Heinemann, Isabel (2003): Rasse, Siedlung, deutsches Blut. Das Rasse- und Siedlungshauptamt der SS und die rassenpolitische Neuordnung Europas. Göttingen.

Heinemann, Isabel (2005): "Ethnic Resettlement" and Inter-Agency Cooperation in the Occupied Eastern Territories. In: Networks of Nazi Persecution. Bureaucracy, Business and the Organisation of the Holocaust, Feldman, Gerald/Seibel Wolfgang (eds.). Oxford.

Henke, Josef (1993): Quellenschicksale und Bewertungsfragen. Archivische Probleme bei der Überlieferungsbildung zur Verfolgung der Sinti und Roma im Dritten Reich. In: Vierteljahrshefte für Zeitgeschichte 41, 1, pp. 61–77.

Hentschel, Klaus (1996): Physics and National Socialism: An Anthology of Primary Sources. Translated by Ann Hentschel. Basel.

Herbert, Ulrich (2000): Forced Laborers in the Third Reich: An Overview. In: International Labor and Working-Class History, 58, pp. 192–218.

Herzog, Dagmar (2005): Sex after Fascism: Memory and Morality in Twentieth-Century Germany. New Jersey.

Hildebrandt, Sabine (2014): The Anatomy of Murder. Ethical Transgressions and Anatomical Science during the Third Reich. New York.

Hipp, Dietmar (2020): Von NS-Konzentrationslagern erzählen. Angeklagte vor Gericht über Dachau, Mauthausen, Ravensbrück und Neuengamme. Bielefeld.

Hubenstorf, Michael (1994): "Aber es kommt mir doch so vor, als ob Sie dabei nichts verloren hätten". Zum Exodus von Wissenschaftlern aus den staatlichen Forschungsinstituten Berlins im Bereich des öffentlichen Gesundheitswesens. In: Fischer, Wolfram/Hierholzer, Klaus/Hubenstorf, Michael/Walther, Peter T./Winau, Rolf (ed.), Exodus von Wissenschaften aus Berlin. Berlin, pp. 355–461.

Huebner, Todd (2009): Flossenbürg Main Camp. In: Megargee, Geoffrey P. (ed.) The United States Holocaust Memorial Museum Encyclopedia of Camps and Ghettos, 1933–1945, Volume I: Early Camps, Youth Camps, and Concentration Camps and Subcamps under the SS-Business Administration Main Office (WVHA). Indiana, pp. 559–566.

Jardim, Tomaz (2012): The Mauthausen Trial. Cambridge.

Jobst, Clemens/Czech, Herwig (2022): Erwin Deutsch, the Eppinger Clinic and the Legacy of the Second Vienna School of Medicine–Continuities of a Career. In: Wiener Klinische Wochenschrift 136, 7–8, pp. 224–233.

Kaiser, Stephanie/Schmidt, Mathias (2020): Ludwig Stumpfegger (1910–45). A Career at the Interface of Hitler, Himmler, and Ravensbrück Concentration Camp. In: Recognising the Past in the Present. New Studies on Medicine before, during and after the Holocaust, Hildebrandt, Sabine/Offer, Miriam/Grodin, Michael A. (eds.). Oxford, pp. 154–171.

Kater, Michael (1989): Doctors Under Hitler. Chapel Hill.

Klimpel, Volker (2005): Ärzte-Tode. Unnatürliches und gewaltsames Ableben in neun Kapiteln und einem biographischen Anhang. Würzburg.

Kurlander, Eric (2019): Nazism and Religion. Oxford Research Encyclopedia of Religion. Oxford.

Lachman, Ernest (1977): Anatomist of Infamy: August Hirt. In: Bulletin of the History of Medicine 51, 4, pp. 594–602.

Lasik, Aleksander (1998): Historical-Sociological Profile of the Nazi SS. In: Gutman, Y./Berenbaum, M. (eds.), Anatomy of the Auschwitz Death Camp. Bloomington, pp. 271–287.

Lovell, Richard (1992): Churchill's Doctor. A Biography of Lord Moran. Carlton.

Löwen, Mario zur (2005): Robert Kempner, Ankläger einer Epoche. Lebenserinnerungen. München.

Madajczyk, Piotr (2024): The Biographical Landscapes of Raphael Lemkin. Abingdon.

Margalit, Gilad (1997): Die deutsche Zigeunerpolitik nach 1945. In: Vierteljahrshefte für Zeitgeschichte 45, 4, pp. 557–588.

Miles, Steven (2005): The Hippocratic Oath and the Ethics of Medicine. Oxford.
Miller, Franklin/Moreno, Jonathan (2021): Human Infection Challenge Experiments: Then and Now. In: Ethics and Human Research 43, 3, pp. 42–44.
Milton, Sybil (1995): Vorstufe zur Vernichtung. Die Zigeunerlager nach 1933. In: Vierteljahrshefte für Zeitgeschichte 43, 1, pp. 115–130.
Morrison, Jack (2000): Ravensbrück. Everyday Life in a Women's Concentration Camp, 1939–45. Princeton.
Moskowitz, Merle (1977): Hugo Münsterberg. A study in the history of applied psychology. In: American Psychologist 32, 10, pp. 824–842.
Neliba, Günter (1992): Wilhelm Frick: Der Legalist des Unrechtsstaates. Paderborn.
Neufeld, Michael J. (2009): Mittelbau Main Camp (Aka Dora). In: Megargee, Geoffrey P. (ed.). The United States Holocaust Memorial Museum Encyclopaedia of Camps and Ghettos, 1933–1945, Volume 1: Early Camps, Youth Camps, and Concentration Camps and Subcamps under the SS-Business Administration Main Office. Indiana, pp. 966–971.
Nuremberg Military Tribunal (1949): Trials of War Criminals Before the Nuernberg Military Tribunals Under Control Council Law No. 10, Nuernberg, Vol. XV, October 1946–April 1949. Washington D.C., p. 407.
Pilzweger-Steiner, Stefanie/Riedle, Andrea (2018): Beweise für die Nachwelt/Evidence for Posterity: Die Zeichnungen des Dachau-Überlebenden Georg Tauber/The Drawings of the Dachau Survivor Georg Tauber. Berlin.
Pugliese, Elizabeth (2013): Taylor, Telford. In: Mikaberidze, Alexander (ed.), Atrocities, Massacres and War Crimes, An Encyclopedia. Volume 1: A–L. Santa Barbara.
Raim, Edith (2009): Kaufering I–XI. In: Megargee, Geoffrey P. (ed.). The United States Holocaust Memorial Museum Encyclopaedia of Camps and Ghettos, 1933–1945, Volume 1: Early Camps, Youth Camps, and Concentration Camps and Subcamps under the SS-Business Administration Main Office. Translated by Stephen Pallavicini. Indiana, pp. 488–490.
Reginbogin, Herbert/Breger, Marshall J. (eds.) (2024): Nuremberg Principles and Ukraine. The Contemporary Challenges to Peace, Security, and Justice. Lanham (in press).
Roth, Karl Heinz/Schmidt, Ulf/Weindling, Paul (2001): Documents and Material Pertaining to the Trial History, Background and Consequences of the Nuremberg Medical Trial. In: Eltzschig, Johannes/Walter, Michael (eds.): The Nuremberg Medical Trial 1946/47. Guide to the Microfiche Edition. Berlin.
Schalm, Sabine (2009): Überleben durch Arbeit? Außenkommandos und Außenlager des KZ Dachau 1933–1945. Berlin.
Schaller, Dominik/Zimmerer, Jürgen. Eds. (2009): The Origins of Genocide: Raphael Lemkin as a historian of mass violence. Abingdon.
Schikorra, Christa (2001): Kontinuitäten der Ausgrenzung. "Asoziale" Häftlinge im Frauen-Konzentrationslager Ravensbrück. Berlin.
Schikorra, Christa (2009): "Herumtreiberei" und "liederlicher Lebenswandel". Frauen im Zugriff von Fürsorge und Polizei im NS-Staat. In: A. Allex and D. Kalkan (eds), Ausgesteuert—ausgegrenzt ... angeblich asozial. Neu-Ulm, pp. 55–61.
Schmidt, Ulf (2004): Justice at Nuremberg. Leo Alexander and the Nazi Doctors' Trial. Basingstoke.
Schmidt, Ulf (2005): The Scars of Ravensbrück. In: German History 23, 1, pp. 20–49.
Schmidt, Ulf (2008): Karl Brandt: The Nazi Doctor: Medicine and Power in the Third Reich. London.
Schmidt, Ulf (2015): Secret Science. A Century of Poison Warfare and Human Experiments. Oxford.
Schmidt, Ulf (2024): Thanatology and the Nuremberg Doctors' Trial: Conceptualizing the "Science of Killing". In: Reginbogin/Breger (in press).
Schmuhl, Hans-Walter (2008): The Kaiser Wilhelm Institute for Anthropology, Human Heredity and Eugenics, 1927–1945. Dordrecht.
Schwartz, Johannes (2018): Weibliche Angelegenheiten. Handlungsräume von KZ-Aufseherinnen in Ravensbrück und Neubrandenburg. Hamburg.

Siegel, Sari (2014): Treating an Auschwitz Prisoner-Physician: The Case of Dr. Maximilian Samuel. In: Holocaust and Genocide Studies 28, 3, pp. 450–481.

Sommer, Robert (2009): Das KZ-Bordell. Sexuelle Zwangsarbeit in nationalsozialistischen Konzentrationslagern. München.

Sondhaus, Lawrence (2000): Franz Conrad von Hötzendorf. Architect of the Apocalypse. Boston.

Stackelberg, Roderick (2007): The Routledge Companion to Nazi Germany. New York.

Stoltzenberg, Dietrich (2004): Fritz Haber. Chemist, Nobel Laureate, German, Jew. Philadelphia.

Strebel, Bernhard (2003): Das KZ Ravensbrück. Paderborn.

Sydnor, Charles (2009): Auschwitz I Main Camp. In: Megargee, Geoffrey P. (ed.), The United States Holocaust Memorial Museum Encyclopedia of Camps and Ghettos, 1933–1945, Volume I: Early Camps, Youth Camps, and Concentration Camps and Subcamps under the SS-Business Administration Main Office (WVHA). Indiana, pp. 204–208.

Taylor, Telford (1952): Sword and Swastika: Generals and Nazis in the Third Reich. New York.

Taylor, Telford (1970a): Nuremberg and Vietnam: An American Tragedy. New York.

Taylor, Telford (1970b): Guilt, Responsibility and the Third Reich. Cambridge.

Taylor, Telford (1974): Perspectives on Justice. Evanston.

Taylor, Telford (1992): The Anatomy of the Nuremberg Trials: A Personal Memoir. New York.

Torrey, Edwin/Yolken, Robert (2010): Psychiatric Genocide: Nazi Attempts to Eradicate Schizophrenia. In: Schizophrenia Bulletin 36, 1, pp. 26–32.

Trittel, Katharina (2022): Zwischen Erkenntnisstreben und Entgrenzung. Das Selbstverständnis der Flugmediziner im Dienst der Wehrmacht als Grundlage ihrer Elitenkontinuität. In: Rauh, Philipp/Voggenreiter, Marion/Ude-Koeller, Susanne/Leven, Karl-Heinz (eds.), Medizintäter. Ärzte und Ärztinnen im Spiegel der NS-Täterforschung. Köln, pp. 397–419.

Wagner, Jens-Christian (2009): Mittelbau Subcamp System. In: Megargee, Geoffrey P. (ed.), The United States Holocaust Memorial Museum Encyclopaedia of Camps and Ghettos, 1933–1945, Volume 1: Early Camps, Youth Camps, and Concentration Camps and Subcamps under the SS-Business Administration Main Office. Translated by Stephen Pallavicini. Indiana, pp. 973–974.

Waltrich, Hans (2001): Aufstieg und Niedergang der Heilanstalten Hohenlychen (1902 bis 1945). Blankensee.

Waite, Robert G. (2009): Mauthausen Main Camp. In: Megargee, Geoffrey P. (ed.), The United States Holocaust Memorial Museum Encyclopedia of Camps and Ghettos, 1933–1945, Volume I: Early Camps, Youth Camps, and Concentration Camps and Subcamps under the SS-Business Administration Main Office (WVHA). Indiana, pp. 900–904.

Weindling, Paul (1993): Health, race and German politics between national unification and Nazism, 1870–1945. Cambridge.

Weindling, Paul (2004): Nazi Medicine and the Nuremberg Trials. Basingstoke.

Weindling, Paul (2010): John W. Thompson: Psychiatrist in the Shadow of the Holocaust. Rochester.

Weindling, Paul (2014): Victims and Survivors of the Nazi Human Experiments. London.

Weindling, Paul (2017): From Clinic to Concentration Camp. Reassessing Nazi Medical and Racial Research, 1933–1945. London.

Wickert, Christl (2002): Tabu Lagerbordell. In: Eschebach, Insa/Jacobeit, Sigrid, Wenk/Silke (eds.), Gedächtnis und Geschlecht. Frankfurt/M., pp. 41–59.

Zegenhagen, Evelyn (2009): Buchenwald Main Camp. In: Megargee, Geoffrey P. (ed.), The United States Holocaust Memorial Museum Encyclopedia of Camps and Ghettos, 1933–1945, Volume I: Early Camps, Youth Camps, and Concentration Camps and Subcamps under the SS-Business Administration Main Office (WVHA). Translated by Stephen Pallavicini. Indiana, pp. 296–289.

TABLE OF DEFENDANTS

Name   **Sentence**

Hermann Becker-Freyseng   20 years imprisonment, commuted to 10 years, released 1952

Wilhelm Beiglböck   15 years imprisonment, commuted to 10 years, released 1951

Kurt Blome   Acquitted

Viktor Brack   Death by hanging

Karl Brandt   Death by hanging

Rudolf Brandt   Death by hanging

Fritz Fischer   Life imprisonment, commuted to 15 years, released 1954

Karl Gebhardt   Death by hanging

Karl Genzken   Life imprisonment, commuted to 20 years, released 1954

Siegfried Handloser   Life imprisonment, commuted to 20 years, released 1954

Waldemar Hoven   Death by hanging

Joachim Mrugowsky	Death by hanging
Herta Oberheuser	20 years imprisonment, commuted to 10 years, released 1954
Adolf Pokorny	Acquitted
Helmut Poppendick	10 years imprisonment, released 1951
Hans-Wolfgang Romberg	Acquitted
Gerhard Rose	Life imprisonment, commuted to 20 years, released 1955
Paul Rostock	Acquitted
Siegfried Ruff	Acquitted
Konrad Schäfer	Acquitted
Oskar Schröder	Life imprisonment, commuted to 15 years, released 1954
Wolfram Sievers	Death by hanging
George August Weltz	Acquitted

Note: Seven defendants were executed by hanging at Landsberg/Lech Prison (Landsberg am Lech, Allied-occupied South Germany) on 2 June 1948.

TABLE OF CONCENTRATION CAMPS MENTIONED IN ALEXANDER'S DIARY

Name	Location	Date Opened
Dachau	Germany	March 1933
Oranienburg	Germany	March 1933
Sachsenhausen	Germany	July 1936
Buchenwald	Germany	July 1937
Flossenbürg	Germany	May 1938
Mauthausen	Austria	August 1938
Neuengamme	Germany	Subcamp established in Dec. 1938; became a main camp in June 1940
Ravensbrück	Germany	May 1939
Auschwitz	Poland	May 1940
Natzweiler-Struthof	France	July 1940
Majdanek	Poland	October 1941
Kaufering (a series of Dachau subcamps)	Germany	June 1944
Mittelbau-Dora	Germany	Made an independent concentration camp in October 1944; originally part of Buchenwald's system of subcamps

INDEX OF PERSONS

A

Agmon 115
Alajoneusne 115
Alexander, Leo 31–33, 35, 38, 41, 42, 45, 47, 50, 51, 56, 65, 71, 75–77, 85–87, 101, 103, 105, 115, 120, 126, 128
Alexander, Phyllis 111, 131, 138, 140, 142, 144
Andrews, M. Neil 111, 125

B

Bach, Erich von dem / Bach-Zelewski, Erich 148, 149
Balicki, Chaim 44, 59
Baron de Meyer, Adolph 80
Baur, Eleonore aka 'Schwester Pia' 94
Bausch 115
Bayer-Pokorny, von 128
Bayle, François 86, 101, 108, 112, 114, 127
Beals, Walter B. 151
Becker, Franz 55
Becker, Josephine, geb. Danner 55
Becker-Freyseng, Hermann 54, 63, 123
Beiglböck, Wilhelm 54, 55, 62, 66, 67, 115, 127, 140
Belicki 61
Benzinger, Theodor 51
Beseat, Amnie 99
Bessing, Bernd 54
Bier, August 66
Binz, Dorothea 104
Blaha, Franz 90, 125
Bourgignon, Alfred Georges 115
Blome, Kurt 44, 49, 72, 82, 83, 126, 130, 132, 138, 146
Böhmer, Erna 102
Bolovsky 49
Bontecomp 112
Bormann, Martin 146
Borst, Maximilian 69, 89, 94, 100, 146
Boschloo, Dirk 131
Bouhler, Philipp 79
Brachtel, Rudolf 106, 108
Brack, Viktor 43, 54, 78, 79
Brandt, Karl 37, 43, 45, 47, 49, 52, 53, 66, 79, 80, 93, 111, 118, 123, 124, 127, 128, 130, 139
Brarde, Aline 136
Brecht 95
Broel-Plater, Maria Janina 101, 103
Brutel de la Rivière, J. J. 131
Buchta, Franz 143
Büchner, Franz 51, 124, 145–146
Bühning 134
Bürger, Max Ferdinand 84
Busche 116

C

Charcot, Jean-Martin 115
Christianson [Christensen] 62
Churchill, Winston 83, 114
Clauberg, Carl 132–134, 136
Clay, Lucius D. 138
Cohen 58
Conti, Leonardo 36, 83
Copplius 115
Cornelis, Jan 131
Crawford, Johnson T. 150

D

Daffner, Abram 59
Daffner, Manick 59
Daniels, George Eaton 126, 128
Deeping, George Warwick 120
Diehl, Karoline, see Rascher, Mrs.
Diehl, Mose 90, 94
Diehl 91, 94, 100
Diehl, Nini 90, 91, 95, 146
Ding-Schuler, Erwin 73, 111
Diepken [Diepgen], Paul 67
Dill, D. B. 124
Dirr, Karl 112
Dönitz, Karl 70
Doll 116
Dohmen, Arnold 124
Dosterewyk, J. C. 128, 130
Drost, Johannes 127
Dubrow 127
Dzido, Jadwigo 101, 102, 104, 105

E

Eichmann, Adolf Otto 148
Enderlein 81
Eppinger, Hans 55, 56, 62
Ewers, H. H. 145

F

Fauber 86
Fegelein, Hermann 149
Feix, Robert 83, 91–93, 122
Fey, J. 124
Fialkowski, Bruno 112
Field 61
Finke, Erich 96
Finler 121
Fischer, Fritz 43, 45, 46, 63, 68, 102, 108, 109, 112, 128, 129, 142
Fleck, Ludwik 58
Forbes 116, 124
Forst, August Wilhelm 145
Foss 86, 88
Frick, Anneliese 114

Frick, Wilhelm 33, 36, 114
Fried, John H. E. 34
Fritz, Hubert 140
Fuchs, Otto Paul 144

G

Ganzer, Gerda, née Quernheim 78
Gehren 118
Genzken, Karl August 43, 63, 86, 118
George 108
George, R. S. 127
Gildemeister, Eugen 107
Grawitz, Ernst Robert 41, 45, 54, 73, 123, 124
Gebhardt, Karl 41–43, 46, 68, 69, 102, 108, 109, 117, 128, 130, 134, 138
Gerl, Albert 144, 145
Gerlach, Walther 37
Gerstein, Kurt 122, 123
Globocnik, Odilo 147, 148
Gobel [Goebel] 132
Goebbels, Paul Joseph 52, 67
Goebel, Johannes 132–136
Goering / Göring, Hermann 33, 61, 85, 123, 127
Gottlieb, Sidney 44
Gottschalk, Rudolf 57
Greiner, Josef 143
Grosse-Brochhoff, [Franz?] 56
Gstettenbauer, August 141, 143
Gütt, Arthur 72
Guillein 115
Guleke 66
Gusthoff 148

H

Haagen, Eugen 66, 111, 128, 130, 144
Haber, Fritz 111
Hadelmeyer, Roman 143
Hagen, Eugen 73, 108
Hal, Hans H. 145

Index of Persons

Halder, Franz 118
Handloser, Siegfried 63, 118, 125, 138
Hardy, Alexander G. 38, 86, 109, 128
Haremza, Ignatz 112
Harris, Whitney Robson 126, 127
Haydn, Josef 141
Heberlein 100
Hedweg 135
Hegel, Georg W. F. 108
Heras, Willy de las 139, 140
Heringer 131
Herzberger 143
Hess, Rudolf 72, 146
Heubner, Wolfgang O. L. 54, 62
Heyde, Werner 80
Heydrich, Reinhard 40, 41, 63, 71, 146, 148
Himmler, Heinrich 35–37, 41, 44, 49, 52, 54, 59, 63, 71, 73, 89, 95, 111, 121–123, 125, 130, 134, 136, 144, 146–149
Hinterarches, Therese 148
Hintermayer, Fritz 130
Hippke, Erich 120, 122, 123
Hippocrates 38, 117, 119, 122, 123
Hirner 146
Hirschfeld, Magnus 145
Hirt, August 94
Hirtz, Georg 111, 130
Hitler, Adolf 36, 37, 41, 42, 52, 58, 70, 79, 83, 85, 89, 90, 92, 94, 118, 121, 123, 127, 138, 143
Hochwald, Ernst, see Anorst Horlik-Hochwald
Höppler 62, 65
Hoff 84
Hohlbaum, Joseph 71
Holzlöhner, Ernst 55, 56, 66, 96, 106, 121, 122
Hop, Willem 137
Horlik-Hochwald, Anorst, also known as Ernst Hochwald 49
Horst, Erika 141
Horst, Robert 141
Hoven, Waldemar 46, 57, 59, 79, 92, 118, 119, 122, 128, 143

Hulst, Steffen 131

I

Ivy, Andrew Conway 113, 115, 116

J

Jackson, Robert Houghwout 33, 35
Jahn, Walter 139
Janosch 121
Jauk, Franz 96
Joerdens, Elisabeth 127
Kaduk 135
Kalk, Heinrich Otto 145
Kaltenbrunner, Ernst Karl 149
Karołewska, Władislawa 101
Kattowitz 60
Katzenellenbogen, Edwin (aka Katzen-Ellenbogen, Edwin) 118, 119
Kempner, Robert 33
Kirchheimer, [Otto] 112
Kirschbaumer 143
Kitchener, Horatio Herbert 88
Klaber, Edith 130
Klaber, Felix 130
Klaber, Isidor 130
Klause 135
Klein, Gustav 144
Klein, Sheve 137
Klinghand 140, 141
Klüppel, Karl 88
Knote 116
Kogon, Eugen 111, 112
Kollmann, Alfred 141
Kollmann, Georg 142
Kollmann 143
Koster, F. 134
Kottenhof, 121
Kraine, Boris 96
Kreisel, Alfons 93
Kruskall, Sarah 37
Kubic, Charlie 115
Kuśmierczuik, Maria 101

L

Ladell, W. S. S. 123
Lammers, Heinrich 124
Lampe, Hannah 89
Larisch, Heribert von 71, 78
La Rouche, Marie 33
Laves 144
Lederer 139, 140
Leib-Cohen 138
Leibbrand, Werner 63, 65, 113
Leiter, Ferdinand 145
Lemkin, Raphael 33, 35
Leeuw-Bernard, Frankje Caroline de 136
Levi 126
Limic 125
Linden 142
Lützelburg, Philipp Xaver von 82, 83
Lutz, Lili 88
Lutz, Wolfgang 86, 91

M

Mac Kove 111
Maczka, Zofia 112
Magnus, Georg 66, 70
Malleret 115
Manasse, Paul 65
Mant, Arthur Keith 42, 44, 78, 86, 114, 115
Mapes, Robert W. 141, 145
McCarthy, Joseph 33
McHaney, James Monroe 33, 38, 87, 103, 111, 117, 123
Meckauf, Valerie 140
Mentzel, Rudolf 37
Meyer, Baron Adolph de 80
Meyer, Herbert 49, 109
Michalowsky 107
Michielsen 132
Mielke, Fred 120
Milch, Erhard 93, 121, 126
Miller, Virginia 111
Mitscherlich, Alexander 120
Molisch 144

Moran, Charles 114
Morell, Theodor 41, 118
Morse, Wayne L. 38
Mrugowski, Joachim 46, 71, 122
Münsterberg, Hugo 118

N

Nales, Gerrit Hendrik 128
Natheiss 95
Nat 132
Nati 124
Neff, Walter 47, 63, 91–93, 95, 96, 106, 112
Nestlewood 38

O

Ochozki, Jan 109
Oberhäuser, Herta, see Oberheuser
Oberheuser, Herta 41, 42, 46, 74, 77, 98, 102, 103, 109, 139
Ohlendorf, Otto 111, 146, 147, 149
Olah, Franz 143
Olbricht 137
Oliver, Feketh 142
Oliviera Salazar, Antonio de 38
Otto 108

P

Papelka 142
Peltibone 140
Pernat, Maya 89
Pfältzer, Bernhard 131
Phoetus 112
Pichowiak, Harry 96
Pick 58
Pillwein, Fritz 143
Pinel, Phillippe 115
Piodrowski 141
Pirker, Josef 144
Platen-Hallermund, Alice von 120
Pluvinage 115
Pokorny, Adolf 35, 58, 127

Poppendick, Helmut 64
Punger 109
Punzengruber, Gisa, née Wagner 108, 113, 118
Punzengruber, Rudolf Emanuel 113, 114, 125, 141

Q

Quernheim, Gerda, see Gerda Ganzer
Quim, W. 107

R

Rascher, Brigitte 89
Rascher, Hans 88
Rascher, Hans-Michel 89
Rascher, Karoline, see Diehl, Karoline
Rascher, Rose, née Klüppel 88
Rascher, Sigmund 44, 51, 52, 54, 57, 63, 82–86, 88–97, 100, 106, 111–114, 120–122, 124–126, 144, 146
Rascher, Sigrid 88
Rascher, Sigurd 88–90
Raymond, Bernhard 49
Reed, Walter 85, 116
Rein, Hermann 51, 117
Reinhardt 124
Reininghaus, Peter Edler von 92
Reisinger, Paul 140
Ritter, Robert 139
Rockwell 140, 141
Roeder / Röder, Karl 44, 140, 142
Roemheld, Karl Wolff von 147
Rogge 119
Rössle, Robert 69
Romberg, Hans-Wolfgang 51, 84, 85, 93, 96, 121, 127, 146
Romen 97
Roosevelt, Franklin D. 83
Rose, Gerhard 43, 81, 108, 127, 130, 138, 139
Rosenthal, Rolf 42, 78, 102
Rosenzweig 142

Rosner 143
Rostock, Paul 43, 54, 66, 127
Roy, Hazel 64
Ruff, Siegfried 43, 51, 84, 85, 93, 116, 118, 121, 122

S

Sachs, Abraham, see Abram Zaks
Saks, Abram 59, 60
Saks, Chzia, née Rothschild 60
Saks, Joshua, see Joshua (Szyja) Zaks
Saks, Moses 60
Samuel, Maximilian 133, 136
Saper, Leroy D. 139
Sauckel, Fritz 138
Sauerbruch, Ferdinand 70, 83, 111
Sawade, Fritz, see Werner Heyde
Schäfer, Konrad 54–56, 61, 66, 67, 116, 143
Schiedlausky, Gerhard 38, 40
Schilling, Klaus / Claus 81, 106, 130
Schittenhelm, Alfred 112, 113
Schmidt, Edith 111, 130
Schmidt, Ludwig 141
Schmidt, Paul 72
Schneeweiss 125
Schreiber 57
Schreiber, Walter 72
Schröder, Oskar 54, 62, 65, 115, 127, 128
Schütterhelm [Schittenhelm, Alfred] 112
Schumann, Horst 133, 136, 137
Schwarz 140
Schweitzer, Albert 52
'Schwester Pia', see Eleonore Baur
Schwind, Herbert 92
Scithers, George R. 126
Scithers, Ruth Mc Kelway 126–128
Sebring, Harold L. 123, 150
Seemann 137
Shally 44
Shelley, Marian 33, 57, 111, 112, 115, 127

Shopinsky 140
Sievers, Wolfram 37, 44, 49, 50, 83, 93, 96, 112, 113, 115, 125, 138, 146
Simony 62
Singelenberg, Anne 131
Singelenberg, Christian 131
Singer 111, 121, 123–125
Sippingen 54
Sillevis-Smit 131
Skritek 143
Smith, L. W. 124
Sneller, Zeger Willem 128
Sobek, Franz 141
Somerhough 115
Spann, Othmar 72
Spanjaard van Esso, Ima 132
Speer, Albert 52, 70, 128
Spohr 97
Steijns, Michel Jean Emile Marie 132, 137
Steinbauer, Gustav 123, 143
Steiner, Rudolf 97, 99
Steyns, Michel J. M. 127, 136
Stockton 124
Stöhr, Heinrich 141
Straaten, Wim van 131
Strime 56
Strughold, Hubertus 51, 55, 61, 84, 116
Stuckgold 100
Stumpfegger, Ludwig 42, 69, 71
Swearingen, Victor C. 150

T

Talbott, J. H. 124
Tauber, Georg 88, 100, 106
Tauböck, Karl 144, 145
Taylor, Telford 33–35, 44, 45, 65, 86, 87, 112, 114, 115
Teubmann 143
Thiele, Gerhard 131
Thompson, John 114, 115, 120, 122, 127
Tillatson, K. J. 124
Trommer, Richard 42

Trump 89, 94, 112
Tschofenig, Josef 144
Twichell 138
Tyn, Brouco van 136

U

Umschweif 137

V

Valentin, Erwin 134
Vassen 92
Vorbicek, Joseph 140, 141, 143
Vorwald 146

W

Wachsmuth, Werner 138
Wagner 118
Wagner, Gerhard 36, 72, 95
Walters 132
Washiniak, Kasmirz 94
Wasileaski 132
Wasilewski 135, 137
Wawrcziniac, Kasimir 96
Weissmann, Relly 130
Weltz, F. H. 84
Weltz, Georg Augustus 43, 44, 49, 51, 83–86, 93, 109, 112, 114, 116, 120–122, 125
Wendt, Günter 86, 114
Wenger, Joseph Numa 38
Wessel, Horst 143
Wessely, Otto 141–143
Wetzel, Erhard 54
Wind, Eliazar de 127
Wirths, Eduard 133, 136, 137
Wiskott, Alfred 51
Witfield, Helen 88
Wolff, Karl F. O. 121, 122, 147
Wollrab 108
Wright, Robert 111
Wüst 146

Z

Zaks, Abram 56
Zaks, Joshua (Szyja) 57
Zamoyska, Christine 93

Zeiss, Heinrich 73
Zeeuw, Henrik de 130
Zoon, Johannes 131

INDEX OF PLACES AND COUNTRIES

A

Aachen 78, 84
Aberdeen 78
Aegypten / Egypt 81, 88, 133
Africa / Afrika 52, 65, 70, 81, 92, 95
Alexandria 88
America / Amerika 67, 73, 123, 149
Ammersee 90
Amsterdam 128, 131, 132, 134, 136
Apfelmeierhof 92
Ascona 88, 89, 91
Athen 65
Augsburg 92, 97, 143
Austria / Österreich 92, 94, 125, 139, 142 144
Avranches 65, 72
Azores 38

B

Baden 61, 79
Balkan 79
Bamberg 138
Basel 81
Bavaria(n) Alps 95
Bayern / Bavaria 112, 113
Bedzin 57
Beelitz 67
Belgium 133, 135
Belvedere 142
Bergen-Belsen 132
Berlin 35, 36, 38, 42, 45, 52, 55, 61, 64, 66–68, 70–73, 81, 83–85, 93, 95, 107, 111, 120, 133, 134, 136-138, 144, 146
Bernburg 119
Bethel 97
Biarritz 66
Bielefeld 97
Birkenau 133–137
Bochum 52, 66, 81
Bodensee 60, 90
Bogenhausen 127
Bohemia (Böhmen) 36, 70
Bonn 68, 74, 84
Braunschweig 66, 68
Breda 131
Breisgau 58, 80
Breslau 81
Bruck (a.d. Mur) 92
Buchenwald 40, 41, 44, 46, 57, 63, 73, 80, 82, 109, 111, 118, 119, 131, 143, 145
Budapest 92, 116
Burgenland 141, 142

C

Caestrochow 60
Chemnitz 59
China 81
Chulm 108
Constanz 89
Corfu 88
Cuba 85
Częstochowa 56, 57

D

Dachau 41, 44, 51, 54, 55, 60, 62, 65, 66, 81, 83–86, 88, 90, 92, 94, 96, 100, 104, 106, 107, 113, 118, 121, 122, 125, 127, 130, 131, 139, 141, 143, 145
Dahlem 64
Dallas 126
Danzig 54, 120

Darmstadt 147
Debreczen 116
Denmark 80
Deutschland (see Germany)
Dornach 88, 90, 91, 97, 100
Dorne 143
Dresden 72, 139
Dupont 91
Dunaföldvor 92
Düsseldorf 74
Dzialoszyc 44

E

Eastern Europe 54
Egene / Egern 149
Elberfeld 97, 99
Elsass 61
England 37, 58, 69, 148
Erlangen 144
Europa / Europe 89, 91, 118, 126, 136, 141

F

Feldberg Württemberg 92
Flensburg 70, 80
Florida 123
Floridsdorf 142
Flossenbürg 40, 42, 60
France 68, 72, 81, 92, 116
Frankfurt am Main / Frankfurt 33, 38, 97, 138, 145
Frankfurt/Oder 61
Freiburg 58, 79, 80, 89
Friedrichshain 38
Friemershein 84
Fuerth / Fürth 86, 140
Fürstenfeldbruck 88

G

Gaisach 95
Gardelegen 131

Garmisch(-Partenkirchen) 126
Gdansk 102, 108
Geneva 63
Germany / Deutschland 33–35, 39, 43, 50–53, 58, 59, 63, 66, 70, 72, 77, 80–84, 87, 92, 95, 101, 105, 109, 110, 114, 119, 123, 124, 126, 129, 131, 132, 134, 135, 139, 145, 146, 149, 150
Ghana 133
Gleiwitz 57, 60
Giessen 72, 82, 106
Göttingen 64, 82
Goldbach 60
Gräfelfing 112
Grafeneck 81
Graz 92
Greek (Islands) 88
Greifswald 66
Grünberg 60
Grunewald 144

H

Haag am Hausruck 88
Haagen 78
Haaren 132
Halle 71–73, 83
Hamburg 38, 40, 65, 68, 88, 90, 92, 97, 100, 120
Hannover (-Stöcken) 65, 131
Herrenhüten 79
Hersbruck 93
Heidelberg 55, 81, 83, 116, 138
Hohenlychen 41, 42, 68, 70, 74
Holland 66, 72, 116, 128, 132, 135
Hongchow 81
Hungary 92, 116

I

Innsbruck 121
Island of Terceira 38
Italy / Italien 33, 65, 84, 147, 149

J

Jena 66

K

Kampenwand 95
Kaufering 60
Kiel 42, 132, 146
(District of) Kielce 44
Kitzbühl 145
Klagenfurt 144
Kochem a.d. Mosel 145
Kohlendey 142
Köln 74, 83
Komotew / Komotau 58
Konstanz 91
Kopenhagen 88

L

Lagos Island 38
Lajes Field 38
Lambarene 52
Landsberg (a.d. Warthe) 37, 38, 56, 57, 59–61
Landshut 69, 92
Lech 56, 59, 60, 92
Leopoldsberg 142
Leipzig 68, 71, 84, 145
Leiden 131
Leyden 127
Lichtenburg 77
Linz / Lienz 68, 144
Lübeck 137
Lublin 66, 147
Lugano 88, 97
Ludwigshafen 55
Lukow / Lukuw 102
Lund 54
Lüneburg 137

M

Madagaskar 79
Maidanek [Majdanek] 60
Malchow 133
Malibaan / Maliebaan 127, 137
Marburg 100
Marrenburg 148
Massachussetts 38
Mauthausen 40, 41, 132
Mecklenburg 83
Merkirch 145
Minneapolis 80
Minsk 141
Mittelbau(-Dora) 119, 131
Montreal 35
Moravia 36
Mösterberg [Österberg] 144
Mühlhausen 61
Mühlheim 131
München-Schwabing 94
Munich / München 37, 44, 51, 64, 66, 69, 79, 80, 85, 89, 90, 92, 94, 96, 97, 99, 100, 108, 109, 112–114, 120, 123, 126, 127, 139, 140, 145
Münster 82, 106
Münstergraben 143

N

Natzweiler / Natzweiler-Struthof 40, 58, 66, 94, 111, 128, 130, 145
Neckar-Eck 145
Neckar-Gernech (Neckargerach) 145
Netherlands 131
Neu-Brandenburg 131
Neuengamme 42, 137
New York (City) 33, 35, 128
New Jersey 118
Niederrhein 84
Nieuw Port 131
Nordhausen 119
North Africa 52, 81

Nürnberg / Nuremberg 4, 33–39, 41–46, 49–51, 53, 62–65, 66, 70, 85–88, 90, 96, 98, 101, 103, 105, 110, 111, 114, 117, 120, 126, 129, 138, 144, 145, 146

O

Oldenburg 64
Oppen 144
Oranienburg 40, 132
Orly Field 38
Oświęcim / Auschwitz / („Ausschwitz') 41, 44, 49, 56, 57, 60, 78, 127, 130–138, 140, 145
Ottoman Empire 88

P

Paris 38, 66, 73, 80, 111, 112, 114, 118, 136, 148
Passau 92, 126
Phyn Pass [Pyhrnpass] 144
Pleskow 68
Poland / Polen 41, 44, 57, 68, 114, 118, 138, 141, 146
Portugal 38
Prag / Prague 41, 58, 71, 94, 118, 146
(East) Prussia / Kingdom of Prussia 63, 67, 97
Pomerania (Pommern) 67
Posen / Poznan 40, 82, 84
Potsdam 38
Pötzlinsdorf 140

Q

Quedlinburg 52

R

Rathenow 71
Ravensbrück / Ravensbruck 40–42, 45, 63, 74, 77, 78, 92, 101–104, 106, 131–133
Reckenfeld 106
Rhine Raderhorst (Kreis Minden) 106
Rieden a.d. Kötz 112
Rijks 131
Roltenbuch (Rottenbuch) 112
Rosenberg 69
Rostock 82
Rotterdam 127, 128, 130, 137
Russia / Russland 41, 52, 65, 67, 68, 79, 82, 114, 118, 120, 122, 146, 149

S

Saacherd 83
Sachsenhausen 73, 107, 117, 132
San Antonio 61
Salzburg 139
Salzgries 141
Saxony 58
Schering 61
Schöngau 112
Schwabing 124
Schwäbisch-Gmünd 100
Schweiz (see Switzerland)
Schwerinbach 125
Scotland 69
Sicily 65, 84, 95
Sonnenstein 133
Soviet Union 132
Spain 92
Stalingrad 52, 64, 70, 72, 79
Stettin 81
Strasbourg / Strassburg 94, 128
Stocksee 42
Stryia 92
Stuttgart 88, 89, 97, 100, 145
Stutthof 107
St. Valentin 143
Suchowah 102

Sudetenland 59, 94
Sweecie 108
Sweden 54, 80, 137, 138
Switzerland / Schweiz 81, 88, 89, 92, 97, 116, 148
Syrakus 65

T

Tauche 133
Tauern 144
Tegernsee 149
Tel Aviv 130
Texas 61, 126
The Hague 128, 131
Thorn 108
Tirol 144
Tölz 95
Törnis 68
Tübingen 66
Tunis 92
Turin 55
Turkey 120

U

United States / US / U.S. / USA 33, 35, 38, 44, 62, 80, 83, 84, 86, 88, 91, 107, 116, 131, 146
Unterkärnten 125
Überlingen 60
Upper Austria / Ober-Österreich 40, 86, 143
Upper Bavaria / Oberbayern 60, 69, 112
Utrecht 127, 131, 132, 135–138

V

Vatican 96
Vienna / Vienne / Wien 35, 58, 61–62, 88, 130, 137, 139–145, 147
Vietnam 33
Vistula / Weichsel 108
Vright 131
Vught 132

W

Warsaw 102, 104
Warschau 149
Washington (D.C.) 33, 38, 84, 88, 138
Weimar 57
Westerburg 132
West Germany 132
Wesseling 145
Westheim 92
Westphalen 106
West Point 126
Wien (see Vienna)
Wolfgangsee 149
Wisconsin 33
Würzburg 65, 80, 83, 97

Z

Zeist 132, 136
Zhitomiz 66
Zürich 92

*Fig. 21: Leo Alexander at the Nuremberg Doctors' Trial.
1946/47 (Source: NARA).*

BIOGRAPHICAL NOTES OF THE EDITORS

Kate Docking is a Post-Doctoral Research Associate at the Centre for the Study of Health, Ethics, and Society at the University of Hamburg and is part of the ERC-funded "Taming the European Leviathan" project. Her PhD, completed at the University of Kent, was titled "Reframing Gender: The Experiences of the Female Medical Personnel of Ravensbrück Concentration Camp, 1933–1945" is currently under contract with Bloomsbury publishers and will be published in 2026. In 2021, she published "Gender, Recruitment and Medicine at Ravensbrück Concentration Camp, 1939–1942" in the peer-reviewed German History journal. She has also published on National Socialist ideology in a De Gruyter edited volume. Her current research projects analyse the entanglements between medicine and societal conceptualisations of the body across twentieth century Europe. She integrates analyses of individual subjectivity, agency, and emotions with governmental policies and the professional practices of medical personnel to explore the themes of reproduction, sexology, and bodily enhancement.
Contact: kate.docking@uni-hamburg.de

Andreas Frewer is Professor at the Institute for History of Medicine and Medical Ethics at Erlangen-Nürnberg University. He studied medicine, philosophy, and the history of medicine in Munich, Erlangen, Berlin, Vienna, Oxford, and Jerusalem. Dissertation at the Free University of Berlin (1998) and European Master in Bioethics (Leuven et al., 2003). 1994–1998 Physician in Berlin (Virchow/Charité), 1998–2002 Assistant Professor Goettingen, 2002–2006 Professor in Hannover. 2014–2017 head of the EFI Excellence Project "Human Rights in Healthcare". 2018–2025 chair of the Graduate School "Human Rights and Ethics in Medicine for Older Persons". Author of more than 350 publications. Editor of twelve series of books and co-editor of "History and Theory of Human Experimentation" (Steiner, 2007), "Healthcare as a Human Rights Issue" (transcript, 2017) and "Ethical Research" (OUP, 2020). Prof. Frewer is member of several Ethics Boards and Senior Advisory Consultant of the World Health Organization (WHO).
Contact: andreas.frewer@fau.de

David Peace is a Post-Doctoral Research Associate at the Centre for the Study of Health, Ethics, and Society at the University of Hamburg and is part of the ERC-funded "Taming the European Leviathan" project. His PhD, completed at the University of Kent, was titled "From Galtonian Eugenics to Biosocial Science: The Intellectual Origins and Policy Implications of Quantifying Heredity in Interwar and Post-War Britain". His current projects explore the historical relationship

between developments in quantitative analysis and the medical biosciences across the 20th century, specialising in the influence of both eugenics and human genetics in population health policies. His research also intersects with the history of medical ethics and WMD prevention, such as his publication "Woe to You for Being a Grandchild: Mutations and the Ethical Case Against WMD's Among Post-War Geneticists in the United Kingdom" (Springer Nature, forthcoming 2024). His work is embedded within various historiographical traditions, including the history of ideas, the history of science and medicine, and social and political history.
Contact: david.peace@uni-hamburg.de

Ulf Schmidt is Senior Professor of Modern History at the University of Hamburg, founding-director of the Centre for the Study of Health, Ethics, and Society, and a Fellow of the Royal Historical Society. His research interests are in the history of modern medical ethics, warfare, and policy in twentieth-century Europe and the United States. He is especially interested in the history of authoritarian regimes and modern dictatorships. He is the author, among others, of Justice at Nuremberg: Leo Alexander and the Nazi Doctors' Trial (Palgrave Macmillan, 2004); Karl Brandt: The Nazi Doctor. Medicine and Power in the Third Reich (Continuum, 2007); Secret Science. A Century of Poison Warfare and Human Experiments (OUP, 2015); coeditor of Propaganda and Conflict: War, Media and the Shaping of the Twentieth Century (Bloomsbury, 2019), and Ethical Research: The Declaration of Helsinki, and the Past, Present, and Future of Human Experimentation (OUP, 2020). He is Principal Investigator of a six-year ERC Synergy Grant on "Taming the European Leviathan: The Legacy of Post-War Medicine and the Common Good".
Contact: ulf.schmidt@uni-hamburg.de

Andreas Frewer

Werner Leibbrand: Leben – Weiterleben – Überleben

GESCHICHTE UND PHILOSOPHIE DER MEDIZIN –
BAND 16
2021. 376 Seiten mit 88 s/w-Abbildungen

978-3-515-12940-4 GEBUNDEN

Werner R. Leibbrand (1896–1974) war Arzt, Medizinhistoriker und Musiker. Seine Vita spiegelt Epochen von Kaiserzeit und Weimarer Republik über Nationalsozialismus bis zur BRD. Er praktizierte als Nervenarzt in Berlin und kannte die Intellektuellen- und Theaterszene der Hauptstadt seit den „Roaring Twenties". Leibbrand war polyglott und international hoch geschätzt. Als Nazi-Gegner wurde er drangsaliert, im Zweiten Weltkrieg nach Bayern zwangsversetzt und musste schließlich sogar mit der jüdischen Ehefrau in einer „Odyssee" 1944 untertauchen. Nach dem Krieg wurde Leibbrand Leiter der Heil- und Pflegeanstalt in Erlangen, gründete dort das Universitätsseminar für Medizingeschichte und war der einzige deutsche Sachverständige im Nürnberger Ärzteprozess. 1953 erhielt er einen Ruf auf den Lehrstuhl für Medizingeschichte in München und wirkte mit großer Kreativität bis ins hohe Alter. Leibbrands Biographie zeigt seine vielfältigen Lebenswelten wie auch besondere „Listen", die ihn bei existenziell-gefährlichen Situationen bestehen ließen.

Die kommentierte Edition seiner Vita bringt viele unbekannte Seiten und Bilder einer faszinierenden Persönlichkeit sowie Beiträge zu seinem Nachwirken.

DER HERAUSGEBER

Andreas Frewer ist Professor am Institut für Geschichte und Ethik der Medizin der FAU Erlangen-Nürnberg. Arzt in der Inneren und Intensivmedizin an Virchow-Klinikum und Charité, HU Berlin (1994–1998). Promotion an der FU Berlin (1998). European Master in Bioethics in Leuven et al. (2002–2003). Habilitation für Geschichte, Theorie und Ethik der Medizin und Professor in Hannover (2002–2006). Leitung der Institute für Geschichte und Ethik der Medizin in Frankfurt/M. (2004), Hannover (2006/07) und Erlangen (2008/09). EFI-Exzellenz-Projekt „Human Rights in Healthcare" (2014–2017) und GRK „Menschenrechte und Ethik in der Medizin für Ältere" (seit 2018). 2012 Brocher Award, 2019 Medizinpreis. Senior Advisory Consultant der World Health Organization (WHO).

Hier bestellen:
service@steiner-verlag.de

Andreas Frewer (Hg.)

Gründerzeit der Medizinethik

Hans-Bernhard Wuermeling und die
Fachentwicklung ins 21. Jahrhundert

GESCHICHTE UND PHILOSOPHIE DER MEDIZIN /
HISTORY AND PHILOSOPHY OF MEDICINE – BAND 17
2022. 331 Seiten mit 19 s/w-Abbildungen und 4 Tabellen

978-3-515-13385-2 GEBUNDEN
978-3-515-13388-3 E-BOOK

Konflikte bei Schwangerschaft, Suizid und Sterbehilfe – die Medizinethik befasst sich mit existenziellen gesellschaftlichen Fragen. Nach 50 Jahren dynamischer Entwicklung ist das Fach heute an Kliniken und Forschungseinrichtungen breit vertreten. 1986 wurde die „Akademie für Ethik in der Medizin" in Erlangen als Verein eingetragen. Ihr Gründungspräsident war der Rechtsmediziner Hans-Bernhard Wuermeling, der als Vortragender und beratender Experte für Bundesärztekammer und Politik sehr engagiert war. Fälle wie das erste deutsche IvF-Kind (1982) oder das „Erlanger Baby" einer hirntoten Frau (1992) haben wichtige Debatten bewirkt. Die Akademie gründete die Zeitschrift „Ethik in der Medizin", das Fach wurde professionalisiert und institutionalisiert. Zahlreiche Publikationen fundierten das neue Gebiet mit langer wissenschaftlicher Tradition.
In diesem Band rekonstruieren Expert:innen und Zeitzeug:innen zentrale Entwicklungen der Medizinethik und zeigen geschichtliche Linien des Fachs bis in die Gegenwart.

DER HERAUSGEBER
Andreas Frewer ist Professor am Institut für Geschichte und Ethik der Medizin der FAU Erlangen-Nürnberg. Arzt in der Inneren und Intensivmedizin an Virchow-Klinikum und Charité, HU Berlin (1994–1998). Promotion an der FU Berlin (1998). European Master in Bioethics in Leuven et al. (2002–2003). Habilitation für Geschichte, Theorie und Ethik der Medizin und Professor in Hannover (2002–2006). Leitung der Institute für Geschichte und Ethik der Medizin in Frankfurt/M. (2004), Hannover (2006/07) und Erlangen (2008/09). Brocher Award (2o12), Medizinpreis (2019) und Schöller-Preis (2021).

MIT BEITRÄGEN VON
Andreas Frewer | Mathias Schütz | Gisela Bockenheimer-Lucius | Paula Herrmann | Maria Rupprecht | Martin J. Wuermeling | Hanna-Barbara Gerl-Falkovitz | Monika Muschol Michael Wuermeling | Markus Wuermeling | Kerstin Franzò & Andreas Frewer

Hier bestellen:
service@steiner-verlag.de